WOMEN AT MIDLIFE

LIFE EXPERIENCES AND IMPLICATIONS FOR THE HELPING PROFESSIONS

Ski Hunter, Sandra S. Sundel, and Martin Sundel

NASW PRESS

National Association of Social Workers
Washington, DC

Terry Mizrahi, MSW, PhD, President
Elizabeth J. Clark, PhD, ACSW, MPH, Executive Director

Cheryl Y. Bradley, Publisher
Paula L. Delo, Executive Editor
Susan Fisher, Editor
January Layman-Wood, Acquisitions Editor
Christina Bromley, Editorial Assistant
Louise Goines, Copy Editor
Jodi Bergeman Glasscock, Proofreader
Becky Hornyak, Indexer

LIBRARY OF CONGRESS CATALOGING-IN-PUBLICATION DATA

Hunter, Ski.
    Women at midlife : life experiences and implications for the helping professions / Ski
Hunter, Sandra S. Sundel, Martin Sundel.
        p. cm.
    Includes bibliographical references and index.
    ISBN 0-87101-351-7
    1. Middle aged women. 2. Social work with women. I. Sundel, Sandra Stone, 1948-
    II. Sundel, Martin, 1940- III. Title.

HQ1059.4 .H86 2002
305.244—dc21

                                    2002020026

WOMEN AT MIDLIFE

WOMEN AT MIDLIFE

LIFE EXPERIENCES AND IMPLICATIONS FOR THE HELPING PROFESSIONS

Ski Hunter, Sandra S. Sundel, and Martin Sundel

ABOUT THE AUTHORS

Ski Hunter, MS, MSW, PhD, LMSW-ACP, is professor at the School of Social Work, University of Texas at Arlington. She teaches courses on human behavior and the social environment; adult development; personal relationships; and lesbian, gay, bisexual, and transgender issues. Along with Martin Sundel, she was an editor of *Midlife Myths*, published in 1989. She was the lead author of *Lesbian, Gay, and Bisexual Youths and Adults*, published in 1998 with Coleen Shannon, Jo Knox, and James I. Martin; and a coauthor with James I. Martin of *Lesbian, Gay, Bisexual, and Transgender Issues in Social Work: A Comprehensive Bibliography with Annotations*, published in 2001. She is the lead author of the upcoming NASW Press publication *Affirmative Practice: Understanding and Working with Lesbian, Gay, Bisexual, and Transgender Persons*, with Jane C. Hickerson and the sole author of *Midlife and Older Lesbian and Gay Persons* which is in progress with another press.

Sandra S. Sundel, MSSW, PhD, LCSW, Executive Director of Jewish Family Service of Broward County, Florida. Formerly on the social work faculty at Florida Atlantic University, she taught courses on practice with individuals, families, and groups. She has consulted widely with corporations, government agencies, and nonprofit organizations on change management and interpersonal communication in the workplace. She specializes in the treatment of women and families. She is coauthor (with Martin Sundel) of *Behavior Change in the Human Services* and *Be Assertive*, and has published numerous journal articles and book chapters.

Martin Sundel, MSW, PhD, is president of Sundel Consulting Group, a global management consulting firm specializing in leadership development, behavior change, and futures planning. He received his PhD in social work and psychology from the University of Michigan and was a Postdoctoral Fellow at the Laboratory of Community Psychiatry at Harvard Medical School. For almost a decade he was the Dulak Professor of Social Work at the University of Texas at Arlington, including when he and Ski Hunter were invited speakers at the MacArthur Foundation Research Network on Successful Midlife Development. Most recently, he was professor of Social Work at Florida International University and Faculty Associate at the Southeast Florida Center on Aging. His publication credits include *Midlife Myths, Behavior Change in the Human Services, Individual Change Through Small Groups, (2nd ed.), Be Assertive,* and *Assessing Health and Human Service Needs.*

PREFACE

Women represent a substantial majority of clients served by the helping professions. Many of these women are at midlife, and their numbers are expanding with the entry of the youngest of the baby boom generation into this life period. This book, *Women at Midlife*, challenges the myths, outdated knowledge, and restrictive viewpoints held about these women. In it, we present research findings on salient topics, including: marriage and family; caregiving of adult family members; single-again and always-single statuses; work and financial issues; physical health concerns; menopause and sexual responses; emotional concerns; personality, identity, and generativity; and psychological well-being and life satisfaction. The book attempts to fill in the knowledge gap about women at midlife and identifies pertinent implications for the helping professions.

Women at Midlife is directed at a wide audience of both graduate and undergraduate students in the social and behavioral sciences. The book can be used as a required text in certain courses (for example, women's studies, women's issues courses in social work, and aging courses), as a supplemental text in other courses (for example, health, aging, women's issues, and families), and as a reference or general information text for students and practitioners in social work, psychology, counseling, mental health, sociology, education, and health care. We refer to these audiences collectively throughout the book as "helping professionals," "professional helpers," or "human services professionals." The book will also be of interest to the growing numbers of midlife women and those who care about them.

The first chapter defines the parameters of midlife for women. Family contexts and relationships are presented in Chapter 2, caregiving of adult family members in Chapter 3, and single-again and always-single statuses in Chapter 4. Work, personal finances, and income security are addressed in Chapter 5. Chapter 6 examines issues associated with physical health concerns, and Chapter 7 covers menopause and outcomes for sexuality. Chapter 8 focuses on emotional concerns; Chapter 9 covers the topics of personality, identity, and generativity; and Chapter 10 addresses psychological well-being and life satisfaction. We conclude with an Epilogue on practice with midlife women and the status of knowledge for this population.

We identify early in Chapters 2–10 the life-span concepts that are addressed here using italic type in order to stand out. After a short introduction, each chapter poses questions for the reader to consider. We then discuss the practice implications. Beginning in Chapter 2, we present exhibits of case vignettes followed by several questions for the reader. The purpose of these questions is for readers to think about the issues, strategies, and services that might be suitable for the situation presented in the vignette and to explore the connections between knowledge and practice.

In the Epilogue, we identify research issues concerning the studies available on midlife women. Because of deficiencies in most studies (noted in the Appendix), a discussion of the changes needed in future research also appears.

Ski Hunter
Sandra S. Sundel
Martin Sundel

ACKNOWLEDGMENTS BY SKI HUNTER

I appreciate the opportunity to work with the NASW Press. I particularly want to thank Paula Delo, Executive Editor; January Layman-Wood, Acquisitions Editor; Lou Goines, our copy editor; Lisa J. Franko, Editor, NASW Press; Susan D. Fisher, Editor, NASW Press, and who brought this book through to publication; Steph Selice, former Senior Editor, Books, and Jane Browning, former Director, Member Services/Publications Division, NASW. I also appreciate and cherish my midlife women friends. They delight me with their intellect, humor, and support. This includes my long-term close friends: Carole, Diana, Jennifer, Stephanie, Sydney, and Vera, and my more recent pals: Barabara, Charlotte, Claudia, Corky, "Yankee" Gail, Jan, Joy, Julia, Linda, Louise, Patty, Raven, Rosemary, Trudy, Sam, Shareen, and Sue. I especially cherish and delight in Bev and the joys of our link.

ACKNOWLEDGMENTS BY SANDRA AND MARTIN SUNDEL

This book benefited from the interest and support of many individuals. We are especially grateful to Gary P. Stone, without whom this book would not have been possible. Harry B. Stone, MD, provided valuable suggestions for the chapter on physical health. Paula Delo, Executive Editor, NASW Press, demonstrated an abiding commitment to this project that allowed us to develop and refine important aspects of the book. We thank Lou Goines, our copy editor, January Layman-Wood, NASW Acquisitions Editor, Lisa Franko, NASW Editor, and Susan Fisher, NASW Editor, for their assistance. Finally, we applaud our sisters and friends who are role models for meeting the challenges for women at midlife, and we celebrate the spirit of our dear friend, FM 2030.

CHAPTER 1

DEFINING WOMEN AT MIDLIFE

Midlife is a contemporary concept created by middle-class Americans of European descent (Gullette, 1998). It happened largely because of the decline in fertility and the dramatic lengthening of life expectancy during the 20th century (Moen & Wethington, 1999). In 1900, life expectancy for men and women in the United States was about 48 years (Hoyer, Rybash, & Roodin, 1999). By 1998 the life expectancy for women in North America was 80 years and 73 years for men ("Life expectancy," 2000). Life expectancy projections by the year 2040 are 83 years for women and 75 years for men (U.S. Bureau of the Census, 1995). For persons who survive to age 65, life expectancy will rise to 85 years for women and 79.9 years for men (U.S. Bureau of the Census, 1990). The advancement in life expectancy for women in the 20th century is remarkable, particularly when compared with the prior century when most women died during their childbearing years (Kastenbaum, 1993). Still, the life expectancy for women in the United States is lower than in 15 other developed countries (National Center for Health Statistics, 1993).

As the stretch of time between birth and death expanded, so did the division of the life course into more periods, including midlife, or the period between the younger and the older generations. Increasingly greater numbers of adults traverse midlife; the numbers expanded in the 1990s with the entrance of the baby-boom generation into this period of life. Midlife adults now comprise about one-third of the U.S. population (Braus, 1995; Rosenblatt, 1996). Starting at age 55, midlife women begin to outnumber midlife men. The current U.S. population includes some 43 million midlife women, who comprise about 31 percent of all females and 16 percent of the total population (U.S. Bureau of the Census, 2001).

This chapter examines the construction of midlife as a life period; provides contrasting definitions of midlife and its variations among midlife women; and describes the concepts that form the theoretical framework of the book. Several vignettes are presented that explore the diversity of experiences among midlife women. Implications for practice are included that relate the chapter material to social work practice.

Questions to Consider:

- *How is midlife defined?*

- *What factors influence the definitions of midlife?*

- *What are some examples of how the life-span developmental perspective applies to midlife women?*

Definitions of Midlife

This book focuses on women experiencing the life period of middle age or midlife. Universally accepted definitions of this life period do not exist, however, making it difficult to define women at midlife or even when they enter or exit this period of life. Two general types of definitions include linear age–stage views and nonlinear views.

Linear Age–Stage Views

The linear age–stage perspective on the life course presumes that life periods are triggered by chronological age. Levinson, Darrow, Klein, Levinson, and McKee (1978) studied a small sample of 40 men and found that the men decided on a career in their 20s, became established in a career in their 30s, and later augmented their personal authority by giving up their mentor. A mentor is a person who was influential in shaping their job perspectives and career. This perspective also fits many women's lives. Women married in their early 20s, bore several children by age 30, experienced "empty nest" depression in their 50s, and were grandmothers in their 60s.

Entry to and exit from the middle period of adulthood, therefore, are usually considered to be marked by chronological ages. In the United States, the general view is that persons are in the middle period of life roughly between the ages of 40 to 60 or 65 (Genovese, 1997; Papalia, Camp, & Feldman, 1996). The entrance and exit ages of midlife, however, vary among researchers (for example, from ages 30 to 69; see Bumpass & Aquilino, 1995; Zal, 1992, respectively). Nonresearchers vary even more than researchers in their perceptions of when midlife begins and ends. Lachman, Lewkowicz, Marcus, and Peng (1994) found that the perceptions in a nonresearcher group ranged from 30 to 55 years for entry to midlife and from 45 to 75 years for exit. Respondents in younger age groups rated the entrance–exit ages as significantly lower than the middle age groups or the older age groups. The expectation of when one enters midlife also varies with historical time and place as well as with the lengthening of the life course. Greater life expectancy pushes both the entrance to and the exit from midlife beyond earlier established ages.

Though researchers use chronological ages for midlife entry and exit, they only regard these ages as approximations because the boundaries of this period of life are ambiguous rather than definitive. Neither a single transition nor a set of transitions defines the entry to or exit from midlife. Instead, there is considerable variability in the timing and sequencing of most transitions in midlife (Bumpass & Aquilino, 1995). For example, there are no age-graded markers tied to participating in school or work. Views other than the linear one may be more applicable to the midlife period as well as other periods of life.

Nonlinear Views

As suggested above, chronological age does not predict one's entry to or exit from midlife or one's particular experiences; many women no longer follow the gender-prescribed life script delineated in the linear age–stage perspective (Tavris, 1989). There is no compelling support for tightly organized adult stages of development associated with certain ages. The variety of adult experiences is not accounted for in fixed stages (Tavris, 1989). In longitudinal work at the Institute of Human Development at Berkeley, the timing and sequencing of most events and transitions varied across persons (Eichorn, Clausen, Haan, Honzik, & Mussen, 1981).

Contrasted with the linear age–stage view of midlife, other definitions seem to be more useful in understanding how women experience midlife. Several of these alternate definitions will be considered, including age identity, biological and social ages, multiple selves, social class and health, occupied or unoccupied roles, midlife content, life events, and subjective feelings.

Age Identity. The boundaries of midlife are often fluid in people's minds. As stated earlier, midlife seems less connected to chronological age than to perceptions, at least for nonresearchers. People seem to sense when they are middle aged based on data such as the age of family members or their social positions (Lachman & James, 1997a). Fiske (1979) characterized midlife as a "state of mind." Another adage also applies: "You are only as old as you feel" (Logan, Ward, & Spitze, 1992). A chronological definition of middle age is thus distinguished from feeling middle aged. These self-perceptions, or feelings, refer to one's age identity (Logan et al., 1992; Sherman, 1994).

Age identity was studied in a midlife and later-life probability sample of men and women (age 40 and older). Logan et al. (1992) interviewed 1,200 persons who lived in a metropolitan area in New York, with a cooperation rate of 67.3 percent. The self-identified age category of the respondents corresponded only roughly with chronological age, and some of the respondents reported large discrepancies. About 40 percent of persons in their 40s identified themselves as young. The percentage who made this identification was much lower at age 50 and older, but a small number of persons ages 70–79 identified themselves as young. Most persons in their 40s, 50s, and 60s considered themselves middle aged. This age identity peaked for 75 percent to 80 percent of the respondents in the 50–59 age group. Still, 40 percent of persons in their 70s continued to place themselves in the middle-age category. The proportion of persons who did this beyond the age of 80 was almost 20 percent.

Biological and Social Ages. Undoubtedly, persons use subjective age perceptions such as how old they feel to determine their age identity, but biological and physical factors (for example, hair turning gray, poorer vision) often influence their age identity. What biological age means, however, depends on other factors such as their social age (Turner, 1994). Our social age is determined by others' perceptions of us (Hendricks, 1992). For example, others may perceive that our biological characteristics indicate that we are middle aged before we do (Turner, 1994). Nevertheless, though social age perceptions are influential in determining one's age identity, they may be disregarded if they are at odds with one's subjective age perceptions. Even if physical changes begin to affect health, strength, and vigor, the person experiencing these changes may not view them as anything critical that signifies aging.

Multiple Selves. A set of selves that persons also use to determine their age identity was identified in a sample of 67 women and 34 men ranging in age from 41 to 96 years. The respondents ranged from blue collar workers to professionals (past or current) and in educational attainment from completing fifth grade to obtaining doctoral degrees. Interviews with the respondents took place in various locations, including offices, nursing homes, and private homes. The sampling was purposive so that the researchers could include a variety of environments and ages. Content analysis of written transcripts of taped interviews generated four selves from which persons appeared to draw conclusions about their age identity: comparative self, reflected self, retrospective self, and mature self (Sherman, 1994).

First, persons used the comparative self when they compared similarities and differences between themselves and others in areas such as health, ages of children, and body changes. Second, persons used the reflected self or what they believed others thought about them. For example, although they might not have considered a particular birthday as anything special, their children might and plan a big celebration. This reflected self is analogous to the social self identified by Logan et al. (1992). Third, persons used the retrospective self when they made comparisons of their current selves with their former selves. This could include, for example, changes observed in health or energy levels. Fourth, persons used the mature self when they determined their age identities by inner standards instead of outer or former self-comparisons. For example, some women who highly value the work ethic might continue to work into their late 60s even though their friends and partners have retired.

Social Class and Health. Perceptions of one's age identity also vary with social class and health (Barbee & Bauer, 1988). Working-class persons are aware of aging earlier than middle-class persons (Troll, 1982). Working-class African American women tend to perceive themselves as aging more quickly because of disproportionate poverty, poor health, and poor nutrition (Spurlock, 1984). Several other researchers found that after chronological age health is the most consistent variable related to age identity (for example, Logan et al., 1992; Markides & Boldt, 1983).

Occupied or Unoccupied Roles. Some persons who are chronologically in the midlife years may or may not view themselves as middle aged because of the roles they occupy or do not occupy. Yet, only childbearing and marriage were strongly and consistently associated with age identity in a sample studied by Logan et al. (1992). There was no association between age identity and retirement or deaths of one's parents.

Midlife Content. Midlife is defined not only by its boundaries but also by its content. The negotiation of changing roles and statuses largely constitutes the midlife experience (Bumpass & Aquilino, 1995). Researchers interviewed a representative sample of 13,017 adults, 19 years and older, during 1987 and 1988 in a project called the National Survey of Families and Households (NSFH). This project was supported by the MacArthur Foundation Research Network on Successful Midlife Development and the Center for Demography and Ecology at the University of Wisconsin. Much of the information from this large sample described the midlife population in the United States. Based on their analysis of data from this project, Bumpass and Aquilino (1995) discovered that for most midlife persons, a prominent part of their experiences included the negotiation of changes in roles and statuses in family and work. Although most persons enter midlife with jobs, young children, and living parents, they usually leave this period with no children still at home, widowed par-

ents or no living parents, and retired from work or anticipating retirement.
More specifically, the findings showed:

1. The proportion of households with children still present steadily declines
   throughout midlife. The NFHS data showed that the proportion of
   households in which the children were gone expanded from 20 percent to
   80 percent between the early 40s and early 60s (Bumpass & Aquilino,
   1995). Parents between ages 45–54 experienced the highest rate of children still at home. This rate was highest for married versus single parents,
   single mothers versus single fathers, and African American and Latino
   parents versus white parents (Marks, 1993). There is considerable variability in the timing of this decline of children in the home and whether
   the departure of children is a permanent arrangement. For example,
   Bumpass and Aquilino found that at the end of midlife there were still
   children present in some households (about one-fifth). These children
   were largely young adults (19 years or older) who either never left or left
   and returned. A growing trend for midlife parents involves an adult child
   over the age of 19 who returns home (see Chapter 2).

2. Persons at midlife having a widowed parent peaks for almost half of the
   population between ages 45–49 (Bumpass & Aquilino, 1995).

3. The loss of fathers happens for half of the midlife population before
   the age of 40; a quarter lose mothers by that age. Parents still living are
   probably in declining health. The declining health and possible
   increasing dependence of one's parents and in-laws significantly affect
   women because they are most often the caregivers when the need
   arises (Bumpass & Aquilino, 1995; see Chapter 3).

4. Most people withdraw from the work force in late midlife. This transition was closer to a true "stage" of midlife than any other midlife
   changes examined in the survey. Usually, this happened at the ages
   linked to the receipt of Social Security payments, that is, 62 and 65
   years (Bumpass & Aquilino, 1995).

5. Around the age of 50, grandparenthood sharply increases. A large
   majority of midlife parents studied in the NSFH project were grandparents by ages 55–64. A third of these parents experienced the birth of
   a first grandchild by their late 40s, and the proportion rose to half by
   the early 50s. The onset of grandparenthood often happens faster for
   remarried parents with stepchildren. African Americans and Latinos
   also often experience an earlier transition to grandparenthood because
   of earlier ages of childbearing (Marks, 1996). The effect of education
   on age of grandparenthood is most striking. By ages 45–49, 55 percent
   of persons not finishing high school are already grandparents. This
   contrasts with only 16 percent of persons who were college graduates.

The delay of childbearing (associated with educational attainment) delays grandparenthood (Bumpass & Aquilino, 1995).

Life Events. The life-events perspective proposes that persons are more focused on the events they are experiencing in their lives than their chronological ages. Women who are going through a divorce, starting a new career, launching children, entering menopause, or experiencing grandchildren have many issues in common, despite their ages. The effect of events may vary, however, such as when they happen off time, that is, when events do not happen at the expected time in the life course (Neugarten & Hagestad, 1976).

Subjective Feelings. Subjective feelings associated with being in the middle period of life are also common, such as the wish to assess how things are going and leaving something for the next generation. There is often a sense of now or never about getting things done because of the feeling that time is running out. Midlife women can also feel responsible for both their children and their parents (Lachman & James, 1997a).

We faced a dilemma in developing a working definition of midlife. The scientific literature uses a linear definition of midlife but, as discussed above, the persons studied tend to prefer nonlinear views. We also prefer nonlinear views and recognize the merits of these views of midlife. But most of the studies on midlife addressed in this book defined midlife in linear terms, beginning at about age 40 and ending at about age 60. The U.S. Bureau of the Census (2001) also uses this definition to define midlife. Recently, there have been discussions in some literature (for example, Staudinger & Bluck, 2001) of using the terms "early" and "late" midlife but this distinction is rare. So, the working definition of midlife in this book is also linear, though we are cognizant of the practical limitations of that definition.

In addition to our working definition of midlife, we want to comment on the definitions of "sex" and "gender." In standard usage, sex distinguishes males and females mostly by biological characteristics, whereas gender is a cultural and social category often including the roles, characteristics, and stereotypes associated with the particular biological and anatomical sex a person is or with one's masculine or feminine characteristics (Stein, 1999). Yet, many factors used to classify persons in regard to masculine or feminine characteristics, such as genitalia, secondary sex characteristics, and hormones, do not divide persons into two distinct groups (Coombs, 1997). Because current views about which biological features distinguish males from females might be erroneous and are far from being resolved, Stein (1999) used the term "sex–gender" characteristics to encompass both sex and gender as standard usage. Sex–gender characteristics include all the characteristics (that is, biological, psychological, cultural) that supposedly distinguish males/men from females/women. In this text, therefore, we consider Stein's use of sex–gender as an appropriate term to convey the conventional use of both sex and gender.

VARIATIONS AMONG MIDLIFE WOMEN

Midlife women are far from a homogenous group. Instead, the reality of midlife women's lives is variation, a phenomenon that has increased due to the historical trend of greater fluidity in life events. This is evident in major life arenas such as childbearing, parenting, and work. For example, although an often designated entry marker for midlife is when one's children are teenagers, some women are in their 30s when this happens. They bore their children when they themselves were teenagers. Other women delayed childbirth until their 30s or later. Midlife parents may have children who are between ages 1–40. There is no one typical age when women experience common parental and family tasks (Berman & Napier, 2000; Huyck, 1999). In addition, some married women never bore children; some lesbian women bore children, others did not. In the work arena, some women followed the "masculine" career script of beginning careers in young adulthood. Other women experienced interrupted careers, especially in the child-rearing years. Serious commitment to paid work did not start for some women until their late 40s or beyond, when they were not focusing as intensively on their families (Droege, 1982). The point is not that age is unimportant but that certain life events are not experienced for all adults at the same age, if they are experienced at all. In addition, midlife women who experience the same events may not experience the same effects (Tavris, 1989).

The midlife experiences of women are also variable because of the diversity of race and ethnicity, social class, sexual orientation, sex-gender identification, disability, educational attainment, and marital status. Impaired health and severely limited financial resources are also likely to affect the postretirement period of later midlife (Bumpass & Aquilino, 1995). Further, within each of these categories, there is diversity (Browne, 1994; Bumpass & Aquilino, 1995). Different representations of midlife women also exist among different cultural traditions, particularly in the non-Western world. Midlife in this book reflects the cultural representations primarily of European Americans or how this cultural context imagines, produces, and understands midlife (Shweder, 1998). Eventually, however, the growing numbers and diversity of black, Latino, and Asian immigrants and refugees will likely have a larger influence on the variation in midlife experiences for women.

COHORT FACTOR IN VARIABILITY

An added source of variability among women in midlife is their cohort membership. A cohort is a group of people that share significant life experiences in common because of the time and place they were born (Gilbert, 1993). Sometimes a label attaches to a cohort such as the baby-boom generation (born between 1946 and 1964) or generation X (born after 1965; see Cavanaugh, 1997). Cohorts can also have subgroups, and patterns of development can happen within cohorts and subgroups influenced, for example, by social class and educational status (Elder, 1979).

Much of the knowledge about midlife women came from studies of earlier cohorts of women who grew up with more restrictive social norms than did recent ones (Unger & Crawford, 1992). For example, most women in the pre-baby-boom cohort, born during the late 1920s and 1930s, developed traditional values regarding home and family. They rarely worked outside the home (Jacobson, 1995). They experienced fewer educational opportunities and they had limited or no access to male-dominated professions such as business, law, and medicine (Kessler-Harris, 1982). When this older cohort of women faced the postparental period, or the time when the last child left home, they often did not know how to refocus their lives. Some of these women experienced anxiety and depression when their "job" of active parenting ended. Eventually, however, many of these women found alternatives to child rearing, such as returning to school or work or getting involved in volunteer work (Jacobson, 1995). Most of these women were financially secure. Those who were not faced poverty during later midlife and beyond. Numerous social constraints that perpetuate poverty for women include the disparity in men's and women's responsibilities in the family system, such as caregiving demands, no-fault divorce laws, welfare policies, employment conditions, costs of child care, costs of health care, and the low economic value of economic support systems (Fitzpatrick & Gomez, 1997).

Members of the baby-boom generation were born after World War II, or more specifically, after January 1, 1946. This group, which includes women who are now in their early 50s, grew up differently from the women who preceded them into midlife. In contrast to the older pre-baby-boom cohort, the baby-boom women seemed less conforming and more liberal. They married later and experienced more sexual freedom. Many of these women benefited from the move to equal opportunity for women that resulted from the feminist and civil rights movements (Jacobson, 1995). They experienced more educational and career opportunities and were the first cohort that could pursue careers in fields previously closed to women. More of them are likely to attain financial independence. Divorce is now an acceptable personal choice and more of these women are likely to live alone (Unger & Crawford, 1992).

Jacobson (1993, 1995) studied 962 women from the baby-boom generation and from two older cohorts. These women were part of a randomly selected sample of midlife women from 21 graduating classes of an unidentified university in California. Respondents represented almost every state in the

United States. The researcher used mailed questionnaires to collect the data. The sample included three groups: 326 baby-boom women, ages 35–42; 292 women ages 43–48; and 344 women age 49 and beyond. Baby-boom women were comparable to or surpassed the two other cohorts in education, occupational status, and household income. More of them were on career tracks instead of being full-time homemakers. Larger numbers held advanced degrees and participated in higher paying, formerly male-dominated professions. Marriage and childbearing happened later for these women, and they had fewer children.

Another unique historical cohort is the current generation of midlife lesbian and gay persons. They are charting a new path because they are the first generation to reach the midlife period since the arrival of the modern gay liberation movement. Some of these women and men were active participants in the social protests associated with the 1969 Stonewall rebellion. Following a routine police raid the night of June 28, 1969, a riot erupted in the Stonewall Inn, a bar in Greenwich Village, New York. The bar patrons, which included local lesbian and gay persons, along with hundreds of other protesters from the streets, battled with police over several days. Although not the first act of resistance to oppression by lesbian and gay persons, this rebellion emerged as a key historical turning point in political activism for this population (for example, Adam, 1987; D'Emilio, 1983).

Some of the diverse experiences of midlife women are presented in five vignettes in Exhibit 1.1. Other vignettes illustrating the diversity of midlife women are included in Chapters 2–10.

───── Exhibit 1.1
Life Experiences of Midlife Women: Variations ─────────

June is 43 years old, never married, with three children and five grandchildren. She had her first child when she was 17. June is a hairdresser, always struggling to make ends meet. Two of her three children married but eventually divorced. The third child is a 19-year-old single mother, never married, who recently returned home with her child. June always feels tired. Her life follows the same routine day in and day out. She has not had a vacation in many years. Either her own children or her grandchildren are always asking for financial help, which she provides when she can. She feels it is too late to make her own life better, but would like to see her children, or at least her grandchildren, achieve more in life.

Christine is 55 years old, married, and has two children. Joanna, her eldest daughter, is 30, and recently married. Her son Ben is 29 years old and engaged to be married within the year. Both children are professionals who have been living on their own for more than five years. Christine's husband Paul is an attorney at the height of his career. Christine became active in local politics while her children were in college, and she volunteers as an advocate in a program for abused children. Her health is good, her marriage is flourishing, sex has never been better, and her children are successful. She feels that she is in the prime of her life.

Sally is 45 years old and has been in a lesbian partnership for 20 years. Her company does not provide domestic partnership benefits for same-sex couples. Sally's partner Mary works for a company that just added such benefits. In the past, both Sally and Mary lost jobs because of discriminatory policies against lesbian and gay employees. Sally was humiliated upon reaching work one day and finding a notice in her box that she was fired because "types" like her were unwelcome. She had confided in another employee that she was a lesbian, and the woman reported the information to the head of the company. After that experience, neither Sally nor Mary has been willing to discuss her sexual identification at work. They do not attend office parties together or have pictures of each other on their desks. If they decide to take the benefits offered by Mary's employer, this will change. Mary is anxious about sharing details of her private life at work, even though one of the managers of her section is openly gay.

Pat is 53 years old. She worked as a mail carrier for many years, but several years ago asked for an inside job and now works as a postal clerk in a large metropolitan city. Pat lives with her life partner in a lesbian relationship. They have been together for 10 years. Pat's mother has Alzheimer's disease and Pat has been taking care of her, with some paid help. She is at the point, however, where she will have to either place her mother in a nursing home or reduce her work hours to provide more extensive care.

Miranda is a 40-year-old African American woman, divorced, with no children. After graduating from high school, she did not go to the community college in her area because she had to take care of her elderly grandmother. After her grandmother died, Miranda went to work cleaning offices so she could contribute financial support for her family and in-laws. She decided to take some classes at the community college and did well in them. A counselor at the college has been encouraging her to pursue an undergraduate degree and helping her apply for financial aid. For the first time in her life, Miranda is able to plan for her own future.

THEORETICAL FRAMEWORK

In recent years, researchers and theorists substantially revised their conceptions of human development during the life course. One of these views, the life-span development perspective, informs this book and provides its theoretical framework. This perspective embodies newer ways of thinking about adult development and discards the views that stages of development are fixed or immutable and that chronological age determines development (for example, Baltes, 1987; Dannefer & Perlmutter, 1990; Dixon, 1992).

The life-span development perspective is neither a defined theory nor a framework that makes assumptions about the direction of change. Instead, it is a general orientation to development and, along with associated concepts such as *resiliency*, *vitality*, and *adaptation*, fits the reality of midlife women's lives and counters the overemphasis on the negative aspects of aging (Belsky, 1997). For example, a typical view of midlife for women is as a time of loss. This view is fueled by negative myths such as the idea that women will experience depression when their children leave home or when they reach menopause. The current research on this period of life, however, counters these unfavorable portrayals (Hunter & Sundel, 1989).

The life-span perspective attempts to identify various conditions under which persons can attain *optimal development* (Denney, 1982). This perspective focuses on *prevention* and *optimization* instead of remediation of behaviors (for example, Turner & Reese, 1980). Another pertinent concept is *environmental press*, defined as the influence of external conditions that can facilitate optimal development or create barriers (Ansello, 1985; Lawton, 1980). We experience an environmental press in every environment we interact with (Terry, 1992). Another concept, *duration dependence*, also can affect optimal development. According to this concept, the longer one spends in a status or situation, the longer one will remain in the particular status or situation (George, 1993; Hagestad, 1990). The life-span perspective also emphasizes *individual differences* and the *multifaceted and multidirectional nature of developmental change*. These perspectives are *contextual* by recognizing the *historical–cultural context* in which development happens. Some aspects of development are universal because they are the same for everyone, but other aspects are culture specific, cohort specific, or specific to a segment of historical time (Hoyer et al., 1999). Persons respond to these contexts and interact with and actively influence them (Baltes, 1987). In addition, no period of life stands alone without reference to other periods of life; what has already happened influences each period of life and each period will affect what is to come. Each phase of life is also *unique* and has its own importance and value (Brim & Kagan, 1980).

Multiple Influences on Development

The life-span perspective is a *pluralistic* one that emphasizes *multiple influences* (for example, biological, environmental) on persons and *diverse outcomes* from one person to another (Baltes, 1987; Lachman et al., 1994). Explanations of the complexities of adult development require different perspectives from a variety of fields of study.

The MacArthur Foundation Research Network on Successful Midlife Development (MIDMAC) was established in 1989 as an interdisciplinary research project. The purpose was to identify biomedical, psychological, and social factors that characterize adults who are physically fit, psychologically healthy, and socially responsible. This book reports findings from various MIDMAC projects (for example, Lachman & James, 1997b; Ryff & Seltzer, 1996). Information on MIDMAC is available at the project's website.*

Other influences on development include *normative* and *nonnormative events* that interact to produce both regularity and variability between persons and within persons (Baltes & Baltes, 1980). There are three types of these events:

1. *Normative age-graded events* are the result of biological, sociocultural, and other factors that correlate with chronological age. Examples include predictable biological events such as menopause, changes in vision and hearing, and predictable cultural events such as retirement.

2. *Normative history-graded events* closely relate to specific historical eras and events instead of chronological age. Historical, as well as cultural, biological, and psychological, events occur in a uniform way for most members of a cohort because the members grow up at the same historical time and in the same place. Sometimes the effects of these events on persons are intense and persist for a lifetime (Hoyer et al., 1999; Papalia et al., 1996). *Historical events* include wars and economic depressions; *cultural events* include expanding work opportunities for women and the effect of inventions such as computers, the Web, and e-mail; *biological events* include epidemics such as HIV/AIDS (also historical; see Papalia et al.); and *psychological events* include particular stereotypes based, for example, on gender, race, or sexual orientation (Cavanaugh, 1997).

3. *Nonnormative events* are unanticipated, random, or rare or chance events. They do not occur at any predictable time in a person's life. They lead to a high degree of interindividual variability among persons, especially in adulthood. Examples of nonnormative events include loss

* Available: http://midmac.med.harvard.edu.

of a child, accidents, winning the lottery, or failures in business. This category of events also includes anticipated events that happen at unexpected times such as early widowhood or being laid off from work 15 years or more before a woman contemplates retirement. The unpredictability of these events can significantly unsettle one's life (Cavanaugh, 1997; Hoyer et al., 1999).

Some persons might develop quite differently from others because of events they experienced. Predicted events that do not occur, or nonevents, can also be a determinant of behavior. Persons would be different from others if they grew up in a different neighborhood or country; attended different schools; not learned to read or write; met different friends, partners, or teachers; not been in an accident; or not lost a job (Hoyer et al., 1999).

Gains, Losses, and Constraints

Another way in which development throughout life is multidimensional is that it involves growth and gains, as well as constraints and losses. In any age period or category of behavior, however, the rates vary within persons and across persons (Baltes, 1987). Losses in midlife may include relationships, health, and leisure time, but there are also gains such as satisfaction, competence, productivity, and leadership (Brim & Kagan, 1980; Lachman et al., 1994). The same events sometimes lead to both gains and losses. Launching children, for example, can lead not only to a sense of loss but also to a sense of freedom. Some factors are constraints on development such as poor health or lack of financial resources; other constraints include restrictive sex–gender roles and the stereotypes associated with ageism, sexism, racism, and heterosexism (Lachman et al., 1994).

Losses were perceived in a sample of 14 midlife men and 18 midlife women as mainly occurring in the physical arena of appearance, energy, and health (Lachman et al., 1994). In a survey of a sample representative of midlife persons in the United States by the American Board of Family Practice (1990), midlife respondents (both men and women) reported the worst and best aspects of midlife they experienced. The worst aspects included getting older, physical and health changes, and feeling less positive about life. Their top concerns were physical changes such as developing a chronic illness or gaining weight. The best aspects for men included an accumulation of life experience and feeling settled, whereas for women the best aspects included freedom, independence, and more time for themselves. In a study of 103 midlife women ranging in age from 40 to 59 years, McQuaide (1998a, 1998b) found that what these women liked best about this period of life was more freedom and independence. They enjoyed the freedom from menstruation and responsibility for children as well as the freedom to do something new, such as develop links with women friends and pursue a career. What they disliked the most were physical changes such as decreased energy and weight gain, along with the social devaluation that accompanied those changes.

Change

Another key emphasis of the life-span perspective is change over the life course. For example, momentous changes in family and work over midlife were found in the NSFH findings (Bumpass & Aquilino, 1995). Change can occur on many levels (for example, personal, cultural) and in many forms (for example, normative, nonnormative, qualitative, quantitative). Midlife women can experience changes in the social arena (children moving in and out, parents becoming sick and dying), the physical arena (menopause, heart disease, weight gain), and the work arena (going back to work, receiving promotions, getting fired; see Lachman & James, 1997a). Changes often include role transitions such as entry into the labor market, marriage, and departure of the last child from home. Social roles undergo changes several times over the life course (Long & Porter, 1984). Because change is multidirectional, the changes midlife women experience will vary (Lachman et al., 1994).

Another emphasis of the life-span perspective is the complexity of change resulting from the interrelationships among different events and areas of life. The empty nest or postparental phase of family life, for example, is an event that occurs in a certain context. Is the mother working outside the home or does her culture stress focusing on her children (Lachman et al., 1994)? What are the other variations such as social class, race and ethnicity, and cohort membership (Bumpass & Aquilino, 1995)? How do social forces and change enhance or interfere with a "successful" midlife? How are midlife women affected by the continuing societal changes in how family is defined, such as lesbian families, multigenerational families, and single-parent families?

SUMMARY

- Defining midlife by chronological age or stages is problematic. Alternatively, the most useful definitions of midlife draw on age identity, the contents of midlife, life events, and subjective feelings.

- Midlife women experience varied and diverse lives influenced by variables such as race and ethnicity, social class, health, financial resources, sexual orientation, disability, educational attainment, and marital status. The cohort factor, which also influences this variability, is shown in the differences between pre-baby-boom and baby-boom women.

- The life-span development perspective in this book emphasizes optimal development, individual differences, the importance of historical–cultural context, and the multifaceted, multidirectional, and complex nature of change.

IMPLICATIONS FOR PRACTICE

Helping professionals should not assume that all women of a particular age enter midlife sharing the same experiences. For example, some women are grandmothers at 40 years of age and great-grandmothers at age 55, whereas others are single or never married at the same ages. The concerns midlife women present and the services they need from social workers and other helping professionals vary greatly. Helping professionals in health and social services agencies should consider the life-span developmental perspective as a guide in planning and providing services to midlife women. Practitioners can strive to improve their services by becoming informed and by applying pertinent research findings (with recognition of their limitations) to midlife women who need their help.

REFERENCES

Adam, B. D. (1987). *The rise of the gay and lesbian movement*. Boston: Twayne.

American Board of Family Practice. (1990). *Perspectives on middle age: The vintage years*. Princeton, NJ: New World Decisions.

Ansello, E. F. (1985). The activity coordinator as environmental press. *Innovations in Activities of the Elderly, 6*, 87–97.

Baltes, P. B. (1987). Theoretical propositions of life-span development psychology: On the dynamics between growth and decline. *Developmental Psychology, 23*, 611–626.

Baltes, P. B., & Baltes, M. M. (1980). Plasticity and variability in psychological aging: Methodological and theoretical issues. In G. E. Gurski (Ed.), *Determining the effects of aging on the central nervous system* (pp. 41–66). Berlin: Schering.

Barbee, E. L., & Bauer, J. A. (1988). Aging and life experiences of low-income, middle-aged African-American and Caucasian women. *Canadian Journal of Nursing Research, 20*, 5–17.

Belsky, J. (1997). *The adult experience*. St. Paul, MN: West Publishing.

Berman, E., & Napier, A.Y. (2000). The midlife family: Dealing with adolescents, young adults, and marriage in transition. In W. C. Nichols, M. A. Pace-Nichols, D. S. Becvar, & A. Y. Napier (Eds.), *Handbook of family development and intervention* (pp. 208–234). New York: John Wiley & Sons.

Braus, P. (1995). The baby boom at mid-decade. *American Demographics, 17*, 40-45.

Brim, O. G., & Kagan, J. (1980). *Constancy and change in human development*. Cambridge, MA: Harvard University Press.

Browne, C. (1994). Feminist theory and social work: A vision for practice with older women. *Journal of Applied Social Science, 18*, 5–16.

Bumpass, L. L., & Aquilino, W. S. (1995). *A social map of midlife: Family and work over the middle life course*. Vero Beach, FL: MacArthur Foundation Research Network on Successful Midlife Development.

Cavanaugh, J. (1997). *Adult development and aging* (3rd ed.). Pacific Grove, CA: Brooks/Cole.

Coombs, M. (1997). Transgenderism and sexual orientation: More than a marriage of convenience. *National Journal of Sexual Orientation Law* [On-line], *3* (1). Available: http://sunsite.unc.edu/gaylaw/issue5/coombs.html.

Dannefer, D., & Perlmutter, M. (1990). Development as a multidimensional process: Individual and social constraints. *Human Development, 33*, 108–137.

D'Emilio, J. (1983). *Sexual politics, sexual communities: The making of a homosexual minority in the United States, 1940-1970.* Chicago: University of Chicago.

Denney, N. W. (1982). Aging and cognitive changes. In B. B. Wolman (Ed.), *Handbook of developmental psychology* (pp. 807–827). Englewood Cliffs, NJ: Prentice Hall.

Dixon, R. A. (1992). Contextual approaches to adult intellectual development. In R. J. Sternberg & C. A. Berg (Eds.), *Intellectual development* (pp. 350–380). New York: Cambridge University Press.

Droege, R. (1982). *A psychosocial study of the formation of the midlife adult life structure in women.* Unpublished doctoral dissertation, California School of Professional Psychology, Berkeley.

Eichorn, D. H., Clausen, J. A., Haan, N., Honzik, M. P., & Mussen, P. H. (Eds.). (1981). *Present and past in middle life.* New York: Academic Press.

Elder, G. H., Jr. (1979). Historical change in life patterns and personality. In P. B. Baltes & O. G. Brim, Jr. (Eds.), *Life-span development and behavior* (Vol. 2). New York: Academic Press.

Fiske, M. (1979). *Middle age: The prime of life?* New York: Harper & Row.

Fitzpatrick, J. A., & Gomez, T. R. (1997). Still caught in a trap: The continued povertization of women. *Affilia, 12*, 318–341.

Genovese, R. G. (1997). *Americans at midlife: Caught between generations.* Westport, CT: Bergen & Garvey.

George, L. K. (1993). Life events. In R. Kastenbaum (Ed.), *Encyclopedia of adult development* (pp. 274–278). Phoenix, AZ: Oryx.

Gilbert, L. A. (1993). Women at midlife: Current theoretical perspectives and research. *Women & Therapy, 14*, 105–115.

Gullette, M. M. (1998). Midlife discourses in the twentieth-century United States: An essay on the sexuality, ideology, and politics of "middle-ageism." In R. A. Shweder (Ed.), *Welcome to middle age! (and other cultural fictions)* (pp. 3–44). Chicago: University of Chicago Press.

Hagestad, G. O. (1990). Social perspective on the life course. In R. H. Binstock & L. K. George (Eds.), *Handbook of aging and the social sciences* (3rd ed., pp. 151–168). San Diego: Academic Press.

Hendricks, J. (1992). Introduction: Making something of our chromosomes. In L. Glasse & J. Hendricks (Eds.), *Gender and aging* (pp. 1–4). Amityville, NY: Baywood.

Hoyer, W. I., Rybash, J. M., & Roodin, P. A. (1999). *Adult development and aging* (4th ed.). Boston: McGraw-Hill.

Hunter, S., & Sundel, M. (Eds.). (1989). *Midlife myths: Issues, findings, and practice implications*. Newbury Park, CA: Sage Publications.

Huyck, M. H. (1999). Gender roles and gender identity in midlife. In S. L. Willis & J. D. Reid (Eds.), *Life in the middle: Psychological and social development in middle age* (pp. 209–232). San Diego: Academic Press.

Jacobson, J. M. (1993). Midlife baby boom women compared with their older counterparts in midlife. *Health Care for Women International, 14,* 427–436.

Jacobson, J. M. (1995). *Midlife women: Contemporary issues*. Boston: Jones and Bartlett.

Kastenbaum, B. K. (1993). Menopause. In R. Kastenbaum (Ed.), *Encyclopedia of adult development* (pp. 326–328). Phoenix, AZ: Oryx.

Kessler-Harris, A. (1982). *Out to work*. New York: Oxford University Press.

Kornhaber, A. (1996). *Contemporary grandparenting*. Thousand Oaks, CA: Sage Publications.

Lachman, M. E., & James, J. B. (1997a). Changing the course of midlife development: An overview. In M. E. Lachman, & J. Boone James (Eds.), *Multiple paths of midlife development* (pp. 1–17). Chicago: University of Chicago Press.

Lachman, M. E., & James, J. B. (Eds.). (1997b). *Multiple paths of midlife development*. Chicago: University of Chicago Press.

Lachman, M. E., Lewkowicz, C., Marcus, A., & Peng, Y. (1994). Images of midlife development among young, middle-aged, and older adults. *Journal of Adult Development, 1,* 201–211.

Lawton, M. P. (1980). *Environment and aging*. Monterey, CA: Brooks/Cole.

Levinson, D., Darrow, C., Klein, E., Levinson, M., & McKee, B. (1978). *The seasons of a man's life*. New York: Alfred A. Knopf.

Life expectancy by country—North America. (2000). [On-line]. Available: http://www.over-population.com/faq/Health/mortality/lifeexpectancy/north_america.html.

Logan, J. R., Ward, R., & Spitze, G. (1992). As old as you feel: age identity in middle and later life. *Social Forces, 71,* 451–467.

Long, J., & Porter, K. (1984). Multiple roles of midlife women: A case for new direction in theory, research and policy. In G. Baruch & J. Brooks-Gunn (Eds.), *Women in midlife* (pp. 109–160). New York: Plenum Press.

Markides, K. S., & Boldt, J. S. (1983). Change in subjective aging among the elderly: A longitudinal analysis. *Gerontologist, 23,* 422–427.

Marks, N. F. (1993). *Contemporary social demographics of American midlife parents* (NSFH Working Paper No. 54). Madison: University of Wisconsin, Center for Demography and Ecology.

Marks, N. F. (1996). Social demographic diversity among American midlife parents. In C. D. Ryff & M. M. Seltzer (Eds.), *The parental experience in midlife* (pp. 29–75). Chicago: University of Chicago Press.

McQuaide, S. (1998a). Opening space for alternative images and narratives of midlife women. *Clinical Social Work, 26,* 39–53.

McQuaide, S. (1998b). Women at midlife. *Social Work, 43,* 21–31.

Moen, P., & Wethington, E. (1999). Midlife development in a life course context. In S. L. Willis & J. D. Reid (Eds.). *Life in the middle: Psychological and social development in middle age* (pp. 3–23). San Diego: Academic Press.

National Center for Health Statistics (1993). Health in the United States and prevention profile, 1992. Hyattville, MD: U.S. Department of Health and Human Services.

Neugarten, B. L., & Hagestad, G. (1976). Age and the life course. In H. Binstock & E. Shanas (Eds.), *Handbook of aging and the social sciences* (pp. 35–55). New York: Van Nostrand Reinhold.

Papalia, D. E., Camp, C. J., & Feldman, R. D. (1996). *Adult development and aging.* New York: McGraw-Hill.

Rosenblatt, R. (1996, January–February). Boo!mers: The babies face fifty. *Modern Maturity,* 32–34.

Ryff, C. D., & Seltzer, M. M. (Eds.). (1996). *The parental experience in midlife.* Chicago: University of Chicago Press.

Sherman, S. S. (1994). Changes in age identity: Self perceptions in middle and late life. *Journal of Aging Studies, 8,* 397–412.

Shweder, R. A. (Ed.). (1998). *Welcome to middle age! (and other cultural fictions).* Chicago: University of Chicago Press.

Spurlock, J. (1984). Black women in the middle years. In G. Baruch & J. Brooks-Gunn (Eds.), *Women in midlife* (pp. 245–260). New York: Plenum Press.

Staudinger, U. M., & Bluck, S. (2001). A view on midlife development from life-span theory. In M. E. Lachman (Ed.), *Handbook of midlife development* (pp. 3–39). New York: John Wiley & Sons.

Stein, E. (1999). *The mismeasure of desire: The science, theory, and ethics of sexual orientation.* New York: Oxford University Press.

Tavris, C. (1989, July/August). Don't act your age. *American Health,* pp. 50–58.

Terry, E. F. (1992). The freshman year experience as environmental press: The William Jewell experience. *College Student Journal, 26,* 110–118.

Troll, L. E. (1982). *Continuations: Adult development and aging.* Monterey, CA: Brooks/Cole.

Turner, B. F. (1994). Introduction. In B. F. Turner & L. E. Troll (Eds.), *Women growing older: Psychological perspectives* (pp. 1–34). Thousand Oaks, CA: Sage Publications.

Turner, R. R., & Reese, H. W. (1980). *Life-span developmental psychology: Intervention.* New York: Academic Press.

Uhlenberg, P., & Kirby, J. B. (1998). Grandparenthood over time: Historical and demographic trends. In M. E. Szinovacz (Ed.), *Handbook on grandparenthood* (pp. 23–39). Westport, CT: Greenwood Press.

Unger, R., & Crawford, M. (1992). *Women & gender: A feminist psychology.* New York: McGraw Hill.

U.S. Bureau of the Census. (1990). *Statistical abstract of the United States* (110th ed.). Washington, DC: U.S. Government Printing Office.

U.S. Bureau of the Census. (1995). *Sixty-five plus in the United States* (DCESA Pub. No. SB-95-8). Washington, DC: U.S. Government Printing Office.

U.S. Bureau of the Census. (2001). *Resident Population Estimates of the United States by Age and Sex* [On-line]. Available: http://eire.census.gov/popest/archives/national/nation2/intfile2-1.txt

Zal, H. M. (1992). *The sandwich generation: Caught between children and aging parents.* New York: Plenum Press.

ADDITIONAL REFERENCES

Karp, D. A. (1988). A decade of reminders: Changing age consciousness between fifty and sixty years old. *Gerontologist, 28,* 727–738.

Quinn, P., & Walsh, P. K. (1995). Midlife women with disabilities: Another challenge for social workers. *Affilia, 10,* 235–254.

CHAPTER 2

FAMILY CONTEXTS AND RELATIONSHIPS

This chapter focuses on the marital and parental statuses of midlife women. Much of the available data on these topics come from the National Survey of Families and Households (NSFH) project identified in Chapter 1 (for example, Bumpass & Aquilino, 1995; Bumpass & Sweet, 1991; Marks, 1995, 1996). Life-span themes in this chapter include: the inapplicability of a universal use of the linear age–stage approach to marital and parental statuses; the influence of changing historical/cultural/social contexts; the diversity of family structures such as single mothers, lesbian mothers, and households with no children; on-time and off-time happenings, the normative experience of child launching, and continuing relationships with adult children; and the changes in normative timing when children leave and the anticipation that they will remain gone from the parental home.

QUESTIONS TO CONSIDER

- *What are the stressors of midlife parenting?*

- *How does the launching of children affect midlife marriages?*

- *What happens to parent–child relationships when children are gone?*

- *What happens to parent–child relationships if children leave home late or leave and return home?*

- *How do midlife lesbian couples compare to heterosexual couples?*

- *What types of family patterns are evident for midlife lesbian mothers?*

HETEROSEXUAL MARRIAGES AND PRIMARY LESBIAN RELATIONSHIPS

Marriage is the central source of investment and support for most adults. The NSFH data showed that about three-quarters of the current midlife population are married. This figure includes about 20 percent in second or later marriages. Among the variables that affect whether one is married during the midlife period are sex and gender and educational attainment. About 80 percent of men and women between the ages of 30–34 are in a marital or cohabiting status. The proportion of married men is steady throughout midlife, but the proportion of married women declines as they get older. Whereas 86 percent of men are in a marital status at ages 60–64, this characterizes only 66 percent of women (Bumpass & Aquilino, 1995). Census data collected in 1999 found 77 percent of men age 55–64 were married and living with their partner compared to 64 percent of women (U.S. Bureau of the Census, 2000). Slightly over a quarter (26 percent) of the women surveyed in the NSFH study were already widowed compared to only 7 percent of the men. Only half of African American women had a spouse or partner during midlife. Education is also positively associated with being married during midlife; both divorce and widowhood are higher among the less educated (Bumpass & Aquilino, 1995). An analysis of panel data from the 1967–1989 waves of the National Longitudinal Survey of Mature Women showed that a college education for midlife women has a positive influence on remaining married in the second decade of midlife and later (Hiedemann, Suhomlinova, & O'Rand, 1998).

Because information on midlife lesbians is minimal, findings are sometimes presented from studies on lesbians of mixed or unknown ages. To some degree this information applies to midlife lesbians because of the issues related to same-sex sexual orientation, such as experiencing heterosexism in daily life. Heterosexism is the ideological system "that denies, denigrates, and stigmatizes any nonheterosexual form of behavior, identity, relationship, or community" (Herek, 1990, p. 316). The proportion of same-sex couples in the United States is unknown. Peplau and Cochran (1990) reported that based on various nonprobability samples, the proportion of couples in the lesbian population is about 75 percent. Somewhere from 42 percent to 75 percent of the participants in lesbian and gay couples live together (Harry, 1983; Peplau & Amaro, 1982).

Being part of a couple is a desired goal for most lesbians at midlife. Almost three-quarters (74 percent) of the national sample of midlife lesbians studied by Bradford and Ryan (1991) were in a primary or dating relationship. Only about one-fifth (19 percent) of these women claimed that they were single and uninvolved.

Although not all lesbian (or gay) couples want to be married, this option of having the benefits that heterosexual couples receive is desirable. In 1985, for the first time, partners of gay and lesbian city employees in Berkeley, California, received the benefits offered earlier only to married heterosexual couples. Later, several other cities followed this practice including Seattle, New York, San Francisco, Minneapolis, and Madison (Domestic-partner benefits, 1991). Various private companies and universities are also implementing or providing some types of domestic partner benefits. In 1997, Hawaii adopted partner registration, providing gay and lesbian couples many rights that married couples enjoy. A major milestone for same-sex couples happened in April 2000, when the Governor of Vermont signed a bill making civil unions for these couples legal in that state (Hunter & Hickerson, in press).

Because being in a lesbian couple usually follows the unique experience of coming out as lesbian, the discussion here focuses on the outcomes of this experience when it happens in midlife. Many women who self-identify as lesbians in midlife lived a long prior life self-identified as heterosexuals. The identity changes they experienced involved a radical transformation and redirection. Whatever the catalysts, "the reversal of years of habit was momentous" (Charbonneau & Lander, 1991, p. 37) and sometimes the consequences were intensely experienced. Some women felt, "for the first time I am me" (Charbonneau & Lander, 1991, p. 42). For some, when they were with other women, intimacy was experienced at a new or previously unimaginable depth (McGrath, 1990).

There was also a down side to coming out as lesbian in midlife resulting from two basic kinds of costs. First, there were the consequences of no longer being in a primary relationship with a man: giving up privileges associated with a male partner, giving up fantasies of being cared for by a man, giving up the social support associated with a primary partnership with a man, and linking with a woman, which in most social contexts does not garner the respect and status as a relationship with a man (for example, Groves & Ventura, 1983; Kirkpatrick, 1989). Second, there were negative reactions by heterosexuals to disclosures that one now self-identifies as lesbian (Bradford & Ryan, 1991). At the least, a large majority of the women studied by Lander and Charbonneau (1990) experienced verbal harassment from others, such as screaming and painful comments. Many other women experienced rejection from their families of origin, demonstrated in actions such as cancelled invitations to family occasions. The negative reactions were alarming to these women because they were unaware of the intense heterosexism directed to persons with a same-sex sexual orientation. This new reality no doubt led many of these women to start hiding their sexual identification. Charbonneau and Lander underscored, however, that it was important for these women to reconceptualize negative stereotypes about lesbians. For some women, this happened because of a single encounter with another woman but for others it was a slower process.

HOUSEHOLDS WITH NO CHILDREN

Most (90 percent) adults between the ages of 35 and 64 are parents (Marks, 1996). Some couples, however, find themselves at midlife having had no children. The NSFH data showed that there were never any children in about one-fifth of the households of couples in early midlife (ages 35–44; Bumpass & Aquilino, 1995). This sometimes happened because couples could not conceive, a situation that usually resulted in their mourning the loss of the dream of producing their own children. Other couples, however, who were able to have children chose not to, including those who struggled with the reality that time was going to run out on that possibility (Anderson, Dimidjian, & Miller, 1995). When both partners had long-term work histories or well-developed careers, the decision about bearing children could be conflictual and require considerable renegotiation of their investments, especially for women (Gilbert & Davidson, 1989).

In a study using structured interviews with 678 adults age 55 and older, Connidis and McMullin (1993) found that the issue of childlessness for some couples does not get resolved in midlife. Concerns about this issue may not even arise until old age (Alexander, Rubinstein, Goodman, & Luborsky, 1992). Using NSFH data, Koropeckyj-Cox (1998) addressed the psychological effects of childlessness in later life. The researcher compared permanently childless adults with biological parents of at least one surviving child. The ages of these respondents ranged from 50 to 84. Generally, the results indicated that permanent childlessness was not a significant or universal disadvantage (measured by loneliness and depression) for either women or men. Yet, from another sample of 287 childless respondents age 55 and older, Connidis and McMullin (1999) reported that both advantages and disadvantages were associated with being childless. Over two-thirds (67 percent) of the respondents reported advantages (for example, fewer worries or problems, greater freedom, career flexibility, and financial benefits) and about the same proportion (64 percent) reported disadvantages (for example, missing the experience of parenthood, lack of companionship, lack of care and support when older).

HOUSEHOLDS WITH CHILDREN

For couples with children, the longest period of active parenting usually happens during midlife when children grow into adolescence and young adulthood. Though the proportion having children under the age of 10 years dropped rapidly in early midlife, life with teenagers peaked at 60 percent for parents in the 40–44 age group and rapidly declined after that. By the last decade of midlife, ages 55–64, few parents live with children under the age of 19 (Bumpass & Aquilino, 1995). The *linear age–stage script*, however, does not fit all midlife parents. The times when parenting begins and ends are variable. Neither does the anticipated continuum of midlife parenting fit all midlife families, beginning when children reach puberty or enter junior high school and ending when the children leave home (Ryff & Seltzer, 1996). In addition, many midlife persons are parenting with a new partner or parenting alone (Marks, 1991).

The proportion of midlife parents in nontraditional single and remarried parenting statuses will likely increase for cohorts now approaching middle age (Bumpass, 1990; Marks, 1993; Uhlenberg, Cooney, & Boyd, 1990). The NSFH data revealed that about one in five midlife parents were unmarried. The same proportion of midlife mothers characterized themselves as divorced, separated, or always single. In a sample of women ages 35–64, only about one-third of African American midlife mothers (ages 35–64) were still in a first marriage compared to 57.5 percent of Latino midlife mothers (ages 35–64) and 61.1 percent of white mothers. The likelihood of remarriage for Latino mothers was lower (9.5 percent) than for white (17.9 percent) or African American (12.1 percent) mothers (Marks, 1991, 1993, 1996). For mothers who remarried, stepchildren were not rare; about one in seven midlife parents were stepparents (Marks, 1991).

Midlife lesbian mothers are also in a variety of family structures, including blended families, single-parent families, and shared-parent families. Blended families, equivalent to stepfamilies, are probably the most typical family structure for lesbians. They include a lesbian partnership and children from previous marriages of both women. Single-parent families usually involve a lesbian parent raising a child from a previous heterosexual marriage. Shared-parenting families involve a lesbian partnership and at least one child raised by both women (Rohrbaugh, 1992).

Although parenting could affect the well-being of any parent, certain family structures may be more detrimental to well-being than others (McLanahan & Adams, 1987). Single parenting and stepparenting appear to be associated with distress, with single parenting the most likely to result in this consequence (for example, McLanahan & Adams, 1989; Umberson & Gove, 1989). The economic status of single mothers in all racial and ethnic groups is also distressing. Their household incomes are only half the size of the household incomes of married midlife mothers. This situation does not get better with time; in later midlife, the income of single mothers deteriorates even further (Marks, 1993). Poor African American women raising adolescent children in an urban context have a particularly difficult time (Allen, Aber, Seidman, Denner, & Mitchell, 1996). Remarried parents report more psychological distress than parents still married to the same partner (Marks, 1993). Remarried mothers receive significantly less emotional support from their children (Bumpass & Sweet, 1991). Both remarried and single midlife mothers are less happy and more depressed than first married mothers (Marks, 1991).

It is possible that there are reasons other than marital status associated with stressed and unhappy mothers, because most of the studies on this topic are correlational. For example, mothers are more distressed than fathers. Because women feel more responsible for relationships, emotional stress in family relationships may affect them more (Marks, 1993; Scott & Alwin, 1989).

STRESSORS OF MIDLIFE PARENTING

Adolescent children tend to get most of the blame for the stressors of midlife parenting. Stressors in parenting can build up from the time of childbearing to the teenage years (Olson et al., 1989) but the highest point usually occurs during the children's school and adolescent years (Harris, Ellicott, & Holmes, 1986). Typically, during this time the parents experience many demands or role overload (Rollins, 1989). In addition, midlife mothers can experience the added discomfort of the intersection of their own developmental issues with the developmental issues of their adolescent children and ambivalences about these issues.

Intersection of Midlife with Adolescence

The intersection of developmental processes in midlife mothers and adolescent children can create distress for the mothers and intensify their anxieties about aging (for example, Hamill & Goldberg, 1997; Seltzer & Ryff, 1996; Silverberg, 1989). For example, mothers may experience issues such as confronting mortality and declining options while their adolescent children represent endless opportunities and seeming invincibility (Silverberg, 1989; Silverberg & Steinberg, 1987). Mothers of daughters may begin to feel concern about losing their sexual attractiveness as their daughters are developing greater sexual attractiveness (Kidwell, Fischer, Dunham, & Baranowski, 1983). In addition, as their daughters are developing into independent adults, mothers may reassess their own choices and personal commitments (Silverberg, 1996). Unlike their young daughters, however, mothers may feel that they are in a race against time. Compared to the lives of their daughters, they also may feel that their current lives are devoid of passion. They may use what their children represent as the standards for their own satisfaction and come up short (Kidwell et al., 1983).

The children of midlife lesbian mothers are also most likely adolescents or older (Kirkpatrick, 1988, 1989; Rothschild, 1991; Sang, 1992). Besides other issues that can arise because of the intersection of developmental processes in midlife mothers and adolescent children, the intersection of mothers coming out as lesbian in midlife along with their adolescent children's developmental issues can create additional difficulties. These lesbian mothers may fear that their children will become hostile and rejecting because of their sexual orientation. Adolescents typically conform to peer attitudes that can be hostile to same-sex sexual orientation, or they may fear embarrassment and ridicule from peers (Kirkpatrick, 1989).

Ambivalences

Mothers report more closeness and involvement with their children compared to fathers from the early to the later years of midlife parenting (Pruchno, Peters, & Burant, 1996). Mothers particularly report more closeness with daughters (Silverberg, 1996). The mother–daughter relationship is a passionate and central one, forming one of the cores of women's lives (Chodorow, 1978). Yet, most parents experience a mix of positive and negative emotions and reactions regarding their children (Nydegger & Mitteness, 1996; Silverberg, 1996). Mothers report more conflict with their children during the midlife period than fathers (for example, Graber & Brooks-Gunn, 1996). The day-to-day struggles with adolescent children affect them more negatively. Both their disagreements with their adolescents and their husbands' disagreements with these children predict lower well-being for mothers (Silverberg, 1996). Adolescent children who display more signs of psychological autonomy, engagement in adult-type roles, and distancing can provoke distress in their mothers (Hamill & Goldberg, 1997; Steinberg, 1987). Yet, psychological investment of mothers in a nonfamily role, such as work, may lead to an easier accommodation to potentially stressful and provocative signs of the maturation and expanding independence of both sons and daughters. Silverberg and Steinberg (1990) studied mothers' work orientation (investment in paid work) in a study of 129 intact families with a firstborn child between the ages of 10 and 15. Through responses to a questionnaire, the researchers found that if mothers' work–role orientation was low or if there was no strong outside investment of self beyond the parental role, the parent–child relationship was negative, but when work–role orientation was high, the parent–child relationship was often positive.

Mothers who view the changes in their children as an indication that they did a good job of preparing their children for adulthood also view signs of autonomous behaviors in their children as positive. They also experience fewer concerns about issues such as their own aging compared to mothers of children who display fewer signs of autonomous behaviors (Hamill & Goldberg, 1997).

Without a strong investment outside the home and a sense of self-worth and competence, it can be especially difficult for mothers to handle their sons' expanding maturity and the realignments in their relationships. For low work–role-oriented mothers of sons, perceptions of increased challenge or distance in the relationship (for example, arguments about rules or devaluation of mothers' opinions) result in diminished well-being for the mothers. In addition, adolescent sons seem to gain influence in family decision making at the expense of their mothers, and their challenges seem more potent to the mothers than the challenges of daughters (Silverberg, 1996).

Mothers also express concern about losing their adolescent daughters as their social worlds begin to expand beyond the home. Higher levels of involvement in mixed peer group activities and dating by daughters are associated with more intense midlife concerns for their mothers, diminished life satisfaction, and more frequent psychological signs of distress. Greater closeness in mother–daughter pairs, however, can reduce the potency of the changes and conflicts in their relationships (Silverberg, 1996).

EFFECTS OF LAUNCHING CHILDREN ON PARENTAL MARRIAGE, WELL-BEING, AND LIFE SATISFACTION

Studies generally show no discrepancies between lesbian and gay couples and heterosexual couples in couple quality (Kurdek, 1994, 1995a), couple adjustments (Kurdek, 1995b; Kurdek & Schmitt, 1986), or in couple satisfaction (Kurdek, 1994, 1995a; Peplau & Cochran, 1990). As indicated above, however, when couples are parents, their satisfaction may not be as high as at other times. They may neglect communication and companionship with each other because of the stressors of parenting adolescents and other demands of life (Rollins, 1989). Relations may be strained compared to the happier situations of newly married couples (Huyck, 1995) or cohabitating gay and lesbian couples with no children in the home.

What happens to couples after the children are no longer living at home? Research that attempts to provide answers to this question focuses only on heterosexual couples. Rollins (1989) reported that a U-shaped curve of marital satisfaction fits most parents. Marital satisfaction is higher before a couple has children, decreases during the child-rearing years, and rises when the children leave home. An exception is a decrease in satisfaction during the period of launching the children, but the drop is not severe enough to modify the U-shaped-curve interpretation of what transpires over time. After the children leave, the partners no longer are primarily mothers and fathers but husbands and wives again. Revitalization of closeness and love enhances marital quality. Couples usually experience understanding and support from each other over the parenting years and are optimistic about their life together as a couple in the postparental period (Turner & Helms, 1994). This U-shaped picture of midlife marriage, however, has detractors. Not all marriages fit this picture (Davidson & Moore, 1992). In addition, decreased marital satisfaction can result from reasons other than child rearing. For example, as indicated before, it may result from the parents' own developmental stress or concerns about midlife that can strain both marital and parent–child interactions (Rollins,

1989; Steinberg & Silverberg, 1987). When midlife mothers experience identity concerns, marriage satisfaction can decrease (Steinberg & Silverberg, 1987).

Panel studies (involving the same groups of persons over a long time) are one way to study the effects of entering and ending the child-launching process on martial happiness and satisfaction of parents.

Recently, results on marital happiness were reported by VanLaningham, Johnson, and Amato (2001) from a national, 17-year, five-wave panel sample. Declines in marital happiness were found at all marital durations and there was no support for an upturn in marital happiness in the later years. The researchers concluded that the *U*-shaped version of marital happiness (for example, Rollins, 1989), declining in the early years (associated with the presence of children) but rising in the later years, is not typical of U.S. marriages. Instead, marital happiness continues to decline or remain flat. Basically the *U*-shaped version appears to be an artifact of cross-sectional research, often with small nonprobability samples from specific regional and demographic groups (for example, Anderson, Russell, & Schumm, 1983; Rollins & Feldman, 1970). This is not to say that every marriage experiences continual decline in happiness or remains flat; some do not experience this outcome but they differ from the central tendency of the marriages studied in this large, national, long-term panel study.

In situations where marital satisfaction grows over time, there are also alternate explanations other than moving beyond the child-rearing years. The growth in satisfaction could result from the partners learning more about each other, as well as developing skills of accommodation over time (Skolnick, 1981). Changes within the partners themselves can also play a role (Barber, 1989). In a qualitative study of African American midlife marriages, partners felt that their growing maturity over time contributed to stabilizing their marriages (Carolan & Allen, 1999). Yet, not all couples are happier after the children leave. Or, happiness may not happen quickly for them.

White and Edwards (1990) also conducted a panel study but obtained different results from the Van Laningham et al., 2001 study. White and Edwards used three types of theories that indicated certain consequences for parents in the postparental period. Role change theories (for example, Holmes & Rahe, 1967) indicated that any role change, positive or negative, would lead to negative effects on psychological and physical well-being. Launching children, therefore, results in role changes for parents from which they will experience negative effects. Role identity theories (for example, Thoits, 1983) indicate that because role loss will lead to negative effects on psychological functioning, child launching will lead to decreased parental well-being. The portrayal of mothers for a long time was that they experienced reactions to launching their children, such as dissatisfaction, loneliness, and depression (Barber, 1989).

Role conflict theories (for example, Barnett & Baruch, 1985) indicate that the effects of role loss or change depended on how much stress and conflict were associated with the role. If one loses a role associated with strain and conflict, a beneficial effect could occur. It follows then that if the role of parents was stressful, parental well-being should improve when the last child leaves home. The results of the White and Edwards' study, based on interviews in 1983 and 1989, are summarized in Exhibit 2.1.

——— Exhibit 2.1

Effects of Launching Children on Parental Marital Happiness, Well-Being, and Life Satisfaction ————————————————————

- The empty nest was associated with significant improvements in marital happiness.

- Generally, life satisfaction improved significantly under two conditions: frequent contact with launched children and when young teens were in the home at the time of the first interviews in 1983.

- Positive effects of the empty nest for both marital and life satisfaction were strongest immediately after the children left (contradicting role change theory).

- The general positive effects of the empty nest on parental well-being supported stressful role theory. When parents saw an end to children in the home, they experienced relief. Launching teens, compared with older children, produced the most improvement in both marital happiness and life satisfaction.

- When conflict was frequent between parents and children, the empty nest brought significantly greater improvement in life satisfaction (supporting role identity theory).

In summary, White and Edwards (1990) found significant improvements in marital happiness when "the nest was emptied," especially when teens were launched. Marital satisfaction was greatest when all the children were launched. Many other studies reported that marriages benefited when the children were gone. Two other panel studies provided strong evidence of an association between launching the children and positive changes in well-being for parents (McLanahan & Sorensen, 1985; Menaghan, 1983). The satisfaction of successful child rearing and newly attained freedoms outweighed any sadness experienced. Other studies reported analogous findings. Parents felt relief when children were not home to take up their time, energy, and money. Life at home was simpler

(Mitchell & Helson, 1990). Supervision, laundry, cleaning, marketing, and cooking chores decreased. Financial worries often declined (Davidson & Moore, 1992). Unless parents were paying for college educations or other large expenditures, disposable income rose (Schaie & Willis, 1991). Couples reported experiencing the privacy they enjoyed when first married, more intimacy, and more spontaneous sexuality (Perlmutter & Hall, 1992). The sexual behavior of midlife to later-life couples was analogous to their earlier patterns but less active (Weinstein & Rosen, 1988). Communication was more open, and activities were shared together as a couple (Davidson & Moore, 1992). Travels together no longer had to be scheduled around school vacations (Perlmutter & Hall, 1992). Partners also could contribute more equally regarding work and home than during earlier stages (Rexroat & Shehan, 1987). Additional positive outcomes for the parents included greater happiness, higher morale, reduced conflict with other roles, personal growth, and self-direction (for example, Cooper & Gutmann, 1987; Huyck, 1989). These findings supported the U-shaped curve of marital satisfaction. Not all midlife couples, however, are happy with their marriages after the children leave.

Marital Distress

Some parents may fear or actually discover that the children were "the glue" that held their marriage together. They achieved the main goals they shared as parents and now have no other goals they want to share. If they refocus on each other, suppressed conflicts may reemerge. Or they may feel like strangers to each other, necessitating a period to get reacquainted (Anderson et al., 1995). They may find little pleasure in this process, however, or in each other, and decide to separate and divorce. On the other hand, the parents may stay together but live separate lives following their individual interests. Their interactions may be amicable but without much affection (Clausen, 1986).

Distress can also occur because of issues that confront contemporary couples at midlife. In a theoretical discourse on midlife marriage, C. M. Anderson et al. (1995) identified three primary issues that can generate this distress: *social and cultural changes*, *personal developmental issues*, and *outdated marital contracts*. First, distress can result from an expansion of models of marriage. When persons now at midlife initially married, a single model of marriage existed, one of stability and permanence. Because of social and cultural changes, there is no longer strong denouncement of divorce and many former assumptions about marriage and marital roles are no longer universally accepted. There are fewer absolutes and constraints. More choices are available as models of marriage, such as dual-earner or dual-career models.

Second, distress can result from individual or personal developmental issues. The reality of one's mortality, for example, often moves to the foreground in midlife. Life reviews are also common. Often, these reviews cause regrets over the paths one did not take. One partner may blame the other for what one feels was missed in life, such as career, travel, relationships, and the person one might have become. If one wants to pursue missed paths, priorities are often reordered. The new priorities may or may not include the partner (Anderson et al., 1995).

Third, outdated marital contracts can cause distress. The implicit or explicit agreements and patterns of relating established early in the marriage can seem outdated and unnecessarily constricting at midlife. If the partners followed traditional sex–gender-role patterns, these may no longer fit them well (Anderson et al., 1995). Child rearing is a major influence on sex–gender-role prescriptions in marriages (Gutmann, 1987). As the children become young adults, however, parents often recover suppressed aspects of themselves (Huyck & Gutmann, 1992). Wives, for example, may openly assert themselves within their marriages. They may push for more satisfaction for themselves, such as shifting from the nurturing role to a pursuit of more individualistic dreams and goals. If the other partner wants the changing partner to remain committed to the original contract, conflict and tension will likely result. But, if both partners want to renegotiate the original contract, they can feel overwhelmed by all the areas now open for renegotiation (for example, division of labor, patterns of intimacy; see Anderson et al., 1995).

Linked to the areas of potential distress identified above, Anderson et al. (1995) identified three goals for intervention with midlife couples:

- Redefining the past includes addressing the feeling that one made wrong choices or lost former hopes and dreams. Instead of viewing the past as one of losses, reframing or shifting one's perspective on the past to one in which there was learning and growth is more helpful. If one can see oneself as responsible for making choices that made sense at the time, one may avoid blaming one's partner for these choices.

- Redefining the present includes broadening the definition of marital distress by including the effects of typical developmental issues at midlife such as the sense that time is running out.

- Redefining the future includes creating realistic dreams and developing skills and resources to attain them. This will probably involve evaluation and revision of the marital contract to include each partner's needs and goals.

EFFECTS OF LAUNCHING CHILDREN ON MOTHERS

In discussions on what parents experience when their last child leaves, the term empty nest often surfaces (Gullette, 1998; Raup & Myers, 1989). Now part of the common vocabulary of midlife, this term is most often associated with mothers (Huyck, 1989). Yet, it is a demeaning term because of its similarity to other barnyard terms often applied to women such as "chicks," "old hens," or "tough old birds." These terms are both sexist and ageist (Oliver, 1988). Even so, the "empty nest syndrome" has been one of the most prevalent myths about midlife mothers.

Empty Nest Syndrome

It used to be thought that launching the last child, often coinciding with menopause, inevitably precipitated depression in women (Perlmutter & Hall, 1992). This became known as the empty nest syndrome (Huyck, 1989). Some mothers invested so much of their lives and identities in the parenting role that they did not develop any separate interests, friends, or sense of self (Kahana & Kahana, 1982; Orsmond, 1991). In this scenario, mothers do not know what they want to do beyond the parenting role (Lasswell & Lasswell, 1991). They may feel useless and as if their seemingly meaningless lives are as good as over (Keith & Schafer, 1991). It is these mothers who were found to be the most susceptible to the empty nest syndrome (for example, Borland, 1982; Mercer, Nichols, & Doyle, 1989). They may experience extreme grief reactions such as recurrent crying and other signs of depression (Orsmond, 1991). Bart (1972) suggested that depression covered over the anger these mothers feel about their children's independence and autonomy. They may feel that the children do not appreciate the sacrifices they made for them. McGoldrick (1989) explained that ethnic background could influence some mothers to feel like failures if their children moved away. In Puerto Rican and Italian families, for example, child and husband care are the major roles of mothers. Hence, they feel that they are "successful" mothers only when actually performing these roles.

Positive Outcomes from Launching Children

Early research on child launching did not support the empty nest syndrome as a common occurrence for midlife mothers. Neugarten (1976) and her coworkers compared mothers with all of their children still at home, mothers with some children who left but with others still at home, and women whose children were all gone. Mothers with children at home seemed to experience more stress than those whose children were gone. Other studies (for example, Bart, 1972; Black & Hill, 1984; Harris et al., 1986) also showed that the "trauma" view of launching children was inaccurate. Even if the reactions to the loss of the parent role were intense, they were usually temporary if mothers found new investments (Black & Hill, 1984; Raup & Meyers, 1989).

Though the empty nest syndrome characterizes some ethnic mothers, this is not the case for other ethnic mothers. For example, Mexican American

mothers in the postparental stage are not different in physical and psychological well-being from Mexican American mothers with children still at home.
This finding was unexpected because of the high value of the maternal role in
the Mexican American culture and the scarcity of alternative roles for women.
When there were alternatives, however, such as employment, mothers' levels
of depression were lower and life satisfaction higher when their children left
(Rogers & Markides, 1989). For African American women, the work role takes
precedence over both the parental role and the marital role (Coleman,
Antonucci, Adelmann, & Crohan, 1987).

Through comparisons of successive 20-year cohorts of midlife women,
Adelmann, Antonucci, Crohan, and Coleman (1989) demonstrated that the
empty nest syndrome was not an inevitable response to loss of the child-rearing role. Instead, it was more the result of socialization during periods of strong
emphasis on the maternal role. Recent cohorts experienced greater balance
between maternal and other roles so that when the children were launched
they could more easily focus on other roles (Huyck, 1989). These women
viewed "motherhood more as an episode than a lifelong occupation" (Unger &
Crawford, 1992, p. 514). Generally the time when the last child leaves home is
now a *normative* or an anticipated period in the life course. This event does not
upset most mothers' lives. More often than not, the positives of this period of
life outweigh the negatives.

Most women in their early 50s experience the feelings of accomplishment and gratification of successfully reared and launched children. They
find that their lives change for the better with a new sense of freedom and
feelings of well-being. If women were college educated before they raised
their families, their need for challenge and instrumental action is often especially strong (Clausen, 1986). They eagerly want to use the talents and abilities that were not possible for them to employ with children at home
(Adelmann et al., 1989; Reinke, Ellicott, Harris, & Hancock, 1985). Women
with an economic advantage are in a much better position to explore the
opportunities this period can provide, such as returning to school to complete their education or to upgrade skills to enter or reenter the workplace
(Mitchell & Helson, 1990).

How Children Turned Out

Midlife parents usually assess how their children turn out as adults. Four out of
five parents are happy with how their children "turned out," though more than
three out of four are troubled about them occasionally (Umberson, 1992). A
positive assessment of outcomes validates for parents that their investments in
child rearing were successful and increases their sense of well-being. Stressful
outcomes, such as an adult child's divorce, are associated with strained parent–child relations and parental depression (for example, Pillemer & Suitor,

1991a, 1991b). Mothers experience more distress than fathers when there are negative events in a child's life (Pruchno et al., 1996).

Seven measures of well-being for parents were assessed by Ryff, Lee, Essex, and Schmutte (1994) and Ryff, Schmutte, and Lee (1996): autonomy, sense of self-acceptance, purpose in life, environmental mastery, personal growth, depression, and positive relations with others. Two variables were assessed for the children's outcomes: educational and occupational achievements and personal and social adjustment. The parents' positive views of children's personal and social adjustment significantly predicted all the well-being variables, except autonomy. Weaker associations happened between parental well-being and children's educational and occupational attainment. The prediction of parents' well-being came not only from what their children accomplished but also from their perceptions that they were responsible for how the lives of their children turned out. Well-being was lower for parents who felt that their children did not turn out well and for those who felt that they were minimally responsible for their children's positive outcomes. An additional variable, parents' comparisons of themselves with their children, was also a significant predictor of parents' well-being. Parents who saw their children as better adjusted than themselves experienced lower well-being.

Three significant discrepancies occurred between mothers and fathers in how they evaluated their children. First, mothers bestowed greater import to their children's adjustment. Second, mothers felt more responsible for their children's adjustment. Third, mothers felt that their children surpassed them in educational and occupational pursuits. When asked a question about the "hopes and dreams" they held for each of their children, the responses of mothers and fathers did not differ. Their most frequent hopes and dreams included happiness and educational success followed by career success, a happy family, personal fulfillment, being a good/moral person, and good health (Ryff et al., 1996).

Improved Relationships between Parents and Adult Children

Parents may also hope for improved relations with their adult children if there were earlier strains. In a panel study, Thornton, Orbuch, and Axinn (1995) studied the relationships between mothers and their sons and daughters during the transition to adulthood. The data came from interviews with the mothers and the children. Interviews took place in 1980 when the children were age 18 and in 1985 when they were 23 years of age. At both interviews, the children responded to identical questions about their mothers and fathers. The researchers did not indicate how many children in their study were still at home and how many were living independently.

In the initial interviews, when the children were age 18, mothers reported that their relationships with their children were always or usually characterized by respect, understanding, and enjoyment. The levels of enjoyment were higher than the levels of respect and understanding. Almost 80 percent of the children reported that their mothers provided the right amount of affection and always or usually accepted and understood them, but they enjoyed joint activities less (19 percent) than did their mothers (45 percent). Even more problematic was communication with their mothers. Over 40 percent of these children reported that they never or only sometimes felt that their mothers made it easy for them to confide in them or talk over troubles with them. Yet, they generally reported more favorable relationships with their mothers than with their fathers. They reported only two exceptions when interactions with fathers were more favorable than those with mothers. They respected their fathers' opinions more than their mothers' opinions and enjoyed doing things with their fathers more than with their mothers (Thornton et al., 1995).

By the age of 23, improvements were observed in parent–child relationships. There were increases in respect, understanding, affection, confidence, and enjoyment. The improvement was greater for mother–child relationships than for father–child relationships. In addition, there was continuity between the quality of relationships at age 18 and those at age 23. If relationships with parents were positive at age 18, they tended also to be positive at age 23 (Thornton et al., 1995).

RELATIONSHIPS GO ON BETWEEN PARENTS AND ADULT CHILDREN

Parents who eagerly await the freedoms from no children in the home may face various obstacles to the realization of this vision. Though active, everyday parenting (for example, feeding, caring for, and monitoring their children) ends, the parental role continues. Parents are expected to assist their adult children in times of crisis or strong need. These are times such as when children divorce, lose jobs, or experience serious health difficulties (Hagestad, 1982). Parent–child relationships fare best, however, when the parents do not encourage dependency from their launched children. Instead, they encourage their independence as separate individuals. They care about their children but avoid over involvement (Eshleman, 1991). The children maintain relatedness or close attachments with their parents while also developing autonomy from them (O'Connor, Allen, Bell, & Hauser, 1996). Both parental well-being and the parent–child relationship benefit from the children's increasing autonomy (Aquilino, 1996).

Extent of Contact with Children Living outside the Home

Most parents enjoy living apart from their children but like to see them frequently. Their life satisfaction and marital happiness are higher when maintaining contact with their children (White & Edwards, 1990). Bumpass and

Aquilino (1995) reported that about 60 percent of midlife parents lived within 25 miles of an adult child, and over half of the parents visited with an adult child at least once a week. Over two-thirds of the parents had contact including phone calls or letters. If adult children had their own children, about three-quarters of their midlife parents made weekly contact with them.

Relationships with adult children were more central in the lives of the least educated parents. Those with college degrees were less likely to have an adult child who lived nearby and much less likely to see the child on a weekly basis. A possible explanation was the effect of education on geographic mobility of the parents and the children (who probably also attained college educations; see Bumpass & Aquilino, 1995). Race and ethnicity also played a role in contact between parents and adult children. Raley (1995) found, for example, that about 50 percent of never-married, non-cohabitating African American men and women age 19 to 29 studied in the NSFH project saw their mothers several times a week compared to one-quarter of white men and women.

Young adults with a same-sex or bisexual sexual orientation often experience reduced contact with their parents if they cannot accept a nonheterosexual sexual orientation in their children. Although few parents spurn their children, express rage to their children, physically harm their children, or eject their children from the home, some react with one or more of these behaviors (Savin-Williams & Dube, 1998). Parents who are extremely rejecting might not only physically harm their children but also cast out their "unacceptable" children or put them out on the street (Bales, 1985; Hersch, 1988; Martin & Hetrick, 1988). If not ejected from the home, these children may run away from home. Verbal and physical violence and negative outcomes such as running away from home often correlate with each other (Savin-Williams & Cohen, 1996). Though no studies exist on this topic for young adults with same-sex sexual orientations, their contacts with parents may be significantly reduced. These lesbian, gay, and bisexual children may lose touch with their parents as well as with their siblings.

Help-Giving Exchanges

A study of three generations has provided the main source of information on the exchange of help between midlife parents and their adult children (Rossi & Rossi, 1990). Cited here are the pertinent results from this body of work and from the works of Marks (1995) and Umberson (1992, 1996):

- The greatest amount of reciprocity between parents and children occurs during the midlife period (Rossi & Rossi, 1990).

- Parents give more help or support to their children than the reverse (Rossi & Rossi, 1990).

- Parents only give or both give and receive help (Marks, 1995).

- A parent's help is usually advice and instrumental support such as money (Rossi & Rossi, 1990).

- Help from an adult child is typically providing comfort in a crisis or helping with household tasks (Rossi & Rossi, 1990).

- When parents experience stressful life events such as the death of an elderly parent, they receive expanded contact, closeness, and support from their adult children (Umberson, 1996).

- Compared with fathers, mothers report more social support from their adult children (Umberson, 1996).

- Mothers feel more responsible than fathers for their children and experience greater involvement with both their grown sons and daughters (Umberson, 1996).

Various characteristics of the parents' situations can influence both their help giving and that of their adult children, such as divorce, nontraditional statuses, age, education, social status, race and ethnicity, and the marital and parenting status of the children.

Parental Divorce. Low quality of the parents' marriage was not associated with the exchange of help in a longitudinal study of 471 parents and their adult children (Amato, Rezac, & Booth, 1995). Parental divorce was found by Umberson (1996) to change the help-giving picture. It resulted in the parents' decreased satisfaction with adult children and less support and help giving from the children. Even when divorce happened after leaving the parental home, children might feel betrayed by their parents and experience torn allegiances. If parents remarried, this could also cause strain in their relationships with their children.

Parental divorce affected help-giving exchanges between children and fathers more than with mothers. Wright and Maxwell (1991) found that divorcing mothers received more services, financial and socioemotional support, and advice than divorcing fathers. The socioemotional support came more often from daughters and the services and financial support from sons.

Nontraditional Parents. Generally, parents in first marriages are more likely than parents in other marital statuses to provide help. Nontraditional, or remarried and single parents more often do not get involved in any help exchanges, or they are the receivers with no giving. Nontraditional parents particularly indicated less belief in continued financial obligations to adult children. There are inconsistencies in this literature, however, mainly regarding mothers. For example, Amato et al. (1995) reported that single mothers received more and provided less help than mothers in first marriages. Remarried mothers, however, provided as much assistance as first-married mothers, yet they received less. Other researchers found that help giving from a single parent to a single adult child was the most frequent exchange (Rossi & Rossi, 1990) and that always-single mothers did not fit the typical pattern found with other nontraditional parents of no involvement in help-giving exchanges with their adult children (Marks, 1991). Single parents, overwhelmed by their own life demands, however, often cannot provide help (Marks, 1995).

Age. With age, help giving by parents declines. One study reported that help giving by parents declines after age 65 (Rossi & Rossi, 1990). By later midlife, African American parents are less likely than white parents to provide help to a child, such as babysitting (Bumpass & Aquilino, 1995).

Education. Parents with the least education usually did not have the resources to provide help to an adult child in later midlife whereas this was much less the case with college-educated parents (Bumpass & Aquilino, 1995).

Social Status. Though parents of lower socioeconomic status (SES) may not have the resources to provide financial support to their adult children, parents of higher SES reported less social support from their adult children and more dissatisfaction and strain in their relationships with them than parents of lower SES (Bumpass & Aquilino, 1995). Rossi and Rossi (1990) reported that members of families of lower SES may be closer and rely more on one another.

Race and Ethnicity. Using NSFH data, Lee and Aytac (1998) examined financial support between parents and adult children in white, African American, and Latino families. They discovered that financial support between the two generations in these families was low except for transfers from white parents to their children. Only 20 percent of these children, however, reported receiving financial assistance of more than $200 from their parents during the past 5 years. Though Latino and African American parents were less likely to provide financial support to their adult children than were white parents, they provided more financial support to children with higher incomes and education. They invested what resources they had on children who were more likely to deliver the highest returns or exchanges later, or perhaps they wanted to "reward" children who had done well because they were proud of them.

Disrupted Marriages of Adult Children. By their late 50s, about a quarter of all parents face a separated or divorced child (Bumpass & Aquilino, 1995). Adult children with midlife parents that experienced marital disruption tend to experience marital separation and divorce (Marks, 1996). Among adult children, rates of marital disruption are also associated with the educational attainment of the parents. By ages 55–59, one-fifth of the least educated parents had a daughter who was a single parent. This contrasted with less than 10 percent of parents with college degrees (Bumpass & Aquilino, 1995). Rates of marital disruption of one's children are also higher among ethnic parents with the least material resources (Marks, 1996). African Americans in midlife, compared to similar age non-Latino whites, are more likely to experience an always-single adult child; a separated, divorced, or widowed adult child; or an adult daughter who is a single parent (Bumpass & Aquilino, 1995).

Children Who Are Parents. Grandparenthood may strengthen the relationship and augment contact and exchange between midlife parents and their adult children. Parents may respond more to pressing needs of adult children who are parents, especially if they are single parents. Separated, divorced, or widowed children especially turn to single mothers for assistance (Bumpass & Aquilino, 1995; Marks, 1993). Much of the current data on grandparenthood was reviewed by Kivett (1991) including evidence of the value of grandparents to families. Grandparents provide help and support when needed (Hagestad, 1988) but how involved they will be depends on geographic proximity; greater distance increases the likelihood that the grandparent role will be remote instead of active (Uhlenberg & Kirby, 1998).

Effects of Help Giving on Parents' Well-Being

Help-giving exchanges between midlife parents and adult children can provide a sense of meaning and worth for the parents (Marks, 1991, 1995). The influence of participation in help-giving relationships with adult children on mothers' self-esteem is greater than from their marital status (Marks, 1991). Giving to adult children is more beneficial to parents' well-being than only receiving from them. Providing social support to children, whether reciprocated or not, is usually associated with greater well-being than only receiving social support from children. Receiving instrumental support (for example, housekeeping or yard work) is not beneficial to parental well-being (Marks, 1991, 1995).

Launching children followed with on-going relationships with children out of the home is a *normative* event. Increasingly, however, midlife parents and their children do not experience the normative pattern of launching but instead patterns that vary from what the normative pattern prescribes, or *non-normative* patterns (Hagestad, 1984; Perlmutter & Hall, 1992).

When Adult Children Leave too Early, Leave Late, Return Home After Leaving, or Never Leave

Timing can affect the child-launching period. If the children leave *on time*, it will likely be a smoother process (Hagestad, 1984). Also, when this transition occurs gradually, parents have time to anticipate the launching and make preparations for it. This is usually the case when children are in college, the military, or on long-term trips (Turner & Helms, 1994). Some children leave *off time*, however, such as at unexpected early ages (Hagestad, 1984). Children in remarried households tend to leave home at earlier ages but this does not happen as often in the slightly larger families of African Americans and Latinos. Aquilino (1990) also found that children may also leave early in families that gain a stepparent and stepsiblings (especially adolescents; see Goldscheider & Goldscheider, 1998). In contrast, other children are late in leaving home.

Young Adults Who Leave Home Late

A growing segment of young adults in the United States do not move out of the home when anticipated. A new and developing trend for midlife parents is not an empty home but continuation of a "full" home. In the 18–34 age group, about 58 percent of men and 47 percent of women continue to live in their parents' homes (U.S. Bureau of the Census, 1991). Close to half (45 percent) of the NSFH parents ages 45–56 reported that they had children age 19 or older living at home (Aquilino, 1990; Marks, 1996). Children were living in the homes of almost one of seven parents over age 65 (White & Rogers, 1997).

The phenomenon of "adult children still at home" most often happens with divorced and not remarried midlife parents. Coresidence with one's children has traditionally been common in some ethnic and racial families such as African American and Latino, probably reflecting not only financial needs but also family values and norms (Paz, 1993; Ward & Spitze, 1992). Adult children are also more likely to reside longer in the homes of the least educated parents (Bumpass & Aquilino, 1995). Some young adults who are still at home are in college. This includes about 30 percent of college students (Perlmutter & Hall, 1992). Others are still at home because they are still single (Riche, 1989) and some fear loneliness if they move out (Perlmutter & Hall, 1992).

As cited here, there are many reasons for coresidence of adult children and parents, but the main reason is the inability of children to support themselves financially. Social and historical factors particularly affect this situation (Goldscheider & Goldscheider, 1998). The most formidable obstacle to children's achieving autonomy is the depreciated opportunity system of professional and technological jobs that help them attain financial independence (Glick & Lin, 1986). When the professional–technological–occupational structure is more favorable, most young adults move out of a dependent state with parents. The push for leaving is strong because of the internalization of the separation, individuation, autonomy, and achievement values of U.S. culture (Schnaiberg & Goldenberg, 1989). Coresidence opposes both the parent's and the child's expectations about adulthood and independence (Ward & Spitze, 1996b). If a child does not become independent at the anticipated time, parents must continue with often unwanted child-rearing responsibilities. Yet, when leaving the home finally happens, the empty home may not be empty for long.

Young Adults Who Return Home

The anticipated or "ideal" pattern of all the children leaving once and for all may not fit most midlife families. Estimates based on NSFH data suggested that parents with two or more children were more likely than not to experience the return of at least one of them after they left home. More men returned home than women. Men returning home increased over the last 15 years, especially among those ages 19–30 compared to those ages 30–34. Over half of the younger cohort of men returned (Aquilino, 1996). Half of married daughters and sons returned to their parents' home with their partners (Glick & Lin, 1986).

Generally, most of the returns (90 percent) reported in the NSFH data happened within 5 years after leaving or during the children's early to mid-20s. Often, the return happened quickly, within a year or less (40 percent) or within 2 years (60 percent). After the first return home, most of the children (90 percent) left within 4 years. The stay was less than 1 year for about a quarter, and two-thirds remained at home less than 2 years. A quarter of those who left, however, returned for a second time. Among adult children age 19 to 34 who left home at least once, slightly over 42 percent returned home at some time (Aquilino, 1996). These "boomerang kids" returned home for various reasons: leaving school or ending military service, divorce or separation, personal difficulties such as misuse of alcohol or drugs, the high cost of housing, low wages, and underemployment or unemployment. The most frequent difficulty was maintaining financial independence (for example, Aquilino, 1996; Lewis & Lin, 1996). These children have been called "incompletely launched young adults" (Schnaiberg & Goldenberg, 1989, p. 251).

After adult children return home, the loss of the "emptiness" can be troublesome for the parents. Experiencing new freedom, financial relief, and self-fulfilling investments of their time and energy, suddenly their lives are not their own again. The household structure they created for the postparental period gets disrupted because again they share their space with their children (Raup & Meyers, 1989; Schnaiberg & Goldenberg, 1989). They can experience familiar but unwelcome annoyance over noise and telephone calls and conflicts over use of possessions such as the family car. Conflicts can happen because of increased housework or when their adult children expect services such as having their clothes washed (by their mothers!).

Most parents with returned adult children provide them frequent daily or weekly services, such as meal preparation, grocery shopping, and emotional support (Veevers & Mitchell, 1998). Parents may resent the freeloading of their adult children (Goldscheider & Goldscheider, 1994; Schnaiberg & Goldenberg, 1989), but the children may consider it inappropriate to pay room and board as they are "part of the family." They may also dislike being treated like young children who must help out with housework. Based on NSFH data, Ward and Spitze (1996a) found that housework was the most common area of disagreement between parents coresiding with adult children. When the children did help out, the exchange was modest. Daughters reported doing more housework whereas sons were more likely to pay room and board. Most of the parents studied by Veevers and Mitchell (1998) reported that they received daily or weekly help from their children but to a lesser degree than what they themselves provided.

Effects on the Family When Children Return Home or Never Leave

Studies on the relationship between parents and children returning home report mixed results. Most of the parents experience positive relationships with their adult children as coresidents (Aquilino & Supple, 1991). This is especially likely with mothers and daughters. The mothers studied by Graber and Brooks-Gunn (1996) consistently rated themselves as having positive mental health (low score on depression) when their daughters returned. Yet, other studies reported that the coresidence arrangement could affect adult children, their parents, and the relationships between them in negative ways. In a study involving adult children who were still living at home or who returned, White and Rogers (1997) used cross-sectional data from adult children in 1992 and panel data from their parents in 1988 and 1992 to investigate the effect of coresidence on parent–child solidarity. They discovered that compared to children who did not live at home (including those who lived only a few miles away), coresiders exchanged significantly more resources with their parents. But there were costs to relationship quality. Coresident children judged the affective quality of their relationships with their parents more negatively than did children who did not live with their parents. Parents studied by Umberson (1996) received more social support from adult children in the home when they were over age 17 but experienced more strain and dissatisfaction than parents whose children lived elsewhere.

Certain factors influence parent's responses to children returning home. For example, well-educated parents experience less satisfaction than less-educated parents when an adult child returns home (Aquilino, 1996). Parents who are middle class and work in professional, technical, or managerial occupations especially may be distressed about their children's dependency and failure to become autonomous adults (Schnaiberg & Goldenberg, 1989).

Renewed financial dependence from one's adult children not only interferes with the parent's new roles and plans (Raup & Meyers, 1989) but also re-creates old parent–child roles. When adult children revert to dependent roles, parents revert to former caregiving roles (Clemens & Axelson, 1985; Johnson & Wilkinson, 1995). This situation is often not a satisfactory one for parents. They probably hold implicit or explicit ideas about when and how their adult children will negotiate various role transitions. Violation of the parental expectations, such as continued or renewed dependency, contributes to their dissatisfaction with coresidence (White & Rogers, 1997). The parents personalize these troubles through either self-blame or blaming the victim instead of putting the situation in the context of *structural changes in society* (Schnaiberg & Goldenberg, 1989). They may experience anxiety, guilt, and shame about not adequately socializing their children for adult work and marriage, and anger or resentment because of the failure of their children to meet their expectations (Hagestad, Smyer, & Stierman, 1984).

Difficulties such as financial burdens may escalate when adult children return home accompanied by their children or when only the children are in the home. About 1.3 million parents are raising their children's children (Casper & Bryson, 1998). This phenomenon is happening across the United States and across social class, race and ethnicity, and cultural backgrounds. Szinovacz (1998) reported on the extent of this phenomenon from a nationally representative sample. At some point in their lives, 30 percent of African American grandmothers, 19 percent of Latino grandmothers, and 12 percent of white grandmothers had taken over the parenting role of their children's children. Grandparents take on the parental role for different reasons, such as divorce of the parents, parental illness or death, substance misuse by a parent, and incarceration of a parent (Fuller-Thomson, Minkler, & Driver, 1997). African American grandmothers studied by Gibson (1999) experienced an unexpected and unplanned for shift to caregivers of their grandchildren with absent parents. They had to accommodate their lives to the needs of their grandchildren, deferring dreams of life without the care of young children. They also had to cope with the absent middle generation parents.

Of the 716 coresident adult children from the NSFH study, there were almost equal numbers among those who left and those who never left, and few differences emerged in the characteristics of these two groups. In addition, there was little to no association between coresidence and family history, parent's need, or the quality of parent–child relations (Ward & Spitze, 1996b).

Most parents, however, are not willing for a returned adult child to remain in their home indefinitely. They view such living arrangements as temporary (Clemens & Axelson, 1985) and most coresident children plan on leaving within a year or less. Yet, with advancing age the anticipated length of the stay builds. Partly this result reflects the lack of marriage plans by older coresidents as well as their satisfaction with the coresidence situation. About one-third of 716 coresident children age 25 and older studied by Ward and Spitze (1996a) never left. These researchers also found that after age 40, few of either continuing or returning coresidents were likely to report plans to leave, and none of the coresidents who never left reported plans to leave. Coresidence seems, therefore, to become increasingly stable with advancing age. Instead of seeing the parent's home as a transitional safety net until the child establishes an independent household, the child's coresidence with the parents can turn into a permanent situation. With time to work out difficulties and conflicts, satisfaction may increase for these older children and their parents.

As noted here, balancing the desires of the parents to phase out the intense aspects of parenting and the uneven progress of the young to become self-sufficient can be a formidable challenge. For some families, this situation is complicated when an adult child has serious impairments or chronic physical, mental, or emotional disability. Often these children cannot be launched, or if they are the parents worry about their living autonomous lives. Parents in this situation were studied by Seltzer, Krauss, Choi, and Hong (1996). A subsample of an ongoing longitudinal study of 461 families that had a son or daughter with mental disability living at home consisted of 387 mothers between the ages of 57 to 85 (M age = 66.8). The adult children ranged in age from 17 to 68 (M age = 34.5). The researchers found that the mothers experienced a downturn in well-being when launching an adult child with a disability (the 30s age group). They were uncertain whether their children could function autonomously.

LOSING AN ADULT CHILD

No midlife parent anticipates the death of an adult child. Throughout midlife, this unexpected event happens twice as much among African American as among white parents. About a quarter of African Americans experience the death of a child by late midlife (Bumpass & Aquilino, 1995).

The death of an adult child is not often noted in the midlife literature because it is not a usual or normative midlife experience. Clearly, however, for parents who experience this type of life event, it is an extraordinary tragedy. The effect of this *off-time* event was studied by Cacace and Williamson (1996) in a convenience sample of older parents (ages 60–72; four mothers and three fathers). The adult children, ages 18–45, died of cancer. The researchers identified five themes in the experiences of the parents in data collected through interviews: (1) personal disruption or feeling robbed of an adult relationship with their children and experiencing difficulties in interpersonal relationships, concentration, and health; (2) unnatural survivorship or not expecting to outlive one's children; (3) isolation or separation from social contacts and experiencing loneliness, grief, and obsessive thinking about the lost child; (4) reminders of their children, such as in visions, dreams, events (for example, weddings of persons the same age of their child), and physical similarities of their child in someone else; (5) coping strategies to help resolve grief, such as redefining the parental role through strengthening ties with remaining children and grandchildren, seeking interpersonal or spiritual support, and keeping busy. All the respondents indicated that they benefited greatly from relationships with friends, extended families, and support groups. All of these parents questioned why their child died and some expressed anger because God did not cure their child.

In a community-based sample of 171 bereaved parents (M age = 45) who experienced the violent death of an adolescent or young adult child (ages 12–28), Murphy et al. (1999) collected data 4, 12, and 24 months postdeath. At 4 months, 68 percent of the parents reported mental distress as the most pressing difficulty they were experiencing, including feeling or affective states (for example, "being on an emotional roller coaster") and functioning or cognitive states (for example, "not being able to make decisions"). The most change on measures of mental distress happened between 4 and 12 months for both mothers and fathers. During the second year, the distress for mothers continued to decline in contrast to slight heightening for fathers in 5 of 10 distress domains. Yet, 2 years following the deaths, the mental distress scores for mothers were up to five times higher than those of typical U.S. women whereas fathers' scores were up to four times higher than those of typical U.S. men. Higher scores on self-esteem and self-efficacy predicted lower distress for both mothers and fathers whether at 4, 12, or 24 months after the death happened.

SUMMARY

- Marriage and family relationships are important to women throughout midlife. Both marital relations and parenting, however, are often strained during this period.

- The intersection of midlife with adolescent children for many parents can cause distress in both the parent–child and the couple relationship.

- After the children leave home, couples may be happier, but they may also confront uncomfortable issues about their marriages.

- Even when adult children no longer live at home, they are still central to their parents' lives.

- Unless the situation has stabilized with older children, children who never leave, or who leave and return for several years or longer, can create dissatisfactions for the parents who were not expecting renewed dependence by their adult children. Often children return because they cannot finance an autonomous life, but they experience dissatisfaction with their parents' expectations for them to help out in the home or pay rent.

- Midlife lesbians are often coupled and, like all couples, can experience changing satisfaction levels. Their relationships are comparable to heterosexual couples in quality and adjustments.

- Midlife lesbian mothers, like many heterosexual mothers, are in a variety of family structures, such as blended and single-parent families.

IMPLICATIONS FOR PRACTICE

Practitioners and social agencies (for example, mental health clinics, family services agencies) need to be aware that midlife women with adolescents are vulnerable to strained marital relations and parenting difficulties. Professional intervention can help midlife couples improve their parenting skills with adolescents. Older adolescents who will soon be leaving home can evoke a stressful situation for parents who are experiencing their own transitions through midlife. Fathers and mothers also may view what is going on with their older children differently. For example, a father may be worried about losing his roles as parent and primary authority in the family whereas a mother may be ready to disengage from active, full-time parenting to pursue other roles. A counselor can help mothers and fathers discuss their different needs and opportunities, and support them to restore harmony in the family.

Human services practitioners are also likely to encounter families with children who never left home or who left but then returned. Practitioners can help these families by first helping the child focus on developing a plan for maintaining as much independence as possible. The parents can work on deemphasizing the former child–parent relationship and developing adult–adult relationships with this family member. Johnson and Wilkinson (1995) suggested that parents use this situation as an opportunity to address developmental goals in a direct and open manner. Because these families cannot use physical distance to help attain differentiation and other developmental goals, they need to agree upon guidelines regarding private space, responsibilities to the household, and respect for each other's lifestyles. In addition, neither the parents nor the child should focus on each other but, instead, should focus on their own developmental goals. The practitioner can observe the family process and identify situations that evoke developmentally inappropriate behaviors. The goal is then for the parents and the child to change these behaviors and other interactions that stand in the way of creating adult-to-adult relationships.

For marital couples whose relationships become or remain strained after their children leave home, practitioners can help them refocus their energies on the marital relationship and work toward the development of a new marital contract that better fits their midlife status. Practitioners working with midlife lesbian couples need to be aware of their similarities to heterosexual couples and of the unique conditions they experience because of the ideological system of heterosexism (see p. 22 and Herek, 1995).

VIGNETTE

Carol, a 44-year-old homemaker, is married to Henry, an automobile mechanic. Married 22 years, they have two daughters, ages 21 and 17, and a son, age 18. The younger daughter, Kim, is a senior in high school and is making plans to attend the state university 400 miles away. She and her father have been especially close. The older daughter, Carolyn, attended the local community college for 2 years and is now a secretary in a law office. She is single, lives near her parents, and visits them often. Their son, Bradley, is enrolled in the community college and living in a dorm. Carol feels pleased about Kim wanting to go farther away to college to pursue a degree. Also, with all of the children gone, she can pursue her desire to return to work. Not only does she want the challenge of employment outside the home but the family also needs additional money to support college educations for Kim and Bradley. Henry, however, is not happy with Carol's plan to return to work. He also warned Kim that if she goes away to school instead of attending the local community college, he would not help her financially. Before this time, the family was mostly conflict free and relationships among the family members were close. Now, because of Henry's objections to the desires of his daughter and wife, there is considerable conflict and distress in the family. This couple's difficulties may soon be exacerbated because Bradley is not doing well in his first semester in college. It is a month before finals in his first semester, and he is failing two out of four courses. His grades are barely passing in the two other courses. If he fails more than one course, he will not be readmitted for the second semester. If this happens, Carol's main concern is that Bradley will move back home just as she was looking forward to all of the children being gone.

Questions

- *What do you think is behind Henry's objections to the desires of his daughter to attend a college far away from home and of his wife wanting to return to work?*

- *If Bradley returns home, what guidelines should the parents follow in regard to their interactions with him, given that they want to begin to relate to him as an adult child?*

REFERENCES

Adelmann, P. K., Antonucci, T. C., Crohan, S. E., & Coleman, L. M. (1989). Empty nest, cohort, and employment in the well-being of midlife of midlife women. *Sex Roles, 20,* 173–189.

Alexander, B. B., Rubinstein, R. L., Goodman, J., & Luborsky, M. (1992). A path not taken: A cultural analysis of regrets and childlessness in the lives of older women. *Gerontologist, 32,* 618–626.

Allen, L., Aber, J. L., Seidman, E., Denner, J., & Mitchell, C. (1996). Mother's parental efficacy at midlife in a Black and Latina sample: Effects of adolescent change across a school transition. In C. D. Ryff & M. M. Seltzer (Eds.), *The parental experience of midlife* (pp. 301–335). Chicago: University of Chicago Press.

Amato, P. R., Rezac, S. J., & Booth, A. (1995). Helping between parents and young adult offspring: The role of parental marital quality, divorce, and remarriage. *Journal of Marriage and the Family, 57,* 363–374.

Anderson, C. M., Dimidjian, S. A., & Miller, A. (1995). Redefining the past, present, and future: Therapy with long-term marriages at midlife. In N. S. Jacobson & A. S. Gutmann (Eds.), *Clinical handbook of couple therapy* (pp. 247–260). New York: Guilford Press.

Anderson, S. A., Russell, C. S., & Schumm, W. R. (1983). Perceived marital quality and family life-cycle categories: A further analysis. *Journal of Marriage and the Family, 45,* 127–139.

Aquilino, W. S. (1990). The likelihood of parent–adult child coresidence: Effects of family structure and parental characteristics. *Journal of Marriage and the Family, 52,* 405–419.

Aquilino, W. S. (1996). The returning adult child and parental experience at midlife. In C. D. Ryff & M. M. Seltzer (Eds.), *The parental experience in midlife* (pp. 423–455). Chicago: University of Chicago Press.

Aquilino, W. S., & Supple, K. R. (1991). Parent–child relations and parent's satisfaction with living arrangements when adult children live at home. *Journal of Marriage and the Family 53*, 13–27.

Bales, J. (1985, December). Gay adolescents' pain compounded. *APA Monitor*, pp. 16, 21.

Barber, C. E. (1989). Transition to the empty nest. In S. J. Bahr & E. T. Peterson (Eds.), *Aging and the family* (pp. 15–32). Lexington, MA: Lexington Books.

Barnett, R. C., & Baruch, G. K. (1985). Women's involvement in multiple roles and psychological distress. *Journal of Personality and Social Psychology, 49*, 135–145.

Bart, P. B. (1972). Depression in middle-age women. In V. Gornick & B. K. Moran (Eds.), *Women in sexist society* (pp. 163–168). New York: New American Library.

Black, S. M., & Hill, C. E. (1984). The psychological well-being of women in their middle-years. *Psychology of Women Quarterly, 8*, 282–292.

Borland, D. C. (1982). A cohort analysis approach to the empty-nest syndrome among three ethnic groups of women: A theoretical position. *Journal of Marriage and the Family, 44*, 117–129.

Bradford, J., & Ryan, C. (1991). Who we are: Health concerns of middle-aged lesbians. In B. J. Warshow, & A. J. Smith (Eds.), *Lesbians at midlife: The creative transition* (pp.147–163). San Francisco: Spinsters.

Bumpass, L. L. (1990). What's happening to the family? Interactions between demographic and institutional change. *Demography, 27*, 483–498.

Bumpass, L. L., & Aquilino, W. S. (1995). *A social map of midlife: Family and work over the middle life course*. Vero Beach, FL: MacArthur Foundation Research Network on Successful Midlife Development.

Bumpass, L. L., & Sweet, J. A. (1991). *The effects of marital disruption on intergenerational relationships* (NSFH Working Paper No. 44). Madison: University of Wisconsin, Center for Demography and Ecology.

Cacace, M. F., & Williamson, E. (1996). Grieving the death of an adult child. *Journal of Gerontological Nursing, 22*, 16–22.

Carolan, M. T., & Allen, K. R. (1999). Commitments and constraints to intimacy for African American couples at midlife. *Journal of Family Issues, 20*, 3–24.

Casper, L., & Bryson, K. (1998). *Co-resident grandparents and their grandchildren: Grandparent maintained families* (U.S. Population Division, Working Paper No. 26). Washington, DC: U.S. Bureau of the Census. Available on-line: http://purl.access.gpo.gov/GPO/LP53369.

Charbonneau, D., & Lander, P. (1991). Redefining sexuality: Women becoming lesbian in midlife. In B. Sang, J. Warshow, & A. Smith (Eds.), *Lesbians at midlife: The creative transition* (pp. 35-43). San Francisco: Spinsters.

Chodorow, M. (1978). *The reproduction of mothering: Psychoanalysis and the sociology of gender*. Berkeley: University of California Press.

Clausen, J. A. (1986). *The life course: A sociological perspective*. Englewood Cliffs, NJ: Prentice Hall.

Clemens, A., & Axelson, L. (1985). The not-so-empty-nest: The return of the fledgling adult. *Family Relations, 34*, 259–264.

Coleman, L. M., Antonucci, T. C., Adelmann, P. K., & Crohan, S. E. (1987). Social roles in the lives of middle-aged and older Black women. *Journal of Marriage and the Family, 49,* 761–771.

Connidis, I. A., & McMullin, J. A. (1993). To have or have not: Parent status and the subjective well-being of older men and women. *Gerontologist, 33,* 630–636.

Connidis, I. A., & McMullin, J. A. (1999). Permanent childlessness: Perceived advantages and disadvantages among older persons. *Canadian Journal of Aging, 18,* 447–465.

Cooper, K. L., & Gutmann, D. L. (1987). Gender identity and ego mastery style in middle-aged pre-and post- empty nest women. *Gerontologist, 27,* 347–352.

Davidson, J. K., & Moore, N. B. (1992). *Marriage and family.* Dubuque, IA: Brown.

Domestic-partner benefits. (1991, June). *HR Magazine,* pp. 36, 125–126.

Eshleman, J. R. (1991). *The family: An introduction* (6th ed.). Boston: Allyn & Bacon.

Fuller-Thomson, E., Minkler, M., & Driver, D. (1997). A profile of grandparents raising grandchildren in the United States. *Gerontologist, 37,* 406–411.

Gibson, P. A. (1999). African American grandmothers: New mothers again. *Affilia, 14,* 329–343.

Gilbert, L. A., & Davidson, S. (1989). Dual career families in midlife. In S. Hunter & M. Sundel (Eds.), *Midlife myths: Issues, findings, and practice implications* (pp. 195–209). Thousand Oaks, CA: Sage Publications.

Glick, P. C., & Lin, S-L. (1986). More young adults are living with their parents: Who are they? *Journal of Marriage and the Family, 48,* 107–112.

Goldscheider, F. K., & Goldscheider, C. (1994). Leaving and returning home in 20th century America. *Population Bulletin, 48,* 1–35.

Goldscheider, F. K., & Goldscheider, C. (1998). The effects of childhood family structure on leaving and returning home. *Journal of Marriage and the Family, 60,* 745–756.

Graber, J. A., & Brooks-Gunn, J. (1996). Expectations for and precursors to leaving home in young women. *New Directions for Child Development, 71,* 21–38.

Groves, P. A., & Ventura, L. A. (1983). The lesbian coming out process: Therapeutic considerations. *Personnel and Guidance Journal, 62,* 146–149.

Gullette, M. M. (1998). Midlife discourses in the twentieth-century United States: An essay on the sexuality, ideology, and politics of "middle-ageism." In R. A. Shweder (Ed.), *Welcome to middle age! (and other cultural fictions)* (pp. 3–44). Chicago: University of Chicago Press.

Gutmann, D. L. (1987). *Reclaimed powers: Toward a new psychology of men and women in later life.* New York: Basic Books.

Hagestad, G. (1982, Winter). Divorce: The family ripple effect. *Generations: Journal of the Western Gerontological Society,* pp. 24–32.

Hagestad, G. O. (1984). The continuous bond: A dynamic, multigenerational perspective on parent–child relations between adults. In M. Perlmutter (Ed.), *Minnesota symposia on child psychology* (Vol. 17, pp. 247–262). Hillsdale, NJ: Lawrence Erlbaum.

Hagestad, G. O. (1988). Able elderly in the family context: Changes, changes, and challenges. In R. Marri & S. A. Bass (Eds.), *Retirement reconsidered: Economic and social roles for older people* (pp. 171–184). New York: Springer.

Hagestad, G. O., Smyer, M. A., & Stierman, K. L. (1984). Parent–child relations in adulthood: The impact of divorce in middle age. In R. Cohen, B. Cohler, & S. Weissman (Eds.), *Parenthood: A psychodynamic perspective* (pp. 247–262). New York: Guilford Press.

Hamill, S. B., & Goldberg, W. A. (1997). Between adolescents and aging grandparents: Midlife concerns of adults in the "sandwich generation." *Journal of Adult Development, 4*, 135–147.

Harris, R., Ellicott, A., & Holmes, D. (1986). The timing of psychosocial transitions and changes in women's lives: An examination of women aged 45–60. *Journal of Personality and Social Psychology, 51*, 409–416.

Harry, J. (1983). Gay male and lesbian relationships. In E. Macklin & R. Rubin (Eds.), *Contemporary families and alternative lifestyles: Handbook on research and theory* (pp. 216–234). Beverly Hills, CA: Sage Publications.

Herek, G. M. (1990). The context of anti-gay violence: Notes on cultural and psychological heterosexism. *Journal of Interpersonal Violence, 5*, 316–333.

Herek, G. M. (1995). Psychological heterosexism in the United States. In A. R. D'Augelli & C. J. Patterson (Eds.), *Lesbian, gay, and bisexual identities over the lifespan: Psychological perspectives* (pp. 321–346). New York: Oxford University Press.

Hersch, P. (1988, January). Coming of age on city streets. *Psychology Today*, pp. 28–32.

Hiedemann, B., Suhomlinova, O., & O'Rand, A. M. (1998). Economic independence, economic status, and empty nest in midlife marital disruption. *Journal of Marriage and the Family, 60*, 219–231.

Holmes, J. D., & Rahe, R. H. (1967). The social readjustment rating scale. *Journal of the Psychosomatic Research, 11*, 213–218.

Hunter, S., & Hickerson, J. (in press). *Affirmative practice: Understanding and working with lesbian, gay, bisexual, and transgender persons*. Washington, DC: NASW Press.

Huyck, M. H. (1989). Midlife parental imperatives. In R. A. Kalish (Ed.), *Midlife loss: Coping strategies* (pp. 115–148). Newbury Park, CA: Sage Publications.

Huyck, M. H. (1995). Marriage and close relationships of the marital kind. In R. Blieszner (Ed.), *Handbook of aging and the family* (pp. 181–200). Westport, CT: Greenwood Press.

Huyck, M. H., & Gutmann, D. L. (1992). Thirtysomething years of marriage: Understanding experiences of women and men in enduring family relationships. *Family Perspective, 6*, 249–265.

Johnson, P., & Wilkinson, W. K. (1995). The "re-nesting" effect: Implications for family development. *Family Journal: Counseling and Therapy for Couples and Families, 3*, 126–131.

Kahana, B., & Kahana, E. (1982). Clinical issues of middle age and life. In F. M. Berardo (Ed.), *The annuals of the American academy of political and social science: Middle and late-life transitions* (pp. 140–161). Beverly Hills, CA: Sage Publications.

Keith, P. M., & Schafer, R. B. (1991). *Relationships and well-being over the life stages*. New York: Praeger.

Kidwell, J., Fisher, J. L., Dunham, R. M., & Baranowski, M. (1983). Parents and adolescents: Push and pull of change. In H. I. McCubbin & C. R. Figley (Eds.), *Stress and the family: Vol.1.Coping with normative transitions* (pp. 74–89). New York: Brunner/Mazel.

Kirkpatrick, M. (1988). Clinical implications of lesbian mother studies. In E. Coleman (Ed.), *Integrated identity for gay men and lesbians: Psychotherapeutic approaches for emotional well-being* (pp. 201–211). New York: Harrington Park Press.

Kirkpatrick, M. (1989). Middle age and the lesbian experience. *Women's Studies Quarterly, 1–2*, 87–86.

Kivett, V. R. (1991). The grandparent–grandchild connection. *Marriage & Family Review, 16*, 267–290.

Koropeckyj-Cox, T. (1998). Loneliness and depression in middle and old age: Are the childless more vulnerable? *Journal of Gerontology: Social Sciences, 53*, 303–321.

Kurdek, L. A. (1994). The nature and correlates of relationship quality in gay, lesbian, and heterosexual cohabiting couples: A test of the contextual, investment, and discrepancy models. In B.Greene & G. M. Herek (Eds.), *Lesbian and gay psychology: Theory, research, and clinical applications* (pp. 133–135). Thousand Oaks, CA: Sage Publications.

Kurdek, L. A. (1995a). Developing changes in relationship quality in gay and lesbian cohabiting couples. *Developmental Psychology, 31*, 86–94.

Kurdek, L. A. (1995b). Lesbian and gay couples. In A. R. D'Augelli & C. J. Patterson (Eds.), *Lesbian, gay, and bisexual identities over the lifespan: Psychological perspectives* (pp. 243–251). New York: Oxford University Press.

Lasswell, M., & Lasswell, T. (1991). *Marriage and the family* (3rd ed.). Belmont, CA: Wadsworth.

Lee, Y-J, & Aytac, I. A. (1998). Intergenerational financial support among Whites, African Americans, and Latinos. *Journal of Marriage and the Family, 60*, 426–441.

Lewis, R. A., & Lin, L-W. (1996). Adults and their midlife parents. In N. Vanzetti & S. Duck (Eds.), *A lifetime of relationships* (pp. 365–382). Pacific Grove, CA: Brooks/Cole.

Marks, N. F. (1991). *Remarried and single parents in middle adulthood: Differences in psychological well-being and relationships with adult children* (NSFH Working Paper No. 47). Madison: University of Wisconsin, Center for Demography and Ecology.

Marks, N. F. (1993). *Contemporary social demographics of American midlife parents* (NSFH Working Paper No. 54). Madison: University of Wisconsin, Center for Demography and Ecology.

Marks, N. F. (1995). Midlife marital status differences in social support relationships with adult children and psychological well being. *Journal of Family Issues, 16*, 5–28.

Marks, N. F. (1996). Social demographic diversity among American midlife parents. In C. D. Ryff & M. M. Seltzer (Eds.), *The parental experience in midlife* (pp. 29–75). Chicago: University of Chicago Press.

Martin, A. D., & Hetrick, E. S. (1988). The stigmatization of the gay and lesbian adolescent. *Journal of Homosexuality, 15*, 163–183.

McGoldrick, M. (1989). Ethnicity and the family life cycle. In B. Carter & M. McGoldrick (Eds.), *The changing family life cycle: A framework for family therapy* (2nd ed., pp. 69–90). Boston: Allyn & Bacon.

McGrath, E. (1990, August). *New treatment strategies for women in the middle.* Paper presented at the annual convention of the American Psychological Association, Boston.

McLanahan, S., & Adams, J. (1987). Parenthood and psychological well-being. *Annual Review of Sociology, 13*, 237–257.

McLanahan, S., & Adams, J. (1989). The effects of children on adults' psychological well-being: 1957–1976. *Social Forces, 68*, 124–146.

McLanahan, S. S., & Sorensen, A. B. (1985). Life events and psychological well-being over the life course. In G. H. Elder (Ed.), *Life course dynamics* (pp. 217–238). Ithaca, NY: Cornell University Press.

Menaghan, E. (1983). Marital stress and family transitions: A panel analysis. *Journal of Marriage and the Family, 45*, 371–386.

Mercer, R. T., Nichols, E. G., & Doyle, G. C. (1989). *Transitions in a woman's life: Major life events in developmental context.* New York: Springer.

Mitchell, V., & Helson, R. (1990). Women's prime of life. Is it the 50's? *Psychology of Women Quarterly, 14*, 451–470.

Murphy, S. A., Gupta, A. D., Cain, K. C., Johnson, L. C., Lohan, J., Wu, L., & Mekwa, J. (1999). Changes in parents' mental distress after the violent death of an adolescent or young adult child: A longitudinal prospective analysis. *Death Studies, 23*, 129–159.

Neugarten, B. L. (1976). Adaptation and the life cycle. *Counseling Psychologist, 6*, 16–20.

Nydegger, C. N., & Mitteness, L. S. (1996). Midlife: The prime of fathers. In C. D. Ryff & M. M. Seltzer (Eds.), *The parental experience in midlife* (pp. 533–559). Chicago: University of Chicago Press.

O'Connor, T. G., Allen, J. P., Bell, K. L., & Hauser, S. T. (1996, Spring). Adolescent–parent relationships and leaving home in young adulthood. *New Directions for Child Development*, 39–52.

Oliver, R. (1988). "Empty nest" or relationship restructuring? A rational-motive approach to a mid-life transition. *Journal of Rational-Emotive and Cognitive-Behavior Therapy, 6*, 102–117.

Olson, D., McCubbin, H. I., Barnes, H., Larsen, A., Muxen, M., & Wilson, W. (1989). *Families: What makes them work?* Newbury Park, CA: Sage Publications.

Orsmond, J. A. (1991). The empty nest phenomenon. *Medical Journal of Australia, 154*, 608, 612.

Paz, J. J. (1993). Support of Hispanic elderly. In H. P. McAddo (Ed.), *Family ethnicity* (pp. 177–183). Newbury Park, CA: Sage Publications.

Peplau, L. A., & Amaro, H. (1982). Understanding lesbian relationships. In W. Paul, J. D. Weinrich, J. C. Gonsiorek, & M. E. Hotvedt (Eds.), *Homosexuality: Social, psychological, and biological issues* (pp. 233–248). Beverly Hills, CA: Sage Publications.

Peplau, L. A., & Cochran, S. D. (1990). A relational perspective on homosexuality. In D. P. McWhirter, S. A. Saunders, & J. M. Reinisch (Eds.), *Homosexuality/heterosexuality: Concepts of sexual orientation* (pp. 321–349). New York: Oxford University Press.

Perlmutter, M., & Hall, E. (1992). *Adult development and aging* (2nd ed.). New York: John Wiley & Sons.

Pillemer, K., & Suitor, J. J. (1991a). Relationships with children and distress in the elderly. In K. Pillemer & K. McCartney (Eds.), *Paren–child relations throughout life* (pp. 163–178). Hillsdale, NJ: Lawrence Erlbaum.

Pillemer, K., & Suitor, J. J. (1991b). Will I ever escape my child's problems? Effects of adult children's problems on elderly parents. *Journal of Marriage and the Family, 53*, 585–594.

Pruchno, R. A., Peters, N. D., & Burant, C. J. (1996). Child life events, parent–child disagreements, and parent well-being: Model development and testing. In C. D. Ryff & M. M. Seltzer (Eds.), *The parental experience in midlife* (pp. 561–606). Chicago: University of Chicago Press.

Raley, R. K. (1995). Black–white differences in kin contact and exchange among never married adults. *Journal of Family Issues, 16*, 77–103.

Raup, J. L., & Myers, J. E. (1989). The empty nest syndrome: Myth or reality? *Journal of Counseling & Development, 68*, 180–183.

Reinke, B. J., Ellicott, A. M., Harris, R. L., & Hancock, E. (1985). Timing of psychological change in women's lives. *Human Development, 28*, 259–280.

Rexroat, C., & Shehan, C. (1987). The family life cycle and spouses' time in housework. *Journal of Marriage and the Family, 49*, 737–750.

Riche, M. F. (1989). Mysterious young adults. In A. S. Skolnick & J. H. Skolnick (Eds.), *Family in transition: Rethinking marriage, sexuality, child rearing, and family organization* (6th ed., pp. 123–128). Glenview, IL: Scott, Foresman.

Rogers, L. P., & Markides, K. S. (1989). Well-being in the postparental stage in Mexican–American women. *Research on Aging, 11*, 508–516.

Rohrbaugh, J. B. (1992). Lesbian families: Clinical issues and theoretical implications. *Professional Psychology: Research and Practice, 23*, 467–473.

Rollins, B. (1989). Marital quality at midlife. In S. Hunter & M. Sundel (Eds.), *Midlife myths: Issues, findings, and practice implications* (pp. 184–194). Newbury Park, CA: Sage Publications.

Rollins, B. C., & Feldman, H. H. (1970). Marital satisfaction of the family life cycle. *Journal of Marriage and the Family, 32*, 20–28.

Rossi, A. S., & Rossi, P. H. (1990). *Of human bonding: Parent–child relations across the life course.* Hawthorne, NY: Aldine de Gryter.

Rothschild, M. (1991). Life as improvisation. In B. Sang, J. Warshow, & A. Smith (Eds.), *Lesbians at midlife: The creative transition* (pp. 91–98). San Francisco: Spinsters.

Ryff, C. D., Lee, Y. H., Essex, M. J., & Schmutte, P. S. (1994). My children and me: Midlife evaluations of grown children and of self. *Psychology and Aging, 9*, 195–205.

Ryff, C. D., Schmutte, P. S., & Lee, Y. H. (1996). How children turn out: Implications for parental self-evaluation. In C. D. Ryff & M. M. Seltzer (Eds.), *The parental experience in midlife* (pp. 383–422). Chicago: University of Chicago Press.

Ryff, C. D., & Seltzer, M. M. (1996). The uncharted years of midlife parenting. In C. D. Ryff & M. M. Seltzer (Eds.), *The parental experience in midlife* (pp. 3–25). Chicago: University of Chicago Press.

Sang, B. (1992). Counseling and psychotherapy with midlife and older lesbians. In S. Dworkin & F. Gutie'rrez (Eds.), *Counseling gay men and lesbians: Journey to the end of the rainbow* (pp. 35–48). Alexandria, VA: American Association for Counseling and Development.

Savin-Williams, R. C., & Cohen, K. M. (1996). Psychosocial outcomes of verbal and physical abuse among lesbian, gay, and bisexual youths. In R. C. Savin-Williams & K. M. Cohen (Eds.), *The lives of lesbians, gays, and bisexuals: Children to adults* (pp. 181–200). Ft. Worth, TX: Harcourt Brace.

Savin-Williams, R. C., & Dube, E. M. (1998). Parental reactions to their child's disclosure of a gay/lesbian identity. *Family Relations, 47,* 7–13.

Schaie, K. W., & Willis, S. L. (1991). *Adult development and aging* (3rd ed.). New York: HarperCollins.

Schnaiberg, A., & Goldenberg, J. S. (1989). From empty nest to crowded nest: The dynamics of incompletely launched young adults. *Social Problems, 36,* 251–269.

Scott, J., & Alwin, D. F. (1989). Gender differences in parental strain: Parental role or gender role? *Journal of Family Issues, 10,* 482–503.

Seltzer, M. M., Krauss, M. W., Choi, S. C., & Hong, J. (1996). Midlife and later-life parenting of adult children with mental retardation. In C. D. Ryff & M. M. Seltzer (Eds.), *The parental experience in midlife* (pp. 459–489). Chicago: University of Chicago Press.

Seltzer, M. M., & Ryff, C. D. (1996). The parental experience in midlife: Past, present, and future. In C. D. Ryff & M. M. Seltzer (Eds.), *The parental experience in midlife* (pp. 641–661). Chicago: University of Chicago Press.

Silverberg, S. B. (1989, July). *A longitudinal look at parent–adolescent relations and parents' evaluation of life and self.* Paper presented at the Tenth Biennial Meetings of the International Society for the Study of Behavioral Development, Jyvaskyla, Finland.

Silverberg, S. B. (1996). Parents' well-being at their children's transition to adolescence. In C. D. Ryff & M. M. Seltzer (Eds.), *The parental experience in midlife* (pp. 215–254). Chicago: University of Chicago Press.

Silverberg, S. B., & Steinberg, L. (1987). Adolescent autonomy, parent–adolescent conflict, and parental well-being. *Journal of Youth and Adolescence, 16,* 293–312.

Silverberg, S. B., & Steinberg, L. (1990). Psychological well-being of parents with early adolescent children. *Developmental Psychology, 26,* 658–666.

Skolnick, A. (1981). Married lives: Longitudinal perspectives on marriage. In D. H. Eichorn, J. A. Clausen, N. Haan, M. P. Honzik, & P. H. Mussen (Eds.), *Present and past in middle life* (pp. 269–298). New York: Academic Press.

Steinberg, L. (1987) Recent research on the family at adolescence: The extent and nature of sex differences. *Journal of Youth and Adolescence, 16,* 751–760.

Steinberg, L., & Silverberg, S. B. (1987). Influences on marital satisfaction during the middle stages of the family life cycle. *Journal of Marriage and the Family, 49,* 751–760.

Szinovacz, M. E. (1998). Grandparents today: A demographic profile. *Gerontologist, 38,* 37–52.

Thoits, P. (1983). Multiple identities and psychological well-being: A reformulation and test of the social isolation hypothesis. *American Sociological Review, 48,* 174–187.

Thornton, A., Orbuch, T. L., & Axinn, W. G. (1995). Parent–child relationships during the transition to adulthood. *Journal of Family Issues, 16*, 518–564.

Turner, J. S., & Helms, D. B. (1994). *Contemporary adulthood* (5th ed.). Orlando, FL: Holt, Rinehart, and Winston.

Uhlenberg, P., Cooney, T., & Boyd, R. (1990). Divorce for women after midlife. *Journal of Gerontology, 45*, S3–S11.

Umberson, D. (1992). Relationships between adult children and their parents: Psychological consequences for both generations. *Journal of Marriage and the Family, 54*, 664–674.

Umberson, D. (1996). Demographic position and stressful midlife events: Effects on the quality of parent–child relationships. In C. D. Ryff & M. M. Seltzer (Eds.), *The parental experience in midlife* (pp. 493–531). Chicago: University of Chicago Press.

Umberson, D., & Gove, W. R. (1989). Parenthood and psychological well-being: Theory, measurement, and stage in the family life course. *Journal of Family Issues, 10*, 440–462.

Unger, R., & Crawford, M. (1992). *Women & gender: A feminist psychology.* New York: McGraw Hill.

U.S. Bureau of the Census. (1991). *Statistical abstract of the United States* (111th ed.). Washington, DC: U.S. Government Printing Office.

U.S. Bureau of the Census. (2000). *Resident population estimates of the United States by age and sex.* Washington, DC: U.S. Government Printing Office. Available on-line: http://www.census.gov/population/www/cen2000/respop.html.

VanLaningham, J., Johnson, D. R., & Amato, P. (2001). Marital happiness, marital duration, and the U-shaped curve: Evidence from a five-wave panel study. *Social Forces, 78*, 1313–1314.

Veevers, J. E., & Mitchell, B. A. (1998). Intergenerational exchanges and perceptions of support within "boomerang kid" family environments. *International Journal of Human Development, 46*, 91–108.

Ward, R. A., & Spitze, G. (1992). Consequences of parent-adult child co-residence. *Journal of Family Issues, 13*, 553–572.

Ward, R. A., & Spitze, G. (1996a). Gender differences in parent–child coresidence experience. *Journal of Marriage and the Family, 58*, 718–725.

Ward, R. A., & Spitze, G. (1996b). Will the children ever leave? Parent–child coresidence history and plans. *Journal of Family Issues, 17*, 514–539.

Weinstein, E., & Rosen, E. (1988). Sexual attitudes, interests, and activities for senior adults. *International Journal of Aging and Human Development, 27*, 261–270.

White, L., & Edwards, J. N. (1990). Emptying the nest and parental well-being: An analysis of national panel data. *American Sociological Review, 55*, 235–242.

White, L. K., & Rogers, S. J. (1997). Strong support but uneasy relationships: Coresidence and adult children's relationships with their parents. *Journal of Marriage and the Family, 59*, 62–76.

Wright, C., & Maxwell, J. (1991). Social support during adjustment to later-life divorce: How adult children help parents. *Journal of Divorce & Remarriage, 15*, 21–48.

ADDITIONAL REFERENCES

Allen, S. F., & Stoltenberg, C. D. (1995). Psychological separation of older adolescents and young adults from their parents: An investigation of gender differences. *Journal of Counseling & Development, 73*, 542–546.

Cooney, T. M. (1994). Young adult's relations with parents: The influence of recent parental divorce. *Journal of Marriage and the Family, 56*, 45–56.

Kurdek, L. A., & Schmitt, J. P. (1986). Relationship quality of partners in heterosexual married, heterosexual cohabiting, and gay and lesbian relationships. *Journal of Personality and Social Psychology, 51*, 711–720.

Lander, P. S., & Charbonneau, C. (1990). The new lesbian in midlife: Reconstructing sexual identity. In J. Hurtig, K. Gillogly, & T. Gulevich, (Eds.), *Michigan Discussions in Anthropology, 9*, 1–14.

Lewis, R. A. (1990). The adult child and older parents. In T. H. Brubaker (Ed.), *Family relationships in later life* (2nd ed., pp. 68–85). Newbury Park, CA: Sage Publications.

McWhirter, D. P., & Mattison, A. M. (1984). *The male couple.* Englewood Cliffs, NJ : Prentice-Hall.

Uhlenberg, P., & Kirby, J. B. (1998). Grandparenthood over time: Historical and demographic trends. In M. E. Szinovacz (Ed.), *Handbook on grandparenthood* (pp. 23–39). Westport, CT: Greenwood Press.

Wanamaker, N. J., & Bird, G. W. (1990). Coping with stress in dual-career marriages. *International Journal of Sociology of the Family, 20*, 198–211.

Williamson, D. S. (1991). *The intimacy paradox: Personal authority in the family system.* New York: Guilford Press.

CHAPTER 3

CAREGIVING OF ADULT FAMILY MEMBERS

Midlife women are often caregivers for adult family members, particularly older parents. Older parents often live in the community and when they need care from others, families usually provide it. Primarily the caregivers are women: mothers, wives, daughters, daughters-in-law, sisters, and granddaughters. In this chapter we focus on daughters. These women often experience the double role challenge of work and parent care, and sometimes the triple role challenge of parent of children still at home, worker, and caregiver of an elderly parent. Parent care is not a major stressor, however, unless the caregiving is extensive and the parents' difficulties severe. There can also be positive outcomes of caregiving, and caregivers tend to adapt to caregiving over time. Lifespan themes that are covered include: historical context of the expanding life course; role transition to parent caregiver; individual differences; resiliency and adaptation of caregivers; normative event of some degree of caregiving; and gains, losses, and constraints experienced in caregiving.

Questions to Consider:

- *Who provides most of the caregiving for adult family members?*

- *What factors influence family members to provide caregiving?*

- *What are double and triple role challenges, and what are their effects on midlife women?*

- *What are the consequences of caregiving for the midlife women who provide the care?*

- *What is the future of caregiving for older parents?*

Caregiving for dependents follows the life course of women. It is not time bound (Rossi, 1985). Many women experience a career of stages of caregiving that include motherhood, middle-age responsibility for older relatives, and caring for disabled husbands in old age (Hooyman, 1990). In addition, women are increasingly caring for more than one generation. Caring can also extend to blended families and former in-laws (Brody, 1985; Hooyman, 1990). Many midlife women care for grandchildren in the parental home. Active grand-mothering is more common and anticipated in some ethnic and racial groups than in white middle-class culture (Spurlock, 1984). As noted in Chapter 2, recent demographic trends indicate that the home may also refill with returning young adult children and sometimes just their grandchildren. Also noted in Chapter 2, some children never leave home. Among these children are those with mental or physical disabilities. Mothers' caregiving of these children in the home may continue indefinitely. Some midlife and older women also provide caregiving for an adult male family member or friend living with HIV/AIDS (Wight, LeBlanc, & Aneshensel, 1998).

Although many midlife women are caring for other family members, most of the literature on caregiving in midlife focuses on older parents. Caregiving for these adult family members, therefore, is the focus of this chapter. Caregiving of some degree is now *normative* because the population of older parents is expanding as life expectancy increases. Because of the *historical context* of the expanding life course, both the prevalence of caregiving and the ages at which it occurs are likely to increase (Himes, 1994). By year 2030, the older population will more than double to 70 million; the age 85 and over population will increase from 4 million in 2008 to 8.9 million in 2030. Members of ethnic and racial groups will represent 25 percent of the older population in year 2030 (Administration on Aging, 2000). The ratio of older women to older men increases as the population ages. For every 100 women in the age 85 and older population, there are 39 men (U.S. Bureau of the Census, 1995). So, when midlife adults have only one living parent it is usually their mothers.

The National Survey of Families and Households (NSFH) project found that one-half of adults in early midlife (ages 35–44) reported feeling responsible for their parents (Bumpass & Aquilino, 1995). This project was supported by the MacArthur Foundation Research Network on Successful Midlife Development and the Center for Demography and Ecology at the University of Wisconsin. Although the proportions were lower in the oldest midlife decade (ages 55–64) because of fewer living parents, one in four adults in their later midlife years experienced an increasingly dependent parent with health limitations. If an aging parent does not yet require hands-on assistance but is in only fair health, this is, at the least, cause for concern or worry (Marks, 1993).

TYPES OF CAREGIVING NEEDED BY OLDER ADULT FAMILY MEMBERS

Three-fourths of older parents at any given time do not need help in their daily lives. Most of them live in their own homes and do many things for themselves. They usually make their own decisions and retain control of their finances (Brody, 1990). Most adult family members, however, experience some dependency on others for their care before the end of their lives. The need for care may be minimal in the beginning, such as transportation and home maintenance (Piercy, 1998). As health declines, however, because of chronic illness, disability, or functional impairment in activities of daily living such as bathing, dressing, housework, and shopping, the need for assistance becomes more extensive. Older racial and ethnic adults, including those in the African American and Latino populations, tend to experience even more chronic disabilities over time (Markides & Mindel, 1987).

Older parents often do not want help from their children (Newman & Newman, 1991); they capitulate their self-sufficiency and independence only with much regret (Hooyman & Lustbader, 1986; Piercy, 1998). In a study of 53 elderly parents (age 65 and over) and 53 of their adult children, the children only gradually approached their parents with direct offers of assistance. First, they demonstrated concern about their parents' health status. Second, they demonstrated urging when they perceived that their parents' health status was worsening and when they tried to get their parents to do something that might improve their health. Third, they demonstrated direct action or helped their parents deal with their health difficulties after they observed that their parents' functional abilities (for example, mobility, maintenance of daily activities) were getting worse (Cicirelli, 2000).

Caregiving recipients may need a range of assistance. Four categories of assistance were identified by Query and Flint (1996):

1. *Instrumental activities of daily living* (IADL) include tasks such as shopping, transportation, cooking, and financial transactions. Parents who need help with these less demanding tasks are still living fairly independently (Blieszner, Mancini, & Marek, 1996).
2. *Activities of daily living* (ADL) include tasks such as bathing, eating, dressing, and mobility. Increasing frailty of the parents necessitates help with these tasks.
3. *Skilled health care* includes tasks such as giving injections or determining vital signs.
4. *Psychological care* includes tasks such as emotional support and companionship.

Families providing care are usually primary caregivers or general caregivers. Primary caregivers provide most of the care regularly. The range of time of caregiving varies from five to 24 hours daily. General caregivers spend less time (four or fewer hours daily) and on an irregular or occasional basis. In addition, there are lay or informal caregivers who do not have certification or credits for accredited training, and professional or formal caregivers who do have training credits or certification, such as nurses, physicians, social workers, and allied health personnel (Query & Flint, 1996). The focus of this chapter is on primary and general informal caregivers who are family members. These caregivers may, however, participate in indirect management services and enlist the services of other types of caregivers as well as coordinate and supervise them (Blieszner et al., 1996).

FAMILIES DELIVER CARE

Although the role of friends in the care network for older persons is increasing and unrelated to ethnic or racial background (Himes & Reidy, 2000), families are the first and often the only resource parents turn to when in need (Feinauer, Lund, & Miller, 1987). Only one person, however, usually provides most of the caregiving (Brody, 1990; Merrill, 1996; Sangl, 1985). If a wife, husband, or other partner is not available, this person is usually an adult child. The most frequently cited reason for an adult child taking on the role of the principal caregiver is that others (usually siblings) are either unable or are adverse to assuming this role. Some adult children provide the care because they live nearby or have the time or space in their homes for coresidence, if needed. Those who live with the parent indicate that they are already "in place" to provide the care. Some give the reason of a special bond with the parent. Others are "only children" or the only surviving child (Brody, Litvin, Hoffman, & Kleban, 1995; Hooyman & Lustbader, 1986). Sometimes the parent selects a child, such as one who was favored earlier in life (Merrill, 1996). Parents who contemplate moving closer to adult children when in need of their assistance tend to target the child with the greater potential to provide assistance (Silverstein & Angelelli, 1998). When there are no adult children, older African Americans (age 85 and older) are more likely than white childless older persons to have a family member as a caregiver (Johnson & Barber, 1995).

Frequently, there is no explicit negotiation about who takes the caregiver role; an adult child just assumes the responsibility (Gatz, Bengston, & Blum, 1990). This is often the case in some ethnic and racial families (for example, Latino and African American) and the "designated" adult child may also care for aunts, uncles, and in-laws. A feeling of obligation or filial responsibility seems to be the primary motivator for adult children to provide care for their parents (Connidis, 2001). Though closeness and affection between the child and parent are often among the motives for caregiving, such sentiments may not always be present (Walker, Pratt, Shin, & Jones, 1989).

Several factors may override caregiving obligations. For example, divorce of one's parents may decrease the general strength of obligations to primary kin (Rossi & Rossi, 1991). However, this may not be the case for adult children who also experienced the disruption of their own marriages (Cicirelli, 1983). Another overriding factor may be the sexual orientation of the parent. If the older parent in need of caregiving is a lesbian, gay, or bisexual person, adult children may not provide assistance. Adult children upset with a parent who disclosed a lesbian, gay, or bisexual orientation after a long-term heterosexual marriage may still be negative and even openly antagonistic. They may refuse all contact with the parent. For some adult children, however, a parent's later life care needs can provide an opportunity for reconciliation. They may rethink their prior deprecation of the parent and work with their parent's partner in a joint caregiving effort (Hooyman & Lustbader, 1986).

FAMILY CAREGIVERS ARE PRIMARILY WOMEN

Caregiving in the family is provided mostly by women who make the *role transition* to parent caregiver (for example, Dwyer & Coward, 1991; Finley, 1989). Through socialization as caregivers, women find it difficult to refuse requests for attention and caring (Hooyman & Lustbader, 1986). "You just do what has to be done" (Pohl, Boyd, & Given, 1997). Almost 80 percent of caregivers of older parents are women, usually adult daughters (Brody, 1990). Marks (1996a) estimated from the NHSF data that the likelihood of women being caregivers between ages 25–49 was 50 percent and between ages 50–64, 65 percent. The most typical caregiving arrangement is an adult daughter caring for a mother (Brody, 1990). Hardly any of the caregiving literature addresses midlife lesbians as caregivers of their older parents or the effect of such caregiving on their lives. The proportion of this population in a caregiving role, therefore, is unknown. Because daughters are the predominant caregivers, however, some midlife lesbians are surely drafted into this role (Kimmel & Sang, 1995).

Caregiving daughters outnumber caregiving sons three to one (Horowitz, 1985; Stoller, 1994). They provide many more hours of caregiving each week and a more complete range of tasks than sons (Montgomery & Kamo, 1989; Walker, 1992). When sons or husbands of daughters help out, they are most likely to perform tasks with identifiable boundaries, such as providing routine household maintenance and repairs, assisting with financial affairs and providing money if needed, offering advice and supervision, and running errands. They use discretion in both how and when to complete the tasks (Abel, 1990; Chappell, 1990; Hooyman & Lustbader, 1986). Daughters are far more likely to provide indoor household assistance, direct hands-on care such as bathing and dressing, emotional care such as helping a parent deal with depression and feel important and loved, and personal health care (Chappell, 1990; Rossi &

Rossi, 1991; Stephens & Christianson, 1986). The hands-on tasks performed by women are the ones found by researchers to be associated with high levels of stress (Horowitz, 1985).

ARE MIDLIFE WOMEN IN A SQUEEZE?

Various phrases apply to midlife adults who care for both children and parents. The "generation in the middle" (Richards, Bengston, & Miller, 1989) and the "sandwich generation" (Brody, 1981) are typical. Their predicament is a "generational squeeze" (Cherlin, 1981) or "generation overload" (Hagestad, 1984). Another term, midlife "squeeze," is analogous to multiple role responsibilities (for example, Brody, 1981; Spitze & Logan, 1990). Most "squeezed" midlife adults are women. When in a squeeze, they are experiencing the double role challenge of worker and parent caregiver or the triple role challenge of parent, worker, and parent caregiver (Marks, 1993).

Double Role Challenges

Midlife women are most likely squeezed by two major competing responsibilities (Cantor, 1991; Halpern, 1994) in one of three versions of the double role challenge identified by Marks (1993, 1996b). One version does not involve older parents. Instead, the challenge involves work and children at home. The two other double role challenges involve older parents. First, there is the combination of a midlife woman with a child living at home (any age) and at least one parent in fair to poor health. This generational squeeze may happen most frequently during the young (ages 35–44) and middle (ages 45–54) periods of midlife when one's parents are still alive and children are still at home. At some time between the ages 35–54, about one in three midlife mothers is likely providing day-to-day support for one or more children and to some degree experiencing concern for one or both parents. These challenges are experienced by 40 percent of mothers during the first decade of midlife and by 16 percent during the second decade. Latino mothers are more likely to experience these challenges, and with fewer resources. The second type of double role challenge that involves midlife parents includes employment and a limited health parent. Marks (1993, 1996b) determined that this double role challenge or potential for conflict between employment and parent caregiving seems quite real, especially during the later midlife years. Often, it is after the children grow up or are gone from the home that the double challenge of employment and concern for an older parent happens.

Stress of Caregiving When the Caregiver Is Employed. Work force participation across the life course is now normative for women in all demographic groups. Even so, many working women provide caregiving for older parents (for example, Moen, Robinson, & Fields, 1994; Stone, Cafferata, & Sangl, 1987), although with some qualifications. Adult children who work 35–44 hours a week are less likely to elect caregiving compared to those who are unemployed (Marks, 1996a). If employed adult children help out, their hours of assistance are lower if employed full time instead of part time (Doty, Jackson, & Crown, 1998). In addition, adult children employed full time are less likely to provide ADL tasks (Dwyer & Coward, 1991; G. R. Lee, Dwyer, & Coward, 1993).

Working women might deal with their multiple responsibilities by maintaining rigid schedules, negotiating parent caregiving around their work schedules, capitulating their own free time (Cantor, 1983; Lang & Brody, 1983) and opportunities for socialization and recreation (Brody, Kleban, Johnsen, Hoffman, & Schoonover, 1987), and sharing some tasks such as personal care and meal preparation with others (Brody, Johnsen, & Fulcomer, 1984). Compared to employees with no caregiving responsibilities, however, employed caregivers reported more stress effects regarding their health, family, and work (Neal, Chapman, Ingersoll-Dayton, Emlen, & Boise, 1990; Scharlach & Boyd, 1989).

If the older parent's needs are extensive, the conflict between the daughter's own life, especially work, and the parent's caregiving needs is likely to intensify. The daughter may take several actions: pay for care, take time off work, or quit work. There are *individual differences*, however, in the ability to take these actions. Some college-educated, middle-class working women shift some of their caregiving tasks to paid home care aides. The pattern is different, however, for women with only high school educations and who lack the resources to purchase care (Hartman, 1990; Moen et al., 1994). Adult working-class daughters cannot even envision alternatives to their own time and labor for parent caregiving (Ward & Carney, 1994). They are more likely to live near or with parents and have established patterns of helping. Taking care of the needs of their parents is part of their daily life (Stueve & O'Donnell, 1984).

To provide additional care, some women reduce work hours or take time off without pay (Stone et al., 1987). A nationwide survey of caregivers reported that 38 percent of caregivers lost time from work or arrived late because of caregiving tasks (American Association of Retired Persons, 1988). Taking time off for caregiving, however, is not always easy to arrange. Women are often in lower status jobs that do not permit flexibility for taking time off to attend to either child or parent needs (Hooyman & Lustbader, 1986; U.S. Select Committee on Aging, 1987).

Approximately 9 percent to 22 percent of caregivers quit their jobs (Brody et al., 1987; Stone et al., 1987) to care for older parents or a sick husband. This was the second most common reason midlife women reported for leaving work, the first being their own illness (Brody et al., 1987). Some women quit work because of financial barriers to buying nonfamily care. Some put their parents' wishes before their own when the parents refuse to accept nonfamily help (Brody, 1990). Out of economic necessity, however, most women cannot quit work. They enter the workplace or hold on to jobs because they need the money (Brody, 1990; Hooyman & Lustbader, 1986). The pressure is even greater if there is no partner to provide economic support (Pavalko & Artis, 1997) and, in addition, if there are still dependent children to support (Hooyman & Lustbader, 1986).

Effects of Variable Work Status. How do the variations of working or not affect midlife women? Brody (1990) compared four groups of women caregivers: the "quit-work" group (quit work to care for mothers); the "traditional" group (not working now or when parent care first arose); the "conflicted" group (working but with reduced hours or thinking about quitting); and the "persevering" group (working with no consideration of reducing work hours or quitting). The findings appear below:

- Women in the quit-work group held lower status jobs more than the two groups still in the labor force. They worked at jobs instead of pursuing careers. These women also had less education and lower family incomes than women in the other groups. They were older than women in the other groups, had the oldest mothers and those with disabilities, had helped the longest, and most likely were sharing their homes with their mothers. They used the least amount of paid help.

- Women in the conflicted group were the most compelling in showing the competition between parent care and work. They felt strongly pulled between wanting to pursue their careers while also feeling obligated to take care of their parents. They were the most career oriented and attained the highest-level jobs and highest family incomes. Although their parents received the most paid help, these women felt the most tied down because of the time they provided to help care for their parents.

- The persevering women and the traditional nonworking women were better off than women in the other two groups. The persevering women reported the best health status, felt most in control of their own lives, and had the most capable mothers. The traditional women held less egalitarian views about women's roles than either group of working women. They reported the least strain, but along with the women who quit work, they experienced poorer mental health than the two groups of working women.

The importance of work in women's lives stood out in Brody's (1990) study. Most of the women who reduced their hours or left work regretted it.

They missed the people, activity, gratification, and the feeling of making important contributions in their jobs. Some regretted missed opportunities for promotions and further personal development.

Triple Role Challenges

Most samples in the studies on caregiving are ones of convenience, making generalizations of findings to experiences of most midlife women dubious. Caution is especially warranted regarding the prevalence of the triple role challenge. Based on interviews with a probability sample of 1,200 men and women, Spitze and Logan (1990) found that at any given time during their 40s and early 50s only a small percentage of women (and men) were trying to balance child care, paid work, parent care, and marriage. Using results from another probability sample of caregivers for parents and parents-in-law, Penning (1998) concluded that only about one-quarter of the daughters and daughters-in-law were dealing with the challenge of balancing child care, paid work, and parent care. Using a small sample of midlife women in a metropolitan community in Canada, Rosenthal, Matthews, and Marshall (1989) also concluded that most midlife women do not experience multigenerational caregiving responsibilities. Spitze and Logan concluded that child care, parent care, and work may cause conflict when performed simultaneously but for most midlife adults these demands are not occurring simultaneously.

Based on the studies reported here, the triple role challenge is not typical for most women in midlife (Spitze & Logan, 1990). Yet, in another representative study, Marks (1993, 1996b) found much higher rates of this squeeze than those reported by Spitze and Logan. The NSFH data indicated that the three role challenges of employment, children at home, and a parent in poor health do occur during midlife, but frequency varies with age groups and marital status. For example, these challenges are most prevalent during early midlife (ages 35–44). They characterize 35 percent of mothers and 37 percent of fathers. The number of persons experiencing this triple responsibility around age 50 decreases to 16 percent of mothers and 25 percent of fathers. In the middle of midlife (ages 45–54), nonwidowed single mothers are about twice as likely to experience the triple role challenge as first-married mothers (26 percent versus 14 percent). Marks (1993, 1996a) explained that the distinction between her results and those reported by Spitze and Logan (1990) may be different definitions of the triple role challenge. Spitze and Logan defined it as 35 or more hours of employment a week, children living at home or helping an adult child 3 or more hours a week, and living with a parent or parent-in-law and helping 3 or more hours a week. Using this definition, they found only 13 percent of midlife adults involved in the three roles. Marks' analysis included part-time employment and parent health limitations versus hands-on help, resulting in a greater prevalence of squeeze for midlife adults.

What are the effects on persons who are faced with the triple role challenge? Loomis and Booth (1995) analyzed data from a national representative sample of married persons interviewed in 1989 and 1992. The longitudinal data identified the effects of caregiving by comparing the well-being of the caregivers before and after they took on multigenerational care responsibilities. The results showed that the change in family responsibilities resulted in little to no effect on well-being. One explanation may be that those most able to do it are the ones who take on the responsibility of caregiving. The marriages of these caregivers were strong, and they were proficient in balancing time dedicated to family, work, and themselves. The researchers concluded that generally the effects of parent caregiving were minimal, and that multigenerational responsibilities for children and parents were not especially difficult. The notion of the stressed-out "sandwich" generation, to these researchers, is a myth.

Another explanation for this finding of minimal effects of parent caregiving is that women can benefit from multiple roles. From a study of adult daughters who were wives, mothers of children living at home, employees, and providers of care for an impaired parent, Christensen, Stephens, and Townsend (1998) reported that these daughters experienced greater opportunities to experience feelings of mastery about performing various roles. For women who simultaneously occupy the roles of wife, mother, parent caregiver, and employee, emotional support received from the partner or partners in a given role is associated with a greater sense of mastery in that role. A sense of mastery in a given role results partly from encouragement, respect, and understanding expressed by the partner or partners in that role. The benefits from emotional support and mastery in one role, however, do not generalize to the other roles. Benefits are specific to a given role (Martire, Stephens, & Townsend, 1998). In the Christensen et al. (1998) study, mastery in family roles was associated with psychological well-being whereas mastery in the employee role was associated with both psychological and physical well-being. Satisfaction with life, however, was associated with an accumulation of mastery across all these roles. Higher levels of mastery were associated with less depression and more satisfaction with one's life.

Several variables appear to modify the benefits of mastery connected to caregiving. One's age group, for example, has an effect. Caregiving is associated with a sense of mastery for women in their 50s and early 60s but not for women in their late 60s and beyond (Moen, 1997). The duration of caregiving is also an important factor. Caregiving may enhance a woman's sense of purpose if limited to 1 or 2 years, but if it lasts longer the strains of the caregiving role may eventually outweigh any benefits. In addition, some caregiving situations are more demanding than others (Moen, 1997). Spitze and Logan (1990) acknowledged that extensively ill parents or those with disabilities might negatively affect caregivers' well-being. Many studies of nonrepresentative groups provide information on the negative effects of caregiving in these special circumstances.

STRESS OF EXTENSIVE CAREGIVING

What are the consequences of caregiving for a parent who requires more time and effort because of serious illness or disability? The long-term consequences of this type of caregiving are unknown, but many findings delineate adverse consequences at the time of the studies (Lund, 1993). Over two-thirds (68 percent) of a sample of 900 respondents felt that caregiving was the most stressful situation they ever experienced (Harper & Lund, 1990).

Midlife daughters attempt to achieve a balance between their impulse to care for a parent and giving "too much" of themselves to this task. If they neglect the impulse to care, they experience guilt and remorse, but if they overloaded themselves in this task, the consequence is stress (McGrew, 1998). When there is too much overload, caregiving of older parents becomes a burden. Physical burden, such as tangible and concrete physical tasks, leads to subjective burden or the emotional stress and feelings that result from caregiving (Parks & Pillsuk, 1991). Many researchers emphasize that the most pervasive and severe consequences of caregiving are the emotional stress and resultant depression, anxiety, guilt, frustration, anger, helplessness, emotional exhaustion, and lowered morale (for example, Berg-Weger, Rubio, & Tebb, 2000a; Lund, 1993). The emotional stress may be greater for women than for men because of stronger attachments and emotional ties to their parents. Women may feel more responsible for the care of parents and may view caregiving as a reflection of their self-worth (for example, Chang & White-Means, 1991; Penning, 1998).

Types of Stressors

Certain types of stressors can lead to physical and subjective burden. They include: lack of knowledge and preparation, physical challenges, demands on time and space, disruptions and adjustments in the family, coresidence, losses of the parent one once knew, and resentment and conflict. These stressors reflect the burden, the *losses*, and the *constraints* experienced in caregiving.

Lack of Knowledge and Preparation. Midlife daughters can lack knowledge and preparation for caregiving (Haggan, 1998; Hooyman & Lustbader, 1986). Unprepared for a parent's disability, some daughters must develop special skills and perform invasive procedures that can violate intergenerational contact and relationship taboos (Montgomery, 1992). Personal care involving body contact is usually experienced as more stressful than impersonal tasks such as housecleaning and cooking (Montgomery, Gonyea, & Hooyman, 1985; Stoller &

Pugliesi, 1989). Daughters may not anticipate troubling behaviors that can happen with care recipients, such as hallucinations, wandering, agitation, and incontinence (Haley, Brown, & Levine, 1987).

Physical Challenges. Caregivers frequently feel physically exhausted (Brody, 1990). This results from the arduous physical tasks of caring for a parent with a disability such as lifting the parent, doing housecleaning for two houses, and not experiencing enough rest or relaxation (Alford-Cooper, 1993; Hooyman & Lustbader, 1986). The physical care tasks escalate with greater decline and dependency of the care receiver (Hooyman, 1990). The caregiver may reach a breaking point and seek institutionalization for the parent (Kingston, Hirshorn, & Cornman, 1986).

Demands on Time and Space. Caregiving can restrict or confine the caregiver in both time and space (Montgomery et al., 1985; Pot, Deeg, van Dyck, & Jonker, 1998). It can be constant, around the clock, boundless, and all encompassing (Abel, 1990; Brody, 1985), leaving little time and space for thoughts, activities, and roles unrelated to caregiving (Pot et al., 1998; Seltzer & Li, 2000). Women are less likely than men to set limits on the time they spend on caregiving (George & Gwyther, 1986).

Disruptions in the Family. Extensive involvement of a caregiver with a parent can interfere with life with one's other family members and, in addition, the family's lifestyle, patterns of socializing, privacy, income, future plans such as moving away, and vacations (Brody, 1985). Extensive caregiving efforts can divide the family when loyalties to the older parent compete with loyalties to other family members (Abel, 1990). Interpersonal difficulties can erupt between older parents and other family members (Brody, 1990). When parents live in their adult children's homes, some caregivers express concern about their marriages ending (Marks, 1994).

Coresidence. Coresident households are infrequent at any point in time (approximately 20 percent; see Bumpass & Aquilino, 1995; Coward & Cutler, 1991). According to U.S. Bureau of the Census 1990 data, younger parents were more likely to coreside with sons whereas older parents were more likely to coreside with daughters (Schmertmann, Boyd, Serow, & White, 2000). When coresident households exist for daughters, the stress levels of the coresident caregivers are usually high. The coresident caregivers experience significantly higher levels of burden and less social support than caregivers who live elsewhere (for example, Berg-Weger, Rubio, & Tebb, 2000b). The coresidence situation is more stressful when the adult child lives alone with an ill parent (Davis & Silverstone, 1981). The strain worsens if the home is also small or not well equipped for a disabled person (Brody, 1985, 1990).

Loss of the Parent One Once Knew. Caregivers can face a loss of the person they knew as their parent. A formerly kind, cheerful, and happy parent can become uncooperative, upset, and irresponsible (Chiriboga, Yee, & Weiler, 1992). This can happen especially when dementia and Alzheimer's disease are present. A large, specialized literature addresses caregiving for parents with these diseases, which are the most devastating of chronic conditions for older adults (for example, Pett, Caserta, Hutton, & Lund, 1988; Walker & Pomeroy, 1997).

Resentment and Conflict. The task of reestablishing a close parent–child relationship, one that may involve escalating contact and interdependence, or even sharing a household, does not come easily for the children or for the parents (Newman & Newman, 1991). After raising their children, some daughters resent the need to resume caregiving again or the interference with their jobs (Brody, 1985). Caregiving, which can bring daughters into intimate contact with their mothers for the first time since their adolescence, can also bring out issues that they assumed were resolved earlier. Often the intensity of these resentments astounds the daughters. Some daughters who did not feel that they received approval and affection from their mothers may hope that this will happen now (Abel, 1990). A. J. Walker and Allen (1991) found that conflict was common in ambivalent pairs of daughters and mothers; expressions of concern for the other were not mutual, usually not coming from the mother; and daughters sensed that their mothers did not respect them or treated them like children. Other pairs were even more distinctly conflicted with few rewards and heavy costs for both daughters and mothers. The daughters focused on themselves and their autonomy instead of a caregiving partnership.

Modifications of the Stress of Caregiving

Several factors that may modify the costs of caregiving include: coping strategies, adaptation over time, work, racial and ethnic background, supports to counter isolation, and miscellaneous supports. Mixed findings, however, characterize most of these factors.

Coping Strategies. A person's coping strategies, whether resolving difficulties such as managing the care recipient's needs or reframing the situation from a negative one to a positive one (Chiriboga et al., 1992), may help reduce stress. Problem-focused coping strategies, in contrast to emotion-focused coping strategies, were found to reduce depression over 18 months in a probability sample of daughter caregivers (Li, Seltzer, & Greenberg, 1999). Daughters who feel they have more control over their lives or are high on mastery tend to use problem-focused coping strategies. Yet, coping strategies do not address the major need of most caregiving daughters, which is to reduce the responsibility they have for their parents' care (Quayhagen & Quayhagen, 1988). No strategy of coping eliminates the psychological costs of caregiving (Parks & Pillsuk, 1991). Because of anticipated worsening of a parent's health, even problem-focused coping may not be effective in helping caregivers feel in control of the situation (Schwarz & Roberts, 2000). Other researchers found that the psychological distress of caregivers was not modified by using problem-focused coping strategies, emotion-focused coping strategies, or by other aids such as emotional and instrumental supports. It also did not matter whether the persons being cared for had minimal, mild, moderate, or severe dementia (Pot, Deeg, van Dyck, & Jonker, 1998).

Adaptation over Time. The small body of longitudinal research on caregiving indicates that eventually a process of *adaptation* occurs (Townsend, Noelker, Deimling, & Bass, 1989). Although the behavior of the care recipient may worsen over time, the caregiver's ability to cope with difficult behavior improves (Zarit, Todd, & Zarit, 1986) and depression peaks (Townsend et al., 1989). Although daughters caring for their mothers, studied by Pohl et al. (1997), experienced the caregiving role as initially stressful, after one year they reported that they would "do it again." Ryff and Seltzer (1995) proposed that caregiving is a process with a progression of stages. Curvilinear effects may operate, with the early and end stages of caregiving resulting in the most stress, but with adaptational processes working in the middle stage.

Racial and Ethnic Background. African American caregivers report less stress and more positive experiences resulting from caregiving. One reason for this may be the stronger intergenerational obligations in this population (Scott & Black, 1994). African American caregivers also seem to be more *resilient* in the face of the negative psychological effects of caregiving. Depression is higher and life satisfaction lower among white caregivers (Haley, Wadley, West, & Vetzel, 1994). Latino caregivers experience no less distress than white caregivers. Latino families, however, may experience special challenges, such as higher risks for certain chronic diseases, such as diabetes, and younger ages of disability in parents (Aranda & Knight, 1997).

African Americans with higher incomes report more stress than those with lower incomes (for example, Hartung, 1993). Yet, significant caregiver strain was found in a small sample of mostly poor African American women. The combination of high caregiver burden (an average of four hours a day spent caring for a dependent parent) and limited resources left the women feeling unable to cope successfully with the demands of their situations. The inability to master caregiving as well as other family difficulties resulted in a loss of well-being and a sense of being "locked in" (England, 1995).

Supports to Counter Isolation. Support from family and friends, including visits and opportunities to socialize, can help reduce perceived burden in caregiving

(Thompson, Futterman, Gallagher-Thompson, Rose, & Lovett, 1993). In a study of the impact of family structure on caregiving, support that countered caregivers' isolation was more important than ethnic origin or type of family structure (nuclear or extended). What seems to matter more in terms of inducing strain and burden is the traditional role of housewife that restricts a woman's outside connections. These women are isolated and often depressed (Tirrito & Nathanson, 1994).

Miscellaneous Supports. Other possible supports include family counseling (Qualls, 1988), self-help books (for example, Jarvik & Small, 1988), support groups (Gatz et al., 1990), and community services such as adult day care, respite or provision of in-home help that allows the caregiver to leave the house, and short-term residential placement that enables the family to take a vacation. Unfortunately, how helpful these types of support are is not certain (for example, Schwiebert & Myers, 1994). Several researchers reported that psychoeducational interventions may not reduce caregiver stress (for example, Abel, 1991; Hugen, 1993).

Responses from the Workplace. In the workplace, "eldercare," the name used for provision of parent caregiving, is now an employee benefit (Brody, 1990). The Family and Medical Leave Act of 1993 permits 12 weeks of unpaid leave to care for a seriously ill parent or child. Upon return to work, a worker is to resume the same or an equivalent position (Yevak, 1994). Yet, workers often need more assistance. Some corporations are beginning to respond more to the needs of their caregiving employees. For example, some benefit packages now include assistance with eldercare (Mor-Barak & Tynan, 1993). Services that are particularly helpful to employed caregivers include flexible work arrangements (for example, flextime and leave policies), home care services, and assistance in locating eldercare services (Lechner & Gupta, 1996). Increasingly, eldercare services are addressed in the literature on caregiving for older parents (for example, Davis & Krouze, 1994; McDaniel & Via, 1997).

National Organizations. Many national organizations exist that provide helpful information and resources for caregivers of adult family members, including older parents and adult children with disabilities. Two of these organizations are the National Alliance for Caregiving and the American Association of Retired Persons.*

---

*National Alliance for Caregiving: http://www.caregiving.org; American Association of Retired Persons: http://www.AARP.org.

POSITIVE OUTCOMES OF CAREGIVING

Alhough the negative effects of caregiving are probably better known, many positive effects can result for caregivers of older parents. They include a sense of accomplishment and fulfillment, giving back to parents, personal growth, improved relationships with parents, close and appreciative pairs of mothers and daughters, and appreciation of siblings. In addition to the *gains* caregivers can experience, these results reflect their *resiliency* and *adaptation*.

Sense of Accomplishment and Fulfillment. Some studies found that most midlife daughters are happy as caregivers and satisfied with their accomplishments (Colerick & George, 1986; Lewis & Meredith, 1988). Other gains include a sense of self-worth and mastery (Martire, Stephens, & Franks, 1997), a greater sense of purpose in life (Marks, 1998), and a sense of accomplishment from completing difficult and stressful caregiving tasks (Miller, 1989). Even women who frequently combined the roles of caregiver and worker reported a sense of fulfillment from handling the demands of each role (Scharlach, 1994).

Giving Back to Parents. Caregiving communicates love and respect for a parent (Hooyman & Lustbader, 1986). Chinese and Filipino Americans, for example, demonstrate a pattern of paying respect to their parents through caring for and providing for them (Jones, 1995). Latino caregivers desire to give back to parents because the parents took care of them when they were children (Clark & Huttlinger, 1998). The types of support for a parent that may communicate love and respect include: "being there," willing to help when needed, and providing comfort when things go wrong (Nunley, Hall, & Rowles, 2000).

Personal Growth. Caregivers often experience personal growth during caregiving (Fitting, Rabins, Lucas, & Eastham, 1986; Marks, 1998). Some caregivers view their sacrifices as resulting in their being "less self-centered, more empathetic, caring, understanding, and compassionate toward others" (Harper & Lund, 1990, p. 261). Caregiving responsibilities can enhance job performance by encouraging caregivers to be more sensitive and empathetic with their clients and coworkers (Scharlach, 1994).

Better Relationships with Parents. Midlife daughters and their parents have an opportunity to develop better relationships through modification of long-standing rules and patterns of behavior. If prior relationships were strained, conciliatory gestures and remarks may occur. Serious illness, which can provoke a sense of time running out, can quicken the desire for reconciliations or resolutions of conflicts between parents and children. This does not include everything, however, such as physical or emotional abuse by a parent. If parents have not yet granted their daughters equal status with them as adults, this may also happen during caregiving (Hooyman & Lustbader, 1986). The daughter must redefine her role with her mother and relate to her more as an adult than a child (Abel, 1990). This change may lead to a change in her mother's perception of her.

Close and Appreciative Pairs of Mothers and Daughters. Affection and togetherness can deepen between the caregiver and the care recipient (Reinardy, Kane, Huck, Call, & Shen, 1999). Some caregivers reported that they were closer to and more loving of the parent because they believed that the parent appreciated their help (Lund, 1993). A daughter may also talk more intimately with her mother than ever before (Hooyman & Lustbader, 1986). Some fortunate mother and daughter pairs not only feel close to each other and experience rewarding interactions but think of themselves as best friends. They express caring, appreciation, and gratitude to each other and concern for the welfare of the other (Allen & Walker, 1992; A. J. Walker & Allen, 1991). The daughters in these pairs experience less frustration, anxiety, or time pressures than daughters who do not feel close (A. J. Walker, Martin, & Jones, 1992). In addition, they experience few or no conflicts, and contain disagreements (Allen & Walker, 1992).

Appreciation of Siblings. Connections among siblings can intensify when a parent becomes seriously ill. They may also come to appreciate each other in new ways (Hooyman & Lustbader, 1986). But, if the adult children who volunteer for the caregiving role assume their siblings will help out and they do not, conflict can erupt with feelings of anger and frustration over being let down (Merrill, 1996).

A FEMINIST ANALYSIS OF CAREGIVING AND RECOMMENDATIONS FOR PRACTITIONERS

As emphasized in this chapter, though some men are caregivers, it is essentially women's work. Adults in need of care depend heavily on women "laborers" (Hooyman & Gonyea, 1999; Hooyman & Lustbader, 1986). A firmly entrenched belief is that women are naturally better at caregiving than men (Alford-Cooper, 1993; LaBorde, 1994). This belief is reinforced through the frequent observation of women as caregivers (A. J. Walker, Pratt, & Eddy 1995). No value is attributed to this private and personal work of caregiving, and the psychological and financial effects are invisible. Important to the privatization of caregiving is the social and political climate of devolution of the federal government's role in caring for vulnerable members of society, and the transfer of care from formal delivery systems such as hospitals to informal community health care systems. These systems, however, are more focused on acute versus chronic or long-term care situations. This leaves even more to women to provide the long-term care needed for older adults with chronic illnesses. In addition, short-term interventions focused on getting caregivers to function better within existing service systems (community resources) or become more adept in coping with stress (for example, stress management techniques or cognitive restructuring) reinforce solutions focused on the individual caregiver as well as sex–gender-based inequities in caregiving (Hooyman & Gonyea, 1999). Public policy should be the target in addition to assisting individual women with their personal difficulties in coping with the burdens of caregiving (C. Lee, 1999).

Individual solutions do nothing to change the structural causes of caregiver stress that lie in the social policy, funding, or insurance arenas. Collective solutions must address these structural factors to improve the lives of caregivers. Explication of this feminist analysis of caregiving by Hooyman (1999) and Hooyman and Gonyea (1995, 1999) suggests what needs to be done to change the structural inequities of this endeavor. Summarized here, the recommendations include:

- Stronger public and governmental investment in developing a comprehensive range of services and supports for caregivers across an array of arenas: economic, health care, workplace, and social.

- Development of long-term-care policy centered on family support (for example, partnership between families and formal services care, universal comprehensive community-based care, adequate compensation for formal and informal caregivers), empowerment (for example, optimization of individual choice about whether to provide care or not and voice in how to provide care), and choice (for example, encouraging choice by providing information about how to procure care through social services that are accessible and culturally relevant and competent).

- Development of social and economic strategies to change the roles of men and women so that more men are primary caregivers and more women move into the labor force with earnings comparable to men. This goal assures sex–gender justice in caregiving.

- Rebalance the roles of caregivers and care recipients in ways that recognize the worth of both so that exploitation of women caregivers ends and mostly women care recipients are not cared for in a paternalistic manner.

The following measures for practitioners who work with caregivers and recipients were emphasized by Hooyman and Gonyea (1995, 1999):

- Uphold the concept of choice including whether to provide care or not; enhance the quality of life for caregivers and recipients; and develop practitioner care management including needs assessment and location of the most suitable and culturally relevant service options.

- Empower caregivers such as emphasizing caregiver control over preferences for caregiving that is tied into one's cultural context.

- Provide early and ongoing education about options throughout all stages of caregiving and include as large a helping network of family members as possible.

- Act as a partner and collaborator with caregivers and recipients to meet their needs.

- Act as an advocate for mobilizing a more comprehensive range of suitable services.

- Develop support groups to promote consciousness raising of the structural base for personal difficulties such as caregiver burden, development of politicizing techniques, and collective actions to use for social change (Hooyman & Gonyea, 1995).

SUMMARY

- Because of increased life expectancy, more women are taking care of parents and parents-in-law than ever before.

- Although most women now work outside the home, most caregivers of older parents continue to be women. Typically, an adult daughter is caring for a mother.

- Women find it difficult to refuse requests for help from their parents, even when caregiving involves reducing their hours of paid employment.

- Midlife women who care for aging parents are likely to experience some degree of a "squeeze" between their roles of mother with children at home and caregiver of a parent, or between their roles as worker and caregiver of a parent. Some midlife women experience a triple role challenge of worker, mother, and caregiver of an ailing parent.

- Although caregiving for a severely disabled or ill parent can lead to high levels of stress, positive results are also possible.

- Women often spend years out of the paid workforce or disrupt their employment because of caregiving for others, which creates a situation of lost income and financial insecurity.

- In the future, fewer women are likely to quit work for any type of caregiving. More women will attempt to buy caregiving services, though they are costly and have not always been readily available.

IMPLICATIONS FOR PRACTICE

Professional helpers need to be familiar with stressors that can affect women in caregiving roles, especially when the stressors affect their parenting and work roles as well. Time spent in caregiving may adversely affect their quality of life, and these women may need help in securing financial resources and social support. Practitioners can also help these women reduce stress and maintain or improve their role performances as parents and employees. They can provide useful anticipatory guidance, such as helping women recognize the possibility that stressors associated with caregiving may decrease over time as they become more familiar with the role and develop the requisite skills. Practitioners can also discuss positive aspects of caregiving, such as opportunities to enhance their relationships with parents. Social agencies can take an active role in helping secure resources for women who are reluctant to leave their jobs for caregiving. Practitioners can help these women manage their emotional difficulties, such as guilt, anxiety, or depression, as well as develop effective responses for satisfying relationships with their parents and parents-in-law. It needs to be recognized, however, that there are no certain strategies that reduce the stress of caregiving for a seriously impaired parent, and that public policy is the necessary target for significant social changes that can lead to modification of the circumstances that lead to caregiver stress.

VIGNETTE

When women experience negative effects of a triple role overload, they may seek the services of various helping professionals. For example, Ann, a 45-year-old single mother of three children, is the primary caregiver for her 80-year-old mother, who is too frail to be left alone. Ann takes part-time responsibility for the caregiving, by visiting her mother every morning before leaving to go to work at noon. A home health care aide arrives at that hour and stays until Ann returns in the evening to prepare dinner for her mother. Later, the night caregiver arrives and stays until Ann returns in the morning. On the weekends, Ann's sister drives 65 miles to help out with the caregiving. The sisters feel depleted and exhausted, both with their direct caregiving and with managing the paid caregivers. Ann worries that her children are not receiving enough of her time and attention. It seems that she is only home to sleep. Ann finally decides to seek the help of a human services professional. She hopes that this step will provide her with suggestions for reducing the stress of trying to balance child care, paid work, and parent care.

Questions

- *What can the counselor tell Ann to help relieve her guilt about feeling so overwhelmed with caregiving for her mother?*

- *What are some possible resources that Ann can use to lessen the hours she spends helping her mother?*

REFERENCES

Abel, E. K. (1990). Family care of the frail elderly. In E. K. Abel & M. K. Nelson (Eds.), *Circles of care: Work and identity in women's lives* (pp. 65–91). Albany: State University of New York.

Abel, E. K. (1991). *Who cares for the disabled elderly? Public policy and the experiences of adult daughters.* Philadelphia, PA: Temple University Press.

Administration on Aging. (2000). *Annual profile of older Americans shows drop in poverty rate* [On-line]. Available: http://www.aos.gov/pr/Pr2000/OAprofile.html.

Alford-Cooper, F. (1993). Women as family caregivers: An American social problem. *Journal of Women and Aging, 5,* 43–57.

Allen, K. R., & Walker, A. J. (1992). A feminist analysis of interviews with elderly mothers and their daughters. In J. F. Gilgun, K. Daly, & G. Handel (Eds.), *Qualitative methods in family research* (pp. 198–214). Newbury Park, CA: Sage Publications.

American Association of Retired Persons. (1988). *A national survey of caregivers: Final report.* Washington, DC: Opinion Research Corporation.

Aranda, M. P., & Knight, B. G. (1997). The influence of ethnicity and culture on the caregiver stress and coping process: A sociocultural review and analysis. *Gerontologist, 37,* 348–352.

Berg-Weger, M., Rubio, D. M., & Tebb, S. S. (2000a). Depression as a mediator: Viewing caregiver well-being and strain in a different light. *Families in Society: Journal of Contemporary Human Services, 81,* 162–173.

Berg-Weger, M., Rubio, D. M., & Tebb, S. S. (2000b). Living with and caring for older family members: Issues related to caregiver well-being. *Journal of Gerontological Social Work, 33,* 47–63.

Blieszner, R., Mancini, J. A., & Marek, L. I. (1996). Looking back and looking ahead: Life-course unfolding of parenthood. In C. D. Ryff & M. M. Seltzer (Eds.), *The parental experience in midlife* (pp. 607–635). Chicago: University of Chicago Press.

Brody, E. M. (1981). "Women in the middle" and family help to older people. *Gerontologist, 21,* 471–479.

Brody, E. M. (1985). Parent care as a normative family stress. *Gerontologist, 25*, 19–29.

Brody, E. M. (1990). *Women in the middle: Their parent-care years.* New York: Springer.

Brody, E. M., Johnsen, P. T., & Fulcomer, M. C. (1984). What should adult children do for elderly parents? Opinion and preferences of three generations of women. *Journal of Gerontology, 39*, 736–746.

Brody, E. M., Kleban, M. H., Johnsen, P. T., Hoffman, C., & Schoonover, C. B. (1987). Work status and parent care: A comparison of four groups of women. *Gerontologist, 27*, 201–208.

Brody, E. M., Litvin, S. J., Hoffman, C., & Kleban, M. H. (1995). Marital status of caregiving daughters and co-residence with dependent parents. *Gerontologist, 35*, 75–85.

Bumpass, L. L., & Aquilino, W. S. (1995). *A social map of midlife: Family and work over the middle life course.* Vero Beach, FL: MacArthur Foundation Research Network on Successful Midlife Development.

Cantor, M. H. (1983). Strain among caregivers: A study of the experience in the U.S. *Gerontologist, 17*, 597–624.

Cantor, M. H. (1991). Family and community: Changing role in aging society. *Gerontologist, 31*, 337–346.

Chang, C., & White-Means, S. (1991). The men who care: An analysis of male primary caregivers who care for frail elderly at home. *Journal of Applied Gerontology, 10*, 343–358.

Chappell, N. L. (1990). Aging and social care. In R. H. Bimstock & L. K. George (Eds.), *Handbook of aging and the social sciences* (3rd ed., pp. 438–454). San Diego: Academic Press.

Cherlin, A. (1981). A sense of history: Recent research on aging and the family. In B. Hess & K. Bond (Eds.), *Leading edges* (NIH Pub. No. 81-2390, pp. 21–50). Washington, DC: U.S. Government Printing Office.

Chiriboga, D. A., Yee, B.W.K., & Weiler, P. G. (1992). Stress and coping in the context of caring. In L. Montada, S. H. Filipp, & M. J. Lerner (Eds.), *Life crises and experience of loss in adulthood* (pp. 95–118). Hillsdale, NJ: Lawrence Erlbaum.

Christensen, K. A., Stephens, M.A.P., & Townsend, A. L. (1998). Mastery in women's multiple roles and well-being: Adult daughters providing care to impaired parents. *Health Psychology, 17*, 163–171.

Cicirelli, V. G. (1983). A comparison of helping behavior to elderly parents of adult children with intact and disrupted marriages. *Gerontologist, 23*, 619–625.

Cicirelli, V. G. (2000). An examination of the trajectory of the adult child's caregiving for an elderly parent. *Family Relations, 49*, 169–175.

Clark, M., & Huttlinger, K. (1998). Elder care among Mexican American families. *Clinical Nursing Research, 7*, 64–81.

Colerick, E. S., & George, L. K. (1986). Prediction of institutionalization among caregivers of patients with Alzheimer's disease. *Journal of the American Geriatrics Society, 34*, 493–498.

Connidis, I. A. (2001). *Family ties and aging.* Thousand Oaks, CA: Sage Publications.

Coward, R. T., & Cutler, S. J. (1991). The composition of multigenerational households that include elders. *Research on Aging, 13*, 55–73.

Davis, B. G., & Silverstone, B. (1981, November). *The impact of care giving: A difference between wives and daughters?* Paper presented at the joint meeting of the Canadian Association of Gerontology and the Gerontological Society of America, Toronto.

Davis, E., & Krouze, M. K. (1994). A maturing benefit: Eldercare after a decade. *Employees Benefits Journal, 19*, 16–20.

Doty, P., Jackson, M. W., & Crown, W. (1998). The impact of female caregivers' employment status on patterns of formal and informal eldercare. *Gerontologist, 38*, 331–341.

Dwyer, J. W., & Coward, R. T. (1991). Multivariate comparison of the involvement of adult sons versus daughters in the care of impaired parents. *Journal of Gerontology: Social Sciences, 46*, S259–S269.

England, M. (1995). Crisis and the filial caregiving situation of African American adult offspring. *Issues in Mental Health Nursing, 16*, 143–163.

Family and Medical Leave Act of 1993, P.L. 103-3, 107 Stat. 6.

Feinauer, L. L., Lund, D. A., & Miller, J. R. (1987). Family issues in multigenerational households. *American Journal of Family Therapy, 15*, 52–61.

Finley, N. J. (1989). Gender differences in caregiving for elderly parents. *Journal of Marriage and the Family, 51*, 79–86.

Fitting, M., Rabins, P., Lucas, M. J., & Eastham, J. (1986). Caregivers for dementia patients: A comparison of husbands and wives. *Gerontologist, 26*, 248–252.

Gatz, M., Bengston, V. L., & Blum, M. J. (1990). Caregiving families. In J. E. Birren & K. W. Schaie (Eds.), *Handbook of the psychology of aging* (3rd ed., pp. 404–426). New York: Academic Press.

George, L. K., & Gwyther, L. P. (1986). Caregiving well-being: A multidimensional examination of family caregivers of demented adults. *Gerontologist, 26*, 253–259.

Hagestad, G. O. (1984). The continuous bond: A dynamic, multigenerational perspective on parent–child relations between adults. In M. Perlmutter (Ed.), *Minnesota symposia on child psychology* (Vol. 17, pp. 247–262). Hillsdale, NJ: Lawrence Erlbaum.

Haggan, P. S. (1998). Counseling adult children of aging parents. *Educational Gerontology, 24*, 333–348.

Haley, W. E., Brown, S. L., & Levine, E. G. (1987). Family caregiver appraisals of patient behavioral disturbance in senile dementia. *Clinical Gerontologist, 6*, 25–34.

Haley, W. E., Wadley, V. G., West, C. A., & Vetzel, L. L. (1994). How caregiving stressors change with severity of dementia. *Seminars in Speech and Language, 15*, 195–205.

Halpern, J. (1994). The sandwich generation: Conflicts between adult children and their aging parents. In D. D. Cahn (Ed.), *Conflict in personal relationships* (pp.143–160). Hillsdale, NJ: Lawrence Erlbaum.

Harper, S., & Lund, D. (1990). Wives, husbands and daughters caring for institutionalized and noninstitutionalized dementia patients: Toward a model of caregiving burden. *International Journal of Aging and Human Development, 30*, 241–262.

Hartman, A. (1990). Aging as a feminist issue. *Social Work, 35*, 387–388.

Hartung, R. (1993). Black burden and becoming nouveau poor. *Journal of Gerontology, 48*, S33–S34.

Himes, C. (1994). Parental caregiving by adult women: A demographic perspective. *Research on Aging, 16*, 191–211.

Himes, C., & Reidy, E. B. (2000). The role of friends in caregiving. *Reseach on Aging, 22*, 315–336.

Hooyman, N. R. (1990). Women as caregivers of the elderly: Implications for social welfare policy and practice. In D. E. Biegel & A. Blum (Eds.), *Aging and caregiving: Theory, research, and policy* (pp. 221–241). Newbury Park, CA: Sage Publications.

Hooyman, N. R. (1999). Research on older women: Where is feminism? *Gerontologist, 39*, 115–118.

Hooyman, N. R., & Gonyea, J. G. (1995). *Feminist perspectives on family care: Policies for gender justice*. Thousand Oaks, CA: Sage Publications.

Hooyman, N. R., & Gonyea, J .G. (1999). A feminist model of family care: Practice and policy directives. *Journal of Women & Aging, 11*, 149–169.

Hooyman, N. R., & Lustbader, W. (1986). *Taking care: Supporting older people and their families.* New York: Free Press.

Horowitz, A. (1985). Family caregiving to the frail elderly. *Annual Review of Gerontology and Geriatrics, 5*, 194–246.

Hugen, B. (1993). The effectiveness of a psycho-educational support service to families of persons with chronic mental illness. *Research on Social Work Practice, 3*, 137–154.

Jarvik, L., & Small, G. (1988). *Parent care: A commonsense guide for adult children.* New York: Crown.

Johnson, C. L., & Barber, B. M. (1995). Childlessness and kinship organization: Comparisons of very old Whites and Blacks. *Journal of Cross-Cultural Gerontology, 10*, 289–306.

Jones, P. S. (1995). Paying respect: Care of elderly parents by Chinese and Filipino American women. *Health Care for Women International, 16*, 385–398.

Kimmel, D. C., & Sang, B. E. (1995). Lesbians and gay men in midlife. In A. R. D'Augelli & C. J.

Patterson (Eds.), *Lesbian, gay, and bisexual identities over the lifespan: Psychological perspectives* (pp. 190–214). New York: Oxford University Press.

Kingston, E. R., Hirshorn, B. A., & Cornman, J. M. (1986). *Ties that bind: The interdependence of generations.* Washington, DC: Steven Locks.

LaBorde, J. (1994). The gendered division of labor in parental caretaking: Biology or socialization? *Journal of Women & Aging, 6*, 65–89.

Lang, A. M., & Brody, E. M. (1983). Characteristics of middle-age daughters and help to their elderly mothers. *Journal of Marriage and the Family, 45*, 193–202.

Lechner, V. M., & Gupta, C. (1996). Employed caregivers: A four-year follow-up. *Journal of Applied Gerontology, 15*, 102–115.

Lee, C. (1999). Health, stress and coping among women caregivers. *Journal of Health Psychology, 4*, 27–40.

Lee, G. R., Dwyer, J. W., & Coward, R. T. (1993). Gender differences in parent care: Demographic factors and same-gender preferences. *Journal of Gerontology: Social Sciences, 48*, S9–S16.

Lewis, S., & Meredith, B. (1988). Daughters caring for mothers. *Aging and Society, 8*, 1–21.

Li, L.W., Seltzer, M. M., & Greenberg, J. S. (1999). Change in depressive symptoms among daughter caregivers: An 18-month longitudinal study. *Psychology and Aging, 14*, 206–219.

Loomis, L. S., & Booth, A. (1995). Multigenerational caregiving and well-being: The myth of the beleaguered sandwich generation. *Journal of Family Issues, 16*, 131–148.

Lund, D. A. (1993). Caregiving. In R. Kastenbaum (Ed.), *Encyclopedia of adult development* (pp. 57–63). Phoenix, AZ: Oryx.

Markides, K. S., & Mindel, C. H. (1987). *Aging and ethnicity.* Newbury Park, CA: Sage Publications.

Marks, N. F. (1993). *Contemporary social demographics of American midlife parents* (NSFH Working Paper No. 54). Madison: University of Wisconsin, Center for Demography and Ecology.

Marks, N. F. (1994). *Midlife caregiving: Do effects differ by gender?* (NSFH Working Paper No. 64). Madison: University of Wisconsin, Center for Demography and Ecology.

Marks, N. F. (1996a). Caregiving across the lifespan: National prevalence and predictors. *Family Relations, 45*, 27–35.

Marks, N. F. (1996b). Social demographic diversity among American midlife parents. In C. D. Ryff & M. M. Seltzer (Eds.), *The parental experience in midlife* (pp. 29–75). Chicago: University of Chicago Press.

Marks, N. F. (1998). Does it hurt to care? Caregiving, work–family conflict, and midlife well-being. *Journal of Marriage and the Family, 60,* 951–966.

Martire, L. M., Stephens, M.A.P., & Franks, M. M. (1997). Multiple roles of women caregivers: Feelings of mastery and self-esteem as predictors of psychosocial well-being. *Journal of Women & Aging, 9,* 117–131.

Martire, L. M., Stephens, M.A.P., & Townsend, A. L. (1998). Emotional support and well-being of midlife women: Role-specific mastery as a mediational mechanism. *Psychology and Aging, 13,* 396–404.

McDaniel, J. L., & Via, B. G. (1997). Aging issues in the workplace. *American Association of Occupational Health Nurses Journal, 45,* 261–269.

McGrew, K. B. (1998). Daughter's caregiving decisions: From an impulse to a balancing point of care. *Journal of Women & Aging, 10,* 49–65.

Merrill, D. M. (1996). Conflict and cooperation among adult siblings during the transition to the role of filial caregiver. *Journal of Social and Personal Relationships, 13,* 399–413.

Miller, B. (1989). Adult children's perceptions of caregiver stress and satisfaction. *Journal of Applied Gerontology, 8,* 275–293.

Moen, P. (1997). Women's roles and resilience: Trajectories of advantage or turning points? In J. H. Gotlib & B. Wheaton (Eds.), *Stress and adversity over the life course: Trajectories and turning points* (pp. 113–156). New York: Cambridge University Press.

Moen, P., Robinson, J., & Fields, V. (1994). Women's work and caregiving roles: A life-course approach. *Journal of Gerontology: Social Sciences, 49,* S176–S186.

Montgomery, R.J.V. (1992). Gender differences in patterns of child-parent caregiving relationships. In J. W. Dwyer & R. T. Coward (Eds.), *Gender, families, and elder care* (pp. 65–83). Newbury Park, CA: Sage Publications.

Montgomery, R.J.V., Gonyea, J. G., & Hooyman, N. R. (1985). Caregiving and the experience of subjective and objective burden. *Family Relations, 34,* 19–26.

Montgomery, R.J.V., & Kamo, Y. (1989). Parent care by sons and daughters. In J. A. Mancini (Ed.), *Aging parents and adult children* (pp. 213–227). Lexington, MA: D. C. Heath.

Mor-Barak, M. E., & Tynan, M. (1993). Older workers and the workplace: A new challenge for occupational social work. *Social Work, 38,* 45–55.

Neal, M. B., Chapman, N., Ingersoll-Dayton, B., Emlen, A., & Boise, L. (1990). Absenteeism and stress among employed caregivers of the elderly, disabled adults, and children. In D. E. Biegel & A. Blum (Eds.), *Aging and caregiving: Theory, research, and policy* (pp. 160–183). Newbury Park, CA: Sage Publications.

Newman, B. M., & Newman, P. R. (1991). *Development through life: A psychosocial approach.* Pacific Grove, CA: Brooks/Cole.

Nunley, B. L., Hall, L. A., & Rowles, G. D. (2000). Effects of the quality of dyadic relationships on the psychological well-being of elderly care-recipients. *Journal of Gerontological Nursing, 26,* 23–31.

Parks, S. H., & Pillsuk, M. (1991). Caregiver burden: Gender and the psychological costs of caregiving. *American Journal of Orthopsychiatry, 6,* 501–509.

Pavalko, E. K., & Artis, J. E. (1997). Women's caregiving and paid work: Causal relationships in late midlife. *Journals of Gerontology, 52B,* S170–S179.

Penning, M. J. (1998). In the middle: Parental caregiving in the context of other roles. *Journal of Gerontology: Social Sciences, 53B,* 188–197.

Pett, M. A., Caserta, M. S., Hutton, A. P., & Lund, D. A. (1988). Intergenerational conflict: Middle aged women caring for demented older relatives. *American Journal of Orthopsychiatry, 58,* 4054–17.

Piercy, K. W. (1998). Theorizing about family caregiving: The role of responsibility. *Journal of Marriage and the Family, 60,* 109–118.

Pohl, J. M., Boyd, C., & Given, B. A. (1997). Mother–daughter relationships during the first year of caregiving: A qualitative study. *Journal of Women & Aging, 9,* 133–149.

Pot, A. M., Deeg, D.J.H., van Dyck, R., & Jonker, C. (1998). Psychological distress of care-givers: The mediator effect of caregiving appraisal. *Patient Education and Counseling, 34,* 43–51.

Qualls, S. H. (1988). Problems in families of older adults. In N. Epstein, S. Schlessinger, & W. Dryden (Eds.), *Cognitive–behavioral therapy with families* (pp. 215–253). New York: Brunner/Mazel.

Quayhagen, M. P., & Quayhagen, M. (1988). Alzheimer's stress: Coping with the caregiv-ing role. *Gerontologist, 28,* 391–396.

Query, J. L., Jr., & Flint, L. J. (1996). The caregiving relationship. In N. Vanzetti & S. Duck (Eds.), *A lifetime of relationships* (pp. 456–483). Pacific Grove, CA: Brooks/Cole.

Reinardy, J. R., Kane, R. A., Huck, S. C., Call, K. T., & Shen, C-T. (1999). Beyond burden: Two ways of looking at caregiving burden. *Journal of Gerontological Social Work, 31,* 119–141.

Richards, L. N., Bengston, V. L., & Miller, R. B. (1989). The "generation in the middle": Perceptions of changes in adults' intergenerational relationships. In K. Kreppner & R. M. Lerner (Eds.), *Family systems and the life plan* (pp. 341–366). Hillsdale, NJ: Lawrence Erlbaum.

Rosenthal, C. J., Matthews, S. H., & Marshall, V. W. (1989). Is parent care normative? The experiences of a sample of middle-age women. *Research on Aging, 11,* 244–260.

Rossi, A. (1985). Gender and parenthood. In A. S. Rossi (Ed.), *Gender and the life course* (pp. 161–191). Hawthorne, NY: Aldine de Gryter.

Rossi, A. S., & Rossi, P. H. (1991). Normative obligations and parent–child help and change across the life course. In K. Pillemer & K. McCartney (Eds.), *Parent–child relations throughout life* (pp. 201–122). Hillsdale, NJ: Lawrence Earlbaum.

Ryff, C. D., & Seltzer, M. M. (1995). Family relations and individual development in adult-hood and aging. In R. Blieszner & V. H. Bedford (Eds.), *Handbook of aging and family* (pp. 94–113). Westport, CT: Greenwood Press.

Sangl, J. (1985). The family support system of the elderly. In R. J. Vogel & H. C. Palmer (Eds.), *Long-term care: Perspectives from research and demonstration* (pp. 307–336). Rockville, MD: Aspen.

Scharlach, A. E. (1994). Caregiving and employment: Competing or complementary roles? *Gerontologist, 34,* 378–385.

Scharlach, A. E., & Boyd, S. (1989). Caregiving and employment: Results of an employee survey. *Gerontologist, 29,* 382–387.

Schmertmann, C. P., Boyd, M., Serow, W., & White, D. (2000). Elder–child coresidence in the United States. *Research on Aging, 22,* 23–42.

Schwarz, K. A., & Roberts, B. L. (2000). Social support and strain of family caregivers of older adults. *Holistic Nursing Practice, 14,* 77–90.

Schwiebert, V. L., & Myers, J. E. (1994). Midlife care givers: Effectiveness of a psychoedu-cational intervention for midlife adults with parent-care responsibilities. *Journal of Counseling & Development, 72,* 627–632.

Scott, J. W., & Black, A. (1994). Deep structures of African American family life: Female and male kin networks. In R. Staples (Ed.), *The black family* (5th ed., pp. 204–213). Belmont, CA: Wadsworth.

Seltzer, M.M., & Li, L.W. (2000). The dynamics of caregiving: Transitions during a three-year prospective study. *The Gerontologist, 40,* 165-178.

Silverstein, M., & Angelelli, J. J. (1998). Older parents' expectations of moving closer to their children. *Journal of Gerontology: Social Sciences, 53B,* 153–163.

Spitze, G., & Logan, J. R. (1990). More evidence on women (and men) in the middle. *Research on Aging, 12,* 182–198.

Spurlock, J. (1984). Black women in the middle years. In G. Baruch & J. Brooks-Gunn (Eds.), *Women in midlife* (pp. 245–260). New York: Plenum Press.

Stephens, S. A., & Christianson, J. B. (1986). *Informal care of the elderly.* Lexington, MA: Lexington Books.

Stoller, E. P. (1994). Teaching about gender: The experience of family care of frail elderly relatives. *Educational Gerontology, 20,* 679–697.

Stoller, E. P., & Pugliesi, K. L. (1989). Other roles of caregivers: Competing responsibilities or supportive resources. *Journal of Gerontology: Social Sciences, 44,* S231–S238.

Stone, R., Cafferata, G. L., & Sangl, J. (1987). Caregivers of the frail elderly: A national profile. *Gerontologist, 27,* 616–626.

Stueve, A., & O'Donnell, L. (1984). The daughter of aging parents. In G. Baruch & J. Brooks-Gunn (Eds.), *Women in midlife* (pp. 203–225). New York: Plenum Press.

Thompson, E. H., Futterman, A. M., Gallagher-Thompson, D., Rose, J. M., & Lovett, S. B. (1993). Social support and caregiver burdens in family caregivers of frail elderly. *Journal of Gerontology: Social Sciences, 48,* S245–S254.

Tirrito, T., & Nathanson, I. (1994). Ethnic differences in caregiving: Adult daughters and elderly mothers. *Affilia, 9,* 71–84.

Townsend, A., Noelker, L., Deimling, G., & Bass, D. (1989). Longitudinal impact of inter-household caregiving stressors. *Psychology and Aging, 4,* 393–401.

U.S. Bureau of the Census. (1995). *American women: A profile* (No. SB/95-19). Washington, DC: U.S. Government Printing Office.

U.S. Select Committee on Aging. (1987). *Exploding the myths: Caregiving in America* (100th Cong., First Sess., Comm. Pub. No. 99-611). Washington, DC: U.S. Government Printing Office.

Walker, A. J. (1992). Conceptual perspectives on gender and family caregiving. In J. Dwyer & R. Coward (Eds.), *Gender, families, and elder care* (pp. 34–46). Newbury Park, CA: Sage Publications.

Walker, A. J., & Allen, K. R. (1991). Relationships between caregiving daughters and their elderly mothers. *Gerontologist, 31,* 389–396.

Walker, A. J., Martin, S. K., & Jones, L. L. (1992). The benefits and costs of caregiving and care receiving for daughters and mothers. *Journal of Gerontology: Social Sciences, 47,* S130–S139.

Walker, A. J., Pratt, C. C., & Eddy, L. (1995). Informal caregiving to aging family members: A critical review. *Family Relations, 39,* 147–152.

Walker, A. J., Pratt, C. C., Shin, H. Y., & Jones, L.L. (1989). Why daughters care: Perspectives of mothers and daughters in a caring situation. In J. A. Mancini (Ed.), *Aging parents and their adult children* (pp. 199–212). Lexington, MA: Lexington Books.

Walker, R. J., & Pomeroy, E. C. (1997). The impact of anticipatory grief on caregivers of persons with Alzheimer's disease. *Home Health Care Services Quarterly, 16,* 55–76.

Ward, D. H., & Carney, P. A. (1994). Caregiving women and the U.S. welfare state: The case of elder kin care by low-income women. *Holistic Nursing Practice, 8*, 44–58.

Wight, R. G., LeBlanc, A. J., & Aneshensel, C. S. (1998). AIDS caregiving and health among midlife and older women. *Health Psychology, 17*, 130–137.

Yevak, M. E. (1994). Caregivers in a continuum. *Adultspan, 8*, 17.

Zarit, S. H., Todd, P. A., & Zarit, J. M. (1986). Subjective burden of husbands and wives as caregivers: A longitudinal study. *Gerontologist, 26*, 260–266.

ADDITIONAL REFERENCES

Brody, E. M., Litvin, S. J., Albert, S. M., & Hoffman, C. J. (1994). Marital status of daughters and patterns of parent care. *Journal of Gerontology: Social Sciences, 49*, S95–S103.

Franklin, S. T., Ames, B. D., & King, S. (1994). Acquiring the family eldercare role. *Research on Aging, 16*, 27–42.

Globerman, J. (1996). Motivations to care: Daughters-and-sons-in-law caring for relatives with Alzheimer's disease. *Family Relations, 45*, 37–45.

Gottlieb, B. H., Kelloway, E. K., & Fraboni, M. (1994). Aspects of eldercare that place employees at risk. *Gerontologist, 34*, 815–821.

Kramer, B. J., & Kipnis, S. (1995). Eldercare and work–role conflict: Toward an understanding of gender differences in caregiver burden. *Gerontologist, 35*, 340–348.

Liebig, P. S. (1993). Factors affecting the development of employer-sponsored eldercare programs: Implications for employed caregivers. *Journal of Women & Aging, 5*, 59–78.

Loos, C., & Bowd, A. (1997). Caregivers of persons with Alzheimer's disease: Some neglected implications for the experience of personal loss and grief. *Death Studies, 21*, 501–504.

Scharlach, A. E., & Fredriksen, K. I. (1994). Elder care versus adult care: Does care recipient age make a difference. *Research on Aging, 16*, 43–68.

Suitor, J. J., & Pillemer, K. (1994). Family caregiving and marital satisfaction: Findings from 1-year panel study of women caring for parents with dementia. *Journal of Marriage and the Family, 56*, 681–690.

CHAPTER 4

SINGLE-AGAIN AND ALWAYS-SINGLE STATUSES

This chapter focuses on midlife women who were always single or are single again. The two major avenues to single-again are divorced or widowed (Atwood, 1988). The term "always single" is a more neutral description than the negative labels "never married" or "unmarried" (Lewis, 1994). Research that distinguishes single-again and always-single women is not plentiful because often respondents who are unmarried are all grouped together (Davies, 1995; Marks, 1995). Life-span themes in this chapter include: strengths, resiliency, vitality, and adaptation; individual differences; historical–cultural contexts; gains and losses; challenges and opportunities; development, growth, and change; and duration dependence.

Questions to Consider

- *What are the short-term and long-term consequences of divorce on midlife women?*

- *What life changes must be addressed by midlife women following divorce?*

- *What are the advantages and disadvantages of being always single?*

Marital Dissolution at Midlife

Persons who enter midlife married, or cohabitating with a partner, tend to remain in these statuses throughout midlife, a fact that may demonstrate the phenomenon of *duration dependence.* The divorce rates in midlife are less than half the rates experienced by persons in their early 30s. Divorce rates also decline steadily with increasing time after entering midlife; whereas 31 percent of persons ages 40–49 divorce before age 40, only about 15 percent of persons ages 60–69 divorce. But greater numbers of separated and divorced persons are entering midlife, including one in six of the National Survey of Families and Households (NSFH) midlife respondents (Bumpass & Aquilino, 1995). This project was supported by the MacArthur Foundation Research Network on Successful Midlife Development and the Center for Demography and Ecology at the University of Wisconsin. The proportion of those who never marry is also projected to decline and the proportion of always-single persons entering midlife is projected to increase. Forming new partnerships also declines with increasing age; compared to about a quarter of persons at ages 30–34, only one in 10 persons at ages 40–44 formed a new partnership in the five years preceding the NSFH study (Bumpass & Aquilino, 1995; Bumpass, Sweet, & Castro-Martin, 1990).

No comparable data exist on breakups of midlife lesbian couples. The data available on same-sex couples, however, may partly be applicable to this population. Individuals in same-sex couples commit themselves to be together for life or "a long time" just as persons in heterosexual couples (Bryant & Demian, 1994). Yet, same-sex relationships appear generally shorter in duration than heterosexual relationships, though it is not easy to assess how long these relationships last because no records of commitment and breakup are kept (Peplau, 1993). The best comparison of breakup rates among different groups comes from Blumstein and Schwartz's (1983) landmark study that included 3,574 married couples, 642 cohabiting couples, 957 gay couples, and 772 lesbian couples. This study provided rare data over 18 months on the longevity of these couples. In the beginning of the survey period, all groups were about equal in predicting expectations of staying together. Most couples were still together at the end of 18 months; less than one in five couples broke up. The proportions for breakups included: lesbian (22 percent), gay (16 percent), heterosexually cohabiting (17 percent), and heterosexually married (4 percent).

Many same-sex couples are together for long periods. Various studies found lesbian and gay couples together 10 years or longer (for example, Berger, 1982; Bryant & Demian, 1994). For lesbian and gay couples in the Blumstein and Schwartz (1983) study already together for more than 10 years, breakups were rare—a finding that may also reflect the *duration dependence* phenomenon. Many couples are together for decades. Through anecdotal accounts, older lesbian and gay persons reported knowing of relationships of 20 years duration or longer (for example, Adelman, 1986; Silverstein, 1981).

Motives for Divorce

Although the divorce rate in midlife is lower than it is in the 30s, Uhlenberg, Cooney, and Boyd (1990) reported from 1985 data that divorce for women after age 40 is not an uncommon occurrence. One-fifth of all divorces involved women over the age of 40, mostly between the ages of 40 and 60. By year 2025, the researchers projected that about half of the women entering old age would no longer be in a marriage because of divorce. If the divorce rates after age 40 continue, this projected proportion could be even higher.

Many women experience the motivation to divorce when they reassess their marriages following major family transitions. When the children leave, for example, disenchantment and discontent with one's marriage, or issues and deficits denied earlier because of the children, may come into awareness (Kaslow, 1994). Earlier expectations of marriage for some women, however, diverged from the reality years before the postparental period (Schwartz & Kalsow, 1997). With children grown or gone, these women, who long held a desire to leave, may now make their exit. Some women also leave a marriage because the partner was abusive, drug addicted, or alcohol addicted. Another precipitating factor may be the realization of one's own mortality and the sense that time is running out. Before it is too late, women may desire new experiences, adventures, freedom, and fun in contrast with a too predictable and familiar long-term marriage. These women want to live more fully or with a different partner (Kaslow, 1994). Other women married to men for a long time desire to leave their marriages because of a transformation in self-identification from heterosexual to lesbian (for example, Bridges & Croteau, 1994; Sang, 1992).

When lesbian (and gay) couples experience a breakup, along with the typical reasons for couple dissolution such as disenchantment or infidelity, extraordinary challenges or obstacles probably also play a part. Internal challenges include confusion from the lack of role models for same-sex couples, disclosure conflicts, negative self-fulfilling prophecies, hiding and passing, and lower stability resulting from missing forces of commitment. Some obstacles are external to couples but create internal difficulties that can interfere with, if not destroy, satisfaction. These obstacles include fewer binding social arrangements such as legal marriage and the hostile climate of bias against lesbian and gay persons (Hunter and Hickerson (in press); Hunter, Shannon, Knox, & Martin, 1998).

Emotions and Life Changes

Several researchers identified some of the basic issues midlife women may confront when suddenly separated from their partners and with divorce pending (for example, Hayes & Anderson, 1993; Schwartz, 1994). They include the emotions and unavoidable life changes discussed below.

Emotions Accompanying Divorce. When one or both partners feel disillusioned with the marriage, a process of detachment from the marriage begins, along with contemplation of a future without the partner. The initiator of the divorce is usually further along in this process or the only one moving in this direction (Bohannon, 1970). Because women are typically more invested in maintaining the marriage (Baruch, Barnett, & Rivers, 1983), they tend to resist initiating the divorce process. If they are the initiators, however, women may begin an emotional divorce several years before a legal divorce.

When men are not the initiators, they are more likely unaware of difficulties in the marriage and may express astonishment when their wives announce their intention to separate. The initiator of separation attains the advantage of some control over the situation and time to prepare for the final separation. For the partner who was unaware of the other partner's plans, the unexpected events can lead to feeling a loss of control and accompanying anxiety (for example, Lazarus & Folkman, 1984). Although the partner who first decides to leave experiences emotional reactions to separation and divorce, usually the partner who feels rejected endures the most severe emotional reactions because of the unanticipated and undesired reality. Along with other emotions, this partner may experience feelings of self-recrimination mixed with a desire to retaliate for the hurt (Kaslow, 1994; Kaslow & Schwartz, 1987).

Hayes and Anderson (1993) also studied the emotions accompanying divorce. They identified the most typical emotions experienced during the dissolution of a marriage in a national sample of 338 single-again women ages 40 to 75. The mean age was 50. The women were previously in long-term marriages of 20 to 48 years, with a mean of 23 years. The following list shows the emotions identified in this study in the most common contexts; typically these women experienced several of these emotions simultaneously (Hayes & Anderson, 1993):

- *Shock and disbelief*, which were often experienced during the initial phases of divorce, even if the partner's request for divorce was not a surprise.

- *Anger and resentment*, which were experienced by 72 percent of the respondents. These emotions resulted from feeling betrayed when one's husband did not want to save the marriage and from hurtful behavior such as infidelity or emotional or physical abuse. Anger was also directed at the legal system because it was rarely helpful.

- *Fear*, which next to anger was the strongest emotion expressed. This emotion was often experienced throughout the dissolution process. Two main fears were not having enough money and being alone.

- *Loneliness*, which occurred mostly when the husband kept the children or the family split into divided camps.

- *Relief*, which could occur at any period during or after the dissolution process. For some women, relief was immediate after they reached the determination to initiate divorce, for others it came gradually over a long time.

Only a few studies examined the emotions of lesbians when their primary relationships dissolved. Lesbians do not react differently than heterosexual women to endings of their primary relationships (Kurdek, 1991). Emotions, such as sadness, regret, and anger, are experienced by both heterosexual women and lesbians (Blumstein & Schwartz, 1983). Depression is just as common among lesbians as among heterosexual women (Rothblum, 1990).

Personal, Family, and Community Changes. Besides the emotions accompanying divorce, midlife women also experience aloneness and change in self-concept and identity and community. Each of these changes is discussed below:

Living alone. Within the first year following divorce, living alone was a source of anxiety for 56 percent of the Hayes and Anderson (1993) sample. More than half missed an intimate relationship (54 percent) and almost two-thirds (63 percent) missed a regular companion for social events. After at least five years following divorce, the proportion of women experiencing these concerns about living alone decreased to 42 percent.

Self-concept and identity. Women who spent most of their lives defining themselves as wives and mothers are likely to experience the sudden status of being single as a difficult time (Hayes & Anderson, 1993). Breakups can also threaten lesbians' sense of who they are because many of them came out in the context of a relationship with another woman. Their identity can become more ambiguous when no longer in a primary partnership (Browning, Reynolds, & Dworkin, 1991). Whether lesbian or heterosexual, suddenly single-again women must also develop new identities to replace the ones they lost (Schwartz, 1994). They must also come to terms with themselves as valued persons after the rejection of divorce (Philpot, 1994). Living as a single-again person also requires different attitudes and skills from those needed in a traditional marriage (Hayes & Anderson, 1993).

Children. Custody disputes are unusual because children are either old enough to make their own decisions about which parent to live with or are gone from the home. If, however, any children are living with them, mothers must cope with the economic, emotional, and energy demands of child rearing alone (Weitzman, 1985). In addition, they worry about the effects of divorce on their children. Over two-thirds (71 percent) of the midlife women studied by Hayes and Anderson (1993) thought that their children would experience negative effects from the divorce for a long time. Philpot (1994) pointed out that older adolescent and adult children might feel angry about the dissolution of the family as well as being pulled between the parents.

Community. Midlife couples are usually well entrenched in numerous inter-personal systems with long histories; the breakup of their marriages often means the breakup of these systems (for example Hagestad, Smyer, & Stierman, 1984). The support of couple friends usually declines (Peck & Manocherian, 1989). Activities the couple used to do are not always open to single-again women. In some social situations these women are perceived to be a threat to other women's marriages (Schwartz, 1994). Friends can feel torn between the two former partners and may take sides or avoid both of them. Similar responses can happen among former in-laws. These various community breakups necessitate that single-again women develop activities and social networks to replace the ones they lost (Philpot, 1994).

Changed economics. Unless they can support themselves financially, midlife women are usually the losers in the economics of divorce. Financial settlements tend to favor husbands. No-fault divorce laws allow little to no alimony. Most divorce settlements do not even include "rehabilitative alimony" to help women prepare to enter the workplace (for example, Philpot, 1994; Schwartz, 1994). For women who no longer have dependent children, divorce courts usu-ally expect them to support themselves even if they lack the necessary experi-ence and skills. Though they may have helped their husbands establish careers, the income derived from those careers is considered to belong to the husbands (Weitzman, 1985). More than half of the women (60 percent) studied by Hayes and Anderson (1993) felt that the divorce settlement was unfair and that they had agreed to the settlement too fast.

A good lawyer is the key to receiving fair benefits in a divorce settlement, if one can afford this resource. Without good advice from a lawyer or financial planner, Block (2000) observed that women may capitulate a portion of their former husband's pension or other retirement plans such as a 401(k) plan in exchange for more immediately accessible assets such as the house. Block encouraged women approaching divorce to (a) learn about the partner's retire-ment savings, (b) take advantage of spousal Social Security benefits (if married at least 10 years before the divorce is final), and (c) if working, take advantage of 401(k) plans and similar programs that can be rolled over into an individual retirement account if a woman leaves her job.

Issues surrounding money for single-again women studied by Hayes and Anderson (1993) created considerable anxiety for 88 percent of them at least 1 year after the divorce and for 68 percent of them after at least 5 years. More than half (54 percent to 62 percent) of the women were not knowledgeable about joint ownership of marital property, were unaware of or did not under-stand marital investments, and were unaware of insurance or pension coverage.

Many midlife women married in the 1950s when most women did not work outside the home. Few women developed marketable skills because they did not anticipate the need to work later (Clausen & Gilens, 1990). If a woman in her 50s had limited or no work experience outside the home, she was unlikely to find a job that would provide enough income to support the standard of living that she experienced when married (Schwartz, 1994). Even worse, midlife women who were full-time housewives, with no job training and no work experience, might suddenly be poor (Hayes & Anderson, 1993; Schwartz, 1994). The average predivorce couple's income in the Hayes and Anderson sample was $40,000 to $45,000. The average postdivorce income for the women was $10,000 to $15,000. Over half (54 percent) of the women had trouble keeping the mortgage or rent paid and 32 percent needed to find less expensive housing.

A large number of midlife women (5,083) participated in the National Longitudinal Survey of women under the auspices of the U.S. Bureau of Labor Statistics (Blumstein & Schwartz, 1983). This study began in 1967 and by 1982 the women in the sample were between ages 45–59. Both widowed and divorced midlife women experienced greater risk of poverty when their marriages ended. Widowed women immediately reflected the expected change in economic status. For divorced midlife women, however, the highest rate of poverty occurred 3–4 years after divorce, though by the fifth year the rates of poverty were below predivorce levels. Morgan (1989) concluded that the economic status of midlife women seriously erodes after divorce.

One group of midlife women may not experience as serious a financial erosion following divorce: those who worked continuously at a career during their marriages (Morgan, 1991). Many blue-collar women also worked all their lives, but their jobs probably did not provide enough money to be fully self-supporting (Rubin, 1979). Morgan reported that both widowed and divorced midlife women moved in and out of poverty depending on factors such as opportunities to prepare for work and available economic supports.

Reemergence in the Dating World. Eligible men in midlife are rare, and the dating scene can be frustrating after many years of marriage. The last time a midlife woman dated anyone was usually in high school or college (Chiriboga, 1989). After 20 years of marriage, dating can feel like an awkward, alien activity. Singles' groups and singles' bars can feel uncomfortable at the least and, for some women, create panic (Kaslow, 1994). Midlife women often feel rejected in the dating world because of the emphasis on youth in our culture (Peck & Manocherian, 1989). Confidence in their appeal and attractiveness often declines (Kaslow, 1994). They can especially feel sexually unappealing if their husbands left them for younger women (Hayes & Anderson, 1993).

Another concern for women reentering the dating scene is the threat of HIV/AIDS (Schwartz, 1994) although most midlife and older women do not perceive themselves at risk and, so, do not use safe-sex practices (Binson, Pollack, & Catania, 1997). Yet, the most prevalent transmission route for midlife and older men and women is through heterosexual sexual activity, and the rise of new HIV/AIDS cases is growing among the age 50 and older population (Ory & Mack, 1998).

If a woman desires to remarry during midlife, the probability for remarriage is not high (Norton & Moorman, 1987; Uhlenberg et al., 1990). Several reasons for this situation include the realities that men tend to marry younger women and that in every period of life more men than women die (Pillari, 1988).

Supports for Single-Again Women

Supports include information and networks. Examples of information include: (a) laws governing the economic aspects of divorce in all 50 states, (b) divorce and property division specialists, (c) on-line organizations, (d) references on family law, social science, and self-help, and (e) support groups. This information is helpful both for women and for the practitioners who are assisting them (Laughlin, 1995).

Hayes and Anderson (1993) investigated the support networks of single-again midlife women in their national sample. Networks that were particularly helpful included:

- *Supportive friendships* mediated the effects of stress during and after the divorce. Friends provided emotional support, assistance, and companionship in leisure activities. Most (80 percent) of the women felt that women friends were more helpful than family members in coping with the stress of divorce.

- *Support groups* were helpful for 66 percent of the respondents. The benefits included: (a) emotional support from women in similar situations; (b) practical, financial, legal, and mental health information; (c) recommendations of helpful community resources; (d) development of job reentry strategies and employment skills; and (e) dating advice.

- *Marriage counseling* was pursued by 50 percent of couples before the divorce. A majority (63 percent) of the women indicated that it was not useful at that point mainly because their husbands (64 percent) refused to participate. Over a third (37 percent) of the women sought individual counseling following their divorce and thought it was useful.

There is little known about the supports available for midlife lesbians when their primary relationships end. They may not receive the support or sympathy from family, friends, or coworkers that heterosexual women receive. Parents or others who never supported the same-sex arrangement may express happiness and relief about the breakup. If these women are not open about their same-sex sexual orientation, they may suffer and grieve alone (Becker, 1988), although some of them may disclose their sexual orientation as the only way to get support from others (Browning et al., 1991).

Positive Outcomes for Single-Again Women

For some women, divorce is so traumatic that it takes a long time to come to terms with it (for example, Wallerstein, 1986). The chances are good, however, that most women who experience a divorce in midlife will eventually reestablish satisfying lives (Chiriboga, 1982, 1991). This outcome reflects the *resiliency*, *vitality*, and *adaptation* of these women. Several studies reported that in both short- and long-term adjustment to divorce, women experienced a higher quality of life and better psychological functioning than men (Chiriboga, 1991; Hayes & Anderson, 1993). For the women studied by Chiriboga (1991) age 40 and older, quality of life improved appreciably between the time of marital separation and a follow-up rating 3 1/2 years later. At follow-up, these women were also happier than younger women. In another report by Chiriboga (1982) on single-again midlife men and women, the women experienced greater *challenges* and *opportunities* after separation.

Hayes and Anderson's (1993) findings on single-again midlife women were also positive regarding how the women *developed* and *changed*. Their sense of self grew stronger, and their contentment and satisfaction with life increased. More than half of women single again for less than 5 years felt free for the first time to be themselves and were developing new positive identities. They felt a sense of achievement and independence, and they liked their privacy. About two-thirds (67 percent) of these women indicated that a relationship potentially leading to marriage was unimportant; they felt disillusioned with marriage. They preferred their current situation of freedom, friends, and positive self-image gained from work. Most of them eagerly waited for retirement when there would be more time for friends and personal activities.

In a qualitative study, Fox and Halbrook (1994) reviewed the lives of eight divorced and low-income women; six were single again, one was separated, and one was separating. None of the single-again women was remarried. After moving through the disruption of "happily ever after" dreams about marriage and family and a disorienting period of "shattered dreams," they moved into the period of "future realities." In the third period, these women developed new assumptions about the meaning of their lives and the divorce experience. Although feelings of disappointment, anger, and resentment surfaced, many of these women also discovered *new strengths* such as *resilience*. Self-esteem grew as they felt stronger and more in control. They also felt that they could no longer hold the belief that fulfillment resulted from pleasing others. Some of these women were astonished by the positive outcomes in their lives, but these outcomes were tempered because of economic fears and uncertainty.

In sum, midlife women vary widely in how they live through the transition of divorce. For some it is a challenge, for others an overwhelming crisis, and for others a relief. However they experience this transition, divorce changes these women. Those who meet the challenges of divorce discover their recuperative powers. For midlife women who were living the dream script of husband, children, house, and so on, the requirement and opportunity to redefine their identities, attain more education, and pursue a job can turn out as happy and exciting experiences (Chiriboga, 1989, 1993).

ALWAYS-SINGLE WOMEN

Although always-single persons were a small proportion of the U.S. population (5 percent) tracked in the 1992 Census, they comprise the fastest growing proportion (U.S. Bureau of the Census, 1992). Between 1970 and 1994, the proportion of always-single women (ages 30–34) tripled from 6 percent to 20 percent; the proportion between ages 35–39 increased from 5 percent to 13 percent (U.S. Bureau of the Census, 1995). If a person is still single after about age 35, the probability increases for continued singlehood. This prediction is based on the concept of *duration dependence*. Still, it is not an easy status because always-single persons live in a social world oriented to marriage and parenthood (Seccombe & Ishii-Kuntz, 1994). They are inundated with couple-oriented advertisements, songs, and weekend hotel specials (K. G. Lewis, 1994).

Why do some women remain single? In a study of single midlife women by Loewenstein et al. (1981), reasons reported for an always-single status included: drifting into it and "unfortunate circumstances" such as never meeting the "right" man. Nine of the 38 always-single women in the sample indicated they were single by choice, were never interested in marriage, and experienced no regrets. For five of the 38 women, the breakup of one or several unhappy relationships with men was given as the reason for their single state. Three women in this sample thought that their careers would be incompatible with marriage.

In a sample of 30 working-class women born between 1907 and 1914, half of the group that was always single gave one of four accounts for remaining single. They included: responsibilities to care for or support older parents or siblings (12 of these 15 women were the primary caregivers of older parents); wanting to make accomplishments in life without hindrances from marriage and motherhood; never wanting to marry; and hearts "broken" by men they planned to marry (Allen, 1994).

In a small sample of always-single women (average age 41), Dalton (1992) placed the choice of singleness on a continuum. At one end are women who made a deliberate choice to remain single; they never desired marriage. In the middle are women who wanted to marry but made choices that took them in other directions, such as education and careers. Some women in the middle category felt they never met the right person. At the other end of the continuum are women who never desired to remain single but it happened because of situations out of their control. Whether chosen or not, many women preferred singleness to past relationships with men in which their interests and identities were sacrificed.

A rare study of 62 always-single ethnic women included Chinese American women (n = 30) and Japanese American women (n = 32) (Ferguson, 2000). Their ages ranged from 33 to 80; the average age was 46.65 years. The average educational attainment was 17.94 years or some graduate work; almost all these women described themselves as middle class. The reasons reported for not marrying included: (a) not wanting to repeat their parents' traditional marriages; (b) having responsibilities associated with their status as eldest daughters (35 of 62 respondents) such as taking care of younger siblings or older parents, including for some living with their parents until they died; (c) pursuing advanced educations; and (d) lacking eligible suitors because the family usually restricted the type of men they could date and marry (Ferguson, 2000).

Influential Social Trends Associated with Singlehood

Aside from the various reasons women give for remaining single, the *historical–cultural context* or various social trends play a role in their remaining in this status. These trends include attitude shifts and the closing gap between marriage and the always-single status in terms of financial security.

Attitude Shifts. Marriage is normative for adult life (Marks, 1995); persons who do not marry are the subject of misunderstanding and disapproval (Dalton, 1992). Families of origin put intense pressure on midlife single daughters to marry. Even if these women attained good jobs and careers, parents may depreciate such achievements gained outside marriage (Anderson & Stewart, 1994). Yet, the social stigma associated with remaining single has gradually decreased and social acceptance of this status is increasing. Sexual relations outside a marital context are no longer stigmatized (Marks, 1995). As a result of these trends of increasing respectability for a single status, and that it can be as happy a status as being married, more adults may choose to remain single all of their lives (for example, Bumpass, Sweet, & Cherlin, 1991; Ferguson, 2000).

Closing Financial Gap Between Marriage and Always-Single Statuses. Because of the high rate of marital dissolution, marriage also no longer guarantees lifetime financial security. Increased options, such as the ability to support oneself, could influence the decline in marriage rates (Goldscheider & Waite, 1986). Especially for women who are well-educated and professionally employed, the financial strain of single life is lessening (Marks, 1995); an always-single status for women is associated with higher levels of education, occupation, and intelligence (Houseknecht, Vaughan, & Statham, 1987). Highly educated women in the 35–39 age group, studied by Cooney and Uhlenberg (1991), were almost 50 percent more likely than highly educated men to have always been single. It is also possible that the absence of marriage motivates women to attain more education and income (Davies, 1995). Not all studies, however, concur with these findings. Although the women studied by Qian and Preston (1993) wanted a college education, they postponed rather than abandoned marriage as a goal. Another study found that women's educational attainment was positively associated with the probability of marriage (Lichter, McLaughlin, Kephart, & Landry, 1992).

Single women, compared to single men, attain more education, higher status occupations, and greater income (Bernard, 1982). Based on data from NSFH, the mean income for single women between ages 45–64 was higher than the mean income for single men in this age group, although the difference did not reach statistical significance (Davies, 1995). The financial advantages of single life for women may eventually surpass the financial advantages of married life (Marks, 1995).

Advantages and Disadvantages of an Always-Single Status for Midlife Women

During the early 1990s, single midlife persons were lower on a wide range of measures of psychological well-being compared to married persons (Marks, 1995). Studies that compared single women and men, however, indicate that long-term single life is a more positive state for women than men (Macklin, 1987). All except one of the always-single women in Dalton's (1992) sample accepted themselves and their single status. For some women, this involved a process of moving from feeling miserable about their singleness to respecting and valuing themselves as single women.

In most situations in life there are both *gains* and *losses*; this is no different for always-single women. Although each woman experiences being single in a unique, multifaceted way, there are advantages and disadvantages of the always-single status for midlife women.

Possible Advantages of the Always-Single Status:

- *Mental health advantages.* The always-single women (ages 35–44) studied by Davies (1995) were significantly higher in levels of self-esteem than always-single men. Psychological distress was also significantly lower for women than men ages 45–64, although there was no significant difference in a younger group of women ages 35–44. As they become older, however, the younger women will likely experience less distress, as it generally declines with age for women.

- *Not lonely.* The findings on loneliness in the always-single status are mixed, but the trend is in the direction of no strong association of loneliness with this status. In a study of 30 always-single women ages 30–40, the respondents spent much time alone but did not report loneliness. They also did not anticipate loneliness as they got older (Burnley & Kurth, 1992). Other studies found that loneliness decreased among the middle-aged population as a whole (for example, Essex & Nam, 1987; Fischer & Phillips, 1982; Russell, 1982). Burnley and Kurth concluded that marital status is not a useful variable in making distinctions between lonely and nonlonely persons.

- *Freedom and independence.* Women age 50 and over and always single are more independent than women who are married (Essex & Nam, 1987). Separated, single-again, and always-single women are also higher on autonomy than married peers (Marks, 1995). In a sample studied by K. G. Lewis and Moon (1997), always-single (as well as single-again) women (ages 30–65) saw the advantages of their status as "freedom from having to take care of a man; freedom for doing what they want, when they want, how they want; and freedom from having to answer to others in terms of time, decisions, and behaviors" (p. 123). Freedom and independence were highly valued in Dalton's (1992) sample of always-single midlife women. Freedom from responsibility for children was important to some of the women as was the ability to make decisions about themselves for themselves. Some women doubted that they could give up these advantages for a relationship with a man. The women in this sample were self-reliant, learning how to take care of themselves instrumentally (for example, fixing things at home) and emotionally.

- *Personal growth.* Opportunities are more available for personal *growth* and self-discovery than if married (Dalton, 1992).

Possible Disadvantages of the Always-Single Status

- *Negative social views.* Although the stigma of an always-single life is decreasing, negative views persist. Yet, most of the women studied by Dalton (1992) found society's characterizations of single women offensive, such as "man hungry," promiscuous, or, if they do not date a lot, lesbian. Some midlife women are lesbian. Either they entered midlife with a same-sex sexual orientation or discovered and acknowledged same-sex attractions during midlife. Even so, lesbians are often invisible in life course studies on women (Allen, 1994). One reason for this is that researchers do not inquire about women's sexual experiences or do not identify partnerships between women as lesbian partnerships (for example, Rubinstein, Alexander, Goodman, & Luborsky, 1991). Feminist researchers may avoid direct questioning of always-single respondents about lesbian experiences, not wanting to impose their perspectives on them. This questioning is also avoided so as not to offend always-single women who are not lesbian (Allen, 1994).

- *Not so free and independent.* Independence does not mean that single women can do whatever they want. Most single women experience the same daily responsibilities as women in married couples, such as shopping, cleaning, errands, and so on. In addition, they are often called upon to help out other family members because they are single and assumed to have available time (V. G. Lewis, 1992).

- *Regrets and losses.* In a study of professional midlife women, the always-single women experienced some regret about not being married but less regret about never having children. Out of 20 regrets, "Would have gotten married" ranked eighth and "Would have had children" ranked eleventh (V. G. Lewis, 1992). Although the women studied by Dalton (1992) intellectually rejected the negatives society attached to their always-single status, they were still bothered by what their internalized views of culture indicated they missed, such as children, intimacy and sexuality with a partner, and financial security. The always-single and single-again women studied by K. G. Lewis and Moon (1997) showed no differences in the types of losses they experienced: being special to a man, touch, children, ready companionship, someone to grow old with, and someone with whom to share interests. Forty percent of Ferguson's (2000) sample of Chinese American and Japanese American women expressed some regret, primarily about not having children. They expressed no regret about not marrying.

- *Rootlessness.* Singlehood can result in a sense of rootlessness. It is important, therefore, to establish foundations and traditions. Friends provided a sense of family (Dalton, 1992).

SUMMARY

- Although divorce rates decline throughout midlife, many women during this period experience separation or divorce.

- For midlife women who are single again or with divorce pending, many difficulties and adjustments lie ahead in the short run. Their changed financial situation is particularly formidable in both the short run and the long run.
- Women are usually the economic losers in divorce. Even if they work, midlife women often earn poverty or near-poverty wages.
- Most women who experience a divorce at midlife eventually reestablish satisfying lives. Many of them develop new positive identities, including a sense of achievement and independence.
- Single-again women may experience some regrets and disadvantages, but also experience positive outcomes related to their single status.

Implications for Practice

Professional helpers need to be aware of the difficulties and adjustments faced by separated or single-again midlife women, and prepare themselves to help these women address the realities associated with their changed statuses. Counselors can encourage and guide women to explore opportunities to improve their lives, especially educational, job, and career moves that can improve their finances and economic security. Counselors should encourage women still in the process of divorce to attain legal assistance to seek a portion of the husband's pension or 401(k) plan. To promote motivation and possibilities for positive change, practitioners and social agencies can work to overcome negative stereotypes of women who are divorced or otherwise single at midlife, and to recognize their great potential for flexibility and resiliency. Professional helpers can provide diverse examples of women who have achieved positive changes, including a sense of accomplishment and independence. Many such examples can be found among women who have been always single.

VIGNETTE

Tanya, 50 years old, is a midlife woman dealing with the ending of a 28-year marriage to her husband Norman. Their two married children reside in another state. For many years Tanya believed that it was important to keep the marriage together "for the children's sake," though Norman was not faithful to her. Although Tanya expressed feeling relief after the divorce was final, she also reported feeling angry and resentful about what Norman did to destroy the marriage. She experienced anxiety about finances, as her work force participation had been erratic and she had no skills to earn enough money to support herself. The first 3 years after the divorce were difficult for Tanya. She could only find low-wage employment and she could not afford to live in the way she had when married. Her income decreased markedly immediately after the divorce, averaging $12,500 for the first two years postdivorce. She could not afford the mortgage on the house and, for a time, had to move in with an elderly aunt to make ends meet. She had no life insurance and no retirement plans. Eventually, Tanya went back to school to upgrade her job skills. About 3 1/2 years after the divorce she was working at a job she liked and earning a higher salary. She developed new friendships and other mutually supportive relationships.

Questions:

- *Why might women such as Tanya experience mixed feelings associated with divorce such as anger and relief?*

- *What can women do so that they do not end up in the financial situation Tanya did following her divorce?*

REFERENCES

Adelman, M. (1986). *Long time passing.* Boston: Alyson.

Allen, K. R. (1994). Feminist reflections on lifelong single women. In D. L. Sollie & L. A. Leslie (Eds.), *Gender, families, and close relationships: Feminist research journeys* (pp. 97–119). Thousand Oaks, CA: Sage Publications.

Anderson, C. M., & Stewart, S. (1994). *Flying solo: Single women in midlife.* New York: W. W. Norton.

Atwood, J. D. (1988). Sexually single again. In E. Winestein & E. Rosen (Eds.), *Sexuality counseling: Issues and implications* (pp. 59–80). Pacific Groves, CA: Brooks/Cole.

Baruch, G. K., Barnett, R., & Rivers, C. (1983). *Lifeprints: New patterns of love and work for today's women.* New York: McGraw-Hill.

Becker, C. S. (1988). *Broken ties: Lesbian ex-lovers.* Boston: Alyson.

Berger, R. M. (1982). *Gay and gray: The older homosexual man.* Urbana: University of Illinois Press.

Bernard, J. (1982). *The future of marriage.* New Haven, CT: Yale University Press.

Binson, D., Pollack, L., & Catania, J. A. (1997). AIDS-related risk behaviors and safer sex practices of women in midlife and older in the United States: 1990–1992. *Health Care for Women International, 18*, 343–354.

Block, S. (2000, August 8). Golden years bleak for divorcés. *USA Today,* pp. B1–B2.

Blumstein, P., & Schwartz, P. (1983). *American couples.* New York: William Morrow.

Bohannon, P. (1970). The six stations of divorce. In P. Bohannon (Ed.), *Divorce and after* (pp. 29–55). New York: Anchor.

Bridges, K. L., & Croteau, J. M. (1994). Once-married lesbians: Facilitating changing life patterns. *Journal of Counseling & Development, 73*, 134–140.

Browning, C., Reynolds, A. L., & Dworkin, S. H. (1991). Affirmative psychotherapy for lesbian women. *Counseling Psychologist, 19*, 177–196.

Bryant, S., & Demian. (1994). Relationship characteristics of American gay and lesbian couples: Findings from a national survey. *Journal of Gay and Lesbian Social Services, 1,*
101–117.

Bumpass, L. L., & Aquilino, W. S. (1995). *A social map of midlife: Family and work over the
middle life course.* Vero Beach, FL: MacArthur Foundation Research Network on
Successful Midlife Development.

Bumpass, L. L., Sweet, J. A., & Castro-Martin, T. (1990). Changing patterns of remarriage.
Journal of Marriage and the Family, 52, 747–756.

Bumpass, L. L., Sweet, J. A., & Cherlin, A. (1991). The role of cohabitation in the declining
rates of marriage. *Journal of Marriage and the Family, 53,* 913–927.

Burnley, C. S., & Kurth, S. B. (1992). Never married women: Alone and lonely? *Humboldt
Journal of Social Relations, 18,* 57–83.

Chiriboga, D. A. (1982). Consistency in adult functioning: The influence of social stress.
Aging and Society, 2, 7–29.

Chiriboga, D. A. (1989). Stress and loss in middle age. In R. A. Kalish (Ed.), *Midlife loss:
Coping strategies* (pp. 42–80). Newbury Park, CA: Sage Publications.

Chiriboga, D. A. (1991). *Divorce: Crisis, challenge, or relief?* New York: New York University
Press.

Chiriboga, D. A. (1993). Divorce. In R. Kastenbaum (Ed.), *Encyclopedia of adult development*
(pp. 130–134). Phoenix, AZ: Oryx.

Clausen, J. A., & Gilens, M. (1990). Personality and labor force participation across the life
course: A longitudinal study of women's careers. *Sociological Forum, 5,* 595–618.

Cooney, T. M., & Uhlenberg, P. (1991). Changes in work–family connections among
highly educated men and women: 1970–1980. *Journal of Family Issues, 12,* 69–90.

Dalton, S. T. (1992). Lived experience of never-married women. *Issues in Mental Health
Nursing, 13,* 69–80.

Davies, L. (1995). A closer look at gender and distress among the never married. *Women
& Health, 23,* 13–30.

Essex, M. J., & Nam, S. (1987). Marital status and loneliness among older women: The differential importance of close family and friends. *Journal of Marriage and the Family, 49,*
93–106.

Ferguson, S. J. (2000). Challenging traditional marriage: Never married Chinese American
and Japanese American women. *Gender & Society, 14,* 136–159.

Fischer, C., & Phillips, S. (1982). Who is alone? Social characteristics of people with small
networks. In L. A. Peplau & D. Perlman (Eds.), *Loneliness: A sourcebook of current theory,
research, and therapy* (pp. 21–39). New York: John Wiley & Sons.

Fox, C., & Halbrook, B. (1994). Terminating relationships at midlife: A qualitative investigation of low-income women's experiences. *Journal of Mental Health Counseling, 16,*
143–154.

Goldscheider, F. K., & Waite, L. J. (1986). Sex differences in the entry into marriage.
American Journal of Sociology, 92, 91–109.

Hagestad, G. O., Smyer, M. A., & Stierman, K. L. (1984). Parent–child relations in adulthood: The impact of divorce in middle age. In R. Cohen, B. Cohler, & S. Weissman
(Eds.), *Parenthood: A psychodynamic perspective* (pp. 247–262). New York: Guilford Press.

Hayes, C. L., & Anderson, D. (1993). Psycho-social and economic adjustment of mid-life
women after divorce: A national study. *Journal of Women & Aging, 4,* 83–99.

Houseknecht, S. K., Vaughan, S., & Statham, A. (1987). The impact of singlehood on the
career patterns of professional women. *Journal of Marriage and the Family, 49,* 353–366.

Hunter, S., Shannon, C., Knox, & J. Martin (1998). *Lesbian, gay, and bisexual youths and adults: Knowledge for human services practice*. Thousand Oaks, CA: Sage Publications.

Kaslow, F. W. (1994). Painful partings: Providing therapeutic guidance. In L. L. Schwartz (Ed.), *Mid-life divorce counseling* (pp. 67–81). Alexandria, VA: American Counseling Association.

Kaslow, F. W., & Schwartz, L. L. (1987). *The dynamics of divorce: A life cycle perspective*. New York: Brunner/Mazel.

Kurdek, L. A. (1991). The dissolution of gay and lesbian couples. *Journal of Social and Personal Relationships, 8*, 265–278.

Laughlin, B. (1995). Pathfinder: Economic effects of divorce on women. *Legal Reference Services Quarterly, 14*, 57–84.

Lazarus, R. S., & Folkman, S. N. (1984). *Stress, appraisal, and coping*. New York: Springer.

Lewis, K. G. (1994). Single heterosexual women through the life cycle. In M. P. Mirkin (Ed.), *Women in context: Toward a feminist reconstruction of psychotherapy* (pp. 170–187). New York: Guilford Press.

Lewis, K. G., & Moon, S. (1997). Always single and single again women: A qualitative study. *Journal of Marital and Family Therapy, 23*, 115–134.

Lewis, V. G. (1992). *Life satisfaction of single middle-aged professional women*. Unpublished doctoral dissertation, University of North Carolina at Greensboro.

Lichter, D. T., McLaughlin, D. K., Kephart, G., & Landry, D. J. (1992). Race and the retreat from marriage: A shortage of marriageable men? *American Sociological Review, 57*, 781–799.

Loewenstein, S. F., Bloch, N. E., Campion, J., Epstein, J. S., Gale, P., & Salvatore, M. (1981). A study of satisfactions and stresses of single women in midlife. *Sex Roles, 7*, 1127–1141.

Macklin, E. D. (1987). Nontraditional family forms. In M. B. Sussman & S. X. Steinmetz (Eds.), *Handbook of marriage and the family* (pp. 317–353). New York: Plenum Press.

Marks, N. F. (1995). *Flying solo at midlife: Gender, marital status, and psychological well-being* (CDE Working Paper No. 95-03). Madison: University of Wisconsin, Center for Demography and Ecology.

Morgan, L. A. (1989). Economic well-being following marital termination: A comparison of widowed and divorced women. *Journal of Family Issues, 10*, 86–101.

Morgan, L. A. (1991). *After-marriage ends: Economic consequences for midlife women*. Newbury Park, CA: Sage Publications.

Norton, A. J., & Moorman, J. E. (1987). Current trends in marriage and divorce among American women. *Journal of Marriage and the Family, 49*, 3–14.

Ory, M. G., & Mack, K. A. (1998). Middle-aged and older people with AIDS. *Research on Aging, 20*, 653–664.

Peck, J. S., & Manocherian, J. (1989). Divorce and the changing family life cycle. In B. Carter & M. McGoldrick (Eds.), *The changing family life cycle* (pp. 335–369). Boston: Allyn & Bacon.

Peplau, L. A. (1993). Lesbian and gay relationships. In L. D. Garnets & D. C. Kimmel (Eds.), *Psychological perspectives on lesbian & gay male experiences* (pp. 395–419). New York: Columbia University Press.

Philpot, C. L. (1994). Mid-life divorce: His and hers. In L. L. Schwartz (Ed.), *Mid-life divorce counseling* (pp. 3–27). Alexandria, VA: American Counseling Association.

Pillari, V. (1988). *Human behavior in the social environment*. Pacific Grove, CA: Brooks/Cole.

Qian, Z, & Preston, S. H. (1993). Changes in American marriage 1972 to 1987: Availability and forces of attraction by age and education. *American Sociological Review, 58*, 482–495.

Rothblum, E. D. (1990). Depression among lesbians: An invisible and unresearched phenomenon. *Journal of Gay and Lesbian Psychotherapy, 1*, 67–87.

Rubin, L. B. (1979). *Women of a certain age: The midlife search for self.* New York: Harper & Row.

Rubinstein, R. L., Alexander, B. B., Goodman, M., & Luborsky, M. (1991). Key relationships of never-married, childless older women: A cultural analysis. *Journal of Gerontology: Social Sciences, 46*, S270–S277.

Russell, D. (1982). The measurement of loneliness. In L. A. Peplau & D. Perlman (Eds.), *Loneliness: A sourcebook of current theory, research, and therapy* (pp. 81–104). New York: John Wiley & Sons.

Sang, B. (1992). Counseling and psychotherapy with midlife and older lesbians. In S. Dworkin & F. Gutie'rrez (Eds.), *Counseling gay men and lesbians: Journey to the end of the rainbow* (pp. 35–48). Alexandria, VA: American Association for Counseling and Development.

Schwartz, L. L. (1994). Separation and divorce in mid-life: Variations on a theme. In L. L. Schwartz (Ed.), *Mid-life divorce counseling* (pp. 89–98). Alexandria, VA: American Counseling Association.

Schwartz, L. L., & Kaslow, F. W. (1997). *Painful partings: Divorce and its aftermaths.* New York: John Wiley & Sons.

Seccombe, K., & Ishii-Kuntz, M. (1994). Gender and social relationships among the never-married. *Sex Roles, 30*, 585–603

Silverstein, C. (1981). *Man to man: Gay couples in America.* New York: William Morrow.

Uhlenberg, P., Cooney, T., & Boyd, R. (1990). Divorce for women after midlife. *Journal of Gerontology, 45*, S3–S11.

U.S. Bureau of the Census. (1992). *Statistical abstract of the United States: 1992.* Washington, DC: U.S Government Printing Office.

U.S. Bureau of the Census. (1995). *American women: A profile* (No. SB/95-19). Washington, DC: U.S. Government Printing Office.

Wallerstein, J. (1986). Women after divorce: Preliminary report from a ten-year follow-up. *American Journal of Orthopsychiatry, 56*, 65–77

Weitzman, L. (1985). *The divorce revolution: The unexpected social and economic consequences for women and children in America.* New York: Free Press.

CHAPTER 5

WORK, PERSONAL FINANCES, AND INCOME SECURITY

The diverse work patterns of women, including dual-earner and dual-career patterns, are addressed in this chapter. The challenges of integrating family and work are discussed as are the substantial benefits from this arrangement compared to women who remain at home. The family–work arrangement also creates high stress levels, however, and these women need various personal, interpersonal, and environmental supports. Issues regarding children and working mothers are discussed. The difficulty of planning a secure retirement is underscored because of the low financial resources of most midlife women. Issues addressed include lifelong sex–gender inequities, systematic inequities in retirement policies that discriminate against women, and women's lifelong involvement in caregiving that interrupts their work histories and relegates them to a lower socioeconomic status. Life-span themes evident here include social change; historical context; normative events; on-time, off-time; cohort; prevention and optimization; innovation and flexibility.

QUESTIONS TO CONSIDER

- *What factors contribute to the various work patterns of midlife women?*

- *What are the conflicts and stressors in dual-earner and dual-career families?*

- *What are the effects of dual-earner and dual-career families on children?*

- *What factors are associated with the low-income security of many midlife women?*

- *How can low-income security of midlife women best be addressed?*

WOMEN'S WORK FORCE PARTICIPATION

It is now the *norm* for women in almost all demographic groups to work out-side the home (Seccombe, 1992). Women's participation in the U.S. workplace has increased substantially since the 1940s (U.S. Bureau of the Census, 1990). In 1995, about 75 percent of women ages 25–54 were in the workplace (U.S. Department of Labor, 1996). The year 2000 figure was expected to be 80 percent (U.S. Department of Labor, 1991). Three trends, delineated by Guy and Erdner (1993), are responsible for the historic shift of women's movement into the workplace:

- The first and primary trend is economic necessity. A large percentage of women in the workplace (44 percent) are single, divorced, or widowed (U.S. Department of Labor, 1991). The earnings of married women are also a critical contribution to total family income (Guy & Erdner, 1993).

- The second trend is women's increasing education. Over half (55 percent) of college students were women in 1993, up from 44 percent two decades earlier (U.S. Bureau of the Census, 1995). Women became the majority of students in the college population in 1988 (53.3 percent). In that year, women earned 52 percent of the bachelor's degrees and 51 percent of the master's degrees (U.S. Department of Education, 1991). Recent census data reported that 24 percent of women ages 25 and over had completed a bachelor's degree or more (U.S. Bureau of the Census, 2000). Educated women are also rapidly moving into traditionally male-dominated occupations such as law and medicine.

- The third trend is the changing norms regarding women's roles in society. Increasingly, it is more acceptable for women to bear fewer children, bear no children, remain single (Guy & Erdner, 1993), and/or work outside the home.

Diverse Work Patterns of Midlife Women

The numbers of working midlife women, including married and older midlife women, are also noteworthy. By 1988, more than half (53 percent) of married women between ages 45–64 worked outside the home and mostly full time (U.S. Bureau of the Census, 1990). Rates for women ages 55–65 rose from 40 percent in 1974 to 49 percent in 1995. The estimated proportion for this group of women in the year 2005 is 54 percent (U.S. Bureau of the Census, 1992; U.S. Department of Labor, 1974, 1996). For women under the age of 50, rates of full-time employment are higher for African American women than for white women. For example, the rates are 69 percent for African American women compared to 55 percent for white women between ages 45–49 (Bumpass & Aquilino, 1995).

Motherhood still makes a difference in work rates between men and women, based on 1987–1988 data from the National Survey of Families and Households (Bumpass & Aquilino, 1995) (a project supported by the MacArthur Foundation Research Network on Successful Midlife Development and the Center for Demography and Ecology at the University of Wisconsin). Marks (1993) reported that more midlife fathers were in the workplace than midlife mothers. The rates for fathers versus mothers were categorized into three midlife age groups: ages 35–44 (male = 94 percent; female = 70 percent); ages 45–54 (male = 88 percent; female = 69 percent); and ages 55–64 (male = 65 percent; female = 41 percent). Although lower than the rates for fathers, the rates of work reported for midlife mothers ages 35–54 were still high. The somewhat lower levels of employment among older versus younger mothers probably reflected a *cohort difference*.

The effect of one's marital/parenting status on workplace participation appears mixed in comparisons of married and single non-Latino white women and Latino and African American women. Marks (1993, 1996) reported that single non-Latino white mothers were more likely to work than married non-Latino white mothers. Married African American mothers, however, were employed at higher rates than were single African American mothers or married non-Latino white mothers. Married Latino mothers were the least likely to be in the labor force, especially among the older cohort (ages 55–64). A greater number of younger married Latino mothers (ages 35–44) are now in the labor force. Their employment rates also outnumber the employment rates of younger single Latino mothers.

Many midlife single mothers studied by Meyer (1996) did not work or worked only part time. Both their unemployment and disability rates were more than double that of midlife married mothers. Midlife single mothers fare worse financially in the labor market as compared to midlife single fathers. These mothers earn substantially less income both on an annual and an hourly basis. Because they worked more hours, however, these mothers earn more income than midlife married women.

Midlife women's degree of participation in the workplace is not only lower than that of men but also more diverse. Some women delay entry into the workplace until midlife. Others enter the workplace earlier in their lives but not all of them are continuous workers. Pienta, Burr, and Mutchler (1994) proposed the following typology to reflect the diversity of women's work histories: (a) a continuous work pattern, in which one works throughout adulthood to the point of retirement; (b) an intermediate work pattern, in which one is generally work oriented but takes brief exits from work for family reasons;

and (c) a family work pattern, in which one works during one or more stages of adulthood but takes extended exits from work for family reasons.

The "attachment hypothesis" explains why some midlife women follow the continuous work pattern. Using this hypothesis, Pienta et al. (1994) proposed that there is a momentum that develops in early work experiences that follows a person through the later stages of their life course. Women with a strong attachment to paid work at early points in their lives, therefore, are more likely to maintain their workplace attachment in their later years. Even when workplace participation was not *normative* for women, those with a strong attachment to work still maintained their attachment to employment. Without social norms that support them, other kinds of conducive experiences probably operate such as intrinsically rewarding work, a supportive partner, or economic needs. The counterparts to the work-attached group of women are those who established no work attachment earlier in their lives and, hence, experienced less attachment to work in their later years.

The two other work patterns, intermediate and family oriented, characterize many midlife women. The difference between the two patterns is the length of time away from the workplace. The reasons for the departures, however, are usually the same—family responsibilities such as rearing young children or caring for older adult family members (Pienta et al., 1994). Women who are not in a continuous work pattern usually make transitions back into the workplace that are linked also to family events such as the exit of the last child from home, marital dissolution, or death of a parent (Smith & Moen, 1988).

Women who experience an interrupted or discontinuous work force pattern and later return to the workplace are identified as "reentry women." This term usually refers to women who reenter educational institutions or the workplace following an absence from a few to as many as 35 years (Lewis, 1988). Most reentry women are between the ages of 25 and 54 (U.S. Bureau of the Census, 1990). Women in this group include those who are married and with children in the home, mothers whose children are grown or launched, single heads of households, and displaced homemakers. Most reentry women studied are white and middle class (Padula, 1994), and they are frequently in social services, education, and health occupations (Staney, 1986).

Sometimes women's work histories are interrupted for reasons other than family responsibilities. This can happen, for example, when *social, economic,* and *political changes* result in job displacement. The displacement rate of women from the labor force between 1987 and 1992 was 38 percent. The rate of displacement for women ages 55–64 years was 39 percent compared to 32 percent for males in the same age group (U.S. Department of Labor, 1992). The reemployment rate for men happened 12 percent faster than for women (Herz, 1988). Both women and African American displaced workers are less likely to be reemployed than are white men. African American men and women are often displaced for a year, which is two to three times longer than the displacement periods for white men or women (Moore, 1990).

Unless forced to withdraw because of displacement, increasingly fewer women withdraw from the workplace after marriage, during childbearing or child rearing, or when providing caregiving for older parents and in-laws. African American women showed less of the typical sex–gender differences in their work experiences (Gibson, 1988). Their work histories are not necessarily continuous, but they stay on the job much longer than white women (Andersen, 1988). Lesbians also seem less likely to show the traditional sex–gender differences in work patterns. Midlife lesbians who are mothers often derive their identity from work and other investments, as well as from motherhood (Kimmel & Sang, 1995). In addition, both partners in lesbian couples almost always work. This work pattern in lesbian couples existed long before the now rapidly growing trend of dual-earner or dual-career patterns among heterosexual couples. The dual-track heterosexual family began to emerge during the *social changes* of the 1960s (Gilbert & Davidson, 1989).

Dual-Earner and Dual-Career Families

The integration of work and family is now one of the major contemporary challenges for marital partners throughout midlife (for example, Bumpass & Aquilino, 1995; Echenrode & Gore, 1990). Dual-earner/dual-career families are now *normative*, and the proportion of these families continues to advance (Reeves & Darville, 1992). Partners who work full time, with or without children, are on either a dual-earner or dual-career track (Gilbert & Davidson, 1989). Most marital partners are on the dual-earner track—both partners work full time in jobs that do not provide a career sequence. About one-quarter of partners are on the dual-career track (Persell, 1990). On this track, both partners are pursuing careers that entail systematic steps to advancement in an organizational hierarchy. Both partners are managers or professionals and experience high work involvement. On the other hand, dual-earner couples are usually in clerical, administrative, technical, retail, or production positions and experience lower work involvement. Another difference is that the career track usually requires more education than the earner track (Duxbury & Higgins, 1994; Reeves & Darville, 1992).

In a study of professional midlife women, over three-quarters (78 percent) felt a pressing need to try to balance work and family (Gordon & Whelan, 1998). Consensus between wives and their husbands on how to balance work and family roles was a major factor in their morale (Kessler & McRae, 1982). Three basic arrangements for combining work and family in dual-career families include: traditional, role sharing, and participant. In the traditional dual-career family, the wife is primarily responsible for the family. Usually, her husband's salary is much higher than her salary. In the role-sharing family, a polar opposite to the traditional family, both partners are actively involved in work and family responsibilities. This is the most egalitarian approach and the ideal image of dual-career families. Neither partner is more responsible for home chores nor child care. Salaries of the partners are usually equal. The participant dual-career family may be a transitional arrangement. Both partners share parenting, but wives take primary responsibility for home chores such as cleaning, cooking, and shopping. Husbands often show little motivation to do housework and seem unlikely to change (Gilbert, 1985; Gilbert & Davidson, 1989).

COMBINING FAMILY AND WORK: BENEFITS

Most women of all social classes prefer to combine work and household roles (Kessler & McRae, 1982). Midlife women receive substantial benefits from employment outside the home, as long as they have at least part-time employment (Vandewater & Stewart, 1997), and despite whether they are in high status occupations (Verbrugge, 1987) or in low-level jobs (Belle, 1982). These women experience both better physical and mental health (Barnett, 1997; Bernard, 1982; Carr, 1997; Coleman & Antonucci, 1983). Compared to women who are less traditional and who work, more traditional midlife women who married young, reared children, and are full-time homemakers more often reported health difficulties at midlife. They also reported a decline in psychological well-being (Helson & Picano, 1990). In terms of health, national samples reviewed by Barnett (1997) showed that employed women, in comparison to unemployed women, experienced no differences in coronary heart disease (over a 10-year period) or increased risk of mortality (over an 18-year period). Paid employment may offset psychological signs such as depression (for example, Carr, 1997; Kessler & McRae, 1982) and anxiety (Coleman & Antonucci, 1983). Compared to full-time homemakers, employed midlife women reported better heath and lower psychological anxiety and immobilization (for example, difficulty getting up in the morning; see Adelmann, Antonucci, Crohan, & Coleman, 1989). Midlife women in the national samples reviewed by Barnett (1997) reported less depression than unemployed women and higher levels of subjective well-being.

Many of the benefits of working outside the home center on subjective or psychological well-being (Kessler & McRae, 1984). For example, most married women who work report an increase in happiness (Gove & Zeiss, 1987). In addition, a positive association between employment and self-esteem for women is often reported (for example, Coleman & Antonucci, 1983; Verbrugge, 1982). The single strongest factor influencing self-esteem for both men and women studied by Reitzes, Mutran, and Fernandez (1994) was commitment to the worker role. In a study of women and men ages 58–64 by Reitzes and Mutran (1994), there were no differences in the self-esteem of working midlife men and women or in their commitment to the work role. This was the case although the men were healthier, better educated, wealthier, and in higher prestige occupations.

Eighty-three midlife women from the Mills Longitudinal Study were placed by Roberts and Friend (1998) into three categories of career momentum: high, maintaining, and decreasing. Measures of career momentum were objective, such as years since one's last promotion, and subjective, such as a woman's feeling that she is either *on time* or *off time* in her career stage. The women were also compared on various outcomes including health and psychological functioning. The results for women in each category include the following:

- Women in the high momentum group, or those who were continuing to invest in their career, experienced greater occupational attainment and rated their work as more important than women in the other two groups. Work was more central to their identity. During a previous assessment 30 years earlier, these women were the most confident and independent and, since age 43, rated the highest in effective functioning and well-being. When assessed in their early 50s, these women rated their health better and scored higher on measures of effective functioning, independence, and self-acceptance.

- Women in the maintaining group were relatively high in effective functioning and well-being at age 21, but there were abrupt drops on these variables between ages 21–43.

- During the 30 years prior to the current assessment, women in the low or decreasing momentum group were consistently lowest in well-being, self-acceptance, and independence.

Additional benefits for midlife women, attributed to their involvement in dual-career family arrangements, include opportunities for professional development, economic independence, sense of competence, intellectual companionship, intellectual stimulation, and making a contribution. In addition, there is a strong emphasis on the benefit of establishing a sense of self separate from one's marital partner and one's children (Clausen, 1986; Gilbert, 1993; Gilbert & Davidson, 1989; Gordon & Whelan, 1998). Work is increasing as a primary definer of identity for women. A quarter of the late midlife women in the Berkeley longitudinal studies rated their work roles as equal to their family roles in terms of sense of self. Family relationships for working women were not the sole source of identity and commitment (Clausen, 1986).

Dual-career families challenge the partners to be *innovative* and *flexible* in creating an egalitarian model of marriage (Gilbert & Davidson, 1989). Some researchers claim that the dual-career family results in more sex–gender equality, such as sharing roles in a nontraditional manner (for example, Hertz, 1986; Rapoport & Rapoport, 1971). This represents the role-sharing arrangement identified by Gilbert (1985). Other researchers, however, refute this claim of sex–gender equality (for example, Kerchoff, 1986; Szinovacz, 1982). Only 20 percent of Hochschild's (1989) national sample of working wives experienced egalitarian marriages. One or the other of the two nonegalitarian dual-career arrangements identified by Gilbert (1985)—traditional or participant—was probably operating in the other 80 percent of the marriages.

COMBINING FAMILY AND WORK: CONFLICT AND STRESS

Although women in the workplace can experience many benefits, juggling the demands of family and work is often difficult and conflictual. The stress levels of many mothers and fathers are high. Several theoretical frameworks address work–family conflicts and the perceived stress regarding such conflict. Three of these frameworks are discussed here—rational, sex–gender role expectations, and job strain. Higgins, Duxbury, and Lee (1994) and Duxbury and Higgins (1994) used these frameworks to analyze data obtained in 1990 and 1992 from a Canadian study of dual-career couples. In this discussion, three other components are also addressed: role overload, interference from work to family, and interference from family to work (Duxbury & Higgins, 1991).

The rational framework predicts that the amount of work–family conflict and stress one perceives should rise in proportion to the hours spent in work and family tasks (Greenhaus, Bedeian, & Mossholder, 1987; Gutek, Searle, & Kelpa, 1991). The total time spent in these tasks has been associated with the concept of role overload (for example, Gutek et al., 1991). Another prediction of this framework is that the more hours one spends in work activities, the more likely one will experience interference from work to family. The reverse, interference from family to work, happens when one spends more time in family activities. This rational framework has some support. The more time spent in family and work roles is associated with a greater perception of role overload. Mothers report significantly higher levels of role overload. This is not surprising because they spend more time in work and family roles compared to fathers. Mothers also report both more interference from family to work than do fathers and more interference from work to family than do fathers. Career mothers, however, experience less interference from work to family than dual-earner mothers, though they spend more time at work than dual-earner mothers (Duxbury & Higgins, 1994).

In part, the role overload of mothers is explained by the sex–gender role expectations framework. This framework predicts that women will experience higher levels of interference from work to family whereas men will experience the reverse. Following traditional sociocultural role expectations for the roles of men and women, men take primary responsibility for the work role and women for the family role. These role expectations have essentially not changed over the last 30 years, though large numbers of mothers are now in the workplace (for example, Galinsky, Friedman, & Hernandez, 1991; Hochschild, 1989). Traditionally, work is the way men contribute to the family. Family and household care are still seen as the woman's domain and not the man's domain. Women are expected to fulfill family demands before work demands. They are judged more by their contributions on this front than by their financial contributions to the family (Gutek et al., 1991). Mothers are held responsible for the outcome of child rearing. Hence, they must devote themselves to their children above everything else—certainly above their careers (Sapiro, 1990). Fathers may "help out" at home, but most do not equitably share responsibility for child rearing. Research consistently reports that employed women spend considerably more hours than their husbands on family and household chores (for example, Hochschild, 1989; Pleck, 1985; Voydanoff, 1988). Hence, it is not surprising that they are likely to experience family to work interference. The more hours they spend in paid work, the more likely they will also perceive that work is interfering with family tasks (Duxbury & Higgins, 1994).

The job strain framework proposes that work–family conflict and perceived stress are associated with the control one feels regarding work and family roles (Karasek, 1979). When low control is combined with heavy role demands, stress levels are high (Higgins et al., 1994). Because both earner and career mothers are more responsible for home chores and child rearing than fathers, it follows that these mothers experience more difficulty than fathers in keeping family demands from interfering with work demands. The life stage of the family also plays a role in family role demands and perceived levels of control. When children are young (especially under age 6), mothers experience higher family demands compared to mothers with older children (Hochschild, 1989; Staines & O'Connor, 1980). As tasks related to child care decrease, higher levels of control and lower stress levels should result. Yet, Higgins et al. (1994) reported that the interference from family to work does not begin to decline until the children reach the age of 13. Even when the children are between ages 13 and 18, the overall levels of overload for mothers are significantly higher compared to those for fathers.

As noted earlier, career women are better able to manage the work–family interface than women in noncareer jobs. When their children are young, however, career mothers are no more able to control their family demands than their earner counterparts, but their work hours are often more flexible, and with higher incomes they can purchase support to help out on the home front. Career mothers also reported less interference from work to family and less stress although they spend more hours in paid employment. In line with the job strain framework, career mothers were found to also experience more control over their environments (Higgins, Duxbury, Lee, & Mills, 1992). Yet, they do not experience the same level of control over the distribution of their time as fathers (Barnett, 1997; Duxbury & Higgins, 1994).

In recent studies, the vast majority of husbands and wives reported that when both are employed, husbands should do more than they do of the household and child care work. Yet, these beliefs do not often translate into significant changes in behavior (Rexroat & Shehan, 1987). Compared to samples studied in the 1970s and 1980s, the amount of time dual-career mothers spend on home chores and child care is lower and the amount of time men spend is higher. The total work and family loads of employed mothers, however, are still higher than they are for employed fathers (for example, Higgins et al., 1994; Vanderkolk & Young, 1991).

Effects on Children

A concern about families in which both parents work full time is the consequences for the children. The parents, themselves, are concerned about possible negative effects on their children and attempt to prevent them (for example, Elman & Gilbert, 1984; Scarr, Phillips, & McCartney, 1989). Yet, there are no significant differences in the time these parents spend with their children as compared with families in which only one parent works (Nock & Kingston, 1988). Employed mothers reduce time in other tasks, leisure, or community activities to spend time with their children (Schnittiger & Bird, 1990).

Growing up with working parents may actually provide an advantage for children, including the development of coping skills that help reduce stress, the opportunity to observe less stereotypic sex–gender-role behavior at home (Knaub, 1986), and the parents' encouragement of their autonomy and self-directedness (Hoffman, 1987). Bird and Kemerait (1990) found children in early adolescence and in two-earner families have developed moderate to high levels of self-esteem and mastery. In addition, the parents' dual-earner work histories were not associated with emotional stress across the major life roles of their adolescent children: son/daughter, peer, or student.

Supports for Dual-Career and Dual-Earner Families

Dual-career couples have a higher divorce rate than traditional couples. As indicated in the above discussions, members in these couples (especially the wives) confront many difficulties trying to integrate work and family (Nadelson & Nadelson, 1980). Wives have to develop their own way to care for children and advance their careers because U.S. industries have not generally been responsive to the change in women's lives (Cole, Zucker, & Duncan, 2001). Women and their partners need an array of resources to assist them to cope with the difficulties they face. Gilbert and Davidson (1989) categorized the needed resources into three categories: personal, relationship, and environmental or societal. Personal resources include financial assets, educational attainment, good health, and sociopsychological benefits such as flexible personalities and liberal values about sex–gender roles. Coping strategies are also important. In their study of how dual-career couples coped with stress, Wanamaker and Bird (1990) found that the coping strategy most often used is delegating tasks to other family members and encouraging the children to help out and become more self-sufficient. Family members who reported the least stress used cognitive restructuring more often than members who reported the highest level of stress. This strategy reduced negative emotional states by viewing demands as challenges and viewing dual careers as advantageous to the individuals, partners, and families. Relationship resources include support from one's partner for one's work investments and involvement of each partner in both parenting and housework. A sense of fairness or equity is crucial. Parents experience the least control over societal resources that project cultural views of dual-career couples (Gilbert & Davidson, 1989). As indicated above, there are many pressures against women feeling good about working, such as views of them depriving their families of needed attention (Piotrkowski & Repetti, 1984).

Workplaces with a high proportion of dual-earner mothers should offer programs to help these employees cope with role overload and interference from work to family. Strategies to help mothers increase control over work and family demands can include flex-time work, part-time work, telework, after-school programs, family leave days, work at home, and on-site day care (Duxbury & Higgins, 1994). Although such programs can help these mothers, for women in low-paying, low-status jobs, the role combination of work and family is much more stressful than for women who have careers. Low-status work may not be meaningful or intrinsically rewarding and income may just barely cover child care expenses (for example, Baruch, Barnett, & Rivers, 1983; Cole, Zucker, & Duncan, 2001). Women in low-status work, therefore, will often need a wider range of supports than dual-career mothers.

Income Security for Retirement

Work provides an important means for developing income security for retirement. This goal necessitates preretirement planning involving pensions and other investments.

Preretirement Planning

Retirement planning needs to begin when employees first enter an organization. They should receive information about pension benefit programs and other essential preparations for the retirement years (Turner, Bailey, & Scott, 1994). Employer-sponsored workshops that provide preretirement counseling should be mandatory (White-Means & Hersch, 1993). Local communities and church groups also sponsor retirement planning programs and there are many other seminars and planning programs available (Hayes & Parker, 1993). Many publications also provide useful information for retirement planning such as self-help resources and lists of national organizations that focus on retirement planning (Hayes, 1993), as well as guides to estimating future expenses and sources of retirement income (Rix, 1993).*

Adequate retirement income translates into 65 percent to 70 percent of one's annual salary (Siverd, 1987). Women who successfully attain this level of income for retirement probably have pensions. Pensions are available only in certain occupations, however, such as those that are managerial and professional. About 40 percent of workers in these types of occupations are now women. Many of them will receive pensions and will have a far greater chance of meeting the requirements for retirement funds than other midlife women (Rosenthal & Morith, 1993). Even these women, however, will not receive the benefits they might have accumulated because of the subtle barrier of the "glass ceiling" that prevents women from moving beyond middle management. It is even more unusual for the few women who pass this barrier to move further into senior or top executive levels (Gilbert, 1993).

Only one in five women who work in firms with fewer than 100 employees are on a pension plan (Older Women's League, 2001). Low-income groups have especially low rates of pension coverage. This includes about 80 percent of women earning $10,000 or less and 60 percent earning between $10,000 and $14,999 (Older Women's League, 1998). Pensions rarely cover persons who work part time, and women are more likely than men to work part time.

In the private sector, men are twice as likely to have a pension. Even if women have pension coverage, the benefits are considerably less than those received by men (Johnson, 1998). In 1998 the average private pension per year was $4,679 for women compared to $6,442 for men (Older Women's League, 2001).**

With or without pensions, women can invest in financial products such as 401(k) plans and individual retirement accounts (Rowland, 1987). Unlike tra-

---

*Pre-Retirement Education Planning for Women (Hayes, 1989), one of the most comprehensive seminars, is available at: http://sites.tier.net/aop/prep.htm. An additional web source that addresses women and retirement is available at:
http://www.moneyminded.com/security/retir/a7rgap21.htm. Also, the Women's Institute for a Secure Retirement is available at: www.wiser.heinz.org.

**Women can explore what they need to know and do about pensions on many web sites. One example is available at: http://www.asec.org/wopens.htm.

ditional pensions, women do not have to be in the same job for years to attain benefits from these types of plans (Block, 2000). This option is a help to women because they change jobs on average every 3.5 years (Older Women's League, 2001). Also, when women leave the workplace to care for children or older parents they can roll 401(k) savings into individual retirement accounts (Block, 2000).

Most women have no investments in the most lucrative retirement resources because they are disproportionately in low-paying jobs and generally lack adequate resources to make investments (Richardson & Kilty, 1997). Women retiring in the next 20 years are expected to have less than one-third of the income necessary for a comfortable retirement (Older Women's League, 2001).

Substantial numbers of women depend solely on Social Security benefits during retirement. Social Security includes 90 percent of the income for 40 percent of older women (age 65 and older); for 25 percent of older women there is no other source of income (Older Women's League, 2001). Social Security benefits are also less than what men receive. The average annual Social Security benefit for women age 65 and over in 1998 was $7,452 compared to $9,720 for men, or about $200 less a month than what men received (Rothman, 1998).

Major Obstacles Midlife Women Confront in Preparing for Retirement

As indicated above, the primary difficulty for women preparing for retirement is low salary. Income is the greatest predictor of retirement planning (Kilty & Behling, 1985). More than half (55 percent) of working women are in female-dominated occupations such as sales, clerical, and service (Pienta et al., 1994). Compared to male-dominated occupations, these jobs and those held by women at small firms are low paying (Nadeau, Walsh, & Wetton, 1993; Older Women's League, 1998; Rosenthal & Morith, 1993). In general, earnings of women are about three-fourths that of men (U.S. Bureau of the Census, 1994). In 1996, white women earned 74 cents for every dollar men earned; African American women earned 65 cents and Latino women 57 cents (National Committee on Pay Equity, 1997). Even when women are in the same job categories as men, they earn significantly less (Andersen, 1988). Sex–gender based wage inequity has not changed, and it follows women into retirement even if they are in professional or managerial jobs (Hooyman & Gonyea, 1999).

Most women who face retirement over the next several decades will not have received much education, a factor that contributes to their being in low-paying jobs. Less than a quarter (22 percent) of women ages 45–64 finished one or more years of college. About a third (33 percent) of women ages 55–64 did not attain a high school diploma (Hayes & Parker, 1993). Even a college education, however, has not closed the salary gap between women and men.

Women who are pursuing college educations are now in the majority, but this educational advance has not raised their salaries to equitable levels. Comparisons between genders for those with high school degrees revealed an average salary of $19,168 for women and $26,820 for men. The average salary for women with bachelor's degrees was $32,291 versus $45,987 for men (U.S. Bureau of the Census, 1995). Thirty years after passage of the Fair Pay and Equal Pay Acts, women still earn only three-quarters of what men earn for the same job. The amount will vary but over a lifetime this situation can result in as much as $250,000 less in earnings (Older Women's League, 2001).

Another factor contributing to the wage gap between men and women is that more women than men experience interrupted work histories. Current male-oriented models of work follow a *linear* design that views retirement as a single event ending one's labor force participation. Retirement for women can best be viewed from a *life-span perspective* as a series of movements in and out of the work force (Hooyman, 1999).

Only a third of women work consistently after they leave school, compared to 46 percent of men (National Center of Educational Statistics, 1998). Women are often in work positions that are easier to interrupt and resume later. These "flexible" work positions often include the "feminine" jobs of teaching, secretarial work, nursing, and library work. The other side of these types of jobs, however, is low pay, low prestige, few opportunities for advancement, and little autonomy on the job (James, 1990; Reeves & Darville, 1992). When women move in and out of these or other jobs, they experience a further reduction in income. In addition, they experience lower Social Security and pension benefits in retirement, and lost pension coverage or vesting rights when they change jobs (Gonyea, 1998; Older Women's League, 1998).

Women with continuous work force histories are not necessarily in higher paying jobs. Long work histories also do not pay off unless one has the skills, training, and credentialing to advance in the job (Elman & O'Rand, 1998). Midlife women may delay exit from the work force to compensate for low lifetime earnings and savings, as well as little or no pension or Social Security coverage (Pienta et al., 1994). Some women who have "retired" may return to work (Richardson, 1999). Yet, these actions may not suit other adults in the family who need caregiving as discussed above. More women than men retire for caregiving reasons, often involuntarily (Richardson, 1993). Wives may also retire because their husbands are retired; husbands frequently pressure their wives to retire because they dislike being at home alone (Arber & Ginn, 1995; Matthews & Brown, 1987).

As noted above, most lesbians work. In one of the rare studies of midlife lesbians by Sang (1990), almost all of the 110 respondents were in careers; over three-fourths were professionals and half of the women were in careers and jobs that were nontraditional for women, such as dean, financial analyst, and truck driver. These respondents were recruited from various resources such as conferences, friendship networks, and professional organizations; they were from 24 states, Canada, Holland, and Israel. Almost all midlife lesbian respondents in the Bradford and Ryan (1991) national survey were employed. In comparison with employed midlife women in the general population, lesbians were four times as likely to work in professional or technical fields. They were more likely employed as managers or administrators and less likely employed in clerical positions. One of the reasons for these higher level positions is that many midlife lesbians are well educated. Among the Bradford and Ryan respondents, only 15 percent had no college education. Almost half (48 percent) completed a graduate or professional degree. Yet, even with advanced education and professional and technical jobs, the earned income of this population does not reflect their preparation or positions. More than a quarter (28 percent) of Sang's (1990, 1991) sample indicated that they experienced financial insecurity as a new issue at midlife. Money was also the most common concern of the midlife respondents in the Bradford and Ryan (1991) sample of lesbians. Over half (55 percent) of these respondents experienced current distress because of financial difficulties, and these women were at least five times more likely than heterosexual women their age to experience financial difficulties.

Caregiving Women: Economic Consequences

Women move in and out of the workplace across the life span to provide caregiving for family members. They may reduce their work schedules, abandon employment, or forgo promotions or career development opportunities (Elman & O'Rand, 1998; Neal, Ingersoll-Dayton, & Starrels, 1997). They spend on average 11.5 years out of the workplace because of caregiving; this adds up to 15 percent of missed time in the workplace. For every year out of the workplace, a woman has to work five years to recover lost income and pension coverage, if not career promotion (Older Women's League, 2001; "Women need," 2001).

Women who leave paid employment even temporarily to assume caregiving roles often get locked into a lower socioeconomic status for the rest of their lives (Hooyman & Gonyea, 1995). Some women in late midlife who reduce or stop paid employment to engage in caregiving do not resume employment after the caregiving ends (Pavalko & Artis, 1997). Other women who reenter the workplace after caregiving end up in clerical or low-paying positions because of their limited marketable skills (Hooyman & Kiyak, 1993). Although not as damaged financially as women in low-paying jobs, women in higher status positions who take time off for caregiving can be put at a disadvantage for promotions compared to male colleagues who do not take time off for caregiving (Hooyman & Lustbader, 1986).

POVERTY

Many women are so far away from meeting their financial needs at retirement that they end up in poverty (O'Grady-LeShane, 1990). Women comprise 75 percent of the elderly poor. This includes 26 percent of women ages 65–74, 42 percent of women ages 75–84, and 51 percent of women ages 85 and older (Devlin & Ayre, 1997; Rothman, 1998). The poverty rate for women (11.8 percent) is higher than the rate for older men (6.9 percent). The median income of older persons (65 years and older) in 1999 was $19,079 for males and $10,943 for females (Administration on Aging, 2000a).

Women without husbands and without their own earnings are most likely to experience the worst economic conditions (James, 1990). Many poor midlife women were socialized to be financially dependent on their husbands. They usually do not have adequate training to get well-paying jobs when they lose their husbands either through divorce or death (Butler & Weatherley, 1992). The poverty rates among unpartnered midlife women are: separated—37 percent, widowed—25 percent, divorced—19 percent, and always single—17 percent. These poverty rates contrast with a 5 percent rate for married women (U.S. Bureau of the Census, 1989).

About 31 percent of older persons live alone; three out of five older women age 85 and over live alone (Administration on Aging, 2000a). Older persons living alone are much more likely to be poor (20.2 percent) than those living with families (5.2 percent). Older Latino women who live alone have the highest poverty rates (58.8 percent; see Administration on Aging, 2000b).

African American women are twice as likely as older white women to be poor and five times more likely than older white men. About one-third (34 percent) of African American women between ages 65–74 live in poverty; 44 percent of those over 75 live in poverty (Devlin & Ayre, 1997). These numbers would expand if they included women close to the poverty line (Devlin & Ayre, 1997). For example, Rothman (1998) reported that more than 50 percent of African American women over age 75 live below or near the poverty line.

The status of African American single mothers stands out. Half of these mothers live in debt and are at a considerable disadvantage in meeting unexpected needs, as well as funding for retirement and old age. Single Latino mothers are at a similar economic disadvantage (Marks, 1993). Only 25 percent of African American women and 33 percent of Latino women have income from savings or other assets (Older Women's League, 2001).

Richardson (1999) pointed out that the systematic biases in retirement policies exacerbate the sex–gender inequities in poverty. For example, married women who work pay more to Social Security than they get back. Although dual entitlement policies under Social Security imply that a woman who works will receive benefits for that work, there will be no benefits for her work if her husband's benefits or earnings are larger. Social Security provides dual entitlement benefits when a woman is eligible for a retirement benefit based on her own work history. But women qualify for a higher benefit only as a wife or widow. They receive their own benefit first and if the benefit from their husband's work is higher, they receive an added payment to cover the discrepancy. Hence, they receive no more than if they had never worked. Women who divorce before 10 years of marriage do not receive dual entitlements. To qualify, they must have been in a marriage that lasted for at least 10 years and currently be in an unmarried status.

Another barrier to adequate finances in retirement is the disqualification of midlife women for federal assistance. They do not fall within any of the official assistance categories: caregivers to dependent children, disabled, blind, elderly, or frail (Butler & Weatherley, 1992). Butler and Weatherley (1992, 1995) addressed the shortcomings of social policies regarding midlife women, and the pathways to homelessness.

The factors characterizing many women, now in midlife or older, such as low-paying jobs and no or low retirement benefits, ensure poverty for many of them (Browne, 1994). The move into poverty begins decades earlier when girls and young women do not realize the importance of consistent work histories and planning for retirement (Hayes, 1989, 1990, 1991). Both requirements are important to help prevent poverty in later life, as well as higher and equitable pay, pensions, and elimination of the barriers of ageism, sexism, classism, and racism. We also need economic and social strategies to integrate women into more jobs with wages comparable to male counterparts (Hooyman & Gonyea, 1999). The threat of poverty will continue for many women in later life unless these social transformations occur.

Structural changes in Social Security and pension systems are also needed to address equity and adequacy issues (Hooyman, 1999). The Social Security program assumes a "traditional" family with a lifelong breadwinner and a lifelong homemaker. It also assumes a 40-year career with a calculation of benefits on one's 35 highest earning years. But for every year not worked, a zero enters the computation for the average indexed monthly earnings. This reduces one's monthly benefit by about $12. So far, there have been no basic changes to help women because of the perennial projections about future funding problems for the Social Security program (Demby, 1996).

TOWARD GREATER INCOME SECURITY FOR WOMEN

Nine out of 10 women will be solely responsible for their financial support at some point in their lives ("Women need," 2001). As noted earlier in this chapter, preventive measures to prepare for this situation are needed and can be found in resources such as workshops, books, and web sites. Practice focused on income security for women, however, must be directed at all system levels: individual, micro, and macro. At the individual level, women must be better informed about retirement policies and encouraged to examine how their life circumstances will affect their retirement. At the micro enviromental or organizational level, preretirement and postretirement groups are useful for looking at the connections between work and family, informal and formal work, and private and public work. At the macro environmental or sociopolitical level, employers should not be allowed to give wages that are discriminatory and unjust based on age, sex–gender, ethnicity, or sexual orientation. Women who work in any occupation, including ones that are female dominated, should receive wages comparable to men. Work of comparable worth should be paid the same amount. Social Security rules should be changed so that women who work are not penalized in benefits because their husbands' earnings were higher than theirs (Richardson, 1999). The ultimate goal is to eradicate poverty for older women by adopting a nonpoverty standard of living for every older American person (Smeeding, 1998). To *prevent* poverty and to *optimize* the lives of midlife women throughout their life span, these structural barriers must be addressed (Richardson, 1999).

Women's years of caregiving must also be addressed on the structural level. Caregiving is essential to society but at the same time it is a devalued task. For their caregiving contributions, women are relegated to socially and economically powerless positions in the private arena (Hooyman, 1990). Economically, they are penalized because caregiving is not compensated by salaries, pensions, or social security (Browne, 1994; Hooyman, 1990). Recommendations for augmenting the economic supports for caregivers, made by Hooyman (1999) and Hooyman and Gonyea (1995, 1999), include:

- *Broaden the definition of work* to include unpaid labor in the home and the community. This would result in direct financial compensation for women who provide caregiving, credit for years lost from the workplace resulting from caregiving, and financing of paid caregiving over the family life span through a social insurance approach.

- *Provide public support* for financial support of women who take on the caregiving role. In addition, modify the Social Security system and private pension systems so that the economic value of all types of caregiving and all types of caregivers is recognized. Compensation should be given for caregiving services to adult family members such as a caregiver wage or allowance.

- *View public resources as supporting both women and men* who do the valued work of caregiving. Women are not to be viewed as the sole providers of care; there should be equitable distribution of caregiving burden among family members.

- *Provide other publicly provided benefits* such as health care, retirement benefits, and workers' compensation.

- *Replace the concept of caregiver* that implies that caregiving is free with more neutral terms. "Attendant care," for example, implies an exchange of care services for an attendant allowance and reinforces the view of caregiving as having an economic value.

- *Facilitate interconnections with other services of the social service system* to help reduce the caregiving burden. This includes, for example, connections with day care, transportation, respite, flexible residential care, and counseling.

In sum, unless the structural arrangements of work and caregiving, including sex–gender based inequities, are addressed and changed, there can be no real new solutions to the burden of caregiving for women and to the financial costs of providing care across the life span. Nor can the real issues that put midlife and older women into poverty be seriously addressed and changed.

SUMMARY

- Work patterns of midlife women include continuous work; intermittent work, with brief exits for family reasons; and work during one or more stages of adulthood, with extended exits for family reasons.

- Some women do not begin work until midlife.

- The challenges of integrating family and work increasingly characterize dual-earner and dual-career families. Most midlife women, however, prefer the combination of work and family. They receive substantial benefits from employment as compared to women who remain at home.

- Stress levels are high for dual-earner and dual-career couples; they need various personal, interpersonal, and environmental resources to help meet the challenges of integrating family and work.

- Concerns about the negative consequences for children and families with both parents working full time seem to be unfounded. Positive consequences for children can result and, as compared with other families, dual-earner and dual-career parents spend a similar amount of time with their children.

- Women often disrupt their work or do not attain the economic benefits of continuous paid work because of caregiving to others throughout the life course; they may find themselves unprepared financially for retirement.

IMPLICATIONS FOR PRACTICE

Social agencies and professional helpers need to recognize the diverse work–family patterns and histories of midlife women. For women who have trouble integrating family and work in dual-earner or dual-career families, practitioners can help reduce stress, secure needed resources, and find ways to help them more effectively manage their roles or make other decisions to lessen their overload. Practitioners can counter negative images of working women with research that refutes the belief that children will suffer negative consequences if their mothers work outside the home.

Practitioners also need to be familiar with how caregiving can affect the financial status of these women and help them secure needed economic and social resources. Both community and clinical practitioners can advocate for changes in the workplace to provide more flexible work arrangements for women, as well as structural changes that result in paying caregivers so that women can be better prepared financially for retirement.

During midlife, law, finances, and psychosocial considerations often become increasingly interrelated and interdependent. In some situations, therefore, it might be appropriate for social workers, accountants, and lawyers to collaborate in helping a woman evaluate her readiness to prepare for retirement (see Sundel & Bernstein, 1995).

VIGNETTE

Kathleen is a midlife woman experiencing conflict between work and parenting. She is 42 years old and the mother of two young sons, ages 8 and 6. She spent her 20s and early 30s developing a successful career as an investment banker. She married Ted, a partner in an accounting firm, when she was 32 and he was 41 years old, and she anticipated continuing her career. After Kathleen's first child was born, though, she discovered that she did not want to return to work immediately. To her surprise, she found that she enjoyed full-time motherhood and wanted a second child. Yet, several years later, Kathleen increasingly felt conflicted about her departure from the world of work to pursue full-time motherhood. She missed the feeling of productivity that she once received from her career. She wants to reenter the work world though she fears that she cannot compete in her field with women who did not take time off from work, or with younger women who are single and do not have children. She worries about possible detrimental effects on her children, but she is nevertheless considering a return to work.

When Kathleen returns to work she will likely experience stressors that often occur for women in dual-career families: continued primary responsibility for child rearing and housekeeping, family–work interference, work–family interference, lack of personal time, and (sometimes) priority of husband's career. She also may experience midlife stressors including assessment of career progress as insufficient or unsatisfactory and a sense that time is running out for what she wants to achieve in her life including her career. On the positive side, studies have shown that children in dual-career families rarely suffer because both parents work and women who work outside the home experience better physical and mental health than women who do not.

Questions

- *What research findings on dual careers can you apply to Kathleen's situation to help her clarify her thoughts and feelings about returning to work?*

- *What do you envision as the most positive outcome for Kathleen?*

REFERENCES

Adelmann, P. K., Antonucci, T. C., Crohan, S. E., & Coleman, L. M. (1989). Empty nest, cohort, and employment in the well-being of midlife of midlife women. *Sex Roles, 20,* 173–189.

Administration on Aging. (2000a). *Annual profile of older Americans shows drop in poverty rate* [On-line]. Available: http://www.aos.gov/pr/Pr2000/OAprofile.html.

Administration on Aging. (2000b). *Profile of older Americans: 2000* [On-line]. Available: http//:www.aoa.dhhs.gov/aoa/stats/profile/#Poverty2.

Andersen, M. L. (1988). *Thinking about women* (2nd ed.). New York: Macmillan.

Arber, S., & Ginn, J. (1995). Choice and constraint in the retirement of older married women. In S. Arber & J. Ginn (Eds.), *Connecting gender & ageing* (pp. 69–86). Philadelphia: Open University Press.

Barnett, R. C. (1997). Gender, employment, and psychological well-being: Historical and life course perspectives. In M. E. Lachman & J. B. James (Eds.), *Multiple paths of midlife development* (pp. 325–342). Chicago: University of Chicago Press.

Baruch, G. K., Barnett, R., & Rivers, C. (1983). *Lifeprints: New patterns of love and work for today's women*. New York: McGraw-Hill.

Belle, D. (Ed.). (1982). *Lives in stress: Women and depression*. Beverly Hills, CA: Sage Publications.

Bernard, J. (1982). *The future of marriage*. New Haven, CT: Yale University Press.

Bird, G. W., & Kemerait, L. N. (1990). Stress among early adolescents in two-earner families. *Journal of Early Adolescence, 10*, 344–365.

Block, S. (2000, August 8). Golden years bleak for divorce's. *USA Today*, pp. B1–B2.

Bradford, J., & Ryan, C. (1991). Who we are: Health concerns of middle-aged lesbians. In B. J. Warshow, & A. J. Smith (Eds.), *Lesbians at midlife: The creative transition* (pp.147–163). San Francisco: Spinsters.

Browne, C. (1994). Feminist theory and social work: A vision for practice with older women. *Journal of Applied Social Science, 18*, 5–16.

Bumpass, L. L., & Aquilino, W. S. (1995). *A social map of midlife: Family and work over the middle life course*. Vero Beach, FL: MacArthur Foundation Research Network on Successful Midlife Development.

Butler, S. S., & Weatherley, R. A. (1992). Women at midlife and categories of neglect. *Social Work, 37*, 510–515.

Butler, S. S., & Weatherley, R. A. (1995). Pathways to homelessness among middle-aged women. *Women & Politics, 15*, 1–22.

Carr, D. (1997). The fulfillment of career dreams at midlife: Does it matter for women's mental health? *Journal of Health and Social Behavior, 38*, 331–344.

Clausen, J. A. (1986). *The life course: A sociological perspective*. Englewood Cliffs, NJ: Prentice Hall.

Cole, E. R., Zucker, A. N., & Duncan, L. E. (2001). Changing society, changing women (and men). In R. K. Unger (Ed.), *Handbook of the psychology of woman and gender* (pp. 410–423). New York: John Wiley & Sons.

Coleman, L. M., & Antonucci, T. C. (1983). The impact of work on women at midlife. *Developmental Psychology, 19*, 290–294.

Demby, E. R. (1996). *Gender gap* [On-line]. Available: http://www.assetpub.com/archive/ps/96-04psapril/april96PS16.html.

Devlin, S., & Arye, L. (1997). The social security debate: A financial crisis of a new retirement paradigm? *Generations, 21*, 27–33.

Duxbury, L., & Higgins, C. (1991). Gender differences in work–family conflict. *Journal of Applied Psychology, 76*, 60–74.

Duxbury, L., & Higgins, C. (1994). Interference between work and family: A status report on dual-career and dual-earner mothers and fathers. *Employee Assistance Quarterly, 9*, 55–80.

Echenrode, J., & Gore, S. (1990). *Stress between work and family*. New York: Plenum Press.

Elman, C., & O'Rand, A. M. (1998). Midlife work pathways and educational entry. *Research on Aging, 20*, 475–505.

Elman, M. R., & Gilbert, L. (1984). Coping strategies for role conflict in married professional women with children. *Family Relations, 33*, 317–327.

Galinsky, E., Friedman, D., & Hernandez, C. (1991). *The corporate reference guide to work family programs*. New York: Families and Work Institute.

Gibson, R. C. (1988). The work, retirement, and disability of older Black Americans. In J. S. Jackson (Eds.), *The black American elderly* (pp. 304–324). New York: Springer.

Gilbert, L. A. (1985). *Men in dual-career families: Current realities and future prospects*. Hillsdale, NJ: Lawrence Erlbaum.

Gilbert, L. A. (1993). Women at midlife: Current theoretical perspectives and research. *Women & Therapy, 14*, 105–115.

Gilbert, L. A., & Davidson, S. (1989). Dual career families in midlife. In S. Hunter & M. Sundel (Eds.), *Midlife myths: Issues, findings, and practice implications* (pp. 195–209). Thousand Oaks, CA: Sage Publications.

Gonyea, J. G. (Ed.). (1998). *Resecuring social security and Medicare: Understanding privatization and risk.* Washington, DC: Gerontological Society of America.

Gordon, J. R., & Whelan, K. S. (1998). Successful professional women in midlife: How organizations can more effectively understand and respond to the challenges. *Academy of Management Executive, 12*, 8–27.

Gove, W. R., & Zeiss, C. (1987). Multiple roles and happiness. In F. J. Cosby (Ed.), *Spouse, parent, worker: On gender and multiple roles* (pp. 125–137). New Haven, CT: Yale University Press.

Greenhaus, J., Bedeian, A., & Mossholder, K. (1987). Work experiences, job performance, and feeling of personal and family well-being. *Journal of Vocational Behavior, 31*, 200–215.

Gutek, B., Searle, S., & Kelpa, L. (1991). Rational versus gender role explanations for work–family conflicts. *Journal of Applied Psychology, 76*, 560–568.

Guy, R. F., & Erdner, R. A. (1993). Retirement: an emerging challenge for women. In R. Kastenbaum (Ed.), *Encyclopedia of adult development* (pp. 405–409). Phoenix, AZ: Oryx.

Hayes, C. L. (1989, October). Financial security: What every woman must know. *McCall's, 117*, 124–126.

Hayes, C. L. (1990). Social and emotional issues facing midlife women: The important role of pre-retirement planning. In C. L. Hayes (Ed.), *Women in mid-life: Planning for tomorrow* (pp. 27–39). New York: Haworth Press.

Hayes, C. L. (1991). Long term care for women. In *Long term care: Visions of the future* (Proceedings of UNUM Life Insurance, pp. 4–7). Portland, ME: UNUM Life Insurance.

Hayes, C. L. (1993). Pre-retirement planning for women resources. In C. L. Hayes (Ed.), *Women in mid-life: Planning for tomorrow* (pp. 117–124). New York: Haworth Press.

Hayes, C. L., & Parker, M. (1993). Overview of the literature on pre-retirement planning for women. In C. L. Hayes (Ed.), *Women in mid-life planning for tomorrow* (pp. 1–17). New York: Haworth Press.

Helson, R., & Picano, J. (1990). Is the traditional role bad for women? *Journal of Personality and Social Psychology, 59*, 311–320.

Hertz, R. (1986). *More equal than others: Women and men in dual-career marriages.* Berkeley: University of California Press.

Herz, D. E. (1988). Employment characteristics of older women, 1987. *Monthly Labor Review, 111*, 3–12.

Higgins, C., Duxbury, L., & Lee, C. (1994). Impact of life-cycle stage and gender on the ability to balance work and family responsibilities. *Family Relations, 43*, 144–150.

Higgins, C., Duxbury, L., Lee, C., & Mills, S. (1992). An examination of work–time and intra-role conflict. *Optimum, 23*, 29–38.

Hochschild, A. (1989). *The second shift.* New York: Viking Press.

Hoffman, L. (1987). The effects on children of maternal and parental employment. In N. Gerstel & H. Gross (Eds.), *Families and work* (pp. 362–393). Philadelphia: Temple University Press.

Hooyman, N. R. (1990). Women as caregivers of the elderly: Implications for social welfare policy and practice. In D. E. Biegel & A. Blum (Eds.), *Aging and caregiving: Theory, research, and policy* (pp. 221–241). Newbury Park, CA: Sage Publications.

Hooyman, N. R. (1999). Research on older women: Where is feminism? *Gerontologist, 39*, 115–118.

Hooyman, N. R., & Gonyea, J. G. (1995). *Feminist perspectives on family care: Policies for gender justice.* Thousand Oaks, CA: Sage Publications.

Hooyman, N. R., & Gonyea, J .G. (1999). A feminist model of family care: Practice and policy directives. *Journal of Women & Aging, 11*, 149–169.

Hooyman, N. R., & Kiyak, H. A. (1993). *Social gerontology* (3rd ed.). Boston, MA: Allyn & Bacon.

Hooyman, N. R., & Lustbader, W. (1986). *Taking care: Supporting older people and their families.* New York: Free Press.

James, J. B. (1990). Women's employment patterns and midlife well-being. In H. Y. Grossman & N. L. Chester (Eds.), *The experience and meaning of work in women's lives* (pp. 103–120.). Hillsdale, NJ: Lawrence Erlbaum.

Johnson, R.W. (1998). The gender gap in pension wealth: Is women's progress in the labor market equalizing retirement benefits [on-line]. Available: http//www.urban.org/retirement/briefs/1/brief_1.html.

Karasek, R. (1979). Job demands, job decision latitude and mental strain: Implications for job redesign. *Administrative Science Quarterly, 24*, 285–307.

Kerchoff, D. (1986). Family pattern and morale in retirement. In I. Simpson & J. McKinney (Ed.), *Toward a sociology of women* (pp. 245–254). Lexington, MA: Xerox College.

Kessler, R. C., & McRae, J. A. (1982). The effects of wives' employment on the mental health of married men and women. *American Sociological Review, 47*, 216–227.

Kessler, R. C., & McRae, J. A. (1984). Sex differences in vulnerability to undesirable life events. *American Sociological Review, 49*, 620–631.

Kilty, K. M., & Behling, J. H. (1985). Predicting retirement intentions and activities of professional workers. *Journal of Gerontology, 40*, 219–227.

Kimmel, D. C., & Sang, B. E. (1995). Lesbians and gay men in midlife. In A. R. D'Augelli & C. J.

Patterson (Ed.), *Lesbian, gay, and bisexual identities over the lifespan: Psychological perspectives* (pp. 190–214). New York: Oxford University Press.

Knaub, P. K. (1986). Growing up in a dual-career family: The children's perceptions. *Family Relations, 35*, 431–437.

Lewis, L. H. (Ed.). (1988). *Addressing the needs of returning women.* San Francisco: Jossey-Bass.

Marks, N. F. (1993). *Contemporary social demographics of American midlife parents* (NSFH Working Paper No. 54). Madison: University of Wisconsin, Center for Demography and Ecology.

Marks, N. F. (1996). Social demographic diversity among American midlife parents. In C. D. Ryff & M. M. Seltzer (Eds.), *The parental experience in midlife* (pp. 29–75). Chicago: University of Chicago Press.

Matthews, S., & Brown, D. (1987). Retirement as a crucial life event: The differential experiences of women and men. *Research on Aging, 9*, 548–551.

Meyer, D. R. (1996). The economic vulnerability of midlife single parents. In C. D. Ryff & M. M. Seltzer (Eds.), *The parental experience in midlife* (pp. 77–102). Chicago: University of Chicago Press.

Moore, T. S. (1990). The nature and unequal incidence of job displacement costs. *Social Problems, 37*, 230–242.

Nadeau, S., Walsh, W., & Wetton, C. (1993). Gender wage discrimination: Methodological issues and empirical results for a Canadian public sector employer. *Applied Economics, 25*, 227–241.

Nadelson, C., & Nadelson, T. (1980). Dual-career marriages: Benefits and costs. In F. Pepitone-Rockwall (Ed.), *Dual-career couples* (pp. 91–109). London: Sage Publications.

National Center of Educational Statistics. (1998). *Gender differences in earnings among young adults entering the labor market* [On-line]. Available: http://www.nces.ed.gov/pub-search/pubsinfos.asp?pubio=98086.

National Committee on Pay Equity. (1997). *The wage gap: 1996.* Washington, DC: Author.

Neal, M. B., Ingersoll-Dayton, B., & Starrels, M. E. (1997). Gender and relationship differences in caregiving patterns and consequences among employed caregivers. *Gerontologist, 37,* 804–816.

Nock, S. L., & Kingston, P. W. (1988). Time with children: The impact of couples' work–time commitments. *Social Forces, 67,* 59–85.

O'Grady-LeShane, R. (1990). Older women and poverty. *Social Work, 35,* 421.

Older Women's League. (1998). *Women, work, and pensions: Improving the odds for a secure retirement.* Washington, DC: Author.

Older Women's League. (2001). *Older women and poverty* [On-line]. Available: http://www.owl-national.org/poverty.html.

Padula, M. A. (1994). Reentry women: A literature review with recommendations for counseling and research. *Journal of Counseling & Development, 73,* 10-16.

Pavalko, E. K., & Artis, J. E. (1997). Women's caregiving and paid work: Causal relationships in late midlife. *Journals of Gerontology, 52B,* S170–S179.

Persell, C. (1990). *Understanding society.* New York: Harper & Row.

Pienta, A. M., Burr, J. A., & Mutchler, J. E. (1994). Women's labor force participation in later life: The effects of early work and family experiences. *Journal of Gerontology: Social Sciences, 49,* S231–S239.

Piotrkowski, C. S., & Repetti, R. L. (1984). Dual-earner families. *Marriage and Family Review, 7,* 3–4.

Pleck, J. (1985). *Working wives/working husbands.* Beverly Hills, CA: Sage Publications.

Rapoport, R., & Rapoport, R. (1971). *Dual-career families.* Harmondsworth, England: Penguin Books.

Reeves, J. B., & Darville, R. L. (1992). Aging couples in dual-career/earner families: Patterns of role sharing. *Journal of Women & Aging, 4,* 39–55.

Reitzes, D. C., & Mutran, E. J. (1994). Multiple roles and identities: Factors influencing self-esteem among middle-aged working men and women. *Social Psychology Quarterly, 57,* 313–325.

Reitzes, D. C., Mutran, E. J., & Fernandez, M. E. (1994). Middle-aged working men and women. *Research on Aging, 16,* 355–374.

Rexroat, C., & Shehan, C. (1987). The family life cycle and spouses' time in housework. *Journal of Marriage and the Family, 49,* 737–750.

Richardson, V. F. (1993). *Retirement counseling.* New York: Springer.

Richardson, V. F. (1999). Women and retirement. *Journal of Women & Aging, 11,* 49–66.

Richardson, V. F., & Kilty, K. M. (1997). A critical analysis of expected and actual finances among retired women and men. *Journal of Poverty, 1,* 19–47.

Rix, S. E. (1993). Who pays for what? Ensuring financial security in retirement. In C. L. Hayes (Ed.), *Women in mid-life: Planning for tomorrow* (pp. 5–25). New York: Haworth Press.

Roberts, B. W., & Friend, W. (1998). Career momentum in midlife women: Life context, identity, and personality correlates. *Journal of Occupational Health Psychology, 3,* 195–208.

Rosenthal, M., & Morith, N. P. (1993). Women and long term care planning: The adverse impact of women's perceptions. In C. L. Hayes (Ed.), *Women in mid-life: Planning for tomorrow* (pp. 67–81). New York: Haworth Press.

Rothman, S. (1998). *Studies show women more likely to live in poverty* [On-line]. Available: http://www.bankrate.com/smm/news/pf/19980319a.asp.

Rowland, M. (1987, February). Rich for life: Using your new money freedom. *Working Women, 12,* 31–34.

Sang, B. (1990). Reflections of midlife lesbians on their adolescence. *Journal of Women and Aging, 2,* 111–117.

Sang, B. (1991). Moving toward balance and integration. In B. Sang, J. Warshow, & A. Smith (Eds.), *Lesbians at midlife: The creative transition* (pp. 206–214). San Francisco: Spinsters.

Sapiro, V. (1990). *Women in American society* (2nd ed.). Palo Alto, CA: Mayfield.

Scarr, S., Phillips, D., & McCartney, K. (1989). Working mothers and their families. *American Psychologist, 44,* 1402–1409.

Schnittiger, M. H., & Bird, G. W. (1990). Coping among dual-career men and women across the family life cycle. *Family Relations, 39,* 199–205.

Seccombe, K. (1992). Employment, the family, and employer-based policies. In J. W. Dwyer & R. T. Coward (Eds.), *Gender, families, and elder care* (pp. 165–180). Newbury Park, CA: Sage Publications.

Siverd, B. (1987, January). How to beat the retirement clock. *Working Women, 12,* 34, 36.

Smeeding, T. M. (1998). Reshuffling responsibility in old age: The United States in a comparative perspective. In J. Gonyea (Ed.), *Resecuring Social Security and Medicare: Understanding privatization and risk* (pp. 24–36). Washington, DC: Gerontological Society of America.

Smith, K. R., & Moen, P. (1988). Passage through midlife: Women's changing family roles and economic well-being. *Sociological Quarterly, 29,* 503-524.

Staines, G., & O'Connor, P. (1980). Conflicts among work, leisure, and family roles. *Monthly Labor Review, 103,* 35–39.

Staney, F. M. (1986). Career indecision in reentry and undergraduate women. *Journal of College Student Personnel, 27,* 114–119.

Sundel, M., & Bernstein, B. E. (1995). Legal and financial aspects of midlife review and their implications for mental health counselors. *Journal of Mental Health Counseling, 17,* 114–123.

Szinovacz, M. (Ed.). (1982). *Women's retirement* . Beverly Hills, CA: Sage Publications.

Turner, M. J., Bailey, W. C., & Scott, J. P. (1994). Factors influencing attitude toward retirement and retirement planning among midlife university employees. *Journal of Applied Gerontology, 13,* 143–156.

U.S. Bureau of the Census. (1989). Poverty in the United States: 1987. *Current Population Reports* (Series P-60). Washington, DC: U.S. Government Printing Office.

U.S. Bureau of the Census. (1990). *Statistical abstract of the United States* (110th ed.). Washington, DC: U.S. Government Printing Office.

U.S. Bureau of the Census. (1992). *Statistical abstract of the United States: 1992.* Washington, DC: U.S Government Printing Office.

U.S. Bureau of the Census. (1994). *Income, poverty, and validation of noncash benefits.* Washington, DC: U.S. Government Printing Office.

U.S. Bureau of the Census. (1995). *American women: A profile* (No. SB/95-19). Washington, DC U.S. Government Printing Office.

U.S. Bureau of the Census. (2000). *Educational attainment in the United States* (Pub. No. 20-563, update, PPL 147). [On-line]. Available: http://www.2000.census.gov/population/www/socdemo/educ-attn.html.

U.S. Department of Education. (1991). *Digest of education statistics, 1990.* Washington, DC: U.S. Government Printing Office.

U.S. Department of Labor, Bureau of Labor Statistics. (1974). *Employment and earnings.* Washington, DC: U.S. Government Printing Office.

U.S. Department of Labor, Bureau of Labor Statistics. (1991). *Employment and earnings.* Washington, DC: U.S. Government Printing Office.

U.S. Department of Labor, Bureau of Labor Statistics. (1992). *Employment in perspective: Women in the labor force* (Report 831). Washington, DC: U.S. Government Printing Office.

U.S. Department of Labor, Bureau of Labor Statistics. (1996). *Employment and earnings.* Washington, DC: U.S. Government Printing Office.

Vanderkolk, B., & Young, A. (1991). *The work and family revolution.* New York: Facts on File.

Vandewater, E. A., & Stewart, A. J. (1997). Women's career commitment patterns and personality development. In M. E. Lachman, & J. Boone James (Eds.), *Multiple paths of midlife development* (pp. 375–408). Chicago: University of Chicago Press.

Verbrugge, L. (1982). Women's social roles and health. In P. Berman & E. Ramey (Eds.), *Women: A developmental perspective* (Pub. No. 82-2298, pp. 49–78). Bethesda, MD: National Institute of Child Health and Human Development.

Verbrugge, L. (1987). Role responsibilities, role burdens, and physical health. In F. Crosby (Ed.), *Spouse, parent, worker: On gender and multiple roles* (pp. 154–166). New Haven, CT: Yale University Press.

Voydanoff, P. (1988). Work role characteristics, family structure demands, and work/family conflict. *Journal of Marriage and the Family, 50,* 749–761.

Wanamaker, N. J., & Bird, G. W. (1990). Coping with stress in dual-career marriages. *International Journal of Sociology of the Family, 20,* 198–211.

White-Means, S. L., & Hersch, J. (1993). Economic viability among post-retirement age women. In C. L. Hayes (Ed.), *Women in mid-life: Planning for tomorrow* (pp. 19–35). New York: Haworth Press.

Women need to focus on saving more than men. (2001). [On-line]. Available: http://www.herbudget.com/focusonwomen.shtml.

CHAPTER 6

PHYSICAL HEALTH CONCERNS

This chapter focuses on the three physical conditions most likely to threaten women in midlife—heart disease, breast cancer, and lung cancer. The health issues of midlife lesbians, as well as the prevalence of heterosexism in health care settings, are addressed. Also discussed is the recent "coming of age" of women's health, a phenomenon that came after years of women being excluded from the major research projects on health. Life-span themes include prevention, and multiple influences.

QUESTIONS TO CONSIDER

- *What are the most common life-threatening conditions that affect women in midlife?*

- *What are the incidence and mortality rates, risk factors, and preventive factors for coronary heart disease in midlife women?*

- *What are the incidence and mortality rates, risk factors, and preventive factors for breast and lung cancer in midlife women?*

- *What knowledge is there about the state of lesbian health care and the treatment of lesbians in traditional health care settings?*

- *What factors are being addressed in the new movement on women's health?*

- *What concerns exist about health insurance for midlife and older women?*

Most midlife women and men consider themselves to be in good health (Bayer, Whissell-Buechy, & Honzik, 1980). Women, however, experience more health difficulties than men in every time frame—daily, annually, or over their life-times (Verbrugge, 1989). In midlife, they experience more acute conditions than men, including "infective/parasitic diseases, respiratory conditions, diges-tive system conditions, injuries, ear diseases, headaches, genitourinary disor-ders, skin diseases, and musculoskeletal diseases" (Ingram Fogel, 1991, p. 511). Acute conditions require one or more days of medical attention or restricted activity and last less than 3 months (Woods, 1993). Chronic conditions, which persist long beyond 3 months because they are irreversible, are also more com-mon among midlife women (Verbrugge, 1989), such as arthritis, diabetes, chronic bronchitis, hypertension, osteoporosis (progressive bone loss), and lupus (for example, Horton, 1995; Whitbourne, 2001; Woods, 1993). Because women live longer than men, they are more likely to develop a chronic illness. Chronic illnesses require considerable medical and self-care to prevent more extensive disability. The adjustment can be difficult especially when the illness or its management interferes with valued roles or employment (Chrisler, 2001).

The focus of this chapter is on chronic conditions that are the most life threatening for women in midlife. Between ages 45 and 64, women can die from cerebrovascular disease, chronic obstructive pulmonary disease, pneumo-nia and influenza, chronic liver disease and cirrhosis, and diabetes mellitus (National Center for Health Statistics, 1990). Heart disease and cancer, how-ever, are the most life threatening. Between ages 35 and 44, women are most likely to die from heart disease or cancer, and these diseases continue as the major causes of death throughout midlife (Hooker & Kaus, 1994; Woods, 1993). Coronary heart disease (CHD), lung cancer, and breast cancer hold the most risk of dying. Most women (and men) will die of CHD.

CORONARY HEART DISEASE

Coronary heart disease is one of several cardiovascular heart diseases; other cardiovascular heart diseases include hypertension (or high blood pressure), cerebrovascular accidents (strokes), and rheumatic heart disease (American Heart Association, 1995; U.S. Bureau of the Census, 1991). CHD is a disorder of the cardiovascular system that includes the heart and blood vessels (Sullivan, 1987). This disorder, or more specifically a heart attack, accounts for about two-thirds (66.3 percent) of cardiovascular disease (American Heart Association, 1995; U.S. Bureau of the Census, 1991). When a heart attack is experienced, an interrupted supply of blood to the heart causes a part of the heart muscle (myocardium) to die. Myocardial infarction refers to destruction of the myocardial tissue. The part of the tissue affected is called an infarct

(Turner & Helms, 1994). The risk of myocardial infarction appears to be increasing for women but declining for men.

The signs of CHD happen 10–20 years later in women than in men. Before menopause, estrogen appears to lower the risk of CHD in women. When estrogen production dramatically drops following menopause, the risk of CHD increases (American Heart Association, 1998; Nachtigall & Nachtigall, 1990; Stuenkel, 1993). The medical profession promotes estrogen replacement as a protection from heart disease for postmenopausal women, but several recent studies question the benefits (Haney, 2000). Most of the studies on the benefits of estrogen replacement did not use clinical trials but instead used cohort studies on mostly self-selected women (Matthews, Kuller, Wing, & Jansen-McWilliams, 1997).

After age 50, CHD is the most common cause of death in women (Stuenkel, 1993). Almost half (49.1 percent) of the deaths of women in 1995 resulted from CHD. This disease causes more deaths among women than the next 16 causes of death combined (American Heart Association, 1998). The death rate for African American women from CHD is 35.3 percent higher than for white women; between ages 35–74 it is more than 71 percent higher (American Heart Association, 1997).

The mortality rates from CHD in women, after menopause, exceed those for men (Amsterdam & Legato, 1993). Women are twice as likely to die because of a heart attack within the first few weeks than are men, and more women (44 percent) than men (27 percent) die within a year following a heart attack (American Heart Association, 1995, 1997). This situation probably results from later diagnosis for women, so that there is more advancement in the disease before it is recognized (Council on Ethical and Judicial Affairs, 1991). Health care professionals ignore, misinterpret, or minimize cardiac signs in women more than in men (Healy, 1991). Even when medical indications are similar to those of men, women may not receive as aggressive treatment (Ayanian & Epstein, 1991) or state-of-the-art medical and surgical management of their heart conditions as men (Young & Kahana, 1994). Surgeons use 28 percent more bypass surgeries and 15 percent more angioplasty procedures on men. On the other hand, the accepted interventions for men are often inadequate or ineffective when used with women (Ayanian & Epstein, 1991). Because the research on heart disease is almost all based on samples of middle-aged men (Healy, 1991), there is no clarity about the most effective interventions for women (Sobel, 1994).

Risk Factors

There are various lists of risk factors for CHD (for example, Holm & Penckofer, 1995; Olson & Labat, 1995). These factors are similar for men and women and although some factors can be modified or eliminated, others cannot. See Exhibit 6.1 for a summary of these factors.

——— Exhibit 6.1
Risk Factors for Coronary Heart Disease*————————————————

Factors that Cannot Be Modified

- Sex–gender differences (males; females age 75 and older)
- Age (increased rates with advancing age)
- Menopause (increased rates in women after menopause)
- Family history of heart disease (having a parent who experienced a heart attack before age 60)
- Race (greater risk for African American men and women)

Factors that Can Be Eliminated

- Cigarette smoking (higher CHD rates in women)
- Hyperlipidemia or high fat levels in the blood (women more susceptible)
- Obesity (women more susceptible in their later years)
- Diet (quantity of fat and quality of fat such as saturated)
- Physical inactivity (both women and men at all ages)
- Stress, hostility, Type A behavior (for example, high achieving, competitive)
- Alcohol and caffeine consumption

Factors that Cannot Be Eliminated but Are Controllable

- Hypertension (high blood pressure)
- Diabetes (higher prevalence in women)

Socioeconomic Factors

- Lower education
- Lower socioeconomic status

*Data compiled from the American Heart Association (1999, 2001); Brown (1999); Holm and Penckofer (1995); Olson and Labat (1995); and Siegler (1993).

It appears that some life patterns must change to reduce the risk of cardiovascular disease in women (Holm & Penckofer, 1995; Kessel, 1998). Yet, each of the risk factors is controversial. Until we know more about these factors, individually and in various combinations, the recommendation of the American Heart Association (2001) is to eliminate as many of them as possible. Several better known risk factors can either be eliminated or modified.

Risk Factor Control

Smoking. Nearly one-fifth of cardiovascular diseases develop from smoking (American Heart Association, 1999). Approximately half of the cases of CHD in women ages 30–55 are attributed to smoking. Women who smoke experience twice the risk of heart attack compared to women who do not smoke (Kessel, 1998) and the risk rises with the number of cigarettes smoked a day (Burkman, 1988). The risk rises if other factors are present with smoking, such as older age, family history of myocardial infarctions, hypertension, obesity, elevated cholesterol levels, or diabetes (Ingram Fogel, 1991). Smoking combined with taking birth control pills escalates the risk 39 times (American Heart Association, 1992, 1993). If exposed to environmental tobacco smoke at home or work, the risk of death from CHD increases up to 30 percent (American Heart Association, 1999).

There is little disagreement about the risks of smoking and heart disease (and diseases of the respiratory system). There is good news, however, for women who stop smoking. Twelve years of follow-up data showed that the risk of heart disease is highest for midlife women who began smoking before the age of 15. If these women stop smoking, however, the risk of heart disease decreases by one-third within 2 years. From 10 to 14 years after quitting smoking, the risk declines to the same level it is for those who never smoked (Kawachi et al., 1994).

Overweight. More than two-thirds (70 percent) of CHD that occurs in women in the heaviest weight categories has been attributed to excess weight (Manson et al., 1990). More Latino, African American, and white women are both overweight and obese than are men (American Heart Association, 1999).

Cholesterol. This factor is more of a risk for women than men because they have significantly higher average total cholesterol. Beginning at age 50, a higher percentage of women than men have a total blood cholesterol of 200mg/dL or greater. Levels from 200 to 239 mg/dL in adults are borderline high, and levels of 240 mg/dL or greater are considered high (American Heart Association, 1999). High levels predict CHD in premenopausal women or women under age 50 but not in older or postmenopausal women (Perlman, Wolf, Finucane, & Madans, 1989). Women also have significantly lower levels of high-density lipoprotein (HDL) that also appears to be a strong risk factor for CHD. Rates of myocardial infarctions rise 2 percent for each 1 percent decrease in HDL.

Various behaviors may increase HDL: regular and vigorous exercise, weight loss, smoking cessation, reduction in calorie intake, and moderate alcohol consumption (Ingram Fogel, 1991).

Low-Fat Diet, Exercise. Decline in heart disease rates is attributed to changed habits in diet and exercise (American Heart Association, 1989). Low-fat diets, combined with rigorous exercise, can reverse blockages in the coronary arteries (Ornish et al., 1990). The American Heart Association (1998, 1999) reported, however, that only about 15 percent of U.S. adults participate in the recommended rigorous exercise three times a week for at least 20 minutes. Physical inactivity is more prevalent among women than men, among older than younger adults, among African Americans and Latinos than whites, among the less affluent than the more affluent, and among persons with less than a 12th grade education. Less physically active adults have a 30 percent to 50 percent greater risk of developing high blood pressure.

Alcohol. Alcohol may have a positive effect for CHD. One report indicates that 0.5 to 2 drinks per day lowers women's risk of CHD by 40 percent compared to women who do not drink (Garg, Wagener, & Madans, 1993).

The Nurses' Health Study that began at Harvard University addressed several of the risk factors for CHD in a study of 85,941 women from 1980 to 1996. The women ranged in age from 34 to 59 and had no earlier diagnosed cardiovascular disease or cancer. Over the study period, the incidence of heart disease dropped by about a third. Two-thirds of this decline was attributed by the investigators to three factors: improvement in diet (16 percent), a 41-percent decline in smoking (13 percent), and an increase in use of postmenopausal hormones (9 percent). Yet, a large increase in obesity offset some of the gains (Hu et al., 2000). From the same sample, Stampfer, Hu, Manson, Rimm, and Willett (2000) reported that a combination of certain factors can lower women's risk of heart disease: healthy diet, moderate to rigorous physical activity for at least half an hour per day, no smoking, and an average alcohol consumption of at least half a drink a day. The risk of heart disease can be lowered as much as 83 percent and stroke by 75 percent. Women cannot usually achieve a similar level of risk reduction through any of these activities alone. Yet, the significant effect of one of the factors stood out in this study: smoking. Women who smoked 15 or more cigarettes were five times more at risk for heart attack than women who never smoked.

Less Conventional Risk Factors

The risk factors for CHD discussed so far are traditional ones. Less-conventional risk factors also exist that are psychosocial in nature. These include Type

A behavior, work stress, and hostility. Weidner (1994) found that though women, as a group, scored lower than men on these factors, each one of them is linked to CHD in both men and women. Exactly how these factors influence CHD, however, is ambiguous. Moreover, only select aspects of a factor may be harmful. Employment, for example, is not unhealthy for women. Employed women tend to report better health compared to unemployed women (for example, Adelmann, Antonucci, Crohan, & Coleman, 1990; Kritz-Silverstein, Wingard, & Barrett-Connor, 1992; Verbrugge, 1986; and see Chapter 5). Employment may reduce the effects of other stressful roles on health (McKinlay & McKinlay, 1989), although certain job characteristics such as high demand and low control may be linked to CHD in women (Karasek, Baker, Marxer, Ahlbom, & Theorell, 1981). Various other social and economic factors may reduce the risks and mortality rates associated with heart disease such as a supportive partner or confidant and adequately developed economic resources (Williams et al., 1992). As reflected in the life-span approach, there are *multiple influences* on the development of CHD.

CANCER—IN GENERAL

Cancer is second only to heart disease as a leading cause of death of midlife women. Cancer includes more than 100 diseases that result from uncontrolled growth and spread of abnormal cells (Papalia, Camp, & Feldman, 1996). There are four types of cancer: (a) carcinomas located in epithelial cells in places such as the lung, colon, pancreas, or skin; (b) sarcomas located in the muscle, bone, fat, or other connective tissue; (c) lymphomas located in the lymphoid tissues; and (d) leukemias located in the hematological system (Turner & Helms, 1994). The rates for all cancers currently experienced by women during midlife rose 50 percent compared to women born in the last several decades of the 19th century (Boring, Squires, & Tong, 1992). The most common sites for cancer in women are the lung, breast, colon and rectum, and uterus (American Cancer Society, 1993).

Short-term survival rates are somewhat better than they were 60 or so years ago. Most persons diagnosed with cancer (four out of five) died within 5 years in the 1930s (Papalia et al., 1996). Four out of 10 persons diagnosed with cancer in 1998 were projected to survive 5 years after diagnosis (American Cancer Society, 1998). This was due to advances in chemotherapy, radiation, and surgery. There is not considerable improvement, however, in longer term survival beyond 5 years (Papalia et al., 1996). Lung cancer and breast cancer hold the greatest threat to life from cancer for midlife women.

The rates of death for women of all ages are lower for uterine cancer, endometrial cancer, and cervical cancer; for women under age 65, the rates of death are lower for ovarian and breast cancer (National Cancer Institute, 1990).

The projected mortality rates for women in year 2000 were approximately 67,600 for lung and bronchial cancer, 40,800 for breast cancer, 24,600 for colon cancer, 3,900 for rectal cancer, 14,000 for ovarian cancer, 4,600 for uterine cervix cancer, and 6,500 for uterine corpus (endometrial cancer) (see American Cancer Society, 2000). Overall, the mortality rates for most types of cancer are lower for white women than for African American women (National Cancer Institute, 1990). Although lower rates of death from some types of cancer are occurring, the overall mortality rates for all women are increasing steadily (American Cancer Society, 1991). This is partly due to the rising rate of deaths from lung cancer (American Cancer Society, 1999; Boring et al., 1992).

BREAST CANCER

Although CHD kills more women than any other disease (one in every two), women fear breast cancer more (American Heart Association, 1999; Matthews et al., 1997). Breast cancer is the most often occurring cancer in women, excluding cancers of the skin, and it accounts for almost one third of the cancer diagnoses in American women (American Cancer Society, 2001). The estimated incidence of breast cancer for women in 2001 was 192,200 (American Cancer Society, 2001). About 90 percent of the incidence of breast cancer in women occurs at age 40 or older; about 80 percent of these women are over age 50 (U.S. Select Committee on Aging, 1992). It is most common in white women of high socioeconomic status and significantly less common in women of color (Apfel, Love, & Kalinowski, 1994). The incidence rates for African American women in 1989 were 17 percent lower than for white women (U.S. Department of Health and Human Services, 1992).

Every 3 minutes, a woman in the United States receives the diagnosis of breast cancer; every 12 minutes a woman in the United States dies of breast cancer ("Breast cancer," 1992). Current predictions are that one in 27 women will die of breast cancer (American Heart Association, 1998). This is the leading cause of death in women ages 40–44 (U.S. Select Committee on Aging, 1992). African American women are more likely to die from breast cancer (and from colon and rectal cancer) than women of any other racial and ethnic group (American Cancer Society, 2000).

On a more positive note, the American Cancer Society (2000) reported that both incidence rates and mortality rates of breast cancer are beginning to decline. Although reasons for the decline in incidence rates are unclear, the decline in mortality rates, between 1991 and 1996, probably resulted from earlier detection and improvements in treatment. The largest decline occurred among both white and African American younger women.

With cancer localized to the breast, many women now survive beyond the 5-year rate. This rate increased from 72 percent in 1940 to 96 percent today.

The current relative survival rate for 10 years is 71 percent, for 15 years, 57 percent. But, the relative survival rate beyond five years decreases to 77 percent if the cancer spreads regionally and to 21 percent if there are distant metastases (American Cancer Society, 2000).

Mortality rates from breast cancer partially reflect economics, race, ethnicity, sexual orientation, and sex–gender factors. Bricker-Jenkins (1994) observed that a disproportionate number of women who die from breast cancer are poor and of color. Poor women experience a 30 percent higher mortality rate than women with the economic means to obtain health care. In addition, poor women confront class and race bias in the health care system (Forsen, 1991). All women face sex–gender bias in the health care system; in addition, lesbians face heterosexism, as discussed later in this chapter.

Risk Factors

Though there are a number of risk factors proposed for breast cancer, essentially there is no known cause (Ellerhorst-Ryan & Goeldner, 1992). The risk factors discussed in Exhibit 6.2, therefore, are largely speculative.

——— Exhibit 6.2
Possible Risk Factors for Breast Cancer* ————————————————

- Other than sex–gender factors, the most critical factor in developing breast cancer is aging (Marshall, 1993).

- Early menstruation (before age 12) and late menopause increase risk (Apfel et al., 1994; Kelsey & Hildreth, 1981; Ott & Levy, 1994).

*The National Cancer Institute developed a breast cancer "risk disk," a computer program that helps assess a woman's risk for breast cancer through a series of questions. The program evolved from a mathematical model developed by Mitchell Gail and Associates at the Institute. Only the strongest risk factors are considered, along with age (over 50 years). Examples of the risk factors include: (a) reproductive history (for example, young age at one's first menstrual period; late menopause; frequent monthly ovulation); (b) older age at one's first childbirth or never bearing a child; (c) multiple benign breast biopsies; and (d) mother, sister, or daughter with breast cancer (Rubin, 1998). The disk is available by calling the Institute at 1-800-422-6237 or ordering it through the Institute's Web site available at: http://www.cancertrials.nci.nih.gov.

• No pregnancy or late pregnancy affects the risk. Early first pregnancy decreases the risk whereas late pregnancy increases the risk (Apfel et al., 1994; Hofer, 1992; Kelsey & Hildreth, 1981). More specifically, a protective effect is associated with first pregnancy at age 20, but after age 30 the risk for breast cancer increases (American Cancer Society, 2000; Hofer, 1992; Kelsey & Hildreth, 1981). The greatest risk results from no pregnancies (Kelsey & Hildreth, 1981).

• Certain patterns of cell growth in women with a prior history of benign breast disease may increase the risk. For most women, however, benign breast disease does not appear to affect risk (Cancer Committee, 1986).

• Only about 5 percent of breast cancer is hereditary (Jacobson, 1995). In these cases, the risk is highest for women in families with several first-degree relatives (mother, sister, or daughter) who developed breast cancer. These women are two times more likely to develop breast cancer than women with no similar history (American Cancer Society, 1996); by age 50 the risk is five times greater (King, Rowell, & Love, 1993). Determining the actual influence of family history, however, is difficult. Most women who develop breast cancer have no family history of close relatives with breast cancer (Jacobson, 1995).

• A consensus does not exist about postmenopausal hormone treatments as a risk for breast cancer although estrogen alone appears to increase risk. With the addition of progesterone to hormone treatments, there is still risk (Apfel et al., 1994; Dahmoush, Pike, & Press, 1994). Long-term estrogen replacement is not easy to evaluate because findings from studies vary from no risk to moderate risk. In addition, a positive association between estrogen and breast cancer shows up in some subgroups but not others (Ingram Fogel, 1991).

• A high-fat diet has been suspected to increase risk (Lindsey, Dodd, & Kaempfer, 1987; Willett & Hunter, 1993). Little attention has been focused on Asian women who tend to be protected from breast cancer in their country of origin. With immigration to the United States, however, and adaptation to the high-fat diet and other aspects of life here, their breast cancer rates became equivalent to those of American women (Jacobson, 1995; Osteen et al., 1990). To date, however, there is no clear association between a high-fat diet and breast cancer. The Nurses' Health Study reported recent longitudinal findings on fat intake and development of breast cancer. No link occurred between fat and breast cancer (Rubin, 1999b).

- Overweight, often associated with a high-fat diet, is also implicated in breast cancer, but the association is not strong (Ellerhorst-Ryan & Goeldner, 1992).

- Alcohol may also be associated with the development of breast cancer. As little as one drink a day increases the risk (Rubin, 1998). A moderate risk (40 percent to 50 percent) is associated with more than 3 drinks a week (Schatzkin et al., 1987). The risk is even higher (59 percent) if women are also younger, thinner, and premenopausal (Willett et al., 1987). The findings on alcohol are the reverse of what was noted in the discussion on CHD, where abstinence from alcohol is the risk factor.

- Additional risk factors listed by the American Cancer Society (1998, 1999, 2000) include biopsy-confirmed atypical hyperplasia, recent use of oral contraceptives, higher education and socioeconomic status, pesticides and other chemicals, induced abortion, physical inactivity, and genes (BRCA1 and BRCA2).

A key factor missing from most of the scientific and medical literature on breast cancer is the relationship between this disease and our physical environments (Bricker-Jenkins, 1994). The legacy of nuclear weaponry, for example, is implicated in areas of the world that 50 years ago were not high in reported breast cancer rates but are now: Hiroshima, Nagasaki, as well as in California and Nevada (Brady, 1991).

Prevention

Risk factor lists for breast cancer are particularly problematic because more than 70 percent of all breast cancers happen in women with none of the declared risk factors (National Breast Cancer Coalition, 1993). Although *prevention* through elimination of risk factors does not yet look hopeful, in April 1998, the National Cancer Institute (NCI) reported the possibility for prevention on another front. The drug Tamoxifen appears to reduce the risk of breast cancer. This drug has been the focus of extensive clinical study since the early 1980s (Healy, 1998). The NCI is evaluating this drug in one of the largest cancer prevention trials in 270 sites in the United States and Canada. The trials include approximately 13,388 women who are at high risk for breast cancer because of a family history of the disease, precancerous breast tumors, and age (over 60). Some of these women received Tamoxifen and others a placebo. Similar studies are also under way in several other countries (Davis, 1998a; Healy, 1998).

Tamoxifen blocks the growth of estrogen that speeds up the development of breast cancer cells (Davis, 1998a, 1998b). In the NCI trials, for the women who took the drug the risk of breast cancer lessened by 45 percent in healthy, high-risk women across all age groups over 60 years (Healy, 1998; Levy, 1998; Meisler, 1998); the mortality rate of women with breast cancer lessened by 17 percent (Meisler, 1998). Tamoxifen also appeared to prevent the recurrence of breast cancer by 25 percent for women who experienced the disease in one breast (Meisler, 1998). The importance of this finding lies in the knowledge that the risk of a second episode of breast cancer is about twice as high for women who already experienced breast cancer than for women with no diagnosis of this cancer ("Breast cancer survivors," 1998).

Although still awaiting final federal Drug Administration (FDA) approval, Tamoxifen is already the most widely prescribed intervention for the treatment of early and advanced breast cancer (Levy, 1998). It is the only drug to date that has been tested in such a rigorous way (Meisler, 1998). Still, it is unclear whether the prevention features of Tamoxifen actually reduce breast cancer deaths or only delay disease development (Ault & Bradbury, 1998). Tamoxifen is also not a boon for all women because of its troubling side effects (Goetinck & Camia, 1998). It can cause blood clots in the lungs; two women in the NCI study died from such clots. In addition, taking the drug almost doubles one's chance of cancer of the uterine lining (endometrial cancer). Thirty-three women who were taking Tamoxifen in the NCI trials received a diagnosis of endometrial cancer, which was more than twice the number of such cases in the placebo group. Other risks involve heart disease, liver cancer, cancer of the digestive system, and vision difficulties such as cataracts. Because Tamoxifen may also harm the fetus in women who are pregnant (Davis, 1998a, 1998b; Jacobson, 1995), women of childbearing age who are taking it must avoid pregnancy. Less serious but unpleasant side effects that occur in some women include menopause-like symptoms (for example, vaginal dryness and hot flashes; see Healy, 1998). The NCI trials will follow the participants for two more years with a particular focus on the side effects of Tamoxifen. The goal now is to find other drugs that also prevent the growth of cancer cells in the breast, but do not have the adverse effects of Tamoxifen (Davis, 1998b).

Other less harmful drugs are on the horizon. One is Raloxifene, a drug closely related to Tamoxifen and used in the treatment of osteoporosis. Raloxifene may also reduce breast cancer but with fewer risks. Trials involving 19,000 postmenopausal women indicate that Raloxifene can prevent breast cancer without the negative side effects accompanying Tamoxifen, especially uterine cancer. Women who took Raloxifene for an average of two years and five months in one of the current trials showed a 74-percent reduction of breast cancer. Although seven women developed new breast cancers, this occurred in 21 women in the control group ("Raloxifene shows," 1998).

Detection Methods

With Tamoxifen, Raloxifene, and other drugs being tested, prevention for breast cancer has taken a momentous turn from where it was just a short time ago when there was no hope for prevention or cures. So far, however, these drugs carry risks of other health difficulties or are too new to indicate how long these interventions will protect women from breast cancer. This is why the American Cancer Society (1998) continues to recommend the established early detection methods: mammography, clinical examination by health care professionals, and self-examination (Horton, 1995). Early detection remains the best way to reduce mortality (American Cancer Society, 1999, 2000).

Most women apparently forget to do breast self-examinations (Ellerhorst-Ryan & Goeldner, 1992). Only about 40 percent of women routinely perform them (Clarke & Sandler, 1989; Rutledge, 1987). Even personal or family histories of breast cancer are not consistently related to frequency of self-examination (for example, Rutledge, 1987). Some things that may promote more self-examination include professional instructions on how to do these examinations (Baines, To, & Wall, 1986) and reminder cards to hang in one's shower that show the steps involved (Ellerhorst-Ryan & Goeldner, 1992).

The American Cancer Society recommended until recently that women between ages 40 and 49 get mammograms every one or two years and once a year after age 50. The current recommendations now include, for women over age 40, an annual mammogram, an annual clinical breast exam by a health care professional, and monthly self-examination. The American Cancer Society recommends that younger women (ages 20–39) undergo a clinical breast exam every three years as well as carry out monthly self-examinations. Self-examinations are crucial because women who did these examinations had smaller tumors and less lymph node involvement at the time of detection than women who did not (Huguley, Brown, Greenberg, & Clark, 1988). Most breast lumps are benign, but only a clinical exam and other diagnostic processes such as biopsy can determine the diagnosis (American Cancer Society, 2000).

The recommendation of the American Cancer Society regarding mammograms under age 50 is controversial. The detection rate is not as good in younger women (American Cancer Society, 1994). Apfel et al. (1994) reported that there is no evidence that mammography reduces death in women under age 50. A panel of experts convened in 1997 by the National Institutes of Health (NIH) did not recommend them for women in their 40s. Instead, women were urged to make up their own minds about whether to begin mammograms this early ("Panel won't," 1997). This recommendation, however, created a storm of criticism, especially about leaving the decision up to the women themselves.

When women over age 50 receive regular mammograms, the consensus of studies predicts a 30 percent to 35 percent decrease in mortality rates (for example, Davis & Love, 1994; Smart, 1990). Breast abnormalities can show up on a mammogram before physical signs occur (American Cancer Society, 1999). But do women follow the recommended screenings for breast cancer? The answer is that only about 15 percent of women between ages 50–70 obtain annual mammograms (Morabia & Wynder, 1990). Participation was even low in a university-sponsored low-cost mammography program (for example, Rutledge, Hartman, Kinman, & Winfeld, 1988).

Women with a family history of breast cancer, more education, and higher incomes are more likely to get mammograms (Breen & Kessler, 1994; King et al., 1993). Women who are older, uninsured, and in a low socioeconomic status are less likely to seek preventive care, such as mammograms and breast examinations by health professionals (Hayward, Shapiro, Freeman, & Corey, 1988). Older, instead of younger, lesbian and bisexual women are more likely to seek mammograms, especially those who are white and have insurance and higher incomes (Rankow & Tessaro, 1998b).

Mammography is the best screening method for breast cancer available, but it is not foolproof. When a mammogram detects cancer cells, many cells are already in other parts of the body. Breast cancers can be present a long time before detection by a mammogram (approximately eight years) or before a lump appears (approximately 10 years). By the first or second year, cancer cells can access the bloodstream. Only if there is no metastatic spread during the time a lump is developing will discovery of cancer cells be lifesaving (Apfel et al., 1994).

About 10 to 15 percent of breast cancers detected manually are missed through mammography ("Breast imaging," 1995). Sometimes tumors are missed by the radiologists who read the mammograms, and sometimes they are not detectable on mammograms (Rubin, 1999a). Even if a mammogram allows a physician to determine that a suspicious lump is normal, the lump should still be biopsied (American Cancer Society, 1996).

Questions are being raised about whether or not mammograms are beneficial in the early detection of breast tumors. An analysis of seven large studies of mammography done over the last several decades by a group of scientists in Denmark found that the studies were significantly flawed. More recent and more rigorous studies found no support for the diagnostic utility of mammograms ("2 doctors assail mammogram studies," 2001). The Physician Data Query Screening and Prevention Editorial Board, an independent panel of experts, concluded that there is insufficient evidence that mammograms can ensure the early detection of breast cancer. This new research complicates the decision-making process for women who are considering whether or not to undergo mammography ("More doubts raised about mammograms," 2001). More recently, however, the U.S. Preventive Services Task Force (convened by the U.S. Public Health Service) conducted a review of the same studies found to be flawed by the Danish scientists and concluded that mammograms reduce death from breast cancer (Stolberg, 2002). Problems with the studies were not considered to be serious enough to rule out the recommendation of mammograms. Compared to women who did not get regular mammograms, those who did were 23% less likely to die from breast cancer (Stolberg, 2002). The task force also reduced the age from 50 to 40 for when women should begin having mammograms.

Interventions

Interventions for breast cancers include surgery, chemotherapy (drug therapy), and radiation.

Surgical Treatments. Two equally effective surgical methods are available: mastectomy and lumpectomy with radiation. The rate of cancer recurrence with either procedure is about 8 percent (Apfel et al., 1994). Some women with a family history of breast cancer choose preventive bilateral mastectomy. Any remaining breast tissue, however, remains at risk (King et al., 1993).

When mastectomy is elected, women can be confronted with more difficult issues than the physical signs such as pain and arm weakness (Silberfarb, Maurer, & Crouthamel, 1980). Many women experience some degree of emotional upset following mastectomy including depression, anxiety, or anger; disorder in life patterns such as marital and/or sexual involvements; and fear of the threat of cancer and further mastectomy (Meyerowitz, 1980). The reality and trauma of a missing breast are probably harder to deny than the cancer. Although women have breasts for breastfeeding, society bestows other values on them (Apfel et al., 1994). Because women internalize what our culture dictates in terms of a standard of beauty for them that includes breasts, it is a challenge to maintain self-esteem and composure when a breast is missing (Bricker-Jenkins, 1994; Zemore & Shepel, 1989). Men define the standards of beauty for women, and routinely used words following mastectomy such as "disfigurement" or "mutilation" reflect men's view that women who experience this surgical procedure have wounded bodies (Wilkinson & Kitzinger, 1994). Mastectomy, then, not only changes one's external appearance but also provokes fears such as losing sexuality, acceptability and worth as a woman, and a sense of belonging (Apfel et al., 1994; Bloom, 1987).

Numerous publications recommend that promptly after mastectomy, breast prostheses, fitted clothes, and makeup can help women look "feminine" again (Meyerowitz, Chaiken, & Clark, 1988). Brinker-Jenkins (1994) wrote a personal account of her experience with the "promise," through a prosthesis or false breast, of looking just as she did when she went into the hospital for a mastectomy. The priority is to correct a defective body with a cosmetic remedy of disguise (Wilkinson & Kitzinger, 1994). Yet, no study has focused on the usefulness of these devices for positive improvement in body image and quality of life. Nor is there much attention to the discomfort of wearing a prosthesis (McCarthy, 1993).

Concerns about body image and appearance should be addressed with women who experience mastectomies, including the trauma of having a vital body part surgically removed. They should receive information about the options available for restoring external appearance. Some women elect and feel satisfied with the option of breast reconstruction (Rowland & Holland, 1984). Still, the quick fix "to look feminine" may not be a universal need among women who experience mastectomies. Concerns about health are far more important than concerns about physical attractiveness (Meyerowitz, 1981). Focusing on physical appearance, if not irrelevant, may even anger some women for whom traditional standards of attractiveness are not central to their self-image or esteem (Lorde, 1980; Meyerowitz et al., 1988). The negative aftereffects of breast reconstruction may also be overlooked. Bleeding and infection can occur, and the recurrence of cancer is harder to detect (Wilkinson & Kitzinger, 1994).

Perhaps most problematic for many women are the reactions of their primary partners to their missing breast and the effects on sexual functioning. Partners may react negatively to the outcomes of the surgery. Close to half (45 percent) of the women studied by Meyerowitz (1981) reported difficulty showing the area of their missing breast to their partners, a finding significantly associated with depression and anxiety. About half of another sample of women experienced sexual difficulties three to four months after a mastectomy (Derogatis, 1980).

Chemotherapy (Drug Therapies). No woman dies from cancer of the breast itself. What kills women is the spread of breast cancer cells to vital organs, especially the lungs, liver, and bones. If there is evidence of spread to other parts of the body, attempts are made to halt or reverse the spread of cells through chemotherapy or drug therapy such as Tamoxifen. Though these interventions increase survival generally, they do not work for all women (Apfel et al., 1994). Also, as noted earlier, there are potential harmful side effects of treatments such as Tamoxifen.

Another drug, Herceptin, shrinks the types of breast tumors that usually progress rapidly and can cause death within months. About one-third of women with breast cancer experience this type of tumor. Herceptin may provide benefits early during this disease and, when given by itself, causes no damaging side effects. This drug could soon be widely available because of the fast review status given by the FDA (McNeil, 1998; Sternberg, 1998). Another drug, Taxol, increases the survival rate in women with early breast cancer and no spread beyond the lymph nodes; it also causes no serious side effects

(Maugh, 1998). Taxol already has approval by the FDA to prevent osteoporosis and for use in treating ovarian cancer.

New Treatments. The standard treatments for most women with breast cancer are surgery, radiation, and chemotherapy (American Cancer Society, 1999). Studies are, however, looking at new treatments for use in special cases of breast cancer, such as high-dose chemotherapy combined with bone marrow transplant or stem cell rescue. Bone marrow transplants have recently lost support because of studies that show that this intervention offers no improvement over traditional chemotherapy. Survival rates for this procedure are lower than with traditional drug and radiation treatments ("Bone marrow transplants," 2001; "Bone marrow transplants and breast," 2000). The largest health insurer, Aetna, dropped most coverage of bone marrow transplants for women with breast cancer in February 2000.

LUNG CANCER

Although breast cancer was the major cause of death from cancer in women for over 40 years, lung cancer is now the leading cause of cancer death in women; breast cancer is the second major cause. The incidence rate for lung cancer in women (74,600) in 1998 was lower than for breast cancer (182,800) and was beginning to ease off, but the mortality estimates for lung cancer (67,600) were higher than for breast cancer (40,800). More women who died from cancer died from lung cancer than from breast cancer beginning in 1987, and the rates have continued to increase (American Cancer Society, 1998, 1999, 2000). In contrast to breast cancer, there are no screening guidelines for early detection of lung cancer. Yet, largely due to improvements in surgical techniques, the one-year relative survival rates increased from 34 percent in 1975 to 41 percent in 1995. The five-year relative survival rate is 49 percent for localized cancer, but only 15 percent of lung cancers are at that early stage (American Cancer Society, 1996, 1998, 2000). When signs are noticeable, lung cancer is typically already in an advanced stage (American Cancer Society, 1991).

Some of the risk factors for lung cancer include exposure to certain industrial substances such as arsenic; radon and asbestos (especially for persons who smoke); certain organic chemicals; radiation exposure; air pollution; tuberculosis; and environmental tobacco smoke (American Cancer Society, 2000). The tragedy of lung cancer is that its main cause is known and is under one's control: smoking. Smoking by women was unacceptable before the 1920s but later when this changed, women began to smoke and die of lung cancer (Dumas, 1992). Increasing numbers of women began to smoke during World War II. These numbers peaked in 1965 at 34 percent and later decreased to about 25 percent in the early 1990s (Ingram Fogel, 1991).

The risk of developing lung cancer for smokers is 10 times more likely (a 900 percent increased risk) compared to nonsmokers (American Cancer Society, 1996). The risk increases with the duration and extent of smoking (Ingram Fogel, 1991). The good news is that if a woman stops smoking, precancerous, damaged lung tissue often returns to a normal condition.

The treatment for lung cancer depends on the type and stage of development when located. When localized, surgery is usually the selected treatment. Because the disease has usually spread upon discovery, however, treatment usually includes a combination of surgery, chemotherapy, and radiation therapy. In cases of small cell lung cancer, chemotherapy alone, or combined with radiation, is now the selected treatment over surgery. Women with this type of lung cancer have a good chance of going into a period of remission that sometimes lasts a long time (American Cancer Society, 1999).

Lesbian Health Issues

Lesbians are not identified in most samples related to midlife women's health, nor does any federal research target their health issues (Rosser, 1993). The little that is known about this group of women is presented here along with the difficulties they experience in the traditional health care system.

Cancer

Although yearly rates of breast cancer and other cancers have not been established for lesbians, these women fall into some of the high-risk categories (Biddle, 1993; White & Levinson, 1995). For example, they are less likely than heterosexual women to have children. There is also some evidence of high levels of alcohol use and smoking in this population (Buenting, 1992; McKirnan & Peterson, 1989).

One estimate related to breast cancer is that one in three lesbians may develop this disease during their lifetimes (Haynes, 1992). Risk for cervical cancer, however, is probably lower for lesbians than for heterosexual and bisexual women (for example, Johnson, Smith, & Guenther, 1987; Robertson & Schachter, 1981). It is speculated that other diseases transmitted through heterosexual intercourse increase the risk of cervical cancer: herpes, trichomoniasis, chlamydia, and the human papilloma virus. Cervical cancer does not develop in celibate women and it is rare in lesbians who engage in little or no heterosexual intercourse when there are no other risk factors (Rosser, 1993). Lesbians are at risk for cervical cancer if they experienced multiple sexual partners (past or present, male or female), early age of first intercourse, a history of sexually transmitted diseases, and a history of smoking (Rankow & Tessaro, 1998a).

Health Care

Studies of the professional health care sought by lesbians show mixed findings. Some reports found that lesbians do not obtain cervical screenings as often as heterosexual women (for example, Biddle, 1993; Bybee, 1991), receive fewer mammograms and clinical breast exams, and are less likely to perform regular breast self-exams (for example, Haynes, 1992; O'Hanlan, 1993). Yet, other studies reported no lower levels of mammography screening among lesbians compared to the levels of heterosexual women (Rankow & Tessaro, 1998b). Rates of mammograms for lesbians over age 50 are as high as the rates for the general population of women, though rates of monthly breast exams are much lower than national averages (Roberts & Sorensen, 1995). System factors such as geographic access and ease of scheduling facilitate mammography screenings for lesbians as well as women generally (Karon et al., 1999).

Cancer activism is an integral part of lesbian communities. The high rates of breast cancer in these communities led to the development of lesbian health programs (Brownworth, 1993) in cities such as Berkeley and Washington, DC (Bricker-Jenkins, 1994). Some projects focus only on lesbian cancer issues, such as the Chicago Lesbian Cancer Project and the Women's Cancer Resource Center in Oakland, California (Denenberg, 1992). These kinds of centers also help to counter the problematic and anxiety-provoking experiences of most lesbians in traditional health care settings if they disclose their sexual orientation.

Lesbians want what all women want: nonjudgmental, sensitive health care (Roberts & Sorensen, 1995). Yet, women frequently experience abusive treatment in health care interactions (Stevens, 1994b; Stevens & Hall, 1990) and lesbians often experience health care providers as hostile and rejecting. These providers tend to hold prejudiced views of lesbians (for example, disgust, revulsion), experience discomfort about treating them, are condemnatory in their views of them (for example, sick, dangerous, and self-destructive), and are uninformed about them (Rosser, 1993; Stevens, 1992). As summarized by Stevens (1994a), when lesbians disclose their sexual orientation in health care settings, they are likely to encounter some of the following reactions: "embarrassment, fear, ostracism, refusal to treat, cool detachment, shock, voyeuristic curiosity, pity, demeaning jokes, avoidance of physical contact, insults, rejection of lesbian partners and friends, invasions of privacy, rough physical handling, and breaches of confidentiality" (p. 640). Many other studies confirmed these kinds of responses to lesbians in health care settings (for example, Stevens & Hall, 1988, 1990).

From a study of lesbians of various ethnic and racial groups, Stevens (1998) reported that negative reactions to them by health care providers were not always overt. Some were subtle such as facial expressions and gestures that signaled disapproval and discomfort. The health care experiences of these women were often frightening and traumatizing, often resulting in "deeply personal, privatized wounds" (p. 91). Stevens (1994a) included in her work on lesbians and health care the experiences of lesbians not only from a variety of ethnic and racial backgrounds but also from diverse economic circumstances. In addition, she studied their experiences across the full spectrum of health settings and providers. The findings were even more distressing than those in earlier studies. More than three-quarters of the sample (77 percent) evaluated their interactions in health settings negatively. Adverse interactions far outweighed positive ones across all types of health concerns, facilities, and providers. Exceptions included feminist women's health clinics and female physicians.

Because of the negative interactions lesbians experience in traditional health care settings, many of them refuse to use these settings. A little under half (44 percent) of women studied by Stevens (1994a) stopped seeking health care. It was usual for many of these women to go as long as seven, 10, and 18 years without seeing a health care provider. Many of them were ill with chronic conditions such as diabetes and cancer, and recognized the consequences of not obtaining preventive services or early detection of disease. But, the health care system drove them away by subjecting them to being "accused, censured, devalued, silenced, or subordinated . . . stereotyped, denied their dignity, transgressed upon, or assaulted" (Stevens, 1994a, p. 655).

COMING OF AGE OF WOMEN'S HEALTH CONCERNS

Years of exclusive focus on men's health left women disadvantaged regarding the development of effective preventive strategies, diagnostic tools, and interventions (Sherman, 1993). Since the mid-to-late 1980s, however, when the American Heart Association and NIH identified the high prevalence of CHD in women, interest in women's health has escalated. Increased attention is now focused on the cardiovascular health of women. For example, under federal mandate, research in this area cannot, without good cause, exclude women and racial and ethnic women and men (Marshall, 1994). Both federal and nonfederal research-funding initiatives are now directed at women's life experiences, such as the transition to menopause and related coronary and vascular outcomes. An additional effort is directed at the suspected bias in diagnosis and treatment of women (Holm & Penckofer, 1995). Yet, in the year 2000, it was reported that although NIH required inclusion of women in studies, it was not enforcing the requirement to examine whether men and women respond differently to a given treatment (Pear, 2000). Also, in a review of 593 studies published between 1966 and March 2000, Lee, Alexander, Hammill, Pasquali, and Peterson (2001) found few gains in female and elderly representation in heart-related studies.

Based on the epidemic incidence and prevalence rates of breast cancer, and stimulated by the women's movement and HIV/AIDS activism, the issues of breast cancer became politicized (Marshall, 1993). Recent pressure from women's groups, such as the Women's Health Initiative, spurred researchers to focus on causative agents of breast cancer (Cotton, 1992). The National Breast Cancer Coalition, combining both grass-roots action and pressure on Congress by medical experts, was also credited with changing the focus of national cancer research to include breast cancer and doubling the allocation of funds for breast cancer research in 1992 (Marshall, 1993).

Besides these changes in the CHD and breast cancer arenas, over the past 10 years women's health moved to the forefront of attention through efforts of the National Institutes of Health, the U.S. Public Health Service Task Force on Women's Health Issues, the formation of the Office of Research on Women's Health, and the development of the NIH Women's Health Research Agenda. The NIH Task Force on Opportunities for Research on Women's Health began in 1991 to assess the status of women's health research (Woods, 1995). Studies collectively known as the Women's Health Initiatives represent the largest and most ambitious assessment of women's health ever conducted. These studies are pursuing the goal of under-standing the determinants of postmenopausal women's health throughout the world. In addition, these studies are evaluating the effectiveness of interventions to prevent the major causes of morbidity and mortality in midlife and older women (Matthews et al., 1997).

Another significant reason for optimizing women's health is to help counter depression. Poor physical health, as well as prior depression, significantly affected current depression levels in Carr's (1997) study of midlife women. Several longitudinal studies also supported an association between health status and depression (Kaufert, Gilbert, & Tate, 1992; J. B. McKinlay & McKinlay, 1987). In one of these studies, women who rated their health as poor were 17 times more likely to report depression than those who rated their health as good. Certain illnesses were more associated with depression (arthritis, high blood pressure) than others (allergies, thyroid difficulties; see Kaufert et al., 1992). Woods and Mitchell (1996) identified a pattern of midlife depression in which women scored above the depressed mood range during the first year of the study but scored below this range in the second year of the study. This pattern, which they called "resolving depressed mood" (RDM), characterized women who experienced poorer health status than women who did not develop depression. These women also experienced higher stress and had fewer family resources. Woods and Mitchell concluded that the RDM women could benefit from services that promote general health, increase social resources, and help them manage stress.

HEALTH INSURANCE CONCERNS

Although women's health care may be improving, and with more health care outlets appropriate for women, more needs to be done for women who cannot afford health care or are poorly covered or uninsured. In a recent report on health insurance issues for women published by the Commonwealth Fund, a nonprofit health research group based in New York, the number of uninsured women was projected to increase (Lambrew, 2001). Lambrew reported that over the last five years, the number of uninsured women has grown three times faster than the number of uninsured men. If this trend continues, the number of uninsured women will exceed the number of uninsured men by 2005. Currently there are 15 million uninsured women in the United States.

Many women in low-paying jobs cannot access health care because their jobs do not provide medical benefits or, if they do, the benefits require large deductibles. Insurance policies that prohibit payment for treatment of preexisting conditions are also discriminatory against women with chronic illnesses (Chrisler, 2001). Women are more likely than men to have chronic illnesses and more likely to make regular use of prescription drugs. For example, among women ages 50–70, 81 percent rely on prescription drugs compared with 71 percent of men in that age group (Lambrew, 2001). Older cohorts of women are projected to have less coverage for prescription drugs and dental care, which will increase their out-of-pocket expenses. The most important determinant of dental or prescription drug coverage is having employer-based insurance (Lillard, Rogowski, & Kington, 1997).

Poverty is associated with the worst outcomes in chronic illnesses (Chrisler, 2001). Exclusion of chronic illness from insurance coverage is an obstacle to women changing jobs. Some insurance benefits are also restricted to legal dependents, which exclude families of lesbian, gay, or cohabiting unmarried heterosexual employees. Ethnic and racial women, who are overrepresented in jobs with low wages and high risks of injuries (such as hairdressers or laundry workers exposed to certain chemicals or factory workers whose jobs involve highly repetitive movements), might not be eligible for medical treatment or disability status. Their injuries often develop over time rather than happening on an exact date, which often must be identified according to the criteria for coverage in worker compensation policies. Health care services are also scarce in rural areas and inner cities. Poor women may not have a car or money for transportation to the services that are available, or they may have conflicts arranging their work schedules to fit in with the services' schedules (Chrisler, 2001; Fitzpatrick & Gomez, 1997).

Access to health care is largely tied to health insurance; health insurance is largely tied to employment and marital status. This is a structural aspect of the U.S. health care system, which shapes how or if women are insured.

Women who are not employed, or those whose jobs provide partial or no insurance, can be insured through a marital partner or family member's job. White women are twice as likely as African American women to be married and have insurance coverage through their partner's job. Midlife and older women are more likely to be insured as wives than as employees, but they are vulnerable to losing coverage if they become divorced or widowed or if the insured family member loses a job. If unmarried women who work take time off or reduce their work hours to care for children or older relatives, they might also lose their insurance (Meyer & Pavalko, 1996). Even more advantaged women who are divorced can end up with limited means for purchasing insurance policies, in part because of their having to accept low-paying jobs (Chrisler, 2001). In the absence of employer-provided insurance, personal wealth becomes the most important factor in the purchase of private insurance (Lillard et al., 1997).

African American women are three times as likely to be uninsured and two times as likely to receive public insurance such as Medicaid (Meyer & Pavalko, 1996). This federal welfare program established in 1965 to provide medical care for the poor and near poor is applied differently from state to state because of variations in formulas for determining eligibility (Chrisler, 2001). Medicaid coverage is further limited due to cuts in the federal budget and increased eligibility standards (Fitzpatrick & Gomez, 1997). This results in many people this program is supposed to help not being covered or receiving only fragmentary care (Chrisler, 2001). Poor midlife women may particularly be affected by the age qualifications for Medicare, the other federal health care program; they not only cannot afford private health insurance but also are too young to qualify for Medicare (Butler & Weatherley, 1992). Even for women who qualify for Medicare, similar to many private insurance policies, this program provides better coverage for conditions more often affecting men than women (Chrisler, 2001).

In the report sponsored by the Commonwealth Fund, Lambrew (2001) concluded that the most promising approach to increasing access to health insurance for women is to build on insurance options that currently exist, such as employer-sponsored insurance, the Children's Health Insurance Program, and Medicaid. These options represent the most targeted and potentially effective approaches for increasing access to affordable coverage for women. Others, however, believe that women will remain disadvantaged in their access to health care as long as health insurance and health care are tied to the labor market. To change this situation either employment-based insurance must be affordable or a national system of guaranteed coverage established (Peterson & Schmidt-Tieszen, 1997). The most stable source of health insurance coverage can only be guaranteed through a universal system that has no link to marital or job status (Meyer & Pavalko, 1996; Peterson & Schmidt-Tieszen, 1997).

On the basis of reported findings in the foregoing discussion, it is evident that midlife and older women are an oppressed group in terms of health care.

They are disempowered legally, politically, and as consumers of health care, despite the fact that they are the primary consumers of health care (Waysdorf, 1995–1996). To improve health care for women, women's access to health care must attain the same status as other civil rights and universal public rights (Waysdorf, 1995–1996).

SUMMARY

- Although midlife women perceive themselves to be in good health, they become increasingly concerned about their health.

- Life-threatening health risks that heighten with age include heart disease and cancer, especially lung and breast cancer.

- Coronary heart disease is the major cause of death of midlife women.

- Breast cancer was the major cause of death from cancer for a long time, but lung cancer is now the foremost cause of cancer death in women.

- Women may encounter sexism, such as inappropriate or insufficient treatments, when they are in need of health care. Lesbians often experience, in addition, overt hostility by health care providers.

- Prior samples in studies of heart disease contained only men but over the past 12 years women's health has moved to the forefront of the national health agenda.

- The interaction of multiple factors must be addressed for a comprehensive assessment of life-threatening diseases, including sex–gender factors, economics, race, ethnicity, sexual orientation, and physical environment.

- Access to health insurance is tied to employment and marriage. This structural feature of the U.S. health system makes many midlife and older women vulnerable to having no health insurance. To change this situation either employment-based insurance must be affordable or a national system of guaranteed coverage established.

IMPLICATIONS FOR PRACTICE

Professional helpers and social policy makers need to be familiar with the multiple factors involved in life-threatening health risks for midlife women, especially heart disease and cancer. Preventive interventions such as promoting regular mammograms, breast clinical and self-examinations, and the cessation of cigarette smoking are important. Community and clinical practitioners can advocate for changes in insurance to ensure prescription drug equity and to cover services such as mammograms and contraception, and in hospital and clinic policies and procedures that are sexist, biased against lesbians, or that withhold treatments from women who need them. Hospital and agency practitioners, as well as citizen boards and professional advisory committees, can work to promote equal and appropriate health care for women, including abolishment of sexist and heterosexist policies and unsuitable practices.

Practitioners can also help women deal with emotional reactions to being diagnosed with or being treated for a life-threatening illness, as well as suggest ways to increase their ability to cope. Feminist practice principles are desirable when working with women with breast cancer, with an emphasis on strengths as well as needs. The role of the practitioner is to work in partnership with these women, with the goal that the women discover their own road to healing because they are the experts on their own lives (Bricker-Jenkins, 1994). A peer group of women who experienced breast cancer is also essential. Besides the solidarity and skills developed in groups of women with breast cancer, peer support groups are useful at critical times. For example, these groups can provide information and skills for taking charge of one's situation prior to biopsy and, later, for identification of helpers in one's own community (Bricker-Jenkins, 1994). Publications are available that list diverse resources for women with breast cancer (for example, Brady, 1991; Kahane, 1990).

Some women may also benefit from anxiety-reducing interventions, such as relaxation exercises and desensitization to anxiety-provoking situations. Cognitive interventions may help in reducing persistent negative thoughts about their situations. For example, one negative thought might be that one's partner may no longer find a woman attractive after a mastectomy. Marital counseling can help enlist a partner's support in a way that is meaningful, such as reducing the woman's fears that she is now unattractive to her partner.

Bricker-Jenkins (1994) urged social workers to consider a woman with breast cancer as embedded within "person-in-environment" or ecological contexts and as affected by factors such as environmental pollution and socioeconomic oppression. Social workers can be allies of women struggling with cancer by using the full bio-psycho-social lens to examine their situations.

Social workers and other health care professionals can advocate for services for midlife and older women who are disadvantaged in their access to health care. They can help sponsor and lobby for needed structural changes in health insurance and health care, such as a national or universal system of affordable, guaranteed coverage that will reduce or eliminate the inequities linked to marital or job status.

VIGNETTE

Vicky is a 48-year-old day care worker with no children. Her husband of 25 years, Steve, works for the telephone company. Last year Vicky was diagnosed with breast cancer that resulted in the surgical removal of the affected breast and radiation treatment. She is taking Tamoxifen and is contemplating a mastectomy of the other breast as a preventive measure, though there was localization of the cancer. Although Vicky is physically able to work part time, she often does not want to leave the house. She reports chronic anxiety and depression. Most unsettling for her are persistently negative thoughts about herself and her life. One of Vicky's most persistent negative thoughts is that Steve will no longer find her attractive now that she appears "disfigured."

Questions:

- *Why is it important for a practitioner to encourage Vicky to become part of a support group for women diagnosed with breast cancer?*

- *What could a practitioner tell Vicky's husband in order for him to be more proactive in reducing his wife's anxiety about his view of her?*

REFERENCES

2 doctors assail mammogram studies, question benefits. (2001, December 9). *Dallas Morning News*, p. A4.

Adelmann, P.K., Antonucci, T.C., Crohan, S.E., & Coleman, L.M. (1990). A causal analysis of employment and health in midlife women. *Women & Health, 16*, 5-20.

American Cancer Society. (1991). *Cancer facts and figures, 1991*. Atlanta, GA.

American Cancer Society. (1993). *Cancer facts and figures, 1993*. Atlanta, GA.

American Cancer Society. (1994). *Cancer facts and figures. 1994*. Atlanta, GA.

American Cancer Society. (1996). *Cancer facts and figures, 1996*. Atlanta, GA.

American Cancer Society. (1998). *Cancer facts and figures, 1998*. Atlanta, GA.

American Cancer Society. (1999). *Cancer facts and figures, 1999*. Atlanta, GA.

American Cancer Society. (2000). *Cancer facts and figures, 2000*. Atlanta, GA.

American Cancer Society. (2001). *Cancer facts and figures, 2002*. Atlanta, GA.

American Heart Association. (1989). *Silent epidemic: The truth about women and heart disease*. Dallas, TX.

American Heart Association. (1992). *Silent epidemic: The truth about women and heart disease*. Dallas, TX.

American Heart Association. (1993). *Heart and stroke fact statistics*. Dallas, TX.

American Heart Association. (1995). *Heart and stroke facts: 1996 statistical supplement*. Dallas, TX.

American Heart Association. (1997). *1998 Heart and stroke statistical update.* Dallas, TX.

American Heart Association. (1998). *1999 Heart and stroke statistical update.* Dallas, TX.

American Heart Association. (1999). *2000 Heart and stroke statistical update.* Dallas, TX.

American Heart Association. (2001). *2001 Heart and stroke statistical update.* Dallas, TX.

Amsterdam, E. A., & Legato, M. J. (1993). What's unique about CHD in women? *Patient Care, 27,* 21–61.

Apfel, R. J., Love, S. M., & Kalinowski, B. H. (1994). Keep abreast: Women and breast cancer. In M. P. Mirkin (Ed.), *Women in context: Toward a feminist reconstruction of psychotherapy* (pp. 218–236). New York: Guilford Press.

Ault, A., & Bradbury, J. (1998). Experts argue about Tamoxifen prevention trial. *Lancet, 351,* 1107.

Ayanian, J. Z., & Epstein, A. M. (1991). Differences in the use of procedures between women and men hospitalized for coronary heart disease. *New England Journal of Medicine, 325,* 221–225.

Baines, C., To, T., & Wall, C. (1986). Women's attitudes to screening after participation in a national breast screening study. *Cancer, 65,* 1663–1669.

Bayer, L., Whissell-Buechy, D., & Honzik, M. (1980). Adolescent health and personality: Significance in adult health. *Journal of Adolescent Health Care, 1,* 101–107.

Biddle, B. S. (1993). *Health status indicators for Washington area lesbians and bisexual women: A report on the Lesbian Health Clinic's first year.* Washington, DC: Whitman Walker Clinic.

Bloom, J. R. (1987). Psychological response to mastectomy. *Cancer, 59,* 189–196.

Bone marrow transplants. (2001). [On-line]. Available: http://breastcancer.about.com/health/breastcancer/library/weekly/aa031300.htm.

Bone marrow transplants and breast cancer. (2000). [On-line]. Available: http://onhealth.webmd.com/women/in-depth/item,88631 1 1.asp.

Boring, C., Squires, T. S., & Tong, T. (1992). *Cancer statistics, 1992.* Atlanta: American Cancer Society.

Brady, J. (Ed.). (1991). *One in three: Women with cancer confront an epidemic.* Pittsburgh: Cleis.

Breast Cancer Fact Sheet. Massachusetts Breast Cancer Coalition. Newton Highlands, MA: 1992.

Breast imaging: Today and tomorrow. (1995, January). *Harvard Women's Health Watch,* p. 2.

Breen, N., & Kessler, L. (1994). Changes in the use of screening mammography: Evidence from the 1987 and 1990 National Health Interview Surveys. *American Journal of Public Health, 84,* 62–67.

Bricker-Jenkins, M. (1994). Feminist practice and breast cancer: "The patriarchy has claimed my right breast . . . ." *Social Work in Health Care, 19,* 17–42.

Brown, D. (1999, July 22). Heart attacks more likely to be fatal for women than men before age 50. *Dallas Morning News,* p. A9.

Brownworth, V. A. (1993, March). The other epidemic: Lesbians and breast cancer. *Out,* pp. 60–63.

Buenting, J. A. (1992). Health life-styles of lesbian and heterosexual women. *Health Care for Women International, 13,* 165–173.

Burkman, R. T. (1988). Obesity, stress, and smoking: Their role as cardiovascular risk factors in women. *American Journal of Obstetrics and Gynecology, 158,* 1592–1597.

Butler, S. S., & Weatherley, R. A. (1992). Women at midlife and categories of neglect. *Social Work, 37,* 510–515.

Bybee, D. (1991). *Michigan lesbian health survey.* Lansing: Michigan Organization for Human Rights.

Cancer Committee, College of American Pathologists. (1986). Is fibrocystic disease of the breast precancerous? *Archives of Pathologist Laboratory Medicine, 110,* 171.

Carr, D. (1997). The fulfillment of career dreams at midlife: Does it matter for women's mental health? *Journal of Health and Social Behavior, 38,* 331–344.

Chrisler, J. C. (2001). Gendered bodies and physical health. In R. K. Unger (Ed.), *Handbook of the psychology of woman and gender* (pp. 289–302). New York: John Wiley & Sons.

Clarke, D. E., & Sandler, L. S. (1989). Factors involved in nurses teaching breast self-examination. *Cancer Nursing, 12,* 41–46.

Cotton, P. (1992). Women's health initiative leads the way as research begins to fill gender gaps. *Journal of the American Medical Association, 267,* 469–470, 473.

Council on Ethical and Judicial Affairs. (1991). Gender disparities in clinical decision making. *Journal of the American Medical Association, 266,* 599.

Dahmoush, L., Pike, M., & Press, M. F. (1994). Hormones and breast-cell proliferation. In R. A. Lobo (Ed.), *Treatment of the postmenopausal woman: Basic and clinical aspects* (pp. 325–337). New York: Raven Press.

Davis, D. L., & Love, S. M. (1994). Mammographic screening. *Journal of the American Medical Association, 271,* 152–153.

Davis, R. (1998a, April 6). Cancer breakthrough comes with big risk. *USA Today,* p. A1.

Davis, R. (1998b, April 7). A cancer drug with promise, and problems. *USA Today,* p. D6.

Denenberg, R. (1992). Invisible women: Lesbians and health care. *Health/PAC Bulletin, 22,* 14–21.

Derogatis, L. R. (1980). Breast and gynecologic cancers: Their unique impact on body image and sexual identity in women. *Frontiers of Radiation Therapy and Oncology, 14,* 1–11.

Dumas, L. (1992). Lung cancer in women: Rising epidemic, preventable disease. *Nursing Clinics of North America, 27,* 859–869.

Ellerhorst-Ryan, J. M., & Goeldner, J. (1992). Breast cancer. *Nursing Clinics of North America, 27,* 821–833.

Fitzpatrick, J. A., & Gomez, T. R. (1997). Still caught in a trap: The continued povertization of women. *Affilia, 12,* 318–341.

Forsen, A. (1991). Psychosocial stress as a risk for breast cancer. *Psychotherapy and Psychosomatics, 55,* 176–185.

Garg, R., Wagener, D. K., & Madans, J. H. (1993). Alcohol consumption and risk of ischemic heart disease in women. *Archives of Internal Medicine, 153,* 1211–1216.

Goetinck, S., & Camia, C. (1998, April 7). Risks come with breast cancer drug. *Dallas Morning News,* p. A1.

Haney, D. Q. (2000, March 14). Study questions estrogen benefits. *Dallas Morning News,* pp. A1, A11.

Haynes, S. G. (1992, July). *Are lesbians at high risk of breast cancer?* Paper presented at the meeting of the 14th National Lesbian and Gay Health Foundation Conference, Los Angeles.

Hayward, R. A., Shapiro, M. F., Freeman, H. E., & Corey, C. R. (1988). Who gets screened for cervical and breast cancer? *Archives of Internal Medicine, 148,* 1177–1181.

Healy, B. (1991). The Yentl syndrome. *New England Journal of Medicine, 325,* 274–275.

Healy, B. P. (1998). Tamoxifen and the breast cancer prevention trial: Women helping women. *Journal of Women's Health, 7,* 279–280.

Hofer, M. (1992). Lifesaving facts about female cancers. *Special Report Home Library, 1,* 3–14.

Holm, K., & Penckofer, S. (1995). Women's cardiovascular health. In B. J. McElmurry & R. S. Parker (Eds.), *Annual review of women's health* (Vol. 2, pp. 187–203). New York: National League for Nursing Press.

Hooker, K., & Kaus, C. R. (1994). Health-related possible selves in young and middle adulthood. *Psychology and Aging*, *9*, 126–133.

Horton, J. A. (1995). *The women's health data book: A profile of women's health in the United States* (2nd ed.). Washington, DC: Jacobs Institute of Women's Health.

Hu, F. B., Stampfer, J. J., Manson, J. E., Grodstein, F., Colditz, G. A., Speizer, F. E., & Willett, W. C. (2000). Trends in the incidence of coronary heart disease and changes in diet and lifestyle in women. *New England Journal of Medicine*, *343*, 530–537.

Huguley, G. M., Brown, R. L., Greenberg, R. S., & Clark, W. S. (1988). Breast self-examination and survival from breast cancer. *Cancer*, *62*, 1389–1396.

Ingram Fogel, C. (1991). Nutrition and health patterns in midlife women. *NAACOG's Clinical Issues in Prenatal and Women's Health Nursing*, *2*, 509–525.

Jacobson, J. M. (1995). *Midlife women: Contemporary issues*. Boston: Jones and Bartlett.

Johnson, S. R., Smith, E. R., & Guenther, S. M. (1987). Comparison of gynecologic health care problems between lesbian and bisexual women. *Journal of Reproductive Medicine*, *32*, 805–811.

Kahane, D. H. (1990). *No less a woman: Ten women shatter the myths about breast cancer*. New York: Prentice Hall.

Karasek, R. A., Baker, D., Marxer, F., Ahlbom, A., & Theorell, T. (1981). Job decision latitude, job demands and cardiovascular disease. *American Journal of Public Health*, *71*, 694–705.

Karon, S. L., Egan, J., Jacobson, M., Nugent, J., Settersten, L., & Shaw, V. (1999). Understanding lesbians' mammography utilization. *Women's Health Issues*, *9*, 264–274.

Kaufert, P. A., Gilbert, P., & Tate, R. (1992). The Manitoba Project: A re-examination of the link between menopause and depression. *Maturitas*, *14*, 143–155.

Kawachi, I., Colditz, G. A., Stampfer, M. J., Willett, W. C., Manson, J. E., Rosner, B., Speizer, F. E., & Hennekens, C. H. (1994). Smoking cessation and time course of decreased risks of coronary heart disease in middle-aged women. *Archives of Internal Medicine*, *154*, 169–175.

Kelsey, J. L., & Hildreth, L. G. (1981). *Breast and gynecologic cancer epidemiology*. Boca Raton, FL: CRC.

Kessel, B. (1998). Alternatives to estrogen for menopausal women. *Society for Experimental Biology and Medicine*, *217*, 38–44.

King, M., Rowell, S., & Love, S. M. (1993). Inherited breast and ovarian cancer. *Journal of the American Medical Association*, *269*, 1975–1980.

Kritz-Silverstein, D., Wingard, D. L., & Barrett-Connor, E. (1992). Employment status and heart disease risk factors in middle-aged women: The Rancho Bernardo study. *American Journal of Public Health*, *82*, 215–219.

Lambrew, J. M. (2001, August). *Diagnosing disparities in health insurance for women: A prescription for change* [On-line]. Available: http://www.commonwealthfund.org/programs/insurance/lambrew_women_493.pdf.

Lee, P. Y., Alexander, K. P., Hammill, B. G., Pasquali, S. K., & Peterson, E. D. (2001). Representation of elderly persons and women in published randomized trials of acute coronary syndromes. *Journal of the American Medical Association*, *286*, 708–713.

Levy, S. (1998). FDA committee recommends cancer drugs. *Drug Topics*, *142*, 22, 24.

Lillard, L., Rogowski, J., & Kington, R. (1997). Long-term determinants of patterns of health insurance coverage in the medicare population. *Gerontologist*, *37*, 314–323.

Lindsey, A. M., Dodd, M., & Kaempfer, S. H. (1987). Endocrine mechanisms and obesity: Influences in breast cancer. *Oncology Nursing Forum*, *14*, 47–51.

Lorde, A. (1980). *The cancer journals*. Argle, NY: Spinsters, Ink.

Manson, J. E., Colditz, G. A., Stampfer, M. J., Willett, W. C., Rosner, B., Monson, R. R., Speizer, F. E., & Hennekens, C. H. (1990). A prospective study of obesity and risk of coronary heart disease in women. *New England Journal of Medicine, 322*, 882–889.

Marshall, E. (1993). The politics of breast cancer. *Science, 259*, 616–621.

Marshall, E. (1994). New law brings affirmative action to clinical research. *Science, 263*, 602.

Matthews, K. A., Kuller, L. H., Wing. R. R., & Jansen-McWilliams, L. (1997, August). *Premenopausal characteristics of long term users of postmenopausal estrogen replacement therapy.* Paper presented at the annual meeting of the American Psychological Association, Chicago.

Maugh, T. H. (1998, May 19). Osteoporosis drug reduces breast cancer risk, researchers say. *Dallas Morning News*, p. A12.

McCarthy, K. (1993, July). Research on women's health doesn't show whole picture. *APA Monitor, 24*, 14–15.

McKinlay, J. B., & McKinlay, S. M. (1987). Depression in middle-aged women: Social circumstances versus estrogen deficiency. In R. Walsh (Ed.), *The psychology of women* (pp. 157–161). New Haven, CT: Yale University Press.

McKinlay, S.M., & McKinlay, J.B. (1989). The impact of menopause and social factors on health. In C. Hammond, F. Hazeltine, & I. Schiff (Eds.), *Menopause: Evaluation, treatment and health concerns* (pp. 137-161). New York: Alan Liss.

McKirnan, D. J., & Peterson, P. L. (1989). Alcohol and drug use among homosexual men and women: Epidemiology and population characteristics. *Addictive Behaviors, 14*, 545–553.

McNeil, C. (1998). Herceptin raises its sights beyond advanced breast cancer. *Journal of the National Cancer Institute, 90*, 882–883.

Meisler, J. G. (1998). Toward optimal health: The experts discuss Tamoxifen and breast cancer prevention. *Journal of Women's Health, 7*, 513–517.

Meyer, M. H., & Pavalko, E. K. (1996). Family, work, and access to health insurance among mature women. *Journal of Health and Social Behavior, 37*, 311–325.

Meyerowitz, B. E. (1980). Psychosocial correlates of breast cancer and its treatments. *Psychological Bulletin, 87*, 108–131.

Meyerowitz, B. E. (1981, August). *Postmastectomy physical concerns of breast cancer patients.* Paper presented at the meeting of the American Psychological Association, Los Angeles.

Meyerowitz, B. E., Chaiken, S., & Clark, L. K. (1988). Sex roles and culture: Social and personal reactions to breast cancer. In M. Fine & A. Asch (Eds.), *Women with disabilities: Essays in psychology, culture, and politics* (pp. 72–89). Philadelphia: Temple University Press.

Morabia, A., & Wynder, E. L. (1990). Epidemiology and natural history of breast cancer. *Surgical Clinics of North America, 70*, 739.

More doubts raised about mammograms. (2001, January 24). *Dallas Morning News*, p. A4.

Nachtigall, L. E., & Nachtigall, L. B. (1990). Protecting older women from their growing risk of cardiac disease. *Geriatrics, 45*, 24–34.

National Breast Cancer Coalition. (1993). *Breast cancer statistics, 1993.* Washington, DC.

National Cancer Institute. (1990). *Cancer statistics review (1973–1987).* Bethesda, MD.

National Center for Health Statistics. (1990). Advance report of final fatality statistics, 1988. In *Monthly vital statistics report.* Hyattville, MD: U.S. Public Health Service.

O'Hanlan, K. A. (1993). *Lesbians in health research: Presentation to the health, scientific meeting: Recruitment and retention of women in clinical studies* (Report No. 95-3756). Washington, DC: U.S. Department of Health and Human Services.

Olson, A., & Labat, J. (1995). Women, diet, and heart disease. In B. J. McElmurry & R. S. Parker (Eds.), *Annual review of women's health* (Vol. 2, pp. 71–92). New York: National League for Nursing Press.

Ornish, D., Brown, S. E., Scherwitz, L. W., Billings, J. H., Armstrong, W. T., Ports, T. A., McLanahan, S. M., Kirkeeide, R. L., Brand, R. J., & Gould, K. L. (1990). Can lifestyle changes reverse coronary heart disease? *Lancet, 336,* 129–133.

Osteen, R. T., Connolly, J. L, Costanza, M. E., Harris, J. R., Henderson, I. C., & McKenney, S. (1990). *Cancer of the breast—Cancer manual.* Boston: American Cancer Society.

Ott, P. J., & Levy, S. M. (1994). Cancer in women. In V. J. Adesso, D. M. Reddy, & R. Fleming (Eds.), *Psychological perspectives on women's health* (pp. 83–98). Bristol, PA: Taylor & Francis.

Panel won't endorse early mammograms. (1997, January 24). *Dallas Morning News,* p. A23.

Papalia, D. E., Camp, C. J., & Feldman, R. D. (1996). *Adult development and aging.* New York: McGraw-Hill.

Pear, R. (2000, May 7). Research on women's health lacking despite law, studies find. *Dallas Morning News,* p. A9.

Perlman, J., Wolf, P., Finucane, F., & Madans, J. (1989). Menopause and the epidemiology of cardiovascular disease in women. In C. B. Hammond, F. P. Hazeltine, & I. Schiff (Eds.), *Menopause evaluation, treatment, and health concerns* (pp. 313-332). New York: A. L. Liss.

Peterson, K. J., & Schmidt-Tieszen, A. (1997). Medicaid as a woman's issue: A conflict of values. *Affilia, 12,* 136–153.

Raloxifene shows promise in breast cancer prevention. (1998). *Consultant Pharmacist, 13,* 620.

Rankow, E. J., & Tessaro, I. (1998a). Cervical cancer risks and pananicolaou screening in a sample of lesbian and bisexual women. *Journal of Family Practice, 47,* 139–143.

Rankow, E. J., & Tessaro, I. (1998b). Mammography and risk factors for breast cancer in lesbian and bisexual women. *American Journal of Health Behavior, 22,* 403–410.

Roberts, S. J., & Sorensen, L. (1995). Lesbian health care: A review and recommendations for health promotion in primary care settings. *Nurse Practitioner, 20,* 42–47.

Robertson, P., & Schachter, J. (1981). Failure to identify venereal disease in a lesbian population. *Sexual Transmission Diseases, 8,* 875–876.

Rosser, S. V. (1993). Ignored, overlooked, or subsumed: Research on lesbian health and health care. *National Women's Studies Association Journal, 5,* 183–203.

Rowland, J. H., & Holland, J. (1984, May). *Women with cancer: Psychologic and immunologic perspectives.* Paper presented at the meeting of the Society of Behavioral Medicine, Philadelphia.

Rubin, R. (1998, September 14). Reducing the risk of breast cancer. *USA Today,* p. D1.

Rubin, R. (1999a, December 21). Do mammograms pass the test? *USA Today,* pp. D1, D2.

Rubin, R. (1999b, March 10). No link found between fat, breast cancer. *USA Today,* p. D1.

Rutledge, D. N. (1987). Factors related to women's practice of breast self-examination. *Nursing Research, 36,* 117–121.

Rutledge, D. N., Hartman, W. H., Kinman, P. O., & Winfeld, A. C. (1988). Exploration of factors affecting mammography behaviors. *Preventive Medicine, 11,* 412–422.

Schatzkin, A., Jones, D. Y, Hoover, R. N., Taylor, P. R., Brinton, L. A., Zeigler, R. G., Harvey, E. B., Carter, C. L., Licitra, L. M., Dufour, M. C., & Larson, D. B. (1987). Alcohol consumption and breast cancer in the epidemiologic follow-up study of the first national health and nutrition examination survey. *New England Journal of Medicine, 316,* 1169–1173.

Sherman, S. S. (1993). Gender, health, and responsible research. *Clinics in Geriatric Medicine, 9,* 261–269.

Siegler, I. C. (1993). Cardiac health. In R. Kastenbaum (Ed.), *Encyclopedia of adult development* (pp. 52–54). Phoenix, AZ: Oryx.

Silberfarb, P. M., Maurer, L. H., & Crouthamel, C. S. (1980). Psychosocial aspects of neo-plastic disease: I. Functional status of breast cancer patients during different treatment regimens. *American Journal of Psychiatry, 137*, 450–455.

Smart, C. R. (1990, June). The role of mammography in the prevention of mortality from breast cancer. *Cancer Prevention*, pp. 1–15.

Sobel, N. B. (1994, June). Progestins in preventive hormone therapy. *Obstetrics and Gynecology Clinics of North America, 21*, 299–319.

Stampfer, M. J., Hu, F. B, Manson, J. E., Rimm, E. B., & Willett, W. C. (2000). Primary prevention of coronary heart disease in women through diet and lifestyle. *New England Journal of Medicine, 346*, 16–22.

Sternberg, S. (1998, May 18). Drug slows division of breast tumors. *USA Today*, p. D1.

Stevens, P. E. (1992). Lesbian health care research: A review of the literature from 1970–1990. *Health Care for Women International, 13*, 91–120.

Stevens, P. E. (1994a). Lesbians' health-related experiences of care and noncare. *Western Journal of Nursing Research, 16*, 639–659.

Stevens, P. E. (1994b). Protective strategies of lesbian clients in health care environments. *Research in Nursing & Health, 17*, 217–229.

Stevens, P. E. (1998). The experiences of lesbians of color in health care encounters: Narrative insights for improving access and quality. In C. M. Ponticelli (Ed.), *Gateways to improving lesbian health and health care: Opening doors* (pp. 77–94). New York: Haworth Press.

Stevens, P. E., & Hall, J. M. (1988). Stigma, health beliefs, and experiences with health care in lesbian women. *IMAGE: Journal of Nursing Scholarship, 20*, 69–73.

Stevens, P. E., & Hall, J. M. (1990). Abusive health care interactions experienced by les-bians: A case of institutional violence in the treatment of women. *Response, 13*, 23–27.

Stolberg, S.G. (2002, February 22). Officials back mammograms for women 40 and older. *The Dallas Morning News*, p. A8.

Stuenkel, C. A. (1993, April). The truth is . . . women do die of heart disease. *Good Health Report*, p. 1.

Sullivan, R. J. (1987). Cardiovascular system. In G. L. Maddox, R. C. Atchley, L. W. Poon, R. S. Roth, I.C. Siegler, & R. M. Steinberg (Eds.), *The encyclopedia of aging* (pp. 84–89). New York: Springer.

Turner, J. S., & Helms, D. B. (1994). *Contemporary adulthood* (5th ed.). Orlando, FL: Holt, Rinehart, and Winston.

U.S. Bureau of the Census. (1991). *Statistical abstract of the United States* (111th ed.). Washington, DC: U.S. Government Printing Office.

U.S. Department of Health and Human Services. (1992). *Health, United States, 1991, and prevention profile* (DHHS Pub. No. PHS 92-1232). Washington, DC: U.S. Government Printing Office.

U.S. Select Committee on Aging. (1992). *Breast cancer: Wining the battles, losing the war* (Aging Comm. Pub. No.102-894). Washington, DC: U.S. Government Printing Office.

Verbrugge, L. (1986). Role burdens and physical health of women and men. *Women Health, 11*, 47–77.

Verbrugge, L. (1989). Gender, aging and health. In K. Markides (Ed.), *Aging and health* (pp. 23–78). Newbury Park, CA: Sage Publications.

Waysdorf, S. L. (1995–1996). Fighting for their lives: Women, poverty, and the historical role of United States law in shaping access to women's health care. *Kentucky Law Journal, 84*, 745–826.

Weidner, G. (1994). Coronary risk in women. In V. J. Adesso, D. M. Reddy, & R. Fleming (Eds.), *Psychological perspectives on women's health* (pp. 57–81). Bristol, PA: Taylor & Francis.

Whitbourne, S. K. (2001). *Adult development & aging: Biopsychosocial perspectives*. New York: John Wiley & Sons.

White, J. C., & Levinson, M. D. (1995). Lesbian health care: What a primary physician needs to know. *Western Journal of Medicine, 162*, 463–466.

Wilkinson, S., & Kitzinger, C. (1994). Towards a feminist approach to breast cancer. In S. Wilkinson & C. Kitzinger (Eds.), *Women and health: Feminist perspectives* (pp. 124–140). London: Taylor & Francis.

Willett, W. C., & Hunter, D. J. (1993). Diet and breast cancer. *Contemporary Nutrition, 18*, 1–4.

Willett, W. C., Stempfer, M. J., Colditz, G. A., Rosner, B. A., Hennekens, C. H., & Speizer, F. E. (1987). Moderate alcohol consumption and the risk of breast cancer. *New England Journal of Medicine, 313*, 1174–1180.

Williams, R. B., Barefoot, J. L., Califf, R. M., Haney, T. L., Saunders, W. B., Pryor, D. B., Hlatky, M. A., Siegler, I. C., & Mark, D. B. (1992). Prognostic importance of social and economic resources in medically treated patients: Survival in patients with angiographically documented coronary artery disease. *Journal of the American Medical Association, 267*, 520–524.

Woods, N. F. (1993). Midlife women's health: There's more to it than menopause. In B. J. McElmurry & R. S. Parker (Eds.), *Annual review of women's health* (pp. 165–196). New York: National League for Nursing Press.

Woods, N. F. (1995). Cancer research: Future agendas for women's health. *Seminars in Oncology Nursing, 11*, 143–147.

Woods, N. F., & Mitchell, E. S. (1996). Patterns of depressed mood in midlife women: Observations from the Seattle midlife women's health study. *Research in Nursing & Health, 19*, 111–123.

Young, R. F, & Kahana, E. (1994). Gender, recovery from late life heart attack, and medical care. *Women & Health, 20*, 11–31.

Zemore, R., & Shepel, L. F. (1989). Effects of breast cancer and mastectomy on emotional support and adjustment. *Social Science & Medicine, 28*, 19–27.

ADDITIONAL REFERENCES

Bradford, J., & Ryan, C. (1987). *The national lesbian health care survey*. Washington, DC: National Lesbian and Gay Health Foundation.

Hanna, E., Dufour, M. C., Elliott, S., Stinson, F., & Harford, T. C. (1992). Dying to be equal: Women, alcohol, and cardiovascular disease. *British Journal of Addiction, 87*, 1593–1597.

Lucas, V. A. (1992). An investigation of the health care preferences of the lesbian population. *Health Care for Women International, 13*, 221–228.

National Cancer Institute. (2001). *Lifetime probability of breast cancer in American women* [Online]. Available: http://www.cis.nci.gov/facy/5_6.htm.

Trippet, S. E., & Bain, J. (1990). Preliminary study of lesbian health concerns. *Health Values, 14*, 30–36.

CHAPTER 7

MENOPAUSE AND SEXUALITY

M enopause has long been a controversial topic that has been portrayed as a dreaded event for women. Research findings have challenged this negative view. Studies have examined the transition to menopause; competing views of interpretations of this event and its consequences; dilemmas of hormonal therapy; and effects of menopause on sexual interest, activity, and enjoyment. Life-span themes include social circumstances, negative myths, historical–cultural contexts, multiple influences, individual differences, normative and nonnormative events, and gains and losses.

QUESTIONS TO CONSIDER

- *How is menopause viewed from the minimalist and the biomedical perspectives?*

- *What evidence supports or refutes each perspective?*

- *What are positive results of menopause for women?*

- *What happens to the sexual responses of women over the life course?*

- *What do research studies report regarding sexual desire, activity, and enjoyment after menopause?*

- *Do midlife lesbians differ from heterosexual women in their sexual desire, activity, and enjoyment after menopause?*

Every woman experiences the biological transition of menopause either as a natural or medical–surgical event (Woods, 1993). Even so, not much longer than a dozen years ago, few women under age 45 knew much about menopause. Baby boomer women who are now in midlife, however, want information about what to anticipate and how to combat the negative effects they hear about this life transition. Most women know the basics, such as falling estrogen levels, erratic menstrual periods, and loss of ability to bear children. Beyond this, however, what are the medical consequences of estrogen loss? What physical and psychological changes can one anticipate? Is menopause a normal process or a disease? Should women take hormone replacements or not (Azar, 1994; Voda, 1992)? Women often feel confused by conflicting answers to these questions (Lemaire & Lenz, 1995).

Although research on menopause, as well as popular works on this topic, has escalated in recent decades (for example, Sheehy, 1998), there is still not much known about the normal range of experiences of menopause. Aside from various methodological issues, most of the studies are also problematic because almost all are cross-sectional, retrospective, and focused on industrialized societies. The samples are largely urban, white, middle class, and healthy. In addition, women may define menopause differently than researchers do (Kaufert, 1996; S. M. McKinlay, 1996).

Transition to Menopause

Population-based epidemiological studies on menopause use certain terms when referring to the transition to menopause. They include perimenopause, natural menopause, and surgical menopause. Another term, premenopause, refers to women, usually in the early middle years, who still experience regular menstrual periods (for example, S. M. McKinlay, 1996; World Health Organization, 1981, 1996). The World Health Organization (1996) defined premenopause more broadly to include not just the 1 or 2 years before menopause but the entire reproductive period before menopause. Perimenopause is the transition that occurs immediately before menopause when the menstrual cycle length changes from the regular premenopausal pattern. It can be longer, shorter, or more variable. Other signs can include less menstrual flow, breast tenderness, and night sweats for some women. Production of estrogen from the ovaries and the adrenal glands will also diminish (Cole, 1994; S. M. McKinlay, 1996).

S. M. McKinlay (1996) reported that there is only one reliable estimate of age for the inception of perimenopause: 47.5 years. The estimated median length of this experience is 3.8 years. Women can anticipate menstrual irregularity or amenorrhea (suppression of menstruation) for almost 4 years before permanent cessation of the menses. Not all women experience this exact process or timing. Some women studied by S. M. McKinlay, Brambilla, and Posner (1992) experienced perimenopause for a shorter or longer time. Smokers and women who were never pregnant usually begin perimenopause earlier; smokers and older women experience shorter perimenopause transitions. Nearly 10 percent of women do not experience perimenopause or any irregularity. Instead, menstruation stops suddenly.

The term menopause comes from two Greek words: *menos*, which means monthly, and *pausis*, which means cessation. It is the time in a woman's life when menstruation and reproductive capacity end (Kastenbaum, 1993). Menopause happens either through a surgical or a natural process. Two types of surgery cause menstruation to stop: (1) removal of the uterus and one ovary or (2) removal of both ovaries, with or without removal of the uterus. Only the second surgery results in a sharp drop in hormone levels. Yet, women in both surgical groups, who experience a *nonnormative* surgical inducement of menopause, are distinct from women who experience a natural menopause process (S. M. McKinlay et al., 1992). If the process is nonnormative, women can experience severe and traumatic responses (for example, J. B. McKinlay, McKinlay, & Brambilla, 1987; Utian, 1990) and high rates of vasomotor and somatic signs (Kuh, Wadsworth, & Hardy, 1997). These results develop because of the abrupt removal of the ovaries and cessation of ovarian functioning and the accompanying severe changes in hormonal levels. Simultaneously, these women experience the trauma of surgery (Carolan, 1994). They may also experience psychological distress, though not every study reports an association between surgical menopause and psychological distress (for example, Busch, Zonderman, & Costa, 1994).

Natural menopause occurs after the cessation of menses for 12 consecutive months (Dennerstein, 1998; S. M. McKinlay, 1996). After this happens, the postmenopause period commences (World Health Organization, 1996). Although menopause indicates for many women the loss of reproductive capacity, it more accurately represents the single physiological event of the last menstrual period (Fishbein, 1992). Recently, the age of the commencement of natural menopause was calculated from estimates based predominantly on white populations in industrialized countries. The estimates were all within an age range of less than 2 years: 49.6–51.5 years. With removal of two of the lowest and least reliable estimates the range narrowed to less than 1.5 years: 50.1–51 years. The only factor clearly (and overwhelmingly) associated with age variance in the onset of menopause that consistently results in a decrease of 1.5 to 2 years in the median time of onset is current cigarette smoking (S. M. McKinlay, 1996).

The definition of menopause, based on absence of menstruation, was recently questioned (Woods, 1993). Utian (1991) reported, for example, continued variable production of ovarian hormones. In addition, how women define menopause may not coincide with any of the biological definitions of clinicians and researchers (S. M. McKinlay, 1996; Taffe, Garamszegi, Dudley, & Dennerstein, 1997; Woods, 1993). Women themselves base their menopausal status on considerably more and different combinations of indicators. Postmenopause, the period that follows the permanent cessation of menstruation (Kaufert, 1986), can seem similarly ambiguous for some women. For example, some women continue to menstruate with hormonal therapy.

DIFFERING PERSPECTIVES ON MENOPAUSE

What are the effects of menopause on women? Perspectives on the effects range from minimalist to maximalist (Carolan, 1994). The minimalist view proposes that menopause is a natural process and has minimal effects. The maximalist view incorporates the biomedical claims that menopause is a disease (a deficiency in hormones) and a major life event with multiple health and psychological consequences. Former maximalist views of menopause were initially that it was a sin, and later a neurosis. The minimalist view attempts to rewrite all maximalist views and to destigmatize menopausal women (Ferguson & Parry, 1998). In line with this goal, Cole and Rothblum (1990) suggested that instead of referring to the "symptoms" of menopause, which implies that menopause is a disease, the term "signs" is preferable. The term signs is used in this book because it is more neutral than symptoms and because the biomedical view is only one of several other competing views of menopause.

Minimalism Counters Maximalism

The maximalist biomedical perspective on menopause is the traditional and dominant perspective in the literature of the medical profession. Cross-sectional studies consistently report a strong association between menopause and hormonal, vasomotor, and other changes. Perimenopausal women can experience five distinct clusters of signs, identified by Mitchell and Woods (1996): vasomotor (for example, hot flashes, night sweats, trouble breathing); dysphoric mood (for example, depressed mood, irritability, mood swings); somatic (for example, nausea, fatigue); neuromuscular (for example, vaginal dryness, joint pain, backache); and insomnia (for example, difficulty getting to sleep, waking during the night). Although women may experience some of these signs, does this mean they have a "menopausal syndrome"? Mitchell and Woods concluded that it does not because the etiologies are different for each of the clusters. In addition, the stability of the clusters in their study varied over a three-year period. They also questioned whether the identified signs resulted from the menopausal transition.

If menopause is a disease, a causal relationship between decreased estrogen levels and clinical signs must exist, but there is little proof of such a connection (Theisen & Mansfield, 1993). Six longitudinal projects studied midlife women in the 1980s and early 1990s. They included the Massachusetts Women's Health Study (S. M. McKinlay et al., 1992), the Manitoba Project (Kaufert, Gilbert, & Tate, 1992), the Healthy Women Study at the University of Pittsburgh (Matthews et al., 1990), the South East England Study (Hunter, 1992), the Norway Study (Holte & Mikkelsen, 1991), and the Tremin Trust Study (Voda, 1991). These studies did not show that menopause causes numerous negative physical and psychological signs (Woods, 1993).

Physical Effects. Just because a midlife woman experiences signs such as insomnia or irritability, this does not indicate that they result from a menopausal transition or from declining hormones. Many situations can lead to these signs other than hormonal changes, such as life stress, acute or chronic physical illnesses, emotional illnesses, or relationship difficulties (Mitchell & Woods, 1996). The severity of menopausal signs has also been exaggerated (Voda, Dinnerstein, & O'Donnell, 1982). Light to moderate discomfort is common because of hot flashes, night sweats, and insomnia, but severe and frequent discomfort is not common (10 percent to 20 percent; see Rossi, 1992).

Only a few signs are unequivocally associated with declining estrogen levels: hot flushes, hot flashes, and vaginal atrophy (for example, Kaufert, Gilbert, & Hassard, 1988; J. B. McKinlay et al., 1987). Hot flushes are visible red blotches on the skin with perspiration. Hot flashes, which are sudden warm sensations in the neck, are not experienced by some women as unsettling, whereas other women experience them as quite disruptive, particularly the night sweats that can cause chronic sleep difficulties (Ingram Fogel & Woods, 1995). Other signs often attributed to menopause, such as irritability, may result from disruptions in sleep patterns (Kessel, 1998).

Hot flashes and hot flushes accelerate during perimenopause, peak at about the time of menopause, and then decline. They do not, as widely thought, begin to increase after menopause (S. M. McKinlay et al., 1992). Women report the most hot flashes and hot flushes three months or more following their final menstrual period (Guthrie, Dennerstein, Hopper, & Burger, 1996). Reassurance that hot flashes and hot flushes will not last forever may be comforting to women, though the exact time of the endpoint for any individual woman is uncertain (Ingram Fogel & Woods, 1995). The projected time period for the disappearance of these signs varies from one to two years to four to six years after menopause (Guthrie et al., 1996; Ingram Fogel & Woods, 1995).

Vaginal atrophy happens when lower estrogen levels are accompanied by thinning of the vaginal walls and decreased lubrication (Bachmann, 1990; Masters, Johnson, & Kolodny, 1991). These difficulties, however, are usually minor and easily modified (Shangold, 1990).

Psychological Effects. Are menopausal women neurotic, grieving, and depressed? These are long-standing stereotypes resulting from the traditional biomedical view of menopause. Hence, until recently, any emotional upset, such as emotional instability or depression, in a woman in her 40s or 50s was attributed to menopause (Clausen, 1986; Hallstrom & Samuelsson, 1985). This attribution, however, does not hold up in the face of the empirical evidence. Although some women may experience a slight heightening of psychological distress during premenopause (Bromberger & Matthews, 1996) and perimenopause (Hunter, 1990b), there is no notable heightening of psychological distress in menopausal or postmenopausal women (for example, Hunter, 1990b; Matthews et al., 1990; Stewart, Boydell, Derzko, & Marshall, 1992). In a nationally representative sample of midlife women, Busch et al. (1994) obtained reliable and valid measures of psychological distress during two interviews with these women over a 10-year period. The results provided evidence that menopausal status was unrelated to psychological distress. No upsurge happened in depression, psychological well-being, or sleep disturbance. When compared to premenopausal women, neither perimenopausal nor postmenopausal women reported more psychological distress.

Many women believe that menopause causes depression (Daly, 1995; Matthews et al., 1994). Yet, representative samples and longitudinal studies have not found evidence that psychological distress is associated with menopause (for example, Dennerstein, Dudley, Guthrie, & Barrett-Connor, 2000). Studies do not find that menopause causes depression or that depression is especially prevalent at menopause (for example, Hallstrom & Samuelsson, 1985; Utian, 1989).

The absence of a link between menopause and depression was strongly reinforced in the longitudinal studies on menopause. Most of these studies included a measure of depression. In the Manitoba Project, depression was not related to the menopausal transition (Kaufert et al., 1992). Depression was associated with surgical menopause but not natural menopause in the Massachusetts Women's Health Study (J. B. McKinlay & McKinlay, 1987). Depression was not associated with biological changes either before the transition to menopause, during the transition, or after menopause. The greatest heightening of depression was associated with multiple worries and multiple roles, such as paid worker, parent of adolescent children, and caregiver for aging parents (J. B. McKinlay et al., 1987). In the Healthy Women Study, a temporary heightening in depressed mood was reported during the menopausal transition (Avis, Brambilla, & McKinlay, 1994). This change, however, was only indirectly associated with the transition itself through signs such as hot flashes and night sweats. Other associations with depressed mood included a longer transition to menopause, prior depression, health difficulties, and social circumstances such as multiple conflicting roles (S. M. McKinlay et al., 1992). In the South East England study, women who were depressed attributed the condition not to menopause but to family difficulties, bereavement, financial worry, work, and illness. Menopausal depressed mood was predicted by premenopausal depressed mood, stereotypes about menopause, unemployment, low social class, stress, and lack of exercise (Hunter, 1990b, 1992). Menopause was only modestly associated with depression in the Norway study; more important predictors of depression included earlier responses to menstruation, negative expectations of menopause, and mother's perimenopause complaints (Holte, 1992; Holte & Mikkelsen, 1991).

The frequency of prior depression found in the longitudinal studies indicates that psychological distress is a stable characteristic over the lifetime. If women report psychological distress at menopause, they are likely to have histories of previous episodes of distress, such as anxiety or depression (Costa et al., 1987; Matthews et al., 1990; Rossi, 1992). The strongest predictor of depression in the Healthy Women Study was prior depression (Avis et al., 1994). The Norway study (Holte, 1992; Holte & Mikkelsen, 1991) also reported continuity of signs of depression over the life course. Women who experienced depressed mood in the Woods and Mitchell (1996) study consistently reported more stress and were more likely to have a history of premenstrual symptoms (PMS) and postpartum blues than women with an absence of depression. The researchers cautioned that these women may be at risk for continuing difficulties with depression and may require intensive counseling with a focus on managing and preventing depression.

The key conclusion from the longitudinal studies on menopause is that there are no adverse effects of the menopausal transition on mental health, including depression. Menopause itself does not create psychological vulnerability (Bromberger & Matthews, 1996).

In addition to psychosocial factors that may affect one's mood, negative beliefs about the effects of menopause can also lead to a depressed mood (Hunter, 1992; Liao & Hunter, 1995). One source of negative beliefs is negative symbolism associated with the changes in a woman's body or how a woman interprets them (Bart, 1972; J. B. McKinlay et al., 1987). She may abhor the whole idea of menopause because she sees it as a sign of old age, that she is no longer attractive, or even that she is useless (Stimpson, 1982; Wilk & Kirk, 1995). She may feel a loss of control over her body and, more generally, over what is happening in her life (Stimpson, 1982). Negative reactions can also result from identification with a mother who experienced a difficult midlife and menopausal transition (Cate & Corbin, 1992). Woods and Mitchell (1996) noted that women who experienced negative socialization regarding midlife exhibited a pattern of depression that they termed as "emerging depressed mood" (EDM). Compared to women who did not experience depression at midlife, the EDM women were also more likely characterized by "a history of PMS, poorer health status . . . fewer family resources, and less social support"

(Woods & Mitchell, 1996, p. 121). During the first year of a two-year study, these women scored below the depressed mood level but above it in the second year. Fortunately, for some women with negative expectations about menopause, the actual experience of menopause resulted in a more positive attitude (Avis et al., 1994). If this change did not occur, Woods and Mitchell (1996) suggested that negative socialization and lack of positive social support may be modifiable through psychoeducational programs that provide accurate information about midlife and menopause, inspire positive attitudes, and provide connections with other women experiencing similar midlife challenges.

Given some exceptions, most women report neutral or positive attitudes about menopause (Avis & McKinlay, 1991; Hunter, 1992). Instead of being a "syndrome" or major event causing health and mental health difficulties, menopause is more a nonevent. If anything, there are *gains* from menopause, such as simply not menstruating anymore. With no worry about pregnancy, a woman's sex life may be revitalized (Chiriboga, 1989; Perlmutter & Bart, 1982; Schlossberg, 1986). Relief about not having to worry about pregnancy is far more commonly experienced than despair over no longer being able to bear children (Clausen, 1986).

The situation for midlife lesbians is also positive. Cole and Rothblum (1991) conducted the first empirical survey of lesbian women at menopause with a nonclinical sample. They asked the respondents about positive changes in their lives since menopause. Aside from the cessation of menstruation, positive changes included more sex, more orgasms, greater self-acceptance, and enjoyment of their maturity. Only 22 percent of the sample indicated that they experienced no positive changes following menopause.

In sum, based largely on the strong counter of the longitudinal studies to the biomedical claims delineated above, the minimalist perspective prevails over the maximalist perspective as the more accurate picture of menopausal women. Both of these views, however, are problematic. The maximalist, biomedical perspective is problematic because it treats menopausal women as deficient. The minimalist perspective is problematic because women may be castigated if they report having experienced difficulties during menopause (Greer, 1992). Many behavioral and social scientists argue, however, that the biomedical view is the most problematic because it sees women as victims of their ovaries, uterus, and hormones (for example, J. B. McKinlay et al., 1987; Suling, Carlson, Snyder, & Holm, 1995) or that they have sick and weak bodies. This view also portrays women as subjects powerless to medical and scientific authority (Rostosky & Travis, 2000).

Sociocultural Perspective

The sociocultural perspective corroborates the minimalist claim that menopause results in few or no direct negative effects on women. Embedded in sociocultural factors, menopause is not just biology. The life-span theme of *multiple influences* suggests that we cannot fully understand the psychological effects of menopause without knowing, aside from the biological changes occurring in a woman's body, how different cultures treat this transition. If anything causes discomfort, it may be, for example, *social circumstances, role changes, negative expectations,* and *negative cultural attitudes* about aging women and menopause.

Three factors stand out among sociocultural influences. First, during certain previous historical periods women interpreted the losses of childbearing and child rearing in negative ways (Bart, 1972; Greenhill, 1940). Dramatic *social* and *historical changes,* however, profoundly altered the psychological meaning of the end of childbearing and child-rearing roles. Few midlife women in more recent cohorts experience the inability to bear or rear children as a major concern (see Chapter 2).

Second, what women anticipate during the menopausal transition can influence the results. During the baseline measures of attitudes in several longitudinal studies, some respondents reported that they thought women became depressed or irritable during menopause. These same women were significantly more likely at follow-up to report depression, irritability, and troubles with hot flashes, night sweats, and/or insomnia. Women at baseline who rejected negative views were much less likely to show any negative signs of menopause (for example, Avis, Brambilla, McKinlay, & Vass, 1992; Woods & Mitchell, 1999). Bareford (1991) also found that midlife women reported more negative signs when they held more negative attitudes about menopause and when they experienced more difficult life events. Educational intervention, however, may reduce the negative attitudes. Liao and Hunter (1998) evaluated a short-term health education intervention (at three and 15 months) that provided information and group discussion about the normal menopausal transition. The women in this study reported fewer negative beliefs about menopause following the intervention.

Third, the values of one's culture influence expectations of experiences during menopause. For example, the negatives associated with menopause are rooted in the devaluation of older women in Western cultures (Theisen & Mansfield, 1993). When women's ability to reproduce ends, their usefulness to the culture also ends (Crowley, 1994b). In the United States psychoanalysts propagated this view. For example, Helene Deutsch (1945) wrote, "Little by little the whole female genital apparatus is transformed into a number of inactive and superfluous structures" (p. 460). "All the organic process devoted to the services of the species stop. Woman has ended her existence as bearer of a future life, and the species. She is now engaged in an active struggle against her decline" (p. 459). Even now the cultural stereotype of menopausal women, derived from Western science, is one of being "irritable, frequently depressed, asexual, and besieged by hot flashes" (Dickson, 1990, p. 16). These negative, socially constructed stereotypes of menopause are both ageist and sexist (Chrisler, Torrey, & Matthes, 1991), largely resulting from patriarchal views and beliefs about women as defective and imperfect compared to men. In the United States, there are more reports of distress and symptomatology among women going through a menopausal transition than in many other countries (for example, Datan, 1986; Kaufert, 1982). In the United States, women's status declines in midlife and there is no gained status associated with menopause (Kittell, Mansfield, & Voda, 1998; Mansfield & Voda, 1993). In contrast, in certain other cultures (for example, Asia, India) women's worth expands with the event of menopause (for example, Chornesky, 1998; Kerns & Brown, 1992). These women attain new freedoms, elevated social status, and social, religious, or political power. They also rarely experience any negative signs of menopause (for example, Datan, 1986; Kerns & Brown, 1992; Theisen & Mansfield, 1993).

This review of various perspectives of menopause shows the *complex interaction* of *biology, culture, and psychological meaning* in how it is experienced. In the end, each woman's experience will vary as a result of her own *body chemistry, psychology,* and *sociocultural context* (Mansfield, Jorgensen, & Yu, 1989). This is in line with the life-span concept of *individual differences.* The medical profession, however, continues to emphasize the biology of menopause and a view of menopause as an estrogen-deficiency disease (MacPherson, 1981). Its typical treatment response is to medicate women with hormonal therapy (Rueda, 1997).

Hormonal Therapy

Physicians first prescribed estrogen in the 1970s to modify or eliminate various menopausal signs such as hot flashes, vaginal dryness, and osteoporosis (Theisen & Mansfield, 1993). Artificial estrogen replaces about nine-tenths of the natural estrogen that is no longer produced (see Papalia, Camp, & Feldman, 1996). Today the use of hormonal therapy for signs of menopause is controversial, although issues with the treatment were not apparent when first prescribed. This early history from 1966 to the 1980s was traced by Cole (1994) and is presented in Exhibit 7.1.

——— Exhibit 7.1

     Early History of Hormonal Therapy ——————————

- Between 1966 and 1975, women heard that menopause was an "estrogen-deficiency disease" with dreadful consequences. Robert A. Wilson's influential book, *Feminine Forever,* published in 1966, delineated the consequences of menopause in negative, misogynist terms such as "estrogen starvation," "disease," "deficiency," "decay," and "loss of womanhood." The women themselves were termed "eunuchs," "functional castrates," "vapid," "dull-minded," "sharp-tongued," "cowlike," and one of the "saddest of human spectacles." Wilson claimed further that at menopause, a woman was "no longer a functional woman" and was just "marking time until she follows her glands into oblivion." Wilson promised, however, that women could avoid these terrible outcomes and remain "feminine forever" by using estrogen therapy. He provided a long list of benefits that would come from this therapy, such as sex appeal, youthful skin and appearance, and prevention of hot flashes, melancholia, and many more signs of menopause. This book had large sales and was serialized in the national magazines *Look* and *Vogue*.

- In 1975, research on estrogen therapy showing dismal findings appeared in two articles in the *New England Journal of Medicine* (Smith, Prentice, Thompson, & Hermann, 1975; Ziel & Finkle, 1975). Women taking this treatment were at five to 14 times greater risk of having uterine cancer. Then came the revelation by Seaman (1977) that Wilson's (1966) book was amply funded by several pharmaceutical companies, including the maker (Ayerst) of the estrogen therapy known as "Premarin." Following this revelation, the sales of estrogen products in the United States dramatically dropped.

- Estrogen treatment remained unpopular until the late 1970s when prescriptions for lower dosages of estrogen became available. Since 1980, promotion of estrogen treatment for menopausal women experienced a resurgence.

Artificial estrogen is the most widely prescribed drug in the United States (Crowley, 1994a), but its use is still grounded in Wilson's basic premise that menopause is a disease (Utian & Lobo, 1990). The promotion of estrogen for menopausal and postmenopausal women is intended to create a collective consciousness that these women need hormonal treatment (Palmlund, 1997a, 1997b). The distinct message to women is that "their bodies are a source of danger to themselves" (Kaufert & Lock, 1997, p. 86). Consequently, menopause is marketed as a risk and estrogen as a way to control the risk (Palmlund, 1997a, 1997b).

Typically a combination of estrogen and synthetic progesterone is used to prevent uterine cancer in women with intact uteri (Sobel, 1994). If only estrogen is prescribed, episodic endometrial biopsies are recommended (Rosenberg, 1993). The combined treatment is often referred to as hormone replacement therapy or HRT (Cole, 1994). An alternate term such as "hormonal therapy," however, is more accurate because oral use of estrogen and progesterone does not reach true replacement levels (Ingram Fogel & Woods, 1995).

Benefits, Risks, and Discomforts of Hormonal Therapy

Controversy over hormonal therapy has been rampant between physicians and naturalists. Naturalists oppose synthetic hormones for healthy women. They also oppose this therapy because, as Exhibit 7.2 shows, it provides benefits but also serious risks and discomforts (for further discussion of the risks, see Grady et al., 1992; Woods & Mitchell, 1995).

──────   Exhibit 7.2
         Benefits, Risks, and Discomforts of Hormonal Therapy   ──────────

Benefits

- Reductions in hot flashes, night sweats, vaginal itching and dryness, vaginal atrophy, loss of vaginal lubrication, and thinning of the vaginal wall (for example, Farmer, White, Brody, & Bailey, 1984).

- Prevention of bone loss related to osteoporosis, risk of bone fractures, loss of height, and back pain (for example, Cutler & Garcia, 1992; Prestwood et al., 1994).

- Possible reductions of the risk of heart disease, but the findings are inconsistent (for example, Barrett-Connor & Bush, 1991; Haney, 2000; Ross, Paganini-Hill, Mack, & Henderson, 1987; Sobel, 1994; World Health Organization, 1981).

- Possible reduction of the risk of Alzheimer's disease (Kessel, 1998).

- Possible reduction of the risk of colon cancer (Kessel, 1998).

Risks

- Increase in the risk of endometrial cancer (cancer of the lining of the uterus) if a woman only uses estrogen (Kaufman et al., 1991).

- Possible increase in the risk of breast cancer with use of progesterone with estrogen (Bergkvist, Adami, Persson, Hoover, & Schairer, 1989; Colditz et al., 1990; Kaufman et al., 1991).

- Possible damage to the liver and gall bladder if estrogen is ingested orally (Struk-Ware, 1991).

Discomforts

- Continuation of monthly bleeding possible for some women (Rossi, 1992).

- Other possible side effects include weight gain, headaches, nausea, vaginal discharge, swollen breasts, and fluid retention (Papalia et al., 1996).

The Decision Dilemma

The consistent message associated with menopause is that women are responsible for making their own choices for their well-being. This includes choosing to take responsibility for what happens to their bodies. For example, will they take care of their bodies or allow them to deteriorate? Photographs used by pharmaceutical companies show that women who take care of themselves are, among other things, lean and fit. Diet, exercise, and estrogen are what they need (Kaufert & Lock, 1997)! In this scenario, the decision to use hormonal therapy or not is usually an uppermost issue (McQuaide, 1998). Yet, the decision of what to do is not an easy one; women must weigh the risks and benefits. This decision-making endeavor is often confusing because information is incomplete and contradictory and lists of risks and benefits vary and periodically change (Cole, 1994). In addition, every week or so, a new study contradicts another one recently reported (Gonyea, 1999). The long-term effects of hormonal therapy are also uncertain (Woods, 1998).

Many women do not consult with health care providers regarding their decisions about whether to initiate hormonal therapy or not or to stop hormonal therapy. This is not remarkable because there is no consistent message from health care providers (Dennerstein, 1998; Newton et al., 1997). Even so, attempts are made to help women with their decisions. For example, various decision aids exist such as one by O'Connor et al. (1998). An audiotape guides women through an illustrated booklet including information on the benefits and risks of hormonal therapy and a values clarification exercise to help make the decision consistent with personal values. The American College of Physicians (1992) provides guidelines that emphasize careful consideration of the benefits of short-term use of hormonal therapy for managing menopausal signs and long-term use of hormonal therapy for disease prevention. The guidelines recommend a limited course of therapy of one to five years for relief of short-term signs of menopause such as hot flashes.

Although it is the most often prescribed drug therapy in the United States, many women decide not to take hormonal therapy. Usage rates range from 10 percent to 35 percent, for a total of 6 million. Reasons women do not take hormonal therapy include fear of the health risks, especially breast cancer (Bastian et al., 1998). Yet, for other women, reduction of the distress of hot flashes may override the threat of possible detrimental health effects (Rothert et al., 1990). This may soon be the sole reason for pursuing hormonal therapy. On July 9, 2002, a landmark study of hormonal therapy involving 16,000 women, part of the ongoing Women's Health Initiative (WHI), was halted by the National Heart, Lung, and Blood Institute. Although this therapy, which combines estrogen with progestin, lowered the risk for bone fractures and colon rectal cancer, these benefits are outweighed by the increased risks for breast cancer, heart attacks, stroke, and blood clots. The investigators concluded that hormonal therapy causes more harm than good and should only be recommended for women with signs such as severe hot flashes (Rubin, 2002).

Ethnic and racial women are less likely than white women to use hormonal therapy (Bartman & Moy, 1998). The federally funded Study of Women Across America, a preliminary report of 10,000 women ages 40–55, showed that the percentage of white women who used hormonal therapy (25 percent) was greater than for African American (15 percent), Asian (13 percent), or Latino women (10 percent; see "Middle-aged women's aches," 1997). Padonu et al. (1996) reported that African American women viewed hormonal therapy in negative terms primarily because of the fear of cancer and other side effects, possible resumption of menstruation, and resistance to taking a lifelong medication.

Alternatives to Hormonal Therapy

An antiphysician attitude grew out of the feminist movement of the 1960s and alternative self-help clinics. Women dismissed male-originated prescriptions for making a normal process into a medical necessity. Voda (1994) cajoled health care providers "to stop trying to cure women of being women" (p. 520). A growing number of women view menopause as normal and believe that they can cope with it without hormones. They question why women who are not sick take the risks associated with hormonal therapy for long periods of time (Hunt, 1994; National Women's Health Network, 1989).

Lower risk alternatives to hormonal therapy may alleviate uncomfortable effects of menopause. One recommendation is weight-bearing exercise at least three times a week. Supplements of Vitamins B and C may also help. A reduction of alcohol, caffeine, and sugar may decrease hot flashes, nervousness, and other signs (Boston Women's Health Collective, 1992; Doress & Siegal, 1994). Although these alternatives to hormonal therapy are appealing to many women, research is a long way from establishing actual benefits (Rossi, 1992). Drug alternatives to estrogen may be on the horizon. Raloxifene, for example, may provide a number of the benefits of estrogen but without the increased risk of cancer (Barrett-Connor et al., 1998).

SEXUAL INTEREST, ACTIVITY, AND ENJOYMENT

Declines in sexual interest, activity, and enjoyment used to be thought of as the natural consequence of aging and hormonal decline. Women were diverging from *normative expectations* if they were still interested in sexual activity. This view changed, however, when technology that measured objective changes in sexual response became available in the 1970s (Bachmann, 1993). Researchers discovered that the female sexual response does not decline with age! Women tend to experience a peak in sexual arousal and orgasmic response in their mid 30s, and this level remains throughout life. A woman at age 70 or older is as capable of orgasm as a woman at age 35 (Starr, 1993). If aging does not hinder women's sexual capabilities, then, what are the effects on sexual interest, activity, and satisfaction during midlife?

Reports of Declines

Some studies on sexual changes among midlife women report declines in sexual interest, activity, or enjoyment whereas others do not report any of these declines. Some studies show mixed results on different measures. Beginning with studies that report declines, the Kinsey research on women's sexual behavior in the 1950s reported a decline in the frequency of orgasm in sexual activities with a partner. But, frequency of orgasm for women continued to age 60 in activities separate from a partner (for example, masturbation; see Kinsey, Pomeroy, Martin, & Gebhard, 1953). A summary of more recently reported declines in sexual interest, activity, and enjoyment in midlife appears in Exhibit 7.3.

—— Exhibit 7.3
    Declines in Sexual Interest, Activity, and Enjoyment in Midlife ——

- Decreased sexual desire is frequent. Although the rates of women who report a loss of sexual desire following menopause vary, they are as high as 90 percent (Bachmann, 1995). About two-thirds (66 percent) of women who attended a menopause clinic reported decreased sexual desire (Cole, 1988). In the sample of women participating in the Midlife Women's Health Survey, 40 percent reported declines following menopause; one of the most frequent declines was a decrease in sexual desire (Mansfield, Koch, & Voda, 1998).

- Decreased sexual enjoyment with a partner was reported from the sample studied by Bachmann (1995), by 40 percent of the sample studied by Mansfield et al. (1998), and by more than one-quarter of the sample of women ages 35–55 studied by Mansfield, Voda, and Koch (1995).

- Decreased frequency of sexual intercourse with orgasm was reported in several samples (for example, Bachmann, 1995; Cole, 1988). About one-quarter of the sample studied by Mansfield et al. (1995) indicated that achieving orgasm was difficult.

- Decreased intensity of orgasms occurred; contractions were both less intense and less frequent (Masters & Johnson, 1966, 1981).

- Changes in sexual response occurred for 85 percent of the women studied by Cole (1988) such as longer arousal time; the sexual response decreased for more than half (54 percent) of women studied by Mansfield et al. (1995).

- A dislike for sexual activity was reported as one reason for declines in sexual responsiveness (Bachmann, 1995).

- Pain with intercourse and changes in touch sensitivity (either hyper- or hyposensitive) were reported by women studied by Cole (1988).

Many declines and changes listed in Exhibit 7.3 appeared in several other samples of menopausal or postmenopausal women. From a sample of 130 menopausal women, Sarrel (1990) reported a decrease in sexual desire for 77 percent. Over one-third reported decreases in clitoral sensitivity (36 percent) and in orgasmic intensity (35 percent); 29 percent reported decreases in orgasmic frequency. Over one-half reported vaginal dryness (58 percent); over one-third reported dyspareunia (painful intercourse) (39 percent). In a sample of postmenopausal midlife women studied by Sarrel and Whitehead (1985), only 14 percent reported no sexual troubles. Difficulties reported by the rest of the sample fell into four categories. Three areas involved the sexual process: desire phase, excitement phase, and orgasmic phase. The fourth area was dyspareunia. Of the 154 women who reported sexual difficulties, 43 percent reported a loss of sexual desire and 10 percent reported sexual dislike in the desire phase. During the excitement phase, changes included weakened touch sensation (36 percent), loss of clitoral sensation (20 percent), vaginal dryness (36 percent), and urinary incontinence (10 percent). Either a primary or secondary nonorgasmic status existed during the orgasmic phase. Women with secondary nonorgasmic responses (27 percent) were orgasmic previously whereas women with primary nonorgasmic responses (10 percent) were never orgasmic. Vaginal dryness and dyspareunia occurred for 43 percent of the sample. Close to two-thirds (62 percent) of 252 postmenopausal women ($M = 52$ years) in a community-based survey reported a decrease in sexual desire. Distress from this change and taking hormonal therapy were associated with women who had the highest interest in sex before the onset of menopause (Sarrel, Giblin, & Block, 1998).

Most declines in sexual behaviors happen in the later stages of the menopausal transition (for example, McCoy & Davidson, 1985). For women who experience declines, Mansfield et al. (1995) cautioned that it is important to know their feelings about the changes. The changes may not bother them. Even if upset, they may modify their attitudes upon finding out that it is not unusual for women to feel a difference in sexual desire in midlife.

Biological Factors Associated with Declines. A popular conclusion about menopause is that sexual behaviors change because of biological changes, especially hormonal changes, and changes in the vaginal canal and in vaginal lubrication. Though hormones play a role in sexual expression, declines in sexual activity, interest, and enjoyment are unlikely to result from the decrease in hormones (Bachmann, 1995; Laan & van Lunsen, 1997). Not all post-menopausal women experience a loss of interest in or lowered levels of sexual activity (for example, Hallstrom & Samuelsson, 1990). Also, a drop in the ovaries' production of estrogen, although suspected as contributing to a decline in sexual desire during the menopausal transition, does not affect sexual desire. This hormone does not control the sex drive or the ability to experience erotic thoughts or orgasms. Posmenopausal women are still quite capable of experiencing desire for and pleasure in sexual activity (Bachmann, 1993, 1995).

The vaginal canal becomes thinner and less elastic following menopause, and vaginal lubrication happens more slowly during sexual arousal and intercourse. The decline in vaginal lubrication seems to be the most noticeable change associated with less sexual interest, activity, and enjoyment. Almost two-thirds (60 percent) of the women Barbach (1993) studied reported a decline in vaginal lubrication. In a sample of women ages 35–55, Mansfield et al. (1995) found that when vaginal dryness occurred, 71 percent reported less sexual desire, 30 percent less sexual enjoyment, and 34 percent more difficulty with orgasms. Discomfort during intercourse due to vaginal dryness was experienced by 26 percent of premenopausal and perimenopausal women and 40 percent of the postmenopausal women studied in England by Hunter (1990b) and Hunter, Battersby, and Whitehead (1986). If there is no treatment of itching and burning after intercourse, women may experience these discomforts throughout the day. If uncomfortable or painful, intercourse not only can affect one's sexual activity but the well-being of one's intimate relationships. Painful intercourse can result in secondary anxiety and sexual inhibition in both partners (Hunter, 1990a). Fortunately, vaginal dryness can be treated by remaining sexually active and by using nonhormonal lubricants and other nonhormonal vaginal therapies (Bachmann, Notelovitz, Gonzales, Thompson, & Morecraft, 1991), vaginal estrogen preparations, or hormonal therapy (Bachmann, 1995; Notman, 1998).

Various other biological factors, independent of menopausal status, can also affect sexual interest, activity, and enjoyment. Advancing age, for example, significantly predicts a decline in sexual enjoyment with a partner (Cole, 1988). Other factors include physical disorders in either partner such as chronic illnesses (for example, arthritis, diabetes) and malignancies that become more prevalent in midlife and in each passing decade (Bachmann, 1993, 1995). Malignancies of the pelvis, genitalia, or breast, especially, have a major negative effect on sexual functioning of both men and women (for example, Glasgow, Halfin, & Akthausen, 1987). Medications used to treat illnesses and malignancies can also have an adverse effect on sexual functioning (Bachmann, 1993).

Psychosocial Factors Associated with Declines. Psychosocial factors can interfere with midlife women's sexual interest, activity, and enjoyment. These factors, which may be more important in postmenopausal women's sexual functioning than the biological factor, include mental distractions, dual careers, busy schedules, and adolescent children (Katchadourian, 1987; Laan & van Lunsen, 1997; Weg, 1989). Marital adjustment is also closely associated with enjoyment of sexual activity and frequency of sexual intercourse and orgasm (Hallstrom & Samuelsson, 1990; Hawton, Gath, & Day, 1994; Hunter, 1990a). The sexual relationship in a midlife marriage is often at a low point (Edwards & Booth, 1994) because of boredom or dissatisfaction with a long-term sexual partner (for example, McCoy & Davidson, 1985). Older cohorts of women tend to derive fewer rewards from the marriage itself and experience more dissatisfaction with sex in marriage (Edwards & Booth, 1994). Loss of closeness in the marital relationship is likely to precede loss of interest in sex for both men and women (Clausen, 1986). Hawton et al. (1994) also suspected that marital difficulties may influence sexual changes instead of the reverse. From their sample of 280 women in the Midlife Women's Health Survey, Mansfield, Koch, and Voda (2000) reported an association between the women's relationships with partners (for example, "my partner is not affectionate enough") and their sexual response. The respondents, however, often attributed changes in their sexual response to bodily changes. They blamed themselves instead of reflecting on relationship concerns.

Women are not always dissatisfied with infrequent sexual intercourse in their marriages (Hawton et al., 1994). Many of these women are disinterested in or turned off by sex (McCormick, 1994). Some of them see their postmenopausal years as a chance to reduce sexual activity. They may think that sexual behavior should end when they get older because it seems awkward or they may feel embarrassed about sexual feelings (Barbach, 1993). For other women, if sexual activities are viewed as primarily just tolerable or worse, these years can be ones of freedom from the burden of obligatory sex and marital duty (Heiman, 1986; Roughan, Kaiser, & Morley, 1993).

Women may not define self-fulfillment as including a sexual relationship with a man. This situation may cause difficulty for the male partner used to his female partner accommodating to his sexual needs (Heiman, 1986; Leiblum, 1990; Roughan et al., 1993). Husbands or other male partners may balk, blame, or try to induce guilt in their partners, but the women may feel no incentive to continue as before (Barbach, 1993). Reduction of or no sexual activity is too much of a relief for them (Leiblum, 1990).

Sexual Satisfaction

Another set of research findings on the sexual functioning and happiness of midlife women looks quite different from the views just presented. A description of a midlife couple might be stated as, "Male, 42, concerned with his vanity and virility, wondering if he has control, hoping his anxiety won't appear in inability to perform, and eager to nurture. Female, 42, feeling sexual and inviting, openly stating what she needs and wishes to do, and willing to lead" (Krupp, 1993, p. 4). Although 42 years of age is younger than the typical age of menopause, women of older ages could also fit the description here of a woman's sexual desires.

In the first longitudinal study of sexual behavior in midlife women, McCoy and Davidson (1985) found small but significant decreases in sexual activity, sexual thoughts, and vaginal lubrication in postmenopausal women. They did not find changes in orgasmic frequency or sexual enjoyment. In a randomly chosen sample of postmenopausal women ages 50–65, a majority (51 percent) reported that their sexual lives were unchanged (Utian & Boggs, 1999). Half of a sample of postmenopausal women who did not use hormones experienced no decline in sexual interest (Bachmann, 1990). Sixty percent of the sample of midlife women studied by Mansfield et al. (1998) experienced no changes in sexual responsiveness during the past year. Most male and female respondents in the study of midlife marriages by Edwards and Booth (1994) were not elated with the sexual part of their link, but issues such as loss of sexual interest appeared to affect only a minority of marriages. Sexual interest in midlife women studied in England (Hunter, 1990b; Hunter et al., 1986) decreased across menopausal stages but approximately 70 percent of these women reported that they were sexually active. No significant discrepancies were observed among premenopausal, perimenopausal, and postmenopausal women, although fewer of the older women (ages 55–65) were sexually active. Over 80 percent of the sample felt satisfied with their sexual relationships. In an Australian study of 2,000 randomly selected midlife women, the majority (62 percent) reported no change in sexual interest; only 11 percent reported experiencing unusual pain during intercourse (Dennerstein, Smith, Morse, & Burger, 1994).

A factor that may affect the continued sexual well-being of many women after menopause is prior sexual activity, either with a partner or from masturbation (Katchadourian, 1987; Spence, 1989). Women who were sexually active at a high level in their earlier years did not show a decrease in sexual interest or activities after menopause (Masters & Johnson, 1981; Starr & Weiner, 1981). This same factor was also the essential influence on sexuality after surgical menopause (Helstrom, 1994). Women who remain sexually active experience better general vaginal health (Leiblum, Bachmann, Kemmann, Colburn, & Swartzman, 1983). Women who do not experience difficulties with sexual arousal before menopause are unlikely to experience vaginal dryness and pain during sexual activity following the menopause transition (Laan & van Lunsen, 1997).

Some midlife women even report that sex is better than ever before. As noted earlier, a woman's sex life may be revitalized after menopause because she no longer worries about becoming pregnant (Chiriboga, 1989; Perlmutter & Bart, 1982). Almost 80 percent of the women studied by Starr and Weiner (1981) reported that menopause not only did not adversely affect their sexual activity but there were also improvements. Most of the 160 midlife women studied by Rubin (1982) reported better sex than ever. They knew their sexual desires better, experienced more interest in sex, and felt freer to take the initiative. About a quarter (26 percent) of a sample of midlife women studied by Mansfield et al. (1995) reported more sexual enjoyment with a partner during the past year. Because of men's slowed response, midlife lovers studied by Edwards and Booth (1994) experienced longer and more leisurely sexual activity. Older women reported in another study that they enjoyed the tenderness and sensuality of the physical communication with their partners (Butler & Lewis, 1982). Similarly, Mansfield et al. (1998) found that one-fifth of the midlife women they studied desired more nongenital contact such as hugging and kissing.

Lesbian Sexuality after Menopause

In the study by Cole and Rothblum (1991) of midlife lesbians, many respondents (44 percent) reported vaginal dryness. No change occurred, however, in the frequency of sexual activity for 46 percent of the sample. More than two-thirds (68 percent) felt no change in clitoral sensation or sensitivity since menopause. Over half (56 percent) experienced no change in orgasms, though for 20 percent they were less frequent and for 22 percent more frequent. For most of the respondents (73 percent), sexual fantasies did not change. The majority (76 percent) reported that they experienced no sexual difficulties and even more (85 percent) indicated that sex was as good as or better than before menopause. In a study of 75 midlife lesbians, Sang (1993) posed a question specific to the effects of menopause on their sex life. Half (50 percent) of this sample indicated that their sex life was better than before. It was more open and exciting because of better communication and more emphasis on touching and sharing more kinds of behaviors than the pressured goal of orgasms.

Not all midlife lesbians experience positive sexual results after menopause. Some (29 percent) of the women studied by Cole and Rothblum (1991) reported a decrease in the quality of sex. The reasons given included changes in physical response (for example, orgasms not as intense as before), possible negative consequences of hormonal therapy, and experiencing lack of sexual desire or passion for one's partner.

WAYS FOR WOMEN TO INCREASE SEXUAL ENJOYMENT

Hormonal therapy ameliorated sexual functioning in the sample of midlife women studied by Sarrel and Whitehead (1985). Improvements included clitoral sensitivity and return of orgasmic capacity. Sexual desire developed for women who had reported a previous lack of sexual desire. Hormonal therapy may also benefit women who underwent a hysterectomy or were not sexually active before menopause (Bachmann, 1994). Yet, even if hormonal therapy enhances lubrication and decreases vaginal discomfort, Leiblum (1992) cautioned that generally it will not increase sexual interest in either premenopausal or postmenopausal women. As discussed earlier there are health risks associated with hormonal therapy so use of this intervention, for any reason, is not without controversy. Viagra has been touted as increasing sexual desire for men. So far, however, it does not appear to change the degree of sexual desire or sexual satisfaction in women ("Viagra doesn't work," 1999; "Viagra strikes out for women," 2000).

Bachmann (1994) recommended several alternatives to hormonal therapy for increased sexual enjoyment. They include: a warm bath before sex, sex in the morning when there is less fatigue, and use of non-hormonal vaginal preparations. Short-acting, water-based lubricants applied immediately before intercourse can provide temporary relief from vaginal dryness. For additional alternatives, including many self-treatments such as stretching the vagina to reduce the painfulness of intercourse, refer to Barbach (1993) and Nachtigall (1997).

Changes in the sexual script were also recommended by Bachmann (1994), such as using noncoital methods of sexual exchange. Inability to alter the sexual script often worsens sexual difficulties and may lead to eventual sexual abstinence (Bachmann, 1993; Leiblum et al., 1983). As suggested earlier, women's sexual satisfaction may depend less on the physical gratification that is central to the male model of sexuality. Women place more emphasis on the emotional and relational qualities of the experience (for example, McCormick,

1994; Poulin, 1992). Sex is not just intercourse but also hugging, kissing, and gentle caressing. Self-stimulation is also an option (Bachmann, 1994).

SUMMARY

- Perspectives on menopause and its effects on midlife women range from the minimalist view of few consequences to the biomedical view of menopause as a disease with multiple negative consequences, both biological and psychological.

- Research findings from six longitudinal studies of midlife women conducted in North America in the 1980s and early 1990s challenge the validity of the biomedical perspective.

- The biomedical perspective is still strong and reinforced by the frequent prescription of hormonal therapy for menopausal women.

- Prescription of hormonal therapy is controversial, especially because of its side effects.

- Research findings on sexuality during and after menopause are contradictory. Some findings show decline in sexual interest, activity, and enjoyment; others show no declines; and still others show improvement in sexual relationships.

IMPLICATIONS FOR PRACTICE

Social agencies and health centers can provide community education programs to inform and counsel women about the research findings on menopause and sexual responses. Professional helpers should be knowledgeable about the contrasting perspectives on menopause and their effects on midlife women. They also need to be able to inform women about the controversial aspects of hormonal therapy for menopause, including its side effects.

Many women experience menopause as a natural event in their lives and do not seek assistance in health care or mental health settings. Some women, however, may experience or anticipate experiencing a range of negative outcomes from menopause and are more likely to seek such services. These women can benefit from both individual and group interventions from a social worker or other mental health practitioner who can challenge their negative cognitions and behaviors. Drawing on research findings, practitioners can encourage women to question the validity of the biomedical perspective and adopt a more positive view of menopause. Counselors can also counter negative images of sexual changes associated with menopause by discussing research findings that report improvement in sexual relationships as well as suggest ways to modifiy discomforts in sexual actitity.

VIGNETTE

Edie and her sister *Wanda* illustrate different beliefs and experiences of midlife women regarding menopause and how their concerns can be addressed. Edie, 55 years old, has been in a marriage with Ted, age 61, for 35 years. They have three adult children, now married with families of their own. Edie and Ted's marriage is strong, and their sex life is satisfying. Edie did not anticipate experiencing difficulties with menopause, and she had only occasional hot flashes for about one year. Edie now says that she feels "better than ever" and is relieved that menstruation has stopped.

Wanda, Edie's sister, is 51 years old, divorced with no children, and is anticipating the onset of menopause. In contrast with Edie, Wanda believes that she will experience all the negative signs of menopause that she reads and hears about. She fears hot flashes, irritability, and losing interest in sex. She visualizes herself as turning into an unattractive woman and fears that men will no longer find her appealing. After hearing Wanda's fears Edie suggested that she attend a free group for premenopausal women offered at a community health clinic.

Questions

- *Midlife women can be on the two extreme ends of the continuum of experiences of menopause. What could you explain to a female client who anticipates many negatives outcomes when she reaches menopause?*

- *What would be the benefits of individual or group interventions for women who expect a negative transition to menopause?*

REFERENCES

American College of Physicians. (1992). Guidelines for counseling postmenopausal women about preventive hormone therapy. *Annuals of Internal Medicine, 117,* 1038–1041.

Avis, N. E., Brambilla, D., & McKinlay, S. M. (1994). A longitudinal analysis of the association between menopause and depression: Results from the Massachusetts Women's Health Study. *Annals of Epidemiology, 4,* 214–220.

Avis, N. E., Brambilla, D., McKinlay, S. M., & Vass, K. (1992). *A longitudinal analysis of the association between menopause and depression: Results from the Massachusetts Women's Health Study*. Watertown, MA: New England Research Institute.

Avis, N. E., & McKinlay, S. M. (1991). A longitudinal analysis of women's attitudes toward the menopause: Results from the Massachusetts Women's Health Study. *Maturitas, 13*, 65–79.

Azar, B. (1994, May). Women are barraged by media on "the change." *APA Monitor, 25*, 24–25.

Bachmann, G. A. (1990). The ideals of optimal care for women at midlife. *Annuals of the New York Academy of Sciences, 592*, 253–256.

Bachmann, G. A. (1993). Sexual function in the perimenopause. *Obstetrics and Gynecology Clinics of North America, 20*, 379–389.

Bachmann, G. A. (1994). The changes before "the change": Strategies for the transition to the menopause. *Postgraduate Medicine, 95*, 113–124.

Bachmann, G. A. (1995). Sexuality in the menopausal years. *Women's Health Digest, 1*, 110–112.

Bachmann, G. A., Notelovitz, M., Gonzales, S. J., Thompson, C., & Morecraft, B. A. (1991). Vaginal dryness in menopausal women: Clinical characteristics and nonhormonal treatment. *Clinical Practice and Sexuality, 7*, 1–8.

Barbach, L. (1993). The pause: A closer look at menopause and female sexuality. *Siecus Report, 21*, 1–6.

Bareford, C. (1991). An investigation of the nature of the menopausal experience: Attitude toward menopause, recent life change, coping method, and number and frequency of symptoms in menopausal women. In D. Taylor & N. Woods (Eds.), *Menstruation, health, and illness* (pp. 223–236). New York: Hemisphere.

Barrett-Connor, E., & Bush, T. L. (1991). Estrogen and coronary heart disease in women. *Journal of the American Medical Association, 265*, 1861–1867.

Barrett-Connor, E., Wenger, N. K., Grady, D., Mosca, L., Collins, P., Kornitzer, M., Cox, D. A., Moscarelli, E. Y., & Anderson, P. W. (1998). Hormone and nonhormone therapy for the maintenance of postmenopausal health: The need for randomized controlled trials of estrogen and raloxifene. *Journal of Women's Health, 7*, 839–847.

Bart, P. B. (1972). Depression in middle-age women. In V. Gornick & B. K. Moran (Eds.), *Women in sexist society* (pp. 163–168). New York: New American Library.

Bartman, B. A., & Moy, E. (1998). Racial differences in estrogen use among middle-aged and older women. *Women's Health Issues, 8*, 32–44.

Bastian, L. A., Couchman, G. M., Rimer, B. K., McBride, C. M., Feaganes, J. R., & Siegler, I. C. (1998). Perceptions of menopausal stage and patterns of hormone replacement therapy use. *Journal of Women's Health, 6*, 467–475.

Bergkvist, L., Adami, H., Persson, J., Hoover, R., & Schairer, C. (1989). The risk of breast cancer after estrogen–progestin replacement. *New England Journal of Medicine, 321*, 293–297.

Boston Women's Health Collective. (1992). *The new our bodies ourselves*. New York: Simon & Schuster.

Bromberger, J. T., & Matthews, K. A. (1996). A longitudinal study of the effects of pessimism, trait anxiety, and life stress on depressive symptoms in middle-aged women. *Psychology and Aging, 11*, 207–213.

Busch, C. M., Zonderman, A. B., & Costa, P. T. (1994). Menopausal transition and psychological distress in a nationally representative sample: Is menopause associated with psychological distress *Journal of Aging and Health, 6*, 209–228.

Butler, R. N., & Lewis, M. I. (1982). *Aging and mental health* (3rd ed.). St. Louis: C. V. Mosby.

Carolan, M. T. (1994). Beyond deficiency: Broadening the view of menopause. *Journal of Applied Gerontology, 13*, 199–205.

Cate, M. A., & Corbin, D. E. (1992). Age differences in knowledge and attitudes toward menopause. *Journal of Women & Aging, 4*, 33–46.

Chiriboga, D. A. (1989). Stress and loss in middle age. In R. A. Kalish (Ed.), *Midlife loss: Coping strategies* (pp. 42–80). Newbury Park, CA: Sage Publications.

Chornesky, A. (1998). Multicultural perspectives on menopause and the climacteric. *Affilia, 13*, 31–46.

Chrisler, J. C., Torrey, J. W., & Matthes, M. M. (1991). Brittle bones and sagging breasts, loss of femininity and loss of sanity: The media describe the menopause. In A. V. Voda & R. Conover (Eds.), *Proceedings of the Society for Menstrual Cycle Research, 8*, 23–35.

Clausen, J. A. (1986). *The life course: A sociological perspective.* Englewood Cliffs, NJ: Prentice Hall.

Colditz, G. A., Stampfer, M. J., Willett, W. C., Hennekens, C. H., Rosner, B., & Speizer, F. E. (1990). A prospective study of estrogen replacement therapy and the risk of breast cancer in postmenopausal women. *Journal of the American Medical Association, 264*, 2648–2653.

Cole, E. (1988). Sex at menopause: Each in her own way. In E. Cole & E. Rothblum (Eds.), *Women and sex therapy: Closing the circle of sexual knowledge* (pp. 159–168). New York: Harrington.

Cole, E. (1994). Over the hill we go: Women at menopause. In M. P. Mirkin (Ed.), *Women in context: Toward a feminist reconstruction of psychotherapy* (pp. 310–329). New York: Guilford Press.

Cole, E., & Rothblum, E. (1990). Commentary on "sexuality and the midlife woman." *Psychology of Women Quarterly, 14*, 509–512.

Cole, E., & Rothblum, E. D. (1991). Lesbian sex at menopause: As good as or better than ever. In B. Sang, J. Warshow, & A. Smith (Eds.), *Lesbians at midlife: The creative transition* (pp. 184–193). San Francisco: Spinsters.

Costa, P. T., Jr., Zonderman, A. B, McCrae, R. R., Cornoni-Huntley, J., Locke, B. Z., & Barbano, H. E. (1987). Longitudinal analysis of psychological well-being in a national sample: Stability of mean levels. *Journal of Gerontology, 42*, 50–55.

Crowley, S. L. (1994a, June). Estrogen: Friend or foe? *American Association of Retired Persons Bulletin*, pp. 2, 5.

Crowley, S. L. (1994b, May). Much ado about menopause: Plenty of information but precious few answers. *American Association of Retired Persons Bulletin*, pp. 2, 7.

Cutler, W., & Garcia, C. (1992). *Menopause: A guide for women and the men who love them.* New York: W. W. Norton.

Daly, J. (1995). Caught in the web: The social construction of menopause as disease. *Journal of Reproductive and Infant Psychology, 13*, 115–126.

Datan, N. (1986). Corpes, lepers and menstruating women: Tradition, transition, and the sociology of knowledge. *Sex Roles, 14*, 693–702.

Dennerstein, L. (1998). The controversial menopause: An overview. In L. Dennerstein & J. Shelley (Eds.), *A woman's guide to menopause and hormone replacement therapy* (pp. 17–30). Washington, DC: American Psychiatric Press.

Dennerstein, L., Dudley, E., Guthrie, J., & Barrett-Connor, E. (2000). *Life satisfaction, symptoms, and the menopausal transition* [On-line]. Available: http://womenshealth.medscape.com.

Dennerstein, L., Smith, A.M.A., Morse, C. A., & Burger, H. G. (1994). Sexuality and menopause. *Journal of Psychosomatic Obstetrics and Gynecology, 15*, 59–66.

Deutsch, H. (1945). *The psychology of women* (Vol. 2). New York: Grune & Stratton.

Dickson, G. L. (1990). A feminist poststructuralist analysis of the knowledge of menopause. *Advanced Nursing Science, 12*, 15–31.

Doress, P. B., & Siegal, D. S. (in cooperation with the Boston Women's Health Collective). (1994). *Ourselves growing older.* New York: Simon & Schuster.

Edwards, J. N., & Booth, A. (1994). Sexuality, marriage, and well-being: The middle years. In A. S. Rossi (Ed.), *Sexuality across the life course* (pp. 233–259). Chicago: University of Chicago Press.

Farmer, M., White, L., Brody, J., & Bailey, K. (1984). Race and sex differences in hip fracture incidence. *American Journal of Public Health, 74*, 1374–1380.

Ferguson, S. J., & Parry, C. (1998). Rewriting menopause: Challenging the medical paradigm to reflect menopausal women's experiences. *Frontiers, 19*, 20–41.

Fishbein, E. G. (1992). Women at midlife: The transition of menopause. *Nursing Clinics of North America, 27*, 951–957.

Glasgow, M., Halfin, V., & Akthausen, A. F. (1987). Sexual response and cancer. *CA: Cancer Journal for Clinicians, 37*, 322–333.

Gonyea, J. G. (1999). Midlife and menopause: Uncharted territories for baby boomer women. *Generations, 22*, 87–89.

Grady, D., Rubin, S., Petitti, D., Fox, C., Black, E., Ettinger, B., Ernster, V., & Cummings, S. (1992). Hormone therapy to prevent disease and prolong life in postmenopausal women. *Annals of Internal Medicine, 117*, 1016–1037.

Greenhill, J. (1940). Gynecology. In J. Delee & J. Greenhill (Eds.), *Yearbook of obstetrics and gynecology* (pp. 331–347). Chicago: Year Book.

Greer, G. (1992). *The change: Women, aging and the menopause.* New York: Alfred A. Knopf.

Guthrie, J. R., Dennerstein, L., Hopper, J. L., & Burger, H. G. (1996). Hot flushes, menstrual status, and hormone levels in a population-based sample of midlife women. *Obstetrics and Gynecology, 88*, 437–442.

Hallstrom, T., & Samuelsson, S. (1985). Mental health in the climacteric: The longitudinal study of women in Gothenburg. *Acta Obstetrica Gynecologia Scandinavica Supplement, 130*, 13–18.

Hallstrom, T., & Samuelsson, S. (1990). Changes in women's sexual desire in middle life: The longitudinal study of women in Gothenberg. *Archives of Sexual Behavior, 19*, 259–268.

Haney, D. Q. (2000, March 14). Study questions estrogen benefits. *Dallas Morning News*, pp. A1, A11.

Hawton, K., Gath, D., & Day, A. (1994). Sexual function in a community sample of middle-aged women with partners: Effects of age, marital, socioeconomic, psychiatric, gynecological, and menopausal factors. *Archives of Sexual Behavior, 23*, 375–395.

Heiman, J. (1986). Treating sexually distressed marital relationships. In N. S. Jacobson & A. S. Gurman (Eds.), *Clinical handbook of marital therapy* (pp. 361–384). New York: Guilford Press.

Helstrom, L. (1994). Sexuality after hysterectomy: A model based on quantitative and qualitative analysis of 104 women before and after subtotal hysterectomy. *Journal of Psychosomatic and Obstetrical Gynecology, 15*, 219–229.

Holte, A. (1992). Influences of natural menopause on health complaints: A prospective study of healthy Norwegian women. *Maturitas, 14*, 127–141.

Holte, A., & Mikkelsen, A. (1991). Psychosocial determinants of climacteric complaints. *Maturitas, 13*, 205–215.

Hunt, K. (1994). A "cure for all ills"? Constructions of the menopause and the chequered fortunes of hormone replacement therapy. In S. Wilkinson & C. Kitzinger (Eds.), *Women and health: Feminist perspectives* (pp. 124–140). London: Taylor & Francis.

Hunter, M. (1990a). Emotional well-being, sexual behavior, and hormone replacement therapy. *Maturitas, 12*, 299–314.

Hunter, M. (1990b). Psychological and somatic experience of the menopause: A prospective study. *Psychosomatic Medicine, 52*, 357–367.

Hunter, M. (1992). The South East England longitudinal study of climacteric and postmenopause. *Maturitas, 14*, 117–126.

Hunter, M., Battersby, R., & Whitehead, M. (1986). Relationships between psychological symptoms, somatic complaints and menopausal status. *Maturitas, 8*, 217–228.

Ingram Fogel, C., & Woods, N. F. (1995). Midlife women's health. In C. I. Fogel & N. F. Woods (Eds.), *Women's health care: A comprehensive handbook* (pp. 79–99). Thousand Oaks, CA: Sage Publications.

Kastenbaum, B. K. (1993). Menopause. In R. Kastenbaum (Ed.), *Encyclopedia of adult development* (pp. 326–328). Phoenix, AZ: Oryx.

Katchadourian, H. (1987). *Fifty: Midlife in perspective*. New York: Freeman.

Kaufert, P. A. (1982). Myth and menopause. *Sociology of Health and Illness, 4*, 141–166.

Kaufert, P. A. (1986). Menstruation and menstrual change: Women in midlife. *Health Care for Women International, 7*, 63–76.

Kaufert, P. A. (1996). The social and cultural context of menopause. *Maturitas, 23*,169–180.

Kaufert, P. A., Gilbert, P., & Hassard, T. (1988). Researching the symptoms of menopause: An exercise in methodology. *Maturitas, 10*, 143–155.

Kaufert, P. A., Gilbert, P., & Tate, R. (1992). The Manitoba Project: A re-examination of the link between menopause and depression. *Maturitas, 14*, 143–155.

Kaufert, P. A., & Lock, M. (1997). Medicalization of women's third age. *Journal of Psychosomatic Obstetrics and Gynecology, 18*, 81–86.

Kaufman, D. W., Palmer, J. R., deMouzon, J., Rosenberg, L., Stolley, P. D., Worshauer, M. E., & Shapiro, S. (1991). Estrogen replacement therapy and risk of breast cancer: Results from the case-control surveillance study. *American Journal of Epidemiology, 134*, 1375–1385.

Kerns, V., & Brown, J. K. (Eds.). (1992). *In her prime: A new view of middle-aged women* (2nd ed.). Urbana: University of Illinois Press.

Kessel, B. (1998). Alternatives to estrogen for menopausal women. *Society for Experimental Biology and Medicine, 217*, 38–44.

Kinsey, A. C., Pomeroy, W. B., Martin, C. E., & Gebhard, P. H. (1953). *Sexual behavior in the human female*. Philadelphia: W. B. Saunders.

Kittell, L. A., Mansfield, P. K., & Voda, A. M. (1998). Keeping up appearances: The basic social process of the menopausal transition. *Qualitative Health Research, 8*, 618–633.

Krupp, J-A. (1993, Spring–Summer). Sexual relations at midlife and beyond. *Adultspan, 7*, 3–5,16–17.

Kuh, D. L., Wadsworth, M., & Hardy, R. (1997). Women's health in midlife: The influence of the menopause, social factors, and health in earlier life. *British Journal of Obstetrics and Gynaecology, 104*, 923–933.

Laan, E., & van Lunsen, R.H.W. (1997). Hormones and sexuality in postmenopausal women: A psychophysiological study. *British Journal of Psychosomatics, Obstetrics, and Gynaecology, 18*, 126–133.

Leiblum, S. (1990). Sexuality and the midlife woman. *Psychology of Women Quarterly, 14*, 495–508.

Leiblum, S. (1992). The sexual difficulties of women. *Journal of the Medical Association of Georgia, 81*, 221–225.

Leiblum, S., Bachmann, G., Kemmann, E., Colburn, D., & Swartzman, L (1983). Vaginal atrophy in the postmenopausal woman: The importance of sexual activity and hormones. *Journal of the American Medical Association, 249*, 2195–2198.

Lemaire, G. S., & Lenz, E. R. (1995). Perceived uncertainty about menopause in women attending an educational program. *International Journal of Nursing Studies, 32*, 39–48.

Liao, K. L. M., & Hunter, M. S. (1995). Knowledge and beliefs about menopause in a general population sample of mid-aged women. *Journal of Reproductive and Infant Psychology, 13*, 101–114.

Liao, K. L. M., & Hunter, M. S. (1998). Preparation for menopause: Prospective evaluation of a health education intervention for mid-aged women. *Maturitas, 29*, 215–224.

MacPherson, K. I. (1981). Menopause as disease: The social construction of a metaphor. *Advances in Nursing Science, 3*, 95.

Mansfield, P. K., Jorgensen, C. M., & Yu, L. (1989). The menopausal transition: Guidelines for researchers. *Health Education, 20*, 44–50.

Mansfield, P. K., Koch, P. B., & Voda, A. M. (1998). Qualities midlife women desire in their sexual relationships and their changing sexual response. *Psychology of Women Quarterly, 22*, 285–303.

Mansfield, P. K., Koch, P. B., & Voda, A. M. (2000). Midlife women's attributions for their sexual response changes. *Health Care for Women International, 21*, 543–559.

Mansfield, P. K., & Voda, A. M. (1993). From Edith Bunker to the 6:00 news: How and what midlife women learn about menopause. *Women & Therapy, 14*, 89–104.

Mansfield, P. K., Voda, A. M, & Koch, P. (1995). Predictors of sexual response changes in heterosexual midlife women. *Health Values, 19*, 10–20.

Masters, W. H., & Johnson, V. E. (1966). *Human sexual response*. Boston: Little, Brown.

Masters, W. H., & Johnson, V. E. (1981). Sex and the aging process. *Journal of the American Geriatrics Society, 29*, 385–390.

Masters, W. H., Johnson, V. E., & Kolodny, R. C. (1991). *Human sexuality*. Boston: Little, Brown.

Matthews, K. A., Kuller, L. H., Wing, R. R., & Meilahn, E. N. (1994). Biobehavioral aspects of menopause: Lessons from the healthy women study. *Experimental Gerontology, 29*, 337–342.

Matthews, K. A., Wing, R., Kuller, L., Meilahn, E., Kelsey, S., Costello, E., & Caggiula, A. (1990). Influences of natural menopause on psychological characteristics and symptoms of middle-aged healthy women. *Journal of Consulting and Clinical Psychology, 58*, 345–351.

McCormick, N. (1994). *Sexual salvation: Affirming women's sexual rights and pleasures*. Westport, CT: Praeger.

McCoy, N. L., & Davidson, J. M. (1985). A longitudinal study of the effects of menopause on sexuality. *Maturitas, 7*, 203–210.

McKinlay, J. B., & McKinlay, S. M. (1987). Depression in middle-aged women: Social circumstances versus estrogen deficiency. In R. Walsh (Ed.), *The psychology of women* (pp. 157–161). New Haven, CT: Yale University Press.

McKinlay, J. B., McKinlay, S. M., & Brambilla, D. J. (1987). The relative contributions of endocrine changes and social circumstances to depression in mid-aged women. *Journal of Health and Social Behavior, 28*, 345–363.

McKinlay, S. M. (1996). The normal menopause transition: An overview. *Maturitas, 23*, 137–145.

McKinlay, S. M., Brambilla, D. J., & Posner, J. G. (1992). The normal menopause transition. *Maturitas, 14*, 103–115.

McQuaide, S. (1998). Women at midlife. *Social Work, 43*, 21–31.

Middle-aged women's aches, pains studied. (1997, October 10). *Dallas Morning News*, p. A4.

Mitchell, E. S., & Woods, N. F. (1996). Symptom experiences of midlife women: Observations from the Seattle midlife women's health study. *Maturitas, 25*, 1–10.

Nachtigall, L. E. (1997). Sexual function in menopause and postmenopause. In C. W. Bardin (Ed.), *Current therapy in endocrinology and metabolism* (6th ed., pp. 632–636). St. Louis: C. V. Mosby.

National Women's Health Network. (1989). *Taking hormones and women's health: Choices, risks and benefits*. Washington, DC: Author

Newton, K. M., LaCroix, A. Z., Leveille, S. G., Rutter, C., Keenan, N. L., & Anderson, L. A. (1997). Women's beliefs and decisions about hormone replacement therapy. *Journal of Women's Health, 6*, 459–465.

Notman, M. T. (1998). Psychosocial aspects of menopause. In L. Dennerstein & J. Shelley (Eds.), *A woman's guide to menopause and hormone replacement therapy* (pp. 81–89). Washington, DC: American Psychiatric Press.

O'Connor, A. M., Tugwell, P., Wells, G. A., Elmslie, T., Jolly, E., Hollingworth, G., McPherson, R., Bunn, H., Graham, I., & Drake, E. (1998). A decision aid for women considering hormone therapy after menopause: Decision support framework and evaluation. *Patient Education and Counseling, 33*, 267–279.

Padonu, G., Holmes-Rovner, M., Rothert, M., Schmitt, N., Kroll, J., Rovner, D., Talarczyk, G., Breer, L., Ransom, S., & Gladney, E. (1996). African-American women's perception of menopause. *American Journal of Health Behavior, 20*, 242–251.

Palmlund, I. (1997a). The marketing of estrogens for menopausal and postmenopausal women. *Journal of Psychosomatics, Obstetrics, and Gynecology, 18*, 158–164.

Palmlund, I. (1997b). The social construction of menopause as risk. *Journal of Psychosomatics, Obstetrics, and Gynecology, 18*, 87–94.

Papalia, D. E., Camp, C. J., & Feldman, R. D. (1996). *Adult development and aging*. New York: McGraw-Hill.

Perlmutter, E., & Bart, P. E. (1982). Changing views of "the change": A critical review and suggestions for an attributional approach. In A. Voda, M. Dinnerstein, & S. R. O'Donnell (Eds.), *Changing perspectives on menopause* (pp. 187–199). Austin: University of Texas Press.

Poulin, C. (1992). Toward a multidimensional and multidirectional model of female sexual arousal. *Canadian Journal of Human Sexuality, 1*, 129–132.

Prestwood, K. M., Pilbeam, C. C., Burleson, J. A., Woodiel, F. N., Delmas, P. D., Deftos, L. J., & Raisz, L. G. (1994). The short-term effects of conjugated estrogen on bone turnover in older women. *Journal of Clinical Endocrinology and Metabolism, 79*, 366–371.

Rosenberg, L. (1993). Hormone replacement therapy: The need for reconsideration. *American Journal of Public Health, 150*, 190–194.

Ross, R. K., Paganini-Hill, J. A., Mack, T. M., & Henderson, B. E. (1987). Estrogen use and cardiovascular disease. In D. R. Mischel, Jr. (Ed.), *Menopause, physiology, and pharmacology* (pp. 209–224). Chicago: Year Book Medical.

Rossi, A. (1992, August). *Closing the gap: Bio-medical vs. social-behavioral factors in the experience of women and research on the menopausal transition*. Paper presented at the meeting of the American Psychological Association, Washington, DC.

Rostosky, S. S., & Travis, C. B. (2000). Menopause and sexuality: Ageism and sexism unite. In C. B Travis & J. W. White (Eds.), *Sexuality, society, and feminism* (pp. 181–209). Washington, DC: American Psychological Association.

Rothert, M., Rover, D., Holmen, M., Schmitt, N., Talarczyk, C., Knoll, J., & Gogato, J. (1990). Use of information regarding hormone replacement therapy. *Research in Nursing and Health, 13*, 355–366.

Roughan, P. A., Kaiser, F. E., & Morley, J. E. (1993). Sexuality and the older woman. *Clinics in Geriatric Medicine, 9*, 87–106

Rubin, L. B. (1982). Sex and sexuality: Women at midlife. In M. Kirkpatrick (Ed.), *Women's sexual experience—Exploration of the dark continent* (pp. 61–82). New York: Plenum Press.

Rubin, R. (July 10, 2002). Halted HRT study raises questions. *USA TODAY*, p. 7D.

Rueda, J. R. (1997). Medicalization of menopause and public health. *Journal of Obstetrics and Gynecology, 18*, 175–180.

Sang, B. (1993). Existential issues of midlife lesbians. In L. D. Garnets & D. C. Kimmel (Eds.), *Psychological perspectives on lesbian and gay male experiences* (pp. 500–516). New York: Columbia University Press.

Sarrel, P. M. (1990). Sexuality and menopause. *Obstetrics and Gynecology, 75*, 26–30.

Sarrel, P. M., Giblin, K., & Block, B. A. (1998, September). *Sexual interest and functioning in postmenopausal women: A community-based national survey.* Paper presented at the meeting of the North America Menopause Society, Toronto.

Sarrel, P. M., & Whitehead, M. I. (1985). Sex and menopause: Defining the issues. *Maturitas, 7*, 217–224.

Schlossberg, N. K. (1986). Mid-life. In C. Tavris (Ed.), *Everywoman's emotional well-being* (pp. 238–257). Garden City, NY: Doubleday.

Seaman, B. (1977). *Women and the crisis in sex hormones.* New York: Bantam Books.

Shangold, M. (1990). Exercise in the menopausal woman. *Obstetrics and Gynecology, 75*, 53S–58S.

Sheehy, G. (1998). *The silent passage.* New York: Pocket Books.

Smith, D. C., Prentice, R., Thompson, D. J., & Hermann, W. L. (1975). Association of exogenous estrogen and endometrial carcinoma. *New England Journal of Medicine, 293*, 1164–1167.

Sobel, N. B. (1994, June). Progestins in preventive hormone therapy. *Obstetrics and Gynecology Clinics of North America, 21*, 299–319.

Spence, A. P. (1989). *Biology of human aging.* Englewood Cliffs, NJ: Prentice Hall.

Starr, B. (1993). Sex in the later adult years. In R. Kastenbaum (Ed.), *Encyclopedia of adult development* (pp. 429–432). Phoenix, AZ: Oryx.

Starr, B., & Weiner, M. (1981). *The Starr-Weiner report on sex and sexuality in the mature years.* New York: McGraw-Hill.

Stewart, D. E., Boydell, K., Derzko, C., & Marshall, V. (1992). Psychologic distress during the menopausal years in women attending a menopause clinic. *International Journal of Psychiatry in Medicine, 22*, 213–220.

Stimpson, C. R. (1982). The fallacy of bodily reductioning. In A. Voda, M. Dinnerstein, & S. O'Donnell (Eds.), *Changing perspective on menopause* (pp. 265–272). Austin: University of Texas Press.

Struk-Ware, R. (1991). Hormonal replacement therapy: What to prescribe, how, and for how long. In J. R. Struk-Ware & J. W. Utian (Eds.), *The menopause and hormonal replacement therapy* (pp. 259–282). New York: Marcel Dekker.

Suling, L., Carlson, E. S., Snyder, D., & Holm, K. (1995). Perspectives on menopause. *Clinical Nurse Specialist, 9*, 145–148.

Taffe, J., Garamszegi, C., Dudley, E., & Dennerstein, L. (1997). Determinants of self rated menopause status. *Maturitas, 27*, 223–229.

Theisen, S. C., & Mansfield, P. K. (1993). Menopause: Social construction or biological destiny? *Journal of Health Education, 24*, 209–213.

Utian, W. (1989). Biosynthesis and physiologic effects of estrogen and pathophysiologic effects of estrogen deficiency: A review. *American Journal of Obstetrics and Gynecology, 161*, 1828–1831.

Utian, W. (1990). The menopause in perspective: From potions to patches. *Annuals of the New York Academy of Sciences, 592*, 1–7.

Utian, W. (1991). Menopause—A proposed new functional definition. *Maturitas, 14*, 1–2.

Utian, W., & Boggs, P. B. (1999). The North American Menopause Society 1998 menopause survey. Part I: Postmenopausal women's perceptions about menopause and midlife. *Menopause, 6*, 122–128.

Utian, W., & Lobo, R. A. (1990). Cardiovascular implications of estrogen replacement therapy. *Obstetrics and Gynecology, 75*, 185.

Viagra doesn't work in women. (1999, March). *Script*, p. 23.

Viagra strikes out for women. (2000). [On-line]. Available: http://www.canoe.com/Health0005/23 sex.html.

Voda, A. M. (1991). The Tremin Trust: An intergenerational research program on events associated with women's menstrual and reproductive lives. In D. Taylor & N. Woods (Eds.), *Menstruation, health, and illness* (pp. 5–18). New York: Hemisphere.

Voda, A. M. (1992). Menopause: A normal view. *Clinical Obstetrics and Gynecology, 35*, 923–933.

Voda, A. M. (1994). Risks and benefits associated with hormonal and surgical therapies for health midlife women. *Western Journal of Nursing Research, 16*, 507–523.

Voda, A. M., Dinnerstein, M., & O'Donnell, S. R. (Eds.). (1982). *Changing perspectives on menopause*. Austin: University of Texas Press.

Weg, R. B. (1989). Sensuality/sexuality of the middle years. In S. Hunter & M. Sundel (Eds.), *Midlife myths: Issues, findings, and practice implications* (pp. 31–50). Newbury Park, CA: Sage Publications.

Wilk, C. A., & Kirk, M. A. (1995). Menopause: A developmental stage, not a deficiency disease. *Psychotherapy, 32*, 233–241.

Wilson, R. (1966). *Feminine forever*. New York: M. Evans.

Woods, N. F. (1993). Midlife women's health: There's more to it than menopause. In B. J. McElmurry & R. S. Parker (Eds.), *Annual review of women's health* (pp. 165–196). New York: National League for Nursing Press.

Woods, N. F. (1998). Menopause: Models, medicine, and midlife. *Frontiers, 19*, 51–9.

Woods, N. F., & Mitchell, E. S. (1995). Midlife women: Decisions about using hormone therapy for preventing disease in old age. In B. J. McElmurry & R. S. Parker (Eds.), *Annual review of women's health* (Vol. 2, pp. 11–33). New York: National League for Nursing Press.

Woods, N. F., & Mitchell, E. S. (1996). Patterns of depressed mood in midlife women: Observations from the Seattle midlife women's health study. *Research in Nursing & Health, 19*, 111–123.

Woods, N. F., & Mitchell, E. S. (1999). Anticipating menopause: Observations from the Seattle midlife women's health study. *Menopause: Journal of the American Menopause Society,   6*, 167–173.

World Health Organization, Scientific Group. (1981). *Research on menopause* (WHO Technical Services Rep. Series No. 670). Geneva: Author.

World Health Organization. (1996). *Scientific group on research on menopause in the 1990s* (Tech. Rep. No. 886). Geneva, Switzerland: Author.

Ziel, H. K., & Finkle, W. D. (1975). Increased risk of endometrial carcinoma among users of conjugated estrogens. *New England Journal of Medicine, 293*, 1167–1170.

ADDITIONAL REFERENCES

Avis, N. E., Brambilla, D., Vass, K., & McKinlay, S. M. The effect of widowhood on health: A prospective analysis from the Massachusetts Women's Health Study. *Social Science & Medicine, 33,* 1063–1070.

Bell, M. L. (1995). Attitudes toward menopause among Mexican American women. *Health Care for Women International, 16,* 425–435.

CHAPTER 8

EMOTIONAL CONCERNS

E xposure to stress at midlife, and the question of whether the notion of "crisis" fits the experience of many midlife women, are discussed in this chapter. The current data on depression and suicide for midlife women are also examined because of the high prevalence of these difficulties during this period. Life-span themes include normative and nonnormative events, losses, adaptation, off-time/on-time, and multiple influences.

QUESTIONS TO CONSIDER

- *What are examples of the stressful biological and social changes experienced by midlife women?*

- *What evidence counters a universal crisis at midlife?*

- *To what extent is depression experienced by midlife women?*

- *What are some of the multiple factors that influence depression?*

- *What is the association between physical health and depression?*

- *What are the risk factors for depression among midlife lesbians, including those who are African American?*

- *What factors affect suicide rates of midlife women?*

- *Which particular risk factors can influence the suicide rates among midlife lesbians?*

Current use of the term midlife instead of middle age expresses the politics of optimism (Gullette, 1998). Yet, the words midlife and crisis for many of us are an automatic association. The link between crisis and midlife permeates the media, self-help books, and the thinking of the general public as well as professional clinicians. What are the facts about the midlife crisis?

PRESUMPTION OF CRISIS

Popular works (for example, Sheehy, 1977, 1996) suggest that crises happen during midlife. Americans have adopted this concept as a way to provide meaning for situations that seem unusual or difficult and for help in appraising and coping with these situations (Wethington, 2000).

Midlife women experience considerable biological and social changes in conjunction with aging. Many of these changes involve *losses* that create stress. For example, as discussed in previous chapters, children grow up and leave, reproductive capacity stops at menopause, and youth is gone. Women also begin grieving over lost friends and family members as they grow older and die (Dunn & Galloway, 1986). One parent most likely is already deceased, and the surviving parent may be in declining health (Bumpass & Aquilino, 1995). Women are also at greater risk than men during midlife of losing their marital partner through death (Lazarus & Delongis, 1983).

Given that women experience stressful events during midlife, do these events create a crisis? The answer to this question is that it all depends. Stress is experienced by midlife women (and men) at a higher than average level (Chiriboga, 1997). Yet, the severity of reactions to stressful events is largely associated with women's perceptions of the stress associated with the events (Lazarus, 1966) and the extent to which the events disrupt their lives (Neugarten, 1976). Substantial research indicates that negative outcomes of life events are more likely and *adaptation* more difficult when the events are not predictable or occur "*off time*" or "off schedule" (Hagestad, 1990; Lazarus & Delongis, 1983).

These *nonnormative events* are likely to disrupt women's lives. Events that occur when anticipated, however, do not markedly disrupt the rhythm of their lives. Most women hold in their minds a time line of their lives. They anticipate and plan for certain life events such as children leaving home, losing parents, and retirement from work. When these events occur "*on time*," they are considered as predictable, *normative*, and *age-graded events*. As such, they do not disrupt women's lives in substantial ways (Neugarten, 1976; Schlossberg, Troll, & Leibowitz, 1978).

Aside from the likelihood of *normative* and anticipated events, rather than *nonnormative* and disruptive events, happening in midlife, no direct evidence supports the presumption of crisis at midlife (Rosenberg, Rosenberg, &

Farrell, 1999). Distress does not peak at this time in life (Baruch, Barnett, & Rivers, 1983; Costa & McCrae, 1978), a necessary circumstance to substantiate the prevalence of midlife crisis. Midlife is neither more nor less traumatic for most people than any other period in life (Chiriboga, 1989; Pearlin, 1985). Generally, severe mental health difficulties are not experienced during midlife (Kessler, Foster, Webster, & House, 1992). At midlife, there may be a preoccupation with issues such as limited time and personal mortality (Neugarten, 1968), and one's values and investments may be reassessed; however, there is usually not the panic and upheaval associated with a crisis. Persons who experience a crisis may have personality traits that make them vulnerable to crises. If these persons experience a crisis at midlife, however, there is no direct association between this experience and entering the middle period of life (McCrae & Costa, 1990).

Many other studies challenge the applicability of the notion of crisis specifically to women's experiences in midlife (for example, Costa & McCrae, 1980; McQuaide, 1998). For example, most of the women in McQuaide's sample of midlife women reported satisfaction with themselves and their lives, but they also experienced midlife as a challenging time. Of the three-quarters of women who reported that they were happy, only about half of them reported that coping with midlife was easy. They did not view this period, however, as one of torment; nor did whatever stress they were coping with prevent happiness. In another study of 500 midlife women, most of them reported positive attitudes about their lives (80 percent to 90 percent) and their futures (80 percent; see Society for Research on Women in New Zealand, 1988). Lachman, Lewkowicz, Marcus, and Peng (1994) reported that about 45 percent of midlife women who believed there was a midlife crisis associated it with fears of aging. Niemela and Lento (1993) reported, however, that older midlife women (ages 52–55), compared to younger midlife women (ages 49–51), viewed their lives more positively. Women studied by Helson and Wink (1992) reported "difficult times" (versus "crisis") in their 40s but experienced personal stability by their 50s.

Women typically view midlife as a time of changes or transitions instead of crises (Woods & Mitchell, 1997). Stewart and Ostrove (1998) called these changes "midcourse corrections" (p. 1188). Often, such corrections are precipitated by regrets about the goals that women pursued. About one-third of the women in the Class of 1964 from the Radcliffe Longitudinal Study (Stewart & Vandewater, 1999) reported at age 37 that they would not repeat their same life patterns. They experienced "traditional role regrets" or wished that they had pursued other goals, such as work or education before making family commitments. These regrets precipitated a renewal of goals given up earlier. Most (two-thirds) of these women made major changes in their educational or work lives between the ages of 37 and 43. Many women who did not experience regrets also made numerous changes during this period in their lives. The women who experienced regrets and a desire for changes in their lives were not more likely than other women in the sample to make changes. The women with regrets who did not make changes, however, experienced lower well-being in their mid-40s whereas the women who did make changes experienced higher well-being. The researchers replicated these findings with the participants in a sample from the Class of 1967 at the University of Michigan (for example, Tangri & Jenkins, 1993). By age 47, the women in this sample who expressed regrets and did not make changes experienced more depression and rumination, and less effective instrumentality. With these exceptions, however, most of the women in both the Radcliffe and Michigan samples experienced high levels of psychological *adaptation* and low levels of depression by age 47 or 48.

DEPRESSION

Despite the mostly positive findings reported above, the image of midlife women as depressed is strong (McKinlay & McKinlay, 1987). Depression is the most common complaint of women who seek mental health care and the most frequent reason they visit physicians (Strickland, 1992). It is also the most common reason for lesbians to seek counseling (McGrath, Keita, Strickland, & Russo, 1992; Rothblum, 1990). The status of midlife women regarding depression and suicide is addressed in the remainder of this chapter.

What signs must occur for an accurate assessment of depression? The *Diagnostic and Statistical Manual of Mental Disorders* (DSM-IV) of the American Psychiatric Association (1994) states that a major depressive episode involves a number of signs that persist for at least two weeks, and a change from previous functioning is noticeable. Most of these signs, which appear in Exhibit 8.1, are observable every day. At least four of the nine signs must be observable for an assessment of depression, according to the DSM-IV.

———— Exhibit 8.1
    Signs of Depression ——————————————————————————————

- Depressed mood throughout the day

- Lack of pleasure in life activities

- More than a 5 percent weight loss or gain in one month

- Sleep disturbances

- Increased unusual and agitated physical activity or decreased physical activity

- Fatigue or lack of energy

- Feelings of worthlessness or guilt

- Inability to make decisions and concentrate

- Recurring thoughts of death or suicide

The signs of depression are moderately reliable across nations (Culbertson, 1997) and do not appear to be associated with education, ethnicity, or marital status (American Psychiatric Association, 1994).

Several other categories of depression exist other than major depression. Dysthymia is a less severe condition but tends to last longer, typically for two or more years. The difficulties are the same as experienced with major depression but are experienced with lower intensity (Hinrichsen, 1993). Cyclothymic disorder is a mood disturbance involving alternate periods of hypomanic symptoms (elevated, expansive, or irritable mood) and depressive symptoms (American Psychiatric Association, 1994). Depression following the loss of someone important, or bereavement, is an anticipated and normative response to such a situation. Yet, sometimes bereavement develops into a major depression (Hinrichsen, 1993). According to the DSM-IV, if bereavement persists longer than two months after a loss, an assessment of major depression is likely (American Psychiatric Association, 1994). Yet, many practitioners believe that the normal bereavement process lasts longer than two months.

The Epidemiological Catchment Area Study, sponsored by the National Institute of Mental Health, provided the first solid information on the prevalence of several categories of depression (Robins & Regier, 1991). Depression of some degree and lasting at least two weeks is experienced by almost one-third of the U.S. population, major depression by 4.9 percent, and dysthymia by 2.7 percent. Many people with dysthymia also experience major depression at some time in their lives (Robins & Regier, 1991).

Only one out of four depressed persons seeks treatment (Sussman, Robins, & Earls, 1987). With no treatment, major depressive episodes eventually end, but depression usually ends earlier with treatment (Hinrichsen, 1993). Treatment is effective in approximately 80 percent of cases (Strickland, 1992). Even with treatment, however, more than half of individuals with an episode of major depression will experience later episodes (Hinrichsen, 1993).

Depression Experienced by Midlife Women

It is uncertain whether sex–gender discrepancies characterize the general prevalence rates of mental health difficulties in adulthood (for example, Gatz & Smyer, 1992; George 1990), but rates of specific difficulties reflect sex–gender discrepancies. Women generally experience higher rates of affective conditions than men, especially depression and anxiety (for example, Gatz & Smyer, 1992; Sprock & Yoder, 1997). Some studies reported that women were at least twice as likely and maybe as much as four times as likely to suffer from depression as men, regardless of social class or race (for example, American Psychiatric Association, 1994). These sex–gender discrepancies are more prevalent in developed than in developing countries (Culbertson, 1997).

Although sex–gender differences may be found in the rates of depression, there is no clear evidence that women experience more depression in midlife than during other life periods (for example, Bebbington et al., 1998). Even so, midlife women do experience depression, and the causes are complex.

The general view of mental health difficulties today, including depression, is that they result from *multiple determining factors*, such as biological, sociocultural, and psychological, and from developmental issues. Biological influences can include hormonal changes due to menopause, neurochemical changes, and genetics. Sociocultural variables can include discrimination, socioeconomic status, social and political structures, and social support systems. Psychological factors can include perceptions of stress, locus of control, effects of divorce and bereavement, and ineffective coping skills (Mishara, 1993; Warren, 1995). Developmental issues can include reassessments of previous life choices and regrets about missed paths.

At the top of the list of additional explanations for depression in midlife women are changes in estrogen levels and vasomotor signs, such as hot flashes and sleep disturbances associated with dropping estrogen levels. As discussed in Chapter 7, however, the more recent view about psychological consequences of menopause, largely developed through longitudinal studies, is that the natural menopausal transition is not a mental-breakdown phenomenon. Instead, it is a *normal transition* in women's development (for example, Voda, 1992). When menopause is a *normative* experience, women rarely perceive it as the crisis depicted by the biomedical perspective and they do not get depressed because of it (Rossi, 1980).

One factor that does seem to influence depression at midlife (discussed in Chapter 6) is a woman's health status (Woods & Mitchell, 1996). Other relevant factors, addressed here, include sex–gender role identification, personality characteristics, and social circumstances.

Sex–Gender Role Identification. Sex–gender role identification and depression were addressed in a study by Tinsley, Sullivan-Guest, and McGuire (1984). The sample of women (ages 35–50) included a clinical group undergoing treatment for depression. A nonclinical group was used for comparison. Depression was associated with traditional feminine sex–gender roles. Almost three-quarters (73 percent) of women in the clinical group scored in the feminine range of a sex–gender role inventory whereas only 12.5 percent of women in the non-clinical group (those not seeking treatment) scored in this range. The second highest range (20 percent) for the clinical group was the near-feminine role. None of the women in the clinical group had scores in the masculine range; only one woman in this group scored in the androgynous range. In contrast, more than a third (37.5 percent) of the nonclinical group scored in the androgynous range, a third (33.3 percent) in the near-feminine range, and about one-sixth (16.7 percent) in the masculine range. Tinsley et al. (1984) concluded that midlife women who adopted androgynous and masculine sex–gender roles were least likely to be depressed. These women displayed traits such as self-reliance, assertion, and independence, whereas women who adopted a feminine sex–gender role displayed traits such as passivity, helplessness, and dependency.

Traits associated with the female sex–gender role and their association with the vulnerability of midlife women to experience depressive signs were also the focus of a study by Bromberger and Matthews (1996a). The sample included 460 premenopausal women, ages 42–50. A reassessment followed three years later. The traits evaluated in the study are more characteristic of women than men: low instrumentality (for example, passive versus assertive and dominant); high expressivity (for example, nurturant and sensitive to the needs and feelings of others); high tendency to internally self-focus on feelings and thoughts when challenged with difficulties (associated with self-consciousness and ruminative coping responses such as dwelling on the negative characteristics of a stressful situation), and the tendency to suppress angry feelings. Three of these four traits were associated with depressive signs. Women who were low on instrumentality, high on self-focus, and who suppressed angry feelings experienced more depressive signs over the three-year period. High expressivity was not associated with these signs. Of the three traits with positive associations, suppression of angry feelings was less important than low instrumentality and high self-focus. Bromberger and Matthews concluded that certain sex–gender linked traits (low instrumentality, high self-focus, and suppression of anger) increase the vulnerability of women characterized by these traits to psychological distress in midlife. These traits may partly be associated with the greater rates (at least double) of depression in women compared to men.

Personality Characteristics. A subset of midlife women with certain personality characteristics may be more vulnerable than others to adverse responses to the common stressors of midlife, such as menopause. Bromberger and Matthews (1996b) specifically evaluated whether pessimism and trait anxiety can create vulnerability in midlife women to depressive signs when they experience stressful situations during this period of life. The sample included the midlife women identified in their three-year study on sex–gender linked traits discussed above. The signs for the disposition of pessimism, identified by Scheier and Carver (1988), included "passivity," the "withdrawal of effort," and "stopping the pursuance of goals" in the face of a stressful situation. In contrast, the disposition of optimism included signs such as "more likely to cope with stressful situations successfully" and "continue to pursue goals" in the face of stress. The pessimistic women reported more depressive signs than did the optimistic women, especially when they identified recent or chronic difficulties that they perceived as stressful. The measure of trait anxiety used the definitions of neuroticism, a stable dimension of personality. It consisted of an array of aspects such as "chronic negative emotions, including sadness, anxiety, guilt, anger, and cognitive and behavioral characteristics, including low self-esteem and self-preoccupation" (Bromberger & Matthews, 1996b, p. 208). Women who were generally anxious reported more depressive signs, regardless of whether or not they experienced any life stress.

Social Circumstances Perspective. Psychological distress is generally more affected by negative life events than is physical distress (George, 1989). Depression in several studies was associated more with external circumstances than internal ones such as the hormonal changes of menopause (for example, Hunter, 1996; Schmidt, Roca, Bloch, & Rubinow, 1997; see Chapter 7). Social and cultural factors unique to women's lives and strongly associated with the higher rate of depression for women include victimization; economic deprivation and restricted occupational mobility; restrictive sex–gender role expectations; less power, respect, and status; and lowered self-efficacy and sense of personal control (Lemme, 1999). In addition, because of their emotional involvement and feelings of responsibility for a wide network of persons (Carter & McGoldrick, 1989), women experience stress throughout their lives. Various studies reported that increased stress and depression are more likely when women experience worries and difficulties about husbands, children, and other relationships (for example, Avis, Brambilla, & McKinlay, 1994; Kaufert, Gilbert, & Tate, 1992; Schmidt et al., 1997). The demand for continual nurturing tasks, at the expense of one's personal well-being, may play a role in women's depression rates (Lemme, 1999).

Buffers against Depression

Negative life events are likely to lead to substantially more negative consequences if women lack personal and social resources (Kastenbaum, 1993a). Four resources identified here can act as buffers for modifying such consequences, including depression.

Education, Employment, and Income. When retired persons were asked what they would do differently if they had their lives to live over, they reported that greater educational attainment would have made a difference in the quality of their lives (DeGenova, 1993). In another study both educational and occupational attainments were significantly associated with emotional well-being (Willis & Schaie, 1986). The more educated women are, the less likely they will suffer from depression (Willits & Funk, 1989). Midlife and older women with less than 12 years of education were found to be at increased risk for major depression (Gallo, Royall, & Anthony, 1993). Many other studies reported that work was positively associated with mental health in women (for example, Baruch & Barnett, 1986; Carr, 1997; Drebing, Gooden, Drebing, Van De Kemp, & Malony, 1995). Drebing et al. (1995) reported that a career consistently boosted mental health and, particularly, a sense of purpose in life. In a study by Bromberger and Mathews (1994) unemployed midlife women reported more depressive signs than employed women. The most depressed unemployed women were those who attained the least education and either experienced low support from family and friends or reported low marital satisfaction. Three years later, depressive signs decreased for women who were unemployed initially but employed at follow-up, except for those women who had the additional factors of low levels of education, social support, or marital satisfaction. The positive effects of employment may not be strong for some women experiencing stressful life circumstances, but for others, under conditions of low life stress, new employment results in a quick and positive effect. Other researchers reported analogous findings (for example, Adelmann, Antonucci, Crohan, & Coleman, 1989; Wilbur & Dan, 1989).

In Carr's (1997) study midlife women who met their career goals, set when they were ages 35– 36, experienced significantly less depression at ages 52–53 than women who did not meet their career goals. For women in the former group, surpassing their career goals was not a significant predictor of depression. For women in the latter group, the larger the gap between their goals and their accomplishments, the greater the psychological harm experienced. Women in this group not only were significantly higher in depression levels but also were lower in purpose-in-life levels.

To a small degree, family characteristics, such as marriage and adult children, compensated for not attaining one's career goals. The success of raising children to adulthood, for example, may "balance" out a less than hoped for work life. Marriage and children may also act to reduce one's early aspirations in the workplace so that they are redirected from work to family. If this occurs, work aspirations may no longer be a significant factor in one's mental health. Another subgroup of women, those who did not know what their future goal was when they were age 35 or 36, experienced significantly higher depression levels and reduced purpose-in-life levels than did women who developed work aspirations. Having no work aspirations was especially persistent over time in reducing purpose-in-life levels. Findings on another subgroup of women, however, were somewhat contradictory. At age 35 or 36, these women, who hoped to be keeping house in 10 years, experienced significantly reduced purpose-in-life levels. Yet, this result disappeared by ages 52–53 when purpose-in-life levels of these women were not significantly low.

Three factors found by Costello (1991) seemed to protect midlife women from depression: choice, stability, and adaptability. Two of the factors, choice and adaptability, were associated with preparation for and participation in work. Choice included making a determination to continue one's education and deciding whether to work for pay. Adaptability was characteristic of women who adjusted to social changes and joined the workplace; the workplace factor was especially pertinent for those who attained managerial or professional positions. Remaining unmarried or married to the same partner reflected stability (Costello, 1991).

Income can also be a crucial factor influencing depression in midlife women. Rawson and Jenson (1995) found that both the husband's and wife's incomes were statistically significant factors in alleviating depression in the wives. In addition, having her own income at the time of entry into midlife contributed to the stability of a wife's well-being as measured by level of depression.

Marriage. In some studies, the rates of depression for always-single women are low and for married women intermediate (Avis et al., 1994; McKinlay & McKinlay, 1987). Yet, other studies show that marriage is associated with lower depression levels in midlife women and contributes other benefits such as higher psychological well-being. Drebing et al. (1995) found that the presence of a marriage/intimacy component in the current life dreams of midlife women is important to their mental health. This component included continued interest in and pursuit of intimate relationships, particularly marital. Married persons also tend to show greater psychological well-being than unmarried persons, as well as other benefits such as better health and greater longevity (Waite, 1995). Marital satisfaction is associated with both mental and physical well-being (Tower & Kasl, 1996).

It may not be just marriage itself that is the necessary factor associated with positive mental health. For example, several studies found that the most depressed midlife women were widowed, divorced, or separated but it was ambiguous which factor had the greatest effect on depression—loss of partner, income, or social support. These women also completed less than 12 years of education (Avis et al., 1994; McKinlay & McKinlay, 1987). In a study by Earle, Smith, Harris, and Longino (1998), it was discovered that although married midlife women were less likely to report depression than unmarried counterparts, other factors such as self-rated health, employment status, and marital satisfaction predicted emotional well-being at midlife better than one's marital status. Happiness with one's marriage seems especially important.

Women who reported marital dissatisfaction in the Earle et al. (1998) study were five times more likely to report depression than were men who reported marital dissatisfaction. In contrast to women who reported happy marriages, unhappily married women were 3.5 times more likely to report depression. Tower and Kasl (1996) reported an association between marital distress and conflict and a greater degree of depression. A good marriage, however, was found to provide support and mediate stress.

It may also be the case that the marriage/intimacy component of one's life dream loses significance over time. In an Australian sample of women the most popular early dream content area was marriage/intimacy (61 percent versus 36 percent for occupation). When these women entered midlife, however, their dream content changed dramatically. Personal or more individualistic goals were the most popular content (43 percent), compared to marriage/family content (26 percent) and occupational content (27 percent). The researchers interpreted this finding as indicating the desire for greater fulfillment of personal goals at this time in life (Minter & Samuels, 1998).

Midlife Lesbians and Depression

The rates of depression among lesbians vary according to the few studies that focused on them. In the National Lesbian Health Care Survey (Bradford, Ryan, & Rothblum, 1994) of almost two thousand (1,925) lesbians, depression characterized 11 percent of the sample. Constant anxiety or fear was experienced by 11 percent. The oldest group of women (age 55 and older) was least likely to report depression or anxiety. In an earlier study, lesbians reported more depressive episodes (44 percent) than heterosexual women (35 percent; Saghir, Robins, Walbran, & Gentry, 1970). In a study of lesbians and gynecological care, Johnson, Smith, and Guenther (1987) also measured the rate of depression. They found that 30 percent of the sample reported difficulties with depression.

Rothblum (1990) identified some of the risk factors for depression among lesbians. First, in line with many studies that associated clinical depression with lack of social support (for example, Brown & Harris, 1978; Surtees, 1980), similar findings were reported for lesbians (for example, Kurdek, 1988; Kurdek & Schmitt, 1987). Second, disruption of a partnership, whether for heterosexual or lesbian women, is a risk factor for depression. Third, though coming out to oneself as a lesbian can result in many positive consequences, there can also be a down side when one informed others. Fears about negative repercussions are often realistic, such as rejection by family or custody fights over one's children (Gartrell, 1981). How open a woman was about her same-sex sexual orientation, and how it was experienced, also affected psychological health in the Bradford and Ryan (1989) survey. Almost half (49 percent) of another sample of lesbians experienced depression and the disclosure to others about their sexual orientation played a part (Saunders, Tupac, & MacCulloch, 1988). Rothblum found that lesbians who came out to themselves in isolation, those who could not risk the disclosure to others, and those geographically isolated were all at risk for alienation and depression.

From a study of a large, heterogeneous group of African American lesbian and gay persons, Cochran and Mays (1994) reported rates of depression. They speculated that higher depressive distress among these persons may be attributable partly to the "interactive nature of stigmatisation" (p. 528) for being a gay, lesbian, racial, or ethnic person, and, if a woman, for being female. Those who carry multiple lower social statuses may be particularly at risk for depression. The women showed higher levels of distress than the men, except for men infected with HIV/AIDS.

SUICIDE

The ninth leading cause of death in the United States is suicide (U.S. Bureau of the Census, 1994). Two-thirds of the approximately 30,000 reported suicides in the United States each year may be related to major depression (Strickland, 1992). For persons with severe major depression, up to 15 percent will die by suicide (American Psychiatric Association, 1994). Various demographic factors affect suicide rates. Among these factors, the four most pertinent are: age, sex–gender, ethnicity, and marital status.

First, suicide rates increase with age and are generally highest in old age. Midlife persons are also at a high risk for suicide with the rates about 25 percent higher for them than for the nation as a whole (McIntosh, 1991).

Second, women attempt suicide more often than men (Canetto & Sakinofsky, 1998), but more men than women commit suicide at every adult age, regardless of ethnic and racial background (Strickland, 1992). During midlife, suicide rates for men are more than twice as high as for women, and they rise sharply from midlife onward. It is not until after age 65 that the suicide rates for men peak (McIntosh, 1991). Suicide rates for women increase moderately until midlife when they peak (approximately between ages 45–54), and then they decline (Adamek & Kaplan, 1996; Kastenbaum, 1993b; McIntosh, 1991).

Third, suicide rates for non-Caucasians are highest at ages younger than 35, peak by age 35, and decline to lower levels in middle and old age (McIntosh, 1991). White suicide rates are higher than African American suicide rates at all adult ages (Gibbs, 1997; Strickland, 1992). Generally, the rates are two times higher for white women in the United States than for African American women (U.S. Department of Health and Human Services, 1992), but suicide attempts are about the same for these two groups (Nisbett, 1996).

McIntosh proposed that the lower rate for non-Caucasians at midlife and later is their frequent experiences with low income, poverty, racism, and discrimination throughout life. Midlife may not pose as drastic a change in status for them as it does for those who do not continually experience these adverse types of life experiences. Gibbs proposed that various protective factors also reduce the suicide rates of African Americans, including religious beliefs and life-affirming philosophies, important roles for elders, extended family and kin networks, and cohesion in ethnic neighborhoods reinforced by the extended family. In addition, African American women play a central role in their community and learn how to cope with adverse situations. They also experience strong social networks and shared resources. Some African American women who experience chronic and intense anger and frustration and, in addition, hopelessness may attempt suicide (for example, Alston & Anderson, 1995).

Fourth, marital status seems to be a factor associated with suicide rates in midlife. Generally, women, African Americans, and married persons are less likely to commit suicide than males, Caucasians, or unmarried persons. In midlife, however, married women are particularly vulnerable to suicide. Compared to married men, they are significantly more likely to commit suicide in midlife than in later years (Humphrey & Palmer, 1990–1991).

Do Midlife Factors Influence Women's Suicide Rates?

Women are more likely to commit suicide in midlife than in younger or later years. Are there identifiable factors associated with midlife that trigger suicide in women? Although women experience many changes in midlife, there are no known reasons for the high suicide rate (McIntosh, 1991). All the reasons discussed here, therefore, are conjecture. Several possible reasons were suggested by Humphrey and Palmer (1990–1991):

- Many midlife women experience loss of their youthful appearances at the same time as they lose their primary roles as mothers when their children leave home. If mothers are not in a career or job they consider worthwhile, they may view their future as bleak.

- Marriage may not provide meaningful support. Husbands may still be overinvolved in careers and other outside activities.

- Children are no longer around to help integrate mothers with the community.

The question of which factors serve as triggers for suicide during midlife remains unanswered. Some of the factors proposed as boosting the suicide

rates for midlife women may be exaggerated. For example, the event of children leaving home is not a stressor for most women. Instead, most women
experience reduced stress and accompanying relief (see Chapter 2).
Menopause may trigger concerns about purpose, self-worth, and attractiveness in a society that values youth. Still, menopause is not depressing to most
women (see Chapter 7). Other factors may lead to suicide, such as the expanding divorce rate, unemployment, and widowhood (McIntosh, 1991). A number of other factors may also be associated with suicidal behaviors in midlife
and older women, including a history of child abuse, rape, battering, interpersonal difficulties, employment and financial difficulties, and alcoholism
(Osgood & Malkin, 1998). A strong association between physical abuse in
childhood and suicidal behavior in African American women was reported by
Manetta (1999). Sexual abuse in childhood was also a more frequent occurrence for those with suicidal behaviors compared to those who did not have
suicidal behaviors (Manetta, 1999).

   Noting that suicide results from *multiple factors*, Mos'cicki (1995) identified broad categories of risk factors. The categories include psychiatric (mental
or addictive disorders), biological, familial, and situational. As an example, in
the familial category, Smith, Mercy, and Conn (1988) found that suicide rates
in all age groups of women are highest among divorced women, peaking
between ages 35–54. The next highest rates occur among widowed women and
after that among always-single women. The patterns are analogous for white
and African American women. Mos'cicki indicated that multiple risk factors
may coexist, with the chance of suicide or suicidal behavior increasing when
there are a greater number of risk factors.

Lesbians and Suicide

In a review of studies on suicide, Saunders and Valente (1987) discovered that
the sexual orientation of individuals who complete suicide is not often known.
It is difficult, then, to determine the exact rates of suicide for lesbians. The currently known suicide attempt rates show that white lesbians are two and a half
times more likely to report suicide attempts compared to heterosexual women.
Data from the National Lesbian Health Care Survey showed that attempted
suicide rates of white lesbians (16 percent) were lower than they were for
African American (27 percent) and Latino lesbians (28 percent). Overall, the
attempted suicide rate for lesbians was 18 percent. Older lesbians (age 55 and
older) were least likely to experience thoughts about suicide or attempt it
(Bradford et al., 1994).

   Use of alcohol in combination with depression and previous suicide
attempts increase the risk potential for suicide among lesbians (Saghir &
Robins, 1973). Other risk factors may include feelings of alienation due to

prejudice and discrimination and not being part of a supportive lesbian community or religious institution (Saunders & Valente, 1987).

SUMMARY

- The association of crisis with midlife is largely unsubstantiated.

- The rate of depression in midlife women is high, and it is also the most common complaint of women of all ages who seek mental health care.

- A woman's health status seems to be an important factor influencing depression at midlife; women in poorer health report higher levels of depression. Other associated factors include sex–gender role identification, personality characteristics, and social circumstances.

- Factors that may reduce the risk of depression include higher educational level, paid employment, marital satisfaction, and higher family income.

- Accurate rates of depression among midlife lesbians are not available because of the limited number of prevalence studies on this population.

- Risk factors for depression among lesbians include a lack of social support, disruption of a partnership, and disclosure of their sexual orientation to others.

- Women are more likely to commit suicide at midlife than during their younger or later years, and married women are particularly vulnerable at midlife.

- The suicide rate is two times higher for white women than for African American women in the United States, though suicide attempts are about the same for these two groups.

- White lesbians are two and one-half times more likely to report suicide attempts than heterosexual women, but suicide attempt rates for white lesbians are lower than for African American and Latino lesbians.

- The causes for suicide among midlife women are unknown; though multiple risk factors are likely, none have the support of research data or support for them is minimal.

IMPLICATIONS FOR PRACTICE

Professional helpers need to be familiar with research knowledge questioning the assumption that women will experience a crisis at midlife. It is more likely that women will seek mental health care for depression than for a midlife crisis. Practitioners need to know the biological, psychological, and social factors associated with depression in midlife women. Particularly, counselors and psychotherapists need to be prepared to encounter higher levels of depression in women with poor health, low education, lack of paid employment, low income, and marital dissatisfaction. Lesbians with depression may be reluctant to seek services in the formal health care system. If they do seek services, practitioners need to pay special attention to making these women feel that they are welcome and that the best help will be provided. Practitioners can also address the risk factors by helping these women develop more social supports and counseling them on their concerns associated with separation from a partner or disclosure as a lesbian. Practitioners also need to be aware of differences among racial and ethnic groups in seeking professional help. Latino persons, for example, tend to rely on family and mutual support systems when they have life difficulties. Latino midlife women are reluctant to contact a mental health professional, even if their safety is an issue.

Practitioners need to be cognizant of the high suicide rates of midlife women. The high rates of suicide attempts among lesbians and even higher attempt rates among African American and Latino lesbians call for special attention and research to determine what can alleviate this situation. Probable contributing factors include negative images and stigmatization from heterosexism.

The practitioner working with a depressed midlife woman should determine if she has suicidal thoughts or if she has made any suicide attempts. If a determination is made that suicide risk is high, the practitioner must immediately link this woman with resources that specialize in developing interventions and supports for individuals who are at high risk of suicide. Usually, this would mean referral to an inpatient facility or specialized suicide prevention unit. If the practitioner assesses the risk of suicide to be low enough for her to remain in the community, the practitioner can work with the client's physician who can prescribe antidepressant medication, if needed. Intervention by a mental health counselor most likely would include behavioral and cognitive–behavioral techniques.

Professional helpers and social policymakers can advocate for conditions that improve educational and employment resources and policies for women at midlife, and for increased research and availability of empirically validated interventions for marital or partner discord and depression. Professional associations, professional helpers, citizen groups, and legislators can advocate for more research studies to account for suicidal behaviors in midlife women.

VIGNETTE

Yolanda, a 53-year-old Latino, complained of feeling depressed. She recently lost weight, was having trouble sleeping, and reported a lack of interest in sex and most other activities. Family members and her life partner, Lila, told her that all she needed to do was think more positively and she would feel better. But, it was all she could do to drag herself out of bed in the mornings. Often, she called in sick to work and was still in her nightgown when Lila returned home from work. Lila, seeing that suggesting positive thoughts was not working, decided that Yolanda needed to see a mental health counselor. Neither Yolanda nor her family supported this at first. Yolanda's mother said she would move in and care for Yolanda while Lila was at work. After a few weeks, Yolanda's mother was more worried than before because her daughter showed no improvement in mood. She convinced Yolanda to see a mental health counselor and told her that the family would accompany her.

Questions

- *Yolanda appears to be depressed. How could you assess this and determine the extent of her depression?*

- *What considerations do you take into account when working with a midlife woman who is Latino?*

REFERENCES

Adamek, M. E., & Kaplan, M. S. (1996). The growing use of firearms by suicidal older women, 1979–1992: A research note. *Suicide and Life-Threatening Behavior, 26*, 71–78.

Adelmann, P. K., Antonucci, T. C., Crohan, S. E., & Coleman, L. M. (1989). Empty nest, cohort, and employment in the well-being of midlife of midlife women. *Sex Roles, 20*, 173–189.

Alston, M., & Anderson, S. (1995). Suicidal behavior in African–American women. In S. Canetto & D. Lester (Eds.), *Women and suicidal behavior* (pp. 133–143). New York: Springer.

American Psychiatric Association. (1994). *Diagnostic and statistical manual of mental disorders* (4th ed.). Washington, DC: Author.

Avis, N. E., Brambilla, D., & McKinlay, S. M. (1994). A longitudinal analysis of the association between menopause and depression: Results from the Massachusetts Women's Health Study. *Annals of Epidemiology, 4*, 214–220.

Baruch, G. K., & Barnett, R. C. (1986). Role quality, multiple role involvement and psychological well-being in midlife women. *Journal of Personality and Social Psychology, 51*, 578–585.

Baruch, G. K., Barnett, R., & Rivers, C. (1983). *Lifeprints: New patterns of love and work for today's women*. New York: McGraw-Hill.

Bebbington, P. E., Dunn, G., Jenkins, J. R., Lewis, G., Brugha, T., Farrell, M., & Meltzer, H. (1998). The influence of age and sex on the prevalence of depressive conditions: Report from the national survey of psychiatric morbidity. *Psychological Medicine, 28*, 9–19.

Bradford, J., & Ryan, C. (1989). *National lesbian health care survey: Final report*. Washington, DC: National Lesbian and Gay Health Foundation.

Bradford, J., Ryan, C., & Rothblum, E. D. (1994). National lesbian health care survey: Implications for mental health. *Journal of Consulting and Clinical Psychology, 62*, 228–242.

Bromberger, J. T., & Matthews, K. A. (1994). Employment status and depressive symptoms in middle-aged women: A longitudinal investigation. *American Journal of Health, 84*, 202–206.

Bromberger, J. T., & Matthews, K. A. (1996a). A "feminine" model of vulnerability to depressive symptoms: A longitudinal investigation of middle-aged women. *Journal of Personality and Social Psychology, 70*, 591–598.

Bromberger, J. T., & Matthews, K. A. (1996b). A longitudinal study of the effects of pessimism, trait anxiety, and life stress on depressive symptoms in middle-aged women. *Psychology and Aging, 11*, 207–213.

Brown, G. W., & Harris, T. (1978). *Social origins of depression: A study of psychiatric disorder in women*. London: Tavistock.

Bumpass, L. L., & Aquilino, W. S. (1995). *A social map of midlife: Family and work over the middle life course*. Vero Beach, FL: MacArthur Foundation Research Network on Successful Midlife Development.

Canetto, S. S., & Sakinofsky, I. (1998). The gender paradox in suicide. *Suicide and Life-Threatening Behavior, 28*, 1–23.

Carr, D. (1997). The fulfillment of career dreams at midlife: Does it matter for women's mental health? *Journal of Health and Social Behavior, 38*, 331–344.

Carter, B., & McGoldrick, M. (1989). Overview: The changing family life cycle: A framework for family therapy. In B. Carter & M. McGoldrick (Eds.), *The changing family life cycle: A framework for family therapy* (2nd ed., pp. 3–28). Boston: Allyn & Bacon.

Chiriboga, D. A. (1989). Stress and loss in middle age. In R. A. Kalish (Ed.), *Midlife loss: Coping strategies* (pp. 42–80). Newbury Park, CA: Sage Publications.

Chiriboga, D. A. (1997). Crisis, challenge, and stability in the middle years. In M. E. Lachman & J. B. James (Eds.), *Multiple paths of midlife development* (pp. 293–322). Chicago: University of Chicago Press.

Cochran, S. D., & Mays, V. M. (1994). Depressive distress among homosexually active African American men and women. *American Journal of Psychiatry, 1251*, 524–529.

Costa, P. T., & McCrae, R. R. (1978). Objective personality assessment. In M. Storant, I. C. Stiegler, & M. F. Elias (Eds.), *The clinical psychology of aging* (pp. 119–143). New York: Plenum Press.

Costa, P. T., & McCrae, R. R. (1980). Still stable after all these years: Personality as a key to some issues in adulthood and old age. In P. B. Baltes & O. G. Brim (Eds.), *Life-span development and behavior* (Vol. 3, pp. 65–102). San Diego: Academic Press.

Costello, E. J. (1991). Married with children: Predictors of mental and physical health in middle-aged women. *Psychiatry, 54*, 292–305.

Culbertson, F. M. (1997). Depression and gender: An international review. *American Psychologist, 52*, 25–31.

DeGenova, M. K. (1993). Reflections of the past: New variables affecting life satisfaction in later life. *Educational Gerontology, 19*, 191–201.

Drebing, C. E., Gooden, W. E., Drebing, S. M., Van De Kemp, H., & Malony, H. N. (1995). The dream in midlife women: Its impact on mental health. *International Journal of Aging and Human Development, 40*, 73–87.

Dunn, C. R., & Galloway, C. (1986). Mental health of the caregiver: Increasing caregiver effectiveness. *Caring, 15*, 36–42.

Earle, J. R., Smith, M. H., Harris, C. T., & Longino, C. F., Jr. (1998). Women, marital status, and symptoms of depression in a midlife national sample. *Journal of Women & Aging, 10*, 41–57.

Gallo, J. J., Royall, D. R., & Anthony, J. C. (1993). Risk factors on the onset of depression in middle age and later life. *Social Psychiatry and Psychiatric Epidemiology, 28*, 101–108.

Gartrell, N. (1981). The lesbian as a "single" woman. *American Journal of Psychotherapy, 34*, 502–510.

Gatz, M., & Smyer, M. A. (1992). The mental health system and older adults in the 1990s. *American Psychologist, 47*, 741–751.

George, L. K. (1989). Stress, social support, and depression over the life course. In. K. S. Markides & C. L. Cooper (Eds.), *Aging, stress, and health* (pp. 241–267). New York: John Wiley & Sons.

George, L. K. (1990). Gender, age, and psychiatric disorders. *Generations, 14*, 22–27.

Gibbs, J. T. (1997). African–American suicide: A cultural paradox. *Suicide and Life Threatening Behavior, 27*, 68–79.

Gullette, M. M. (1998). Midlife discourses in the twentieth-century United States: An essay on the sexuality, ideology, and politics of "middle-ageism." In R. A. Shweder (Ed.), *Welcome to middle age! (and other cultural fictions)* (pp. 3–44). Chicago: University of Chicago Press.

Hagestad, G. O. (1990). The social meanings of age for men and women. In M. R. Stevenson, M. A. Paludi, K. N. Black, & B. E. Whitley, Jr. (Eds.), *Gender roles across the life span* (pp. 151–167). Madison: University of Wisconsin Press.

Helson, R., & Wink, P. (1992). Personality change in women from the early 40s to the early 50s. *Psychology and Aging, 7*, 45–50.

Hinrichsen, G. A. (1993). Depression. In R. Kastenbaum (Ed.), *Encyclopedia of adult development* (pp. 106–111). Phoenix, AZ: Oryx.

Humphrey, J. A., & Palmer, S. (1990–1991). The effects of race, gender, and marital status of suicides among young adults, middle-aged adults, and older adults. *Omega, 22*, 277–285.

Hunter, M. (1996). Menopause, hormones and women's lives. *Sexual and Marital Therapy, 11*, 119–122.

Johnson, S.R., Smith, E.R., & Guenther, S.M. (1987). Comparison of gynecologic health care problems between lesbian and bisexual women. *Journal of Reproductive Medicine, 32*, 805-811.

Kastenbaum, R. (1993a). Mid-life crisis. In R. Kastenbaum (Ed.), *Encyclopedia of adult development* (pp. 346–351). Phoenix, AZ: Oryx.

Kastenbaum, R. (1993b). Suicide. In R. Kastenbaum (Ed.), *Encyclopedia of adult development* (pp. 501–507). Phoenix, AZ: Oryx.

Kaufert, P.A., Gilbert, P., & Tate, R. (1992). The Manitoba Project: A re-examination of the link between menopause and depression. *Maturitas, 14*, 143–155.

Kessler, R. C., Foster, C., Webster, P. S., & House, J. S. (1992). The relationship between age and depressive symptoms in two national surveys. *Psychology and Aging, 7*, 119–126.

Kurdek, L. A. (1988). Perceived social support in gays and lesbians in cohabiting relationships. *Journal of Personality and Social Psychology, 54*, 504–509.

Kurdek, L. A., & Schmitt, J. P. (1987). Perceived emotional support from family and friends in members of homosexual, married, and heterosexual cohabitating couples. *Journal of Homosexuality, 14,* 57–68.

Lachman, M. E., Lewkowicz, C., Marcus, A., & Peng, Y. (1994). Images of midlife development among young, middle-aged, and older adults. *Journal of Adult Development, 1,* 201–211.

Lazarus, R. S. (1966). *Psychological stress and the coping process.* New York: McGraw-Hill.

Lazarus, R. S., & Delongis, A. (1983). Psychological stress and coping in aging. *American Psychologist, 38,* 245–254.

Lemme, R. H. (1999). *Development in adulthood.* Needham Heights, MA: Allyn & Bacon.

Manetta, A. A. (1999). Interpersonal violence and suicidal behavior in midlife African American women. *Journal of Black Studies, 29,* 510–522.

McCrae, R. R., & Costa, P. T., Jr. (1990). *Personality in adulthood.* New York: Guilford Press.

McGrath, E., Keita, G. P., Strickland, B. R., & Russo, N. F. (1992). *Women and depression: Risk factors and treatment issues.* Washington, DC: American Psychological Association.

McIntosh, J. L. (1991). Middle-age suicide: A literature review and epidemiological study. *Death Studies, 15,* 21–37.

McKinlay, J. B., & McKinlay, S. M. (1987). Depression in middle-aged women: Social circumstances versus estrogen deficiency. In R. Walsh (Ed.), *The psychology of women* (pp. 157–161). New Haven, CT: Yale University Press.

McQuaide, S. (1998). Women at midlife. *Social Work, 43,* 21–31.

Minter, L. E., & Samuels, C. A. (1998). The impact of "the dream" on women's experience of the midlife transition. *Journal of Adult Development, 5,* 31–43.

Mishara, B. L. (1993). Mental health in the adult years. In R. Kastenbaum (Ed.), *Encyclopedia of adult development* (pp. 329–332). Phoenix, AZ: Oryx.

Mos'cicki, E. K. (1995). Epidemiology of suicide. *International Psychogeriatrics, 7,* 137–148.

Neugarten, B. L. (1968). The awareness of middle age. In B. Neugarten (Ed.), *Middle age and aging* (pp. 93–98). Chicago: University of Chicago Press.

Neugarten, B. L. (1976). Adaptation and the life cycle. *Counseling Psychologist, 6,* 16–20.

Niemela, P., & Lento, R. (1993). The significance of the 50th birthday for women's individuation. In W. O. Davis, E. Cole, & E. Rothblum (Eds.), *Faces of women and aging* (pp. 117–127). New York: Harrington Park.

Nisbett, P. A. (1996). Protective factors for suicidal Black females. *Suicide and Life-Threatening Behavior, 26,* 325–341.

Osgood, N. J., & Malkin, M. J. (1998) Suicidal behavior in middle-aged and older women. In J. M. Coyle (Ed.), *Handbook on women and aging* (pp. 191–209). Westport, CT: Greenwood Press.

Pearlin, L. I. (1985). Life strains and psychological distress among adults. In A. Monat & R. S. Lazarus (Eds.), *Stress and coping: An anthology* (2nd ed., pp. 192–207). New York: Columbia University Press.

Rawson, K. T., & Jenson, G. O. (1995). Depression as a measurement of well-being in women at midlife. *Family Perspective, 29,* 297–313.

Robins, L. N., & Regier, D. A. (Eds.). (1991). *Psychiatric disorders in America: The epidemiological catchment area study.* New York: Free Press.

Rosenberg, S. D., Rosenberg, H. J., & Farrell, M. P. (1999). The midlife crisis revisited. In S. L. Willis & J. D. Reid (Eds.), *Life in the middle: Psychological and social development in middle age* (pp. 47–73). San Diego: Academic Press.

Rossi, A. (1980). Life-span theories and women's lives. *Signs, 6,* 4–32.

Rothblum, E. D. (1990). Depression among lesbians: An invisible and unresearched phenomenon. *Journal of Gay and Lesbian Psychotherapy, 1*, 67–87.

Saghir, M. T., & Robins, E. (1973). *Male and female homosexuality*. Baltimore: Williams & Williams.

Saghir, M. T., Robins, E., Walbran, B., & Gentry, K. A. (1970). Homosexuality: IV. Psychiatric disorders and stability in the female homosexual. *American Journal of Psychiatry, 127*, 147–154.

Saunders, J. M., Tupac, J. D., & MacCulloch, B. (1988). *A lesbian profile: A survey of 1000 lesbians*. West Hollywood: Southern California Women for Understanding.

Saunders, J. M., & Valente, S. M. (1987). Suicide risk among gay men and lesbians: A review. *Death Studies, 11*, 1–23.

Scheier, M. F., & Carver, C. S. (1988). A model of behavioral self-regulation: Translating intention into action. In L. Berkowitz (Ed.), *Advances in experimental social psychology* (Vol. 21, pp. 303–346). New York: Academic Press.

Schlossberg, N. K., Troll, L. E., & Leibowitz, Z. (1978). *Perspectives on counseling adults: Issues and skills*. Monterey, CA: Brooks/Cole.

Schmidt, P. J., Roca, C. A., Bloch, M., & Rubinow, D. R. (1997). The perimenopause and affective disorders. *Seminars in Reproductive Endocrinology, 15*, 91–100.

Sheehy, G. (1977). *Passages: Predictable crises of adult life*. New York: Bantam Books.

Sheehy, G. (1996). *New passages: Mapping your life across time*. New York: Bantam Books.

Smith, J. C., Mercy, J. A., & Conn, J. M. (1988). Marital status and the risk of suicide. *American Journal of Public Health, 78*, 78–80.

Society for Research on Women in New Zealand (SRWO). (1988). *The time of our lives: A study of mid-life women*. Christchurch, New Zealand: Christchurch Branch of SRWO.

Sprock, J., & Yoder, C. Y. (1997). Women and depression: An update on the report of the APA task force. *Sex Roles, 36*, 269–303.

Stewart, A. J., & Ostrove, J. M. (1998). Women's personality in middle age: Gender, history, and midcourse corrections. *American Psychologist, 53*, 1185–1194.

Stewart, A. J., & Vandewater, E. A. (1999). "If I had it to do over": Women's midlife review and midcourse corrections. *Journal of Personality and Social Psychology, 76*, 270–283.

Strickland, B. R. (1992). Women and depression. *Current Directions in Psychological Science, 1*, 132–135.

Surtees, P. G. (1980). Social support, residual adversity, and depressive outcome. *Social Psychiatry, 15*, 59–73.

Sussman, L. K., Robins, L. N., & Earls, F. (1987). Treatment-seeking for depression by black and white Americans. *Social Science and Medicine, 24*, 187–196.

Tangri, S., & Jenkins, S. (1993). The University of Michigan class of 1967: The women's life paths study. In K. D. Hulbert & D. T. Schuster (Eds), *Women's lives through time* (pp. 259–281). San Francisco: Jossey-Bass.

Tinsley, E. G., Sullivan-Guest, S. & McGuire, J. (1984). Feminine sex role and depression in middle-aged women. *Sex Roles, 11*, 25–32.

Tower, R., & Kasl, S. (1996). Gender, marital closeness, and depressive symptoms in elderly couples. *Journal of Gerontology: Psychological Sciences, 51B*, P115–P129.

U.S. Bureau of the Census. (1994). *Statistical abstracts of the United States: 1992* (11th ed.). Washington, DC: U.S. Government Printing Office.

U.S. Department of Health and Human Services. (1992). *Health, United States, 1991, and prevention profile* (DHHS Pub. No. PHS 92-1232). Washington, DC: U.S. Government Printing Office.

Voda, A. M. (1992). Menopause: A normal view. *Clinical Obstetrics and Gynecology, 35,* 923–933.

Waite, L. (1995). Does marriage matter? *Demography, 32,* 483–507.

Warren, B. J. (1995). The experience of depression in African American women. In B. J. McElmurry & R. S. Parker (Eds.), *Annual review of women's health* (Vol. 2, pp. 267–283). New York: National League for Nursing Press.

Wethington, E. (2000). Expecting stress: Americans and the "midlife crisis." *Motivation and Emotion, 24,* 85–103.

Wilbur, J., & Dan, A. (1989). The impact of work patterns on psychological well-being of midlife nurses. *Western Journal of Nursing Research, 11,* 703–716.

Willis, S. L., & Schaie, K. W. (1986). Training the elderly on the ability factors of spatial orientation and inductive reasoning. *Psychology and Aging, 1,* 239–247.

Willits, F. K., & Funk, R. B. (1989). Prior college experience and attitude change during the middle years: A panel study. *International Journal of Aging and Human Development, 29,* 283–300.

Woods, N. F., & Mitchell, E. S. (1996). Patterns of depressed mood in midlife women: Observations from the Seattle midlife women's health study. *Research in Nursing & Health, 19,* 111–123.

Woods, N. F., & Mitchell, E. S. (1997). Women's images of midlife: Observations from the Seattle midlife women's health study. *Health Care for Women International, 18,* 439–453.

CHAPTER 9

PERSONALITY, IDENTITY, AND GENERATIVITY

The study of personality, identity, and generativity provides important knowledge of changes that occur in midlife for women. Personality studies include sex–gender role traits and sex–gender crossover. Identity studies include identity statuses, effects of sociohistorical changes, stability, and development across cohorts. Generativity studies include motivation, realization, and the link between identity statuses and generativity. Life-span themes in this chapter include social–historical context, normative history-graded events, and change over the life span.

QUESTIONS TO CONSIDER

- *What is the influence of the cohort factor and economic and cultural characteristics in studies of sex–gender role traits?*

- *What are alternative ways to explain midlife personality shifts other than from the perspective of the traditional sex–gender role approaches?*

- *What factors could account for stability and fluidity in identity statuses among midlife women?*

- *What factors can influence generativity, motivation, and realization? How is identity status associated with generativity?*

- *How are identity status and generativity associated with well-being and role satisfaction?*

PERSONALITY DEVELOPMENT

Two studies provide much of the knowledge to date on the personality development of midlife women—a longitudinal study of the graduates of Mills College (in Oakland, CA) from the classes of 1958 and 1960 (Helson, 1993) and a longitudinal study of the class of 1964 from Radcliffe (in Cambridge, MA) (Stewart & Vandewater, 1993). The Mills study tracked *changes* in women's personality development or, more specifically, changes in sex–gender-role traits. Helson and her colleagues followed 140 women from the Mills classes of 1958 and 1960 for three decades. The Mills findings appeared to support the ideas proposed by Jung (1971) and Gutmann (1987) that women's feminine traits expanded in association with young adult roles but around the time of midlife, these traits diminished and masculine traits expanded (Helson, 1993). More specifically, the expanded traits associated with femininity on the California Psychological Inventory (CPI) during the 20s included sympathy, compassion, lack of confidence and initiative, self-criticism, and sense of vulnerability (Helson & Wink, 1992). Between ages 21–43, more masculine traits expanded that included self-discipline, commitment, and coping skills (Helson & Moane, 1987), and between ages 43–53, independence and self-confidence. Comfort and emotional stability expanded through adherence to both personal and social standards. Coping skills also expanded, including intellectuality, logical analysis, tolerance of ambiguity, substitution, and cognitive breadth. On another measure, the Adjective Check List (Gough & Heilbrun, 1983), the lowest score was on succorance (to give aid, help) between ages 43–52 whereas the highest score was congruence between self and ego ideal. With diminishment in feminine traits and expansion in masculine traits, the Mills women seemed to have experienced an integration of the masculine and the feminine (Helson & Wink, 1992).

The particular cohort and economic and cultural characteristics of the Mills samples likely influenced these findings. These women were upper middle class, educated, and primarily white. They also lived during a time of significant changes in women's roles, influenced by the women's movement. At age 52, for example, scores of the Mills women on a measure of women's dependence on their husbands were significantly lower than the scores of their mothers at the same age (Helson & Wink, 1992; Wink & Helson, 1993). The developmental paths of women in the Mills samples are different from those of women today (such as starting careers in their 20s and having children in their 30s). Their *patterns of change* on feminine and masculine traits will also likely be different from those in the Mills studies (Helson & Moane, 1987). Although research findings supported sex–gender trait changes for women in the Mills samples, they may not be comparable for earlier or later groups of women.

Sex–Gender Crossovers between Women and Men

Another personality topic, also focused on sex–gender role traits, is whether a sex–gender crossover happens between women and men in midlife, that is, whether men acquire more feminine traits and women more masculine traits (Jung, 1971). Some studies found support for a sex–gender role crossover; other studies found no support; and still other studies found that the crossover happened only sometimes in some situations or in one sex–gender but not in the other. Most of the studies listed below showed no crossovers in midlife:

More Feminine. Several studies showed an increase in feminine women and androgynous men in the age category of 61 years and older. This suggested that each sex–gender might become more feminine over time (Hyde, Krajnik, & Skuldt-Niederberger, 1991; Hyde & Phillips, 1979).

Mixed Results on Feminity, Masculinity, and Androgyny. Hyde et al. (1991) recontacted 122 participants in the earlier Hyde and Phillips (1979) study to assess the longitudinal results of the development of androgyny over 10 years (1977–1987). Over half (54 percent) of the sample remained in the same sex–gender role category, but a higher number of masculine women fell in the age category of 21–40 than in the earlier research, and a higher number of androgynous women fell in the youngest age category (13–20) and the oldest age category (61 and older). An assessment of being feminine was assigned to over 70 percent of women in the older age category (61 and older) in both samples.

Minimal to No Crossover. Both midlife men and women were higher in the need for intimacy than their younger counterparts. For women, however, these findings indicated no crossover (James, Lewkowicz, Libhaber, & Lachman, 1995). They did not become more dominant or assertive but, instead, extended their relational interests. In a nationally representative sample, Carlson and Videka-Sherman (1990) found little support for either role reversal or androgyny in midlife. James et al. compared 66 men and 84 women in three age groups: 20–30 (young), 40–64 (middle age), and 65–84 (old). Some support for a crossover was evident but only in a projective assessment technique, not in self-report, and only among men. Little variation was found among the groups in need for affiliation or need for power. The younger group was lower in need for power, but discrepancies with the other groups were small and insignificant. Parker and Aldwin (1997) studied findings from the data in two studies: the Davis Longitudinal Study (DLS) and the Transition Study (TS). The sample in the DLS included members of three cohorts of alumni from the University of California at Davis. Cohort 1 was interviewed as seniors in 1969 and as alumni in 1979 and 1991; cohort 2 was interviewed as seniors in 1979 and again in 1991;

cohort 3 graduated in 1989 and was interviewed in 1991 (for example, Regan & Roland, 1985). The sample for the TS was recruited in the late 1960s in San Francisco and followed for 10 years. The criteria used for recruitment was an impending transition such as graduation from high school, marriage, last child leaving home, and retirement (Lowenthal, Thurnher, & Chiriboga, 1975). Parker and Aldwin used only data from the first and last interviews from the TS. Femininity for both men and women in these studies decreased substantially over time from the 20s to the 40s. Masculinity increased for both men and women between their 20s and 30s and remained stable between their 30s and 40s. Regardless of age, cohort, or life period, however, men remained higher in masculinity than women. Sex–gender identity never crossed over between the men and the women (Parker & Aldwin, 1997). Midlife women in the sample studied by James and Lewkowicz (1997) developed greater concern for power, influence, and impact. They did not, however, cross over in this concern (men did not show a general decrease) or in the expression of affiliate needs.

Partly, the findings of minimal to no sex–gender role crossover resulted from the high current involvement of women in the workplace. As discussed in Chapter 5, younger women in the United States now usually combine parenthood with work outside the home. Women who work in male-dominated occupations are especially less likely to experience a crossover compared with women whose work is in more traditional occupations (Wink, 1994). Women studied by Helson and Moane (1987) who committed to career, family, or both in their 20s developed more fully than women who had no children or were in jobs beneath their capabilities. Between the ages of 27 and the early 40s, the more developed women became harder working, independent, disciplined, and interpersonally adept. In addition, they were more achievement motivated, goal oriented, emotionally stable, dominant, and interested in world events.

Crossover changes may happen more in societies with conventional sex–gender roles or where both women and men follow strict traditional values regarding family organization. Gutmann (1985, 1987) reported that after childrearing was over in these types of family situations, there is often a reversal of roles between men and women. Chronological age, therefore, may not be the essential factor in sex–gender role changes. Also supporting this notion, women in the same age cohort in the Mills study were found by Helson and Picano (1990) to vary in sex–gender role *changes* from young adulthood to midlife. Some women, for example, followed traditional roles anticipated for their generation in young adulthood (married and started families). By midlife, they were still in traditional roles and did not develop the dominance and independence characteristics displayed by the rest of the sample.

Women seem to incorporate masculine characteristics during midlife without feeling that they compromise their feminine characteristics. Yet, such *changes* in sex–gender identity during midlife, or other life periods, do not approach androgyny. Instead, what happens is an expansion of sex and gender characteristics (Huyck, 1996). Instead of a switch of roles, James et al. (1995) suggested the notion of balance of agency and communion. Characteristics of agency include "extraverted, energetic, talkative, enthusiastic, bold, active, self-confident, forceful, spontaneous, and sociable." Characteristics of communion include "warm, kind, cooperative, unselfish, polite, agreeable, trustful, generous, flexible, fair" (p. 190). The copresence or balance of agency and communion has been linked in other studies to psychological well-being (for example, Malley, 1989; Malley & Stewart, 1988). James et al. found in their sample that 22 percent of the women experienced this balance on a projective assessment, and with self-report the proportion increased to 36 percent. The balance of agency and communion appears to increase with age and characterizes more women than men.

Numerous difficulties characterize the research designs used to study the sex–gender crossover hypothesis and their measures. Most studies do not use samples that cover a wide age range of the life course from young adulthood to old age, or that include both men and women. Whether change actually happens or not requires longitudinal research, but most of the studies are cross-sectional. Measurements are also dubious, such as low validity projective data from the Thematic Apperception Test (James et al., 1995). The strongest support for the crossover in sex–gender roles developed from these types of data (for example, Gutmann, 1987).

Personality Prototypes

Personality prototypes reflect different groups of personality domains that may differentiate midlife women. In a series of three studies, York and John (1992) identified a set of personality prototypes from a sample of women from the Mills study (Helson, 1967). Using Rank and Taft's (1945) theoretical perspective and Q-sort descriptions (personality descriptors sorted by a judge by how they fit a person's personality), four prototypes emerged: individuated, traditional, conflicted, and assured. More than 80 percent of the women were assigned to one of the four prototypes. The characteristics of the women in the sample matching each of the four prototypes identified by York and John (1992) are:

- *Individuated prototype cluster* included women who displayed characteristics that were useful for creative and enterprising accomplishments, such as an open, inquiring, and exploring approach to life. Other characteristics of this prototype included social poise and status, self-expression, intellectual capacity, and independence.

- *Traditional prototype cluster* included women who scored much higher than women in the other clusters on measures of the traditional feminine sex–gender role. These women were not assertive and showed a strong sense of duty and adherence to social norms. In addition, they were self-denying and conflicted (for example, feelings of guilt) and appeared constricted in socialization.

- *Conflicted prototype cluster* included women who appeared withdrawn. These women seemed to lack social skills that are necessary for success in interpersonal and work relations. They were characterized by feelings of anxiety, insecurity, and hostility.

- *Assured prototype cluster* included women who had characteristics such as introspection, masculine orientation, self-confidence, assertiveness, and lack of internal conflict and negative affect.

Prototypes reflect personality differences in midlife women; it is useful to contrast them in pairs, such as individuated versus traditional. Also, some prototypes are high on certain traits whereas other prototypes are low on those traits. Women matching the individuated and assured prototypes, for example, should be high on traits such as "personal adjustment, positive self-concept, masculinity, and assertiveness" (York & John, 1992, p. 502), whereas women matching the conflicted prototype should score low on the same traits. In another study of the prototypes, John, Pals, and Westenberg (1998) found associations between prototypes and personality concepts used in other studies. For example, women with the individuated prototype reached the highest level of ego development on Loevinger's (1976) stages of ego development (ED)—individualistic, autonomous, and integrated. Women with the traditional prototype reached the middle region of ED stages—conformist, self-aware, and conscientious. Women with the conflicted prototype remained in the low ED region—impulsive and self-protected.

IDENTITY

Erik Erikson (1950) proposed that each of eight psychosocial conflicts is to be resolved at designated periods of life. Identity versus role confusion is the conflict of concern during adolescence and youth. Following these life periods, however, there will still be identity concerns associated with later life tasks and circumstances. The term identity has variable definitions including (a) consistent conceptions about one's physical, psychological, and social characteristics (Whitbourne, 1987); (b) commitment to a way of life or a system of values (Helson, Stewart, & Ostrove, 1995); and (c) a sense of how we are alike and how we are different from others (Baumeister, 1986). Although most identity research has been conducted with students in high schools and colleges, greater interest is being shown in the application of identity constructs over the life course (for example, Josselson, 1987; Waterman & Archer, 1990).

Using Erikson's theory of identity, Marcia (1966, 1980, 1987) developed a four-status typology based on the absence or presence of exploration and commitment. Identity achievement occurs when, after active exploration of various options and examining social norms (maybe rejecting some), one makes a thoughtful, conscious commitment to something (for example, career, personal philosophy). Those who do not engage in either exploration or commitment are given the status of identity diffuse. Commitment without exploration results in the status of identity foreclosure. Individuals actively exploring but with no commitment to a particular identity are given the identity status of moratorium. Based on this typology, Marcia (1966) developed an interview protocol to determine the progress of identity development in late adolescence. Researchers assigned respondents to one of the four identity statuses. Several reports regarding these statuses and midlife women are also available (for example, De Haan & MacDermid, 1994; Helson et al., 1995).

Identity Statuses among Midlife Women

Identity statuses among midlife women reflect that (a) they develop at different rates in different domains, (b) they are continually developing, (c) they are on a continuum, (d) their direction is not predictable, (e) they are fluid, and (f) the status of identity achievement never reaches completion. Findings and issues about these characteristics are addressed as follows:

- First, identity development occurs at different rates in different domains (for example, Archer, 1991; Whitbourne, Zuschlag, Elliot, & Waterman, 1992). In certain domains, such as parenting and career, identity achievement may not be possible until adulthood (Grotevant, 1987) and may never happen in some domains. About half (52 percent) of college seniors are still in the identity diffusion status regarding religion and politics (Waterman, 1985). Few midlife women are identity achieved in religion, politics, or work (Kroger & Haslett, 1991). Whether variability across domains is *normative* or a source of stress is not known (De Haan & MacDermid, 1994).

- Second, because identity appears to be in a continuous process of development over the life span, instead of completed in adolescence, some theorists and researchers in this area recommend eliminating the concept of fixed identity statuses (for example, Archer, 1991; Cote & Levine, 1988; Hamachek, 1990).

- Third, instead of either/or categories, viewing identity as a continuum makes more sense (Archer, 1991). Some individuals get further along on the identity continuum than others.

- Fourth, identity statuses may not move in anticipated directions. For example, exploration (moratorium) may not move to commitment or identity achievement but, instead, move to diffusion or foreclosure (Marcia, 1987; Waterman, 1982).

- Fifth, there may be more fluidity in identity statuses than previously understood. Individuals can move back and forth between identity statuses (Waterman, 1982). Both internal and external variables affect this fluidity (Marcia, 1987; Waterman, 1982). For example, if job loss happens, a woman who is identity achieved in work may move to identity moratorium (Grotevant, 1987).

- Sixth, women continually evaluate their commitments and never fully complete identity achievement (De Hann & MacDermid, 1994).

Few adult women are identity achieved (Whitbourne & Tesch, 1985). Midlife women studied by De Haan and MacDermid (1994) were not more identity achieved than college women. Midlife women also reported significantly fewer moratoriums and more diffusion statuses compared to college women.

Some researchers reported that it is not in a woman's best interest to reach identity achievement. Josselson (1987) and Patterson, Sochting, and Marcia (1992) found identity foreclosure more adaptive for women than identity achievement. Josselson concluded that foreclosure is less stressful than the exploration required in attaining identity achievement. But, other researchers found that identity achievement was the only significant predictor of all measured components of well-being, including locus of control, self-esteem, depression (inverse association), and life satisfaction. This finding pointed to the importance of the exploration that precedes identity commitments. Individuals who made identity commitments without a period of exploration (foreclosure) were less likely to feel they had control over their life circumstances (De Haan & MacDermid, 1994).

Effects of Sociohistorical Changes on Identity Stability and Change

Identity development is influenced by sociohistorical changes, as shown by comparisons of different cohorts. Helson et al. (1995) studied identity development in three cohorts of women in longitudinal studies: the Berkeley Guidance Study (Eichorn, Clausen, Haan, Honzik, & Mussen, 1981), the Mills

Longitudinal Study (Helson & Wink, 1992), and the Radcliffe Longitudinal Study (Stewart & Vandewater, 1993). The main focus was the influence of *sociohistorical periods* on identity *change*. The respondents, mostly white, middle class, married, and mothers, were assessed for this study in their early 40s. They were young adults in the Berkeley study in the 1950s, the Mills study in the early 1960s, and in the Radcliffe study in the late 1960s.

Study of the Berkeley sample began in 1928. The sample included every third birth in Berkeley, California, over an 18-month period and the respondents were assessed during childhood, adolescence, and adulthood. Adult assessments happened at the ages of 30, 40, and 53 (Block, 1971; Clausen, 1993; Eichorn et al., 1981). In the descriptions of findings that follow, the Berkeley sample refers to the older group and the Mills and Radcliffe samples refer to the younger groups.

Across these three samples, Helson et al. (1995) assessed ego identity using the concepts of searchers or promoters of change and, as defined by Marcia (1980), acceptors or "carriers of the culture." Adding the concepts of integrated and unintegrated, four identity patterns were associated with vector scales from the California Psychological Inventory (CPI). The identity patterns included (a) integrated searchers, (b) integrated acceptors, (c) unintegrated acceptors, and (d) unintegrated searchers (Mallory, 1989). The CPI contains three independent vector scales: vector 1—internality (reluctant to take initiative); vector 2—norm favoring (conscientious, self-disciplined, and rule following); and vector 3—realization (reasonably fulfilled or actualized, capable, able to cope with life stressors; see Gough, 1987; Weiser & Meyers, 1993). Unintegrated acceptors tended to show less initiative (high internality) than other women. Unintegrated searchers showed less impulse control (low norm favoring). Integrated acceptors stood out in their support of norms and traditional values (high norm favoring). In the Mills and Radcliffe samples, women with an integrated identity, especially integrated searchers, showed realization. The associations between the identity patterns and the CPI vector scores for these women during the early 40s were practically the same, a result that supports the notion that identity processes tend to be stable over time. Marcia (1980) suggested that most researchers interested in personality processes concur that they are part of a basically stable self-system. Still, the central question of this study was whether exceptions to this pattern were influenced by *sociohistorical periods*. As noted earlier, identity statuses can be fluid.

Helson et al. (1995) hypothesized that more features of the identity of integrated acceptors (carriers of the culture) would be analogous across cohorts than would be the case for integrated searchers (promoters of change). Comparing the younger and older samples, they found the predicted similarities among the younger and older integrated acceptors, as well as the predicted dissimilarities among the younger and older integrated searchers. The researchers suspected that the identity change for integrated searchers would reflect the *sociohistorical changes* affecting women's roles in the 1960s and 1970s. The more recent cohorts did reflect more self and achievement themes. On another measure, the California Adult *Q* Set (Block, 1978), the two items that most strongly differentiated the younger groups from the older group (higher agreement for the younger groups) were: "has higher aspirations for self" and "values own independence." As anticipated, the integrated searchers were the carriers of social change and the integrated acceptors were the carriers of the culture because they showed more consistency across historical time.

The samples in the study by Helson et al. (1995) reflected the influence of different eras on women and the effect of external factors. The Berkeley Guidance Study women, who became adults in the 1950s, were part of a cohort in which most middle and working-class women were homemakers. If this life plan changed for women in their 40s, it was more the result of external factors, such as the death of a husband, than of their internal goals. The more transitional or modern cohorts in the Mills and Radcliffe samples combined marriage and work. This changed *social context*, galvanized by the women's movement, encouraged women's identity development. Instead of capitulating to sex–gender based constraints, this social movement prompted women to pursue work and family interests that personally fulfilled them. New opportunities were also available to them in education and in the types of occupations they could pursue.

The integrated searchers in the Berkeley sample did not feel validated in the wife and mother aspects of their identities, possibly because the criteria for success in family roles are vague. Although they possessed psychosocial and interpersonal strengths, few of these women felt a sense of individual accomplishment. They were psychologically mature, but they did not experience the sense of independence and socially validated success that often accompanies participation in the workplace. Even if the Berkeley women developed an integrated searcher identity in midlife, there were few opportunities for independent interests or careers for their cohort.

GENERATIVITY

Midlife adults supposedly are interested in creating or doing something that will outlast them. Erikson (1950) first addressed this central task of midlife: generativity (versus stagnation). He proposed that generativity develops greater import during midlife and then diminishes somewhat. More recently, researchers in personality and life-span development have become interested in this concept (for example, McAdams, de St. Aubin, & Logan, 1993; Stewart & Gold-Steinberg, 1990).

Each person is thought to develop a generativity narrative, or conscious story about generative successes and defeats (McAdams & de St. Aubin, 1992). Successes meet the goal of providing a legacy for the next generation (Kotre, 1984; McAdams, 1988). Erikson (1950) bestowed special attention to parenting as the most common way to achieve generativity; however, generativity does not take only a biological form (Kotre, 1984). A broader definition of generativity involves extending one's self into both the community and the future (McAdams, 1988). The concept of generativity developed by McAdams, Hart, and Maruna (1998) entails "assuming the role of responsible parent, mentor, shepherd, guide . . . being a responsible citizen, contributing member of a community, a leader, a mover and shaker . . . creating and producing things, people, and outcomes that are aimed at benefiting, in some sense, the next generation, and even the next" (p. 7). For others, generativity comes from the production of lasting physical objects such as planting a tree or writing a book, ideological expressions such as working to get a law passed (Peterson & Klohnen, 1995), technical skills, cultural contributions (Kotre, 1984), transmitting knowledge and values to younger persons such as work colleagues, or involvement in political and social causes that may positively affect future generations. Peterson and Stewart (1996) identified four broad categories and 10 subcategories of generativity themes drawn from various theories of generativity. The categories, with subcategories in parentheses, include: parenting (parental concern, concern for future of child, concern for independence of child); caring for others (concern for others, broad social concern, teaching others); productivity (personal productivity); and insight (tolerance of conflicts, circumspection of layers of meaning).

Actualization of Generative Strivings in Midlife

Research on generativity in midlife shows mixed results. McAdams et al. (1993) found support for an increase in generative commitments and generative narratives between young adulthood and midlife but no support for Erikson's (1950) hypothesis that these generative factors decrease thereafter. Other studies confirmed that the daily lives of midlife adults reflected strivings to be generative more than was reflected in the daily lives of younger adults (for example, Peterson & Stewart, 1996). Women in their 40s studied by Helson and McCabe (1994) wanted to achieve a new generative identity. They were delighted when they accomplished something that was valuable to others. Yet, not all studies on this topic found a stronger desire in midlife to be generative than in earlier life periods. For example, in longitudinal cohorts of women from the Radcliffe Longitudinal Study of the class of 1964 (Stewart & Vandewater, 1993) and from the University of Michigan class of 1967 (Tangri & Jenkins, 1993), generative desires were significantly lower in midlife (middle or late 40s) than in young adulthood.

Generativity Motivation or Desires, Felt Capacity for Generativity, and Generative Realization

Some studies on generativity and midlife women have addressed the topics of generativity motivation, felt capacity for generativity, and generativity realization. In addition, the appearance in the life span of generative desires and felt capacity for generativity was studied by Stewart and Vandewater (1998). They found that generative desires begin to peak in early adulthood and decline in middle and later life; however, felt capacity for generativity rises from early to middle adulthood and then begins to decline to some degree.

A few studies attempted to determine the motivations for generative concerns and their translation into actions. McAdams and de St. Aubin (1992) conducted one of the most comprehensive studies of the motivational basis for generative concerns and actions. They concluded that the motivational basis included inner desires and cultural demands. This motivational basis seems to stimulate generative commitments that get translated into generative actions.

Another antecedent of generativity motivation in midlife is a supportive mentor, such as a teacher or boss during young adulthood who likely encourages one's psychological growth. Parents, spouses, and lovers are not important influences in generativity motivation (Peterson & Stewart, 1996). Other studies showed that many women high in generativity motivation experienced a past and present history of political involvement and were more likely to integrate a social–political consciousness into their identity. They rated the social movements they witnessed during their adolescence as particularly influential (Peterson & Stewart, 1996).

During midlife, women may feel that they can actually make contributions to the social world and to the next generation. This felt capacity for generativity includes an increased sense of efficacy and a view of oneself as making contributions to a wider community (Stewart & Vandewater, 1998). Political activism also seems to play a role in stimulating a felt capacity for generativity. In a sample of African American women (average age 45) and white women (average age 48) who were in college between 1967 and 1973, political activism as students was associated with both politicized identity and felt capacity for generativity for white women. For African American women, student activism was associated with a felt capacity for midlife generativity but not politicized identity (Cole & Stewart, 1996).

Some studies identified factors associated with generativity realization. In one of these studies, Peterson and Klohnen (1995) used the California Q Set that evaluates one's attitudes, behaviors, and personality (Block, 1978). They assessed two samples from the Mills and Radcliffe longitudinal studies. The findings showed that generativity realization was associated with prosocial personality characteristics (including leadership), favorable views of social norms, and responsiveness to varying viewpoints. Women in both samples felt more concern about helping others in their work environments than in earning large sums of money. Their "radius of concern" also extended beyond their families and workplaces to national and international arenas. Exceptionally generative women were psychologically healthy and fulfilled as measured by the California Q Set, but there was no relation between generativity realization and the positive life outcomes assessed such as general life satisfaction. Only one aspect of satisfaction was related to generativity realization: marital satisfaction.

As noted before, a history of political involvement appears to influence generativity motivation and a felt capacity for generativity. Political involvement also has been associated with generative realization. Generatively accomplished women studied by Peterson and Klohnen (1995) were more likely than nongeneratively accomplished women to be involved in political activities. Results of several other studies that concurred with this finding are as follows:

- In a study of several midlife women who expressed generativity through political means, Stewart and Gold-Steinberg (1990) found that social and historical events were important to them throughout their lives but particularly during the periods of early childhood, later adolescence, and young adulthood. During midlife, they seemed motivated by generativity preoccupations and translated their political thinking into action. Women with intensely formed "political identities," such as feminists or pacifists, experienced a sense of urgency to translate their values and beliefs into action.

- Data from several samples of college-educated women, including graduates from the classes of 1967 and 1973 at the University of Michigan and the class of 1964 at Radcliffe College, were the focus of analysis by Stewart, Settles, and Winter (1998). Midlife political attitudes and actions were associated with activism or being an engaged observer of the social movements of the 1960s, including the women's movement, the civil rights movement, and the antiwar movement. Both African American and white social movement activists were more likely to engage in midlife political activities than nonparticipants or engaged observers. The women's movement seemed to be the most consequential, particularly for white women. Yet, Cole and Stewart (1996) found that the women's movement moderately affected the lives of both groups. White women were more likely to participate in the women's movement whereas African American women were more likely to participate in the civil rights movement. Although the women's movement affected them, African American women rated the effect of the civil rights movement as having a much stronger effect on their lives than did white women.

Generativity realization seems to become more significant in midlife for educationally and financially advantaged samples. Other midlife women who are not advantaged in the same ways may not have the opportunities, time, or resources for expanding their radius of generative efforts. Generativity realization by social class and educational attainment, however, has yet to be addressed (Peterson & Klohnen, 1995).

Identity Statuses and Generativity

Identity development and generativity in midlife women was the focus of study by De Haan and MacDermid (1994). The women in the sample were middle to lower middle class and, on average, in their early 40s and married for 20 years with an average of 3.1 children. Over half (52 percent) of the sample finished some college. Another comparison sample included college women representing over 25 subject majors. Significant associations were noted between separate domain-specific measures of identity (lifestyle, occupation, religion, politics) and role-specific generativity (worker, partner, parent, worshipper, citizen). De Haan and MacDermid (1994) and MacDermid, Franz, and De Reus (1998) reported these positive associations: (a) parenting generativity (for example, helping one's children develop) and lifestyle identity achievement, (b) spousal role generativity (for example, taking care of one's partner) and lifestyle identity achievement, (c) religious generativity (for example, teaching one's faith to younger persons) and religious identity achievement, and (d) civic generativity (for example, being a role model to younger persons) and political identity achievement.

The extremes of the identity status continuum, identity achievement and identity diffusion (the complete absence of identity achievement), were the most influential in predicting generativity in the De Haan and MacDermid (1994) study. Commitment without exploration (foreclosure) or exploration without commitment (moratorium), both of which De Haan and MacDermid considered partial levels of identity development, were not associated with generativity. The finding that most stood out in this study was that identity achievement was the dimension of identity development most consistently and strongly associated with both generativity and well-being. Yet, this identity status was uncommon among the midlife women they studied.

SUMMARY

- Although sex–gender trait changes appear in samples of advantaged midlife women, most of the current literature on midlife women does not support a sex–gender crossover.

- Historical events such as the women's movement seem to play an important role in women's display of more masculine traits.

- Studies on identity development and generativity in midlife women show that both identity achievement and generativity realization vary across domains and roles.

- Identity achievement is the dimension of identity development that is most consistently and strongly associated with both generativity and well-being.

- Identity achievement is uncommon among the midlife women studied.

IMPLICATIONS FOR PRACTICE

Sometimes women who have worked in a career since graduation from college want to reconnect with parts of themselves that they have not addressed during their adult years. Often they desire to do something meaningful or to give back something to their community. Practitioners can help these clients explore ways in which they can develop generativity. A social worker can assist these women to reconnect with activities that were meaningful earlier in their lives and help them identify possible courses of action.

Another issue practitioners may confront relates to midlife women who did not involve themselves in the women's movement and who experience difficulties in acting assertively. These women can benefit from cognitive and behavioral interventions such as assertiveness training (for example, Bower & Bower, 1991; Sundel & Sundel, 1980). Midlife women may also seek counseling for concerns about identity achievement that may involve issues related to generativity in parental, partner, and worker roles.

VIGNETTE

Dora, age 48, attended a women's college in the early 1970s and was active in the women's movement. After earning a master's degree in business, she became one of the first women stockbrokers in a Wall Street firm. She still works a 60-hour week, and her colleagues and friends see her as a success. Although she earns a high income that provides all the money she needs, Dora now wonders if she is contributing anything worthwhile to society. She increasingly feels anxious and loses patience with clients and colleagues.

Questions

- *What questions would you ask Dora to help her clarify the source of her anxiety and impatience at work?*

- *Since it is not unusual for persons at midlife to rethink their lives and consider restructuring them, what cues can you listen for that indicate this might be the case for Dora?*

REFERENCES

Archer, S. (1991). A feminist's approach to identity research. In G. R. Adams, T. P. Gullotta, & R. Montemayor (Eds.), *Adolescent identity formation* (pp. 25–49). Beverly Hills, CA: Sage Publications.

Baumeister, R. F. (1986). *Identity: Cultural change and the struggle for self.* New York: Oxford University Press.

Block, J. (1971). *Lives through time.* Berkeley, CA: Bancroft.

Block, J. (1978). *The Q-sort method in personality assessment and psychiatric research.* Palo Alto, CA: Consulting Psychologists Press.

Bower, S. A., & Bower, G. H. (1991). *Asserting yourself: A practical guide for positive change.* Reading, MA: Addison-Wesley.

Carlson, B. E., & Videka-Sherman, L. (1990). An empirical test of androgyny in the middle years: Evidence from a national survey. *Sex Roles, 23,* 305–324.

Clausen, J. A. (1993). *American lives: Looking back at the great depression.* New York: Free Press.

Cole, E. R., & Stewart, A. J. (1996). Meanings of political participation among Black and White women: Political identity and social responsibility. *Journal of Personality and Social Psychology, 71,* 130–140.

Cote, J. E., & Levine, C. (1988). A critical examination of ego identity status paradigm. *Developmental Review, 8,* 147–184.

De Haan, L. G., & MacDermid, S. M. (1994). Is women's identity achievement associated with the expression of generativity? Examining identity and generativity in multiple roles. *Journal of Adult Development, 1,* 235–247.

Eichorn, D. H., Clausen, J. A., Haan, N., Honzik, M. P., & Mussen, P. H. (Eds.). (1981). *Present and past in middle life.* New York: Academic Press.

Erikson, E. (1950). *Childhood and society.* New York: W. W. Norton.

Gough, H. G. (1987). *CPI: California personality inventory administrator's guide.* Palo Alto, CA: Consulting Psychologists Press.

Gough, H. G., & Heilbrun, A. B., Jr. (1983). *The adjective check list manual: 1980 edition.* Palo Alto, CA: Consulting Psychologists Press.

Grotevant, J. D. (1987). Toward a process model of identity formation. *Journal of Adolescent Research, 2,* 677–683.

Gutmann, D. L. (1985). The parental imperative revisited: Towards a developmental psychology of adulthood and later life. *Contributions to Human Development, 14,* 31–60.

Gutmann, D. L. (1987). *Reclaimed powers: Toward a new psychology of men and women in later life.* New York: Basic Books.

Hamachek, D. (1990). Evaluating self-concept and ego status in Erikson's last three psychosocial stages. *Journal of Counseling and Development, 68*, 677–683.

Helson, R. (1967). Personality characteristics and developmental history of creative college women. *Genetic Psychology Monographs, 76*, 205–256.

Helson, R. (1993). Comparing longitudinal studies of adult development: Toward a paradigm of tension between stability and change. In D. C. Funder, R. D. Parke, C. Tomlison-Keasey, & K. Widaman (Eds.), *Studying lives through time: Personality and development* (pp. 93–120). Washington, DC: American Psychological Association.

Helson, R., & McCabe, L. (1994). The social clock project at middle age. In B. F. Turner & L. E. Troll (Eds.), *Women growing older: Psychological perspectives* (pp. 68–93). Thousand Oaks, CA: Sage Publications.

Helson, R., & Moane, G. (1987). Personality change in women from college to midlife. *Journal of Personality and Social Psychology, 53*, 176–186.

Helson, R., & Picano, J. (1990). Is the traditional role bad for women? *Journal of Personality and Social Psychology, 59*, 311–320.

Helson, R., Stewart, A. J., & Ostrove, J. (1995). Identity in three cohorts of midlife women. *Journal of Personality and Social Psychology, 69*, 544–557.

Helson, R., & Wink, P. (1992). Personality change in women from the early 40s to the early 50s. *Psychology and Aging, 7*, 45–50.

Huyck, M. H. (1996). Continuities and discontinuities in gender identity. In V. L. Bengtson (Ed.), *Adulthood and aging: Research on continuities and discontinuities* (pp. 98–123). New York: Springer.

Hyde, J. S., Krajnik, M., & Skuldt-Niederberger, K. (1991). Androgyny across the life span: A replication and longitudinal follow-up. *Developmental Psychology, 27*, 516–519.

Hyde, J. S., & Phillips, D. E. (1979). Androgyny across the life span. *Developmental Psychology, 15*, 334–336.

James, J. B., & Lewkowicz, C. (1997). Themes of power and affiliation across time. In M. E. Lachman & J. Boone James (Eds.), *Multiple paths of midlife development* (pp. 109–143). Chicago: University of Chicago Press.

James, J. B., Lewkowicz, C., Libhaber, J., & Lachman, M. (1995). Rethinking the gender identity crossover hypothesis: A test of a new model. *Sex Roles, 32*, 185–207.

John, O. P., Pals, J. L., & Westenberg, P. W. (1998). Personality prototypes and ego development: Conceptual similarities and relations in adult women. *Journal of Personality and Social Psychology, 74*, 1093–1108.

Josselson, R. (1987). *Finding herself: Patterns in identity development in women*. San Francisco: Jossey-Bass.

Jung, C. G. (1971). The stages of life. In J. Campbell (Ed.), *The portable Jung* (pp. 3–22). Princeton, NJ: Princeton University Press. (Original work published 1931)

Kotre, J. (1984). *Outliving the self: Generativity and the interpretation of lives*. Baltimore: Johns Hopkins University Press.

Kroger, J., & Haslett, S. J. (1991). A comparison of ego identity status transition pathways and change rates across five identity domains. *International Journal of Aging and Human Development, 34*, 303–330.

Loevinger, J. (1976). *Ego development: Conceptions and theories*. San Francisco: Jossey- Bass.

Lowenthal, M. F., Thurnher, M., & Chiriboga, D. (1975). *Four stages in life*. San Francisco: Jossey-Bass.

MacDermid, S. M., Franz, C. E., & De Reus, L. A. (1998). Generativity: At the crossroads of social roles and personality. In D. P. McAdams & E. de St. Aubin, E. (Eds.),

Generativity and adult development: How and why we care for the next generation (pp. 181–226). Washington, DC: American Psychological Association.

Malley, J. E. (1989). The balance of agency and communion: Adjustment and adaptation in single parents. (Doctoral dissertation, Boston University, 1989). *Dissertation Abstracts International, 50*, 2-B.

Malley, J. E. & Stewart, A. J. (1988). Women's work and family roles: Sources of stress and sources of strength. In S. Fisher & J. Reason (Eds.), *Handbook of life stress, cognition, and health* (pp. 175–191). New York: John Wiley & Sons.

Mallory, M. E. (1989). Q-sort definition of ego identity status. *Journal of Youth and Adolescence, 18*, 399–412.

Marcia, J. E. (1966). Development and validation of ego identity status. *Journal of Personality and Social Psychology, 3*, 551–558.

Marcia, J. E. (1980). Identity in adolescence. In J. Adelson (Ed.), *Handbook of adolescence psychology* (pp. 159–187). New York: John Wiley & Sons.

Marcia, J. E. (1987). The identity status approach to the study of ego identity development. In T. Honess & K. Yardley (Eds.), *Self and identity, perspectives across the life-span* (pp. 161–177). London: Rutledge & Kegan Paul.

McAdams, D. P. (1988). *Power, intimacy, and the life story*. New York: Guilford Press.

McAdams, D. P., & de St. Aubin, E. (1992). A theory of generativity and its assessment through self-report, behavioral acts, and narrative themes in autobiography. *Journal of Personality and Social Psychology, 62*, 1003–1015.

McAdams, D. P., de St. Aubin, E., & Logan, R. L. (1993). Generativity among young, midlife, and older adults. *Psychology and Aging, 8*, 221–230.

McAdams, D. P., Hart, H. M., & Maruna, S. (1998). The anatomy of generativity. In D. P. McAdams & E. de St. Aubin (Eds.), *Generativity and adult development: How and why we care for the next generation* (pp. 7–43). Washington, DC: American Psychological Association.

Parker, R. A., & Aldwin, C. M. (1997). Do aspects of gender identity change from early to middle adulthood? Disentangling age, cohort, and period effects. In M. E. Lachman, & J. Boone James (Eds.), *Multiple paths of midlife development* (pp. 67–107). Chicago: University of Chicago Press.

Patterson, S. J., Sochting, I., & Marcia, J. E. (1992). The inner space and beyond: women and identity. In G. R. Adams, T. P. Bullotta, & R. Montemayor (Eds.), *Adolescent identity formation* (pp. 9–24). Newbury Park, CA: Sage Publications.

Peterson, B. E., & Klohnen, E. C. (1995). Realization of generativity in two samples of women at midlife. *Psychology and Aging, 10*, 20–29.

Peterson, B. E., & Stewart, A. J. (1996). Antecedents and contexts of generativity motivation at midlife. *Psychology and Aging, 11*, 21–33.

Rank, O., & Taft, J. J. (1945). *Will therapy and truth and reality*. New York: Knopf.

Regan, M. C., & Roland, H. E. (1985). Rearranging family and career priorities: Professional women and men of the eighties. *Journal of Marriage and the Family, 47*, 985–992.

Stewart, A. J., & Gold-Steinberg, S. (1990). Midlife women's political consciousness: Case studies of psychosocial development and political commitment. *Psychology of Women Quarterly, 14*, 543–566

Stewart, A. J., Settles, I. H., & Winter, N.J.G. (1998). Women and the social movements of the 1960s: Activists, engaged observers, and nonparticipants. *Political Psychology, 19*, 63–94.

Stewart, A. J., & Vandewater, E. A. (1993). The Radcliffe class of 1964: Career and family social clock projects in a transitional cohort. In K. D. Hulbert & D. T. Schuster (Eds.), *Women's lives through time: Educated women of the twentieth century* (pp. 235–258). San Francisco: Jossey Bass.

Stewart, A. J., & Vandewater, E. A. (1998). The course of generativity. In D. P.McAdams & E. de St. Aubin (Eds.), *Generativity and adult development: How and why we care for the next generation* (pp. 75–100). Washington, DC: American Psychological Association.

Sundel, S., & Sundel, M. (1980). *Be assertive: A practical guide for human service workers.* Beverly Hills, CA: Sage Publications.

Tangri, S., & Jenkins, S. (1993). The University of Michigan class of 1967: The women's life paths study. In K. D. Hulbert & D. T. Schuster (Eds), *Women's lives through time* (pp. 259–281). San Francisco: Jossey-Bass.

Waterman, A. S. (1982). Identity development from adolescence to adulthood. An extension of theory and a review of research. *Development Psychology, 18,* 341–358.

Waterman, A. S. (1985). Identity in the context of adolescent psychology. In A. S. Waterman (Ed.), *Identity in adolescence: Processes and contents* (pp. 5–24). San Francisco: Jossey-Bass.

Waterman, A. S., & Archer, S. L. (1990). A life-span perspective on identity formation: Development in form, function, and process. In P. B. Baltes, D. L. Fetherman, & R. M. Lerner (Eds.), *Life-span development and behavior* (Vol. 10, pp. 29–57). Hillsdale, NJ: Lawrence Erlbaum.

Weiser, N. L., & Meyers, L. S. (1993). Validity and reliability of the revised California Psychological Inventory's vector 3 scale. *Educational and Psychological Measurement, 53,* 1045–1054.

Whitbourne, S. K. (1987). Personality development in adulthood and old age: Relationships among identity style, health, and well-being. In K.W. Schaie & C. Eisdorfer (Eds.), *Annual Review of Gerontology and Geriatrics* (Vol. 7) (pp. 189-216). New York: Springer.

Whitbourne, S. K., & Tesch, S. A. (1985). A comparison of identity and intimacy statuses in college students and alumni. *Developmental Psychology, 15,* 1039–1044.

Whitbourne, S. K., Zuschlag, M. K., Elliot, L. B., & Waterman, A. S. (1992). Psychosocial development in adulthood: A 22 year sequential study. *Journal of Personality and Social Psychology, 63,* 260–271.

Wink, L. (1994, Fall). *The moderating effect of work status on personality change in adulthood: Findings from two longitudinal samples of women.* Presented at the Brown Bag Speaker Series, Harvard University, Radcliff Institute of Advanced Study, Cambridge, MA.

Wink, L., & Helson, R. (1993). Personality change in women and their partners. *Journal of Personality and Social Psychology, 65,* 597–605.

York, K. L., & John, O. P. (1992). The four faces of Eve: A typological analysis of women's personality at midlife. *Journal of Personality and Social Psychology, 63,* 494–508.

ADDITIONAL REFERENCE

Cole, E. R., Zucker, A. N., & Ostrove, J. M. (1998). Political participation and feminist consciousness among women of the 1960s. *Political Psychology, 19,* 349—371.

MacDermid, S. M., Heilbrun, G., & De Haan, L. G. (1997). The generativity of employed mothers in multiple roles: 1979 and 1991. In M. E. Lachman & J. Boone James (Eds.), *Multiple paths of midlife development* (pp. 207–240). Chicago: University of Chicago Press.

CHAPTER 10

PHYCHOLOGICAL WELL-BEING AND LIFE SATISFACTION

Many women, both heterosexual and lesbian, rate midlife as a time high in life satisfaction and well-being, or as the "prime time" of their lives. A number of factors contribute to the psychological well-being and life satisfaction of midlife women. Most of the research on this topic was conducted with samples of well-educated and upper-class women. Much less is known about the life experiences of disadvantaged women, but what knowledge does exist points to lower levels of life satisfaction and well-being. Life-span themes in the chapter include optimal development; vitality; individual differences; cohorts; multiple influences and diverse outcomes; gains, losses, and constraints, and opportunities for change and growth.

QUESTIONS TO CONSIDER

- *What factors are attributed to midlife being the prime time for women?*

- *What role does chronological age play in life satisfaction?*

- *How is health a factor in well-being?*

- *How do divorced and always-single women compare with married women on the dimensions of pleasure and mastery?*

- *What are the factors associated with life satisfaction for midlife women?*

The term psychological well-being is often interchangeable with other terms, such as happiness, morale, quality of life, and life satisfaction (Lewis, 1992). Psychological well-being usually means a sense of self-esteem or self-acceptance (Thomas, 1995). It also means having a sense of meaning and pur-pose in life, and experiencing personal growth or realizing one's potential (Ryff, 1989). In defining psychological well-being for themselves, midlife men and women in Ryff's (1989) study emphasized self-confidence, self-acceptance, and self-knowledge.

PRIME TIME FOR MIDLIFE WOMEN: CONTRIBUTING FACTORS TO PSYCHOLOGICAL WELL-BEING AND LIFE SATISFACTION

Maybe the biggest surprise for many midlife women is the unexpected pleasure of this period of life. They exemplify the life-span concepts of *optimal develop-ment* and *vitality*. They experience new and exciting ventures and a sense of personal achievement (for example, McGrath, Keita, Strickland, & Russo, 1992; Mitchell & Helson, 1990), generated to a great extent by *current cohort circumstances* of improved opportunities and choices (Schuster, 1990). Studies generally find that these women also experience high well-being and life satis-faction, optimism, power, gains in personal autonomy, and effective manage-ment of their environments (Apter, 1995; Goode, 1999).

Their early 50s, or early postparental period, was the time the women studied by Mitchell and Helson (1990) proclaimed as the best time of life. This is when they rated their quality of life at its highest. In two studies, one cross-sectional and the other longitudinal, the researchers evaluated the quality of life of midlife women from the Mills Longitudinal Study. The cross-sectional study included three groups of women: youngest midlife women (ages 26–37), prime midlife women (age 51), and late midlife women (ages 56–61). Mitchell and Helson (1990) found in this study that more women at the midpoint age of 51, or prime women, rated their lives as first rate than did the youngest midlife women (ages 26–37), late midlife women (ages 56–61), or a sample of older women (ages 66–76). Though the differences among the groups were not sig-nificant, half (50 percent) of the prime women reported high life satisfaction in contrast to lower proportions of early midlife women (37 percent) and late midlife women (43 percent). In their longitudinal study, Mitchell and Helson found that almost half (47 percent) of the prime women rated their lives as first rate.

Various findings from the studies by Mitchell and Helson (1990) showed that:

- Women living with children (with or without partners) included 70 percent of the younger group, 40 percent of the prime group, and 18 percent of the older group.

- Work force participation included 61 percent of women in the younger group, 43 percent in the prime group, and 34 percent in the older group.

- Women in the prime group rated themselves more financially comfortable than those in the other two groups, but women in the prime and older groups generated less income from their own earnings than did women in the younger group.

- The income of partners was significantly higher for women in the prime group than women in the other two groups.

- Concern for parents was greater for women in the prime and older groups than it was for women in the younger group.

- Satisfaction with one's partner did not vary across the three groups of women.

- Women in the prime group were less interested in sex than women in the other groups, though many (70 percent) of the women in the prime group were either "very much" or "moderately" interested in sex.

- Women in the prime group seemed less concerned with loneliness, ethical issues, philosophical and spiritual issues, and a sense of inner change than women in the other groups.

- Women in the prime and older groups engaged in more political and social issues, their friendships were more important and more satisfying, and their joy in living was greater than women in the younger group.

From a list of 45 "feelings about life," three-quarters or more of the prime women in the longitudinal study done by Mitchell and Helson (1990) rated seven items as more characteristic of themselves in their 50s (compared to 10 years earlier).

- Being selective in what I do (91 percent)

- Having a sense of being my own person (90 percent)

- Feeling established (78 percent)

- Feeling more satisfied with what I have, less worried about what I won't get (76 percent)

- Focusing on reality or meeting the needs of the day and not worrying about them (76 percent)

- Feeling the importance of time passing (76 percent)

- Using feeling and rationality in decision making (76 percent).

Many of the life satisfaction factors reported by Mitchell and Helson (1990) (cross-sectional results) were significantly correlated with quality of life or life satisfaction for the prime group. They included factors that had both positive and negative association with life satisfaction:

Positive Associations with Life Satisfaction:

- Living only with a partner

- Good health

- Financial comfort

- Interest in sex

- Satisfaction with partner

- Occupation

- Family

- Partner's occupation

- Friendships

- Cultural life

- Opportunities for service.

Negative Associations with Life Satisfaction:

- Loneliness

- Aging

- The need to make choices in one's life, to begin something, or to modify something.

Mitchell and Helson (1990) also reported factors from the longitudinal study that highly correlated with life satisfaction for the prime group as follows:

Factors Associated with Life Satisfaction:

- Living with partner only

- Being an "empty nest" parent

- Health

- Satisfaction in work and status level in work

- Marital satisfaction.

Feelings Positively Associated with Life Satisfaction:

- Feeling that one's life is moving well

- Feeling secure and committed

- Feeling a new level of intimacy

- Feeling optimistic and cheerful about the future.

Feelings Negatively Associated with Life Satisfaction:

- Wishing for a wider scope to one's life

- Feeling very much alone

- Coming near the end of a road and not finding another road.

The remainder of this chapter focuses on selected factors that contribute to psychological well-being and life satisfaction for midlife women. The factors appear in five categories, including biological; interpersonal; social–psychological; educational, work, earnings, and job satisfaction; and diversity.

Biological Factors

Age

Age did not affect life satisfaction in the Loewenstein et al. (1981) sample of always-single and single-again midlife women. No association between well-being and age was found in a study of 300 midlife women between ages 35–55 (Baruch, Barnett, & Rivers, 1983). Several studies also showed that well-being and life satisfaction did not vary across midlife age groups. No significant distinctions were found between life satisfaction in three age groups: 35–39, 40–49, and 50 and older in Lewis's (1992) study of 152 single midlife women. Similarly, stability of well-being was found across three stages of women's lives: premidlife, ages 34–44; midlife, ages 45–55; and postmidlife, ages 56–66 (Rawson, McFadden, & Jenson, 1996). In sum, well-being and life satisfaction do not appear to decline with age.

Health

Health was the variable most closely associated with life satisfaction for the always-single and single-again midlife women studied by Loewenstein et al. (1981). McQuaide (1998b) found that the better a woman's health, the higher her reported levels of well-being. In addition, neither menopausal status nor menopausal signs, such as hot flashes, were associated with well-being as discussed in Chapter 7.

INTERPERSONAL FACTORS

Sex Life

A woman's sex life and her well-being were found to be only moderately associated in a study of 103 white midlife women living in the New York City area (McQuaid, 1998b). Neither the presence nor absence of sexual needs, nor the mode of current sexual fulfillment, was associated with life satisfaction for the single women studied by Lowenstein et al. (1981). Yet, other researchers (for example, Baruch et al., 1983; Mitchell & Helson, 1990) found a positive association between sexual satisfaction and life satisfaction. Sexual satisfaction was the second best predictor of life satisfaction for the single women studied by Lewis (1992).

Marriage, Family, and Children

Marriage has been associated with life satisfaction among midlife women (Crohan, Antonnucci, Adelmann, & Coleman, 1989). Based on data from the National Survey of Families and Households, Bumpass and Aquilino (1995) found that the largest discrepancies in happiness were associated with two factors, marital status and education. Single women were almost twice as likely to report that they were unhappy during much of midlife. Yet, McQuaide (1998b) reported no significant effect of marital status on the well-being of midlife women. Baruch et al. (1983) found that many single women regretted not marrying but nonetheless realized that it was probably not a good fit for their goals and temperament. Life satisfaction in the Loewenstein et al. (1981) sample of single women was high, and no discrepancies emerged between the single-again and the always-single midlife women. Even so, the desire for a steady companion was frequent. When loneliness was an issue for single women (23 percent), there was high correlation between this factor and low life satisfaction. Lewis (1992) reported that their current living situation did not make a difference in the life satisfaction of single women. Those living alone were basically as satisfied as those living with others.

Satisfaction with family life was the best predictor of general life satisfaction in a national sample of midlife women and other respondents (Carlson &

Videka-Sherman, 1990). Midlife women, compared to younger women, reported greater satisfaction with family life, more enjoyment of the parent role, and greater satisfaction with homemaking. Both midlife women and younger women, however, rated paid work as equally or more important than homemaking.

Family relationships did not seem to contribute much to life satisfaction for the always-single or single-again women in the Loewenstein et al. (1981) study. An exception was caregiving for an older parent that negatively affected life satisfaction. No association was found between well-being and rearing children in several studies (for example, Baruch et al., 1983; McQuaide, 1998b; Unger & Crawford, 1992). Whether or not there were children living at home made no difference on well-being in McQuaide's (1998b) sample of midlife women. No difference in happiness or satisfaction was found between mothers and women over age 50 who never bore children (Glenn & McLanahan, 1981). In a study of midlife and older women, the subjective well-being of women who were always single and childless was not different from that of married, childless women (Koropeckyj-Cox, 1998). Childlessness for both groups of women did not significantly affect their well-being. Being childless was less a concern for women studied by Baruch et al. (1983) than not having a primary relationship. Single women in this study did not report any permanent sense of loss regarding being childless.

Relationships with Parents

The link between well-being for midlife women and their relations with their parents was the focus of Welsh and Stewart (1998) in an examination of data from the Radcliffe College class of 1964. The women's relationships with both parents were equally positive. Though the women were more similar to their fathers than their mothers in educational attainment, they reported that they did not experience greater influence from either parent. Yet, perceptions of parents as positive influences and positive relationships with parents were associated with similarity of educational and occupational achievements. Positive relationships with both mothers and fathers were associated with higher levels of concurrent self-esteem. Positive relationships with mothers (but not fathers) predicted emotional well-being, possibly because of the more extensive involvement of mothers compared to fathers in the lives of their adult daughters.

Social Support and Attachments

Social support networks are valuable resources that contribute to psychological adjustment, satisfaction with life, and the maintenance of physical health (Unger & Crawford, 1992). Women of all ages are generally effective in creating and sustaining these networks (Grambs, 1989).

The effects of social support on well-being across adult life was the focus of a study by Ishii-Kuntz (1988). Measurements of social support included the frequency and quality of relationships with family members, friends, and neighbors. Across adult life, family support was most associated with well-being, followed by friends, then neighbors. In another study, professional midlife women with no children indicated that support networks that encouraged their personal and professional growth were of immeasurable value to them. Though partners and family members were part of their support systems, these women emphasized the benefits received from close friends who provided support for risk taking and change (Keneipp, 1985). Midlife women studied by McQuaide (1998b) reported higher satisfaction if they were linked to a group of close women friends, and their well-being was higher when they reported having a confidant with whom they could talk freely and honestly about themselves. Yet, Lewis (1992) did not find a significant association between social support and life satisfaction among professional single women.

SOCIAL–PSYCHOLOGICAL FACTORS

Sex–Gender Role Traits

In their report on college alumnae from the Mills Longitudinal Study, Helson and Wink (1992) found support for an increase in "masculinity" and a decrease in "femininity" between the early 40s and early 50s. An increase in masculinity in the 50s age group meant confidence and decisiveness, and the decrease of femininity meant a reduction in dependence and vulnerability. In another study on the effects of sex–gender role traits on psychological well-being in midlife women, Frank, Towell, and Huyck (1985) found that masculine women were higher on self-esteem than feminine, androgynous, or undifferentiated women. Lewis (1992) concluded from a review of literature on sex–gender role orientation that masculine and androgynous women were higher on sense of well-being than feminine and undifferentiated women. In a metaanalysis of 35 studies on the link between sex–gender role orientation and psychological well-being, Whitley (1983) found that a masculine orientation was associated with self-esteem in both men and women. A higher percentage of women in the Lewis study were masculine (40 percent) than were androgynous (38 percent), feminine (10 percent), or undifferentiated (13 percent). In contrast to the other studies cited, however, the women in the Lewis study with a masculine orientation were not higher on life satisfaction. In that study no single type of sex–gender identity was a significant predictor of life satisfaction.

Mastery and Pleasure

Two dimensions of well-being, mastery and pleasure, were the focus of a study of life satisfaction among midlife women by Baruch et al. (1983). They defined mastery as feeling important and worthwhile. If high on mastery, women were also high on self-esteem and internal locus of control. Pleasure, or finding life enjoyable, was associated with emotional life and intimacy. Both mastery and pleasure were essential to well-being, but mastery contributed more.

Though not using the concept of mastery, several other studies addressed internal locus of control. Women in their 50s, studied by Mitchell and Helson (1990), felt more control over their lives than during earlier age periods. The fourth best predictor of life satisfaction in the Lewis (1992) study was internal locus of control, which was reported by 93 percent of the sample.

Paid work is associated with a high rank on mastery. Across various roles, midlife women studied by Christensen, Stephens, and Townsend (1998) experienced the highest level of mastery in the work role. Other variables that correlated with mastery in the Baruch et al. (1983) study were total family income, prestigious job, proportion of money contributed to the family income, and multiple roles. Variables associated with pleasure were total family income and marital status.

Divorced and always-single women scored lower on pleasure than married women, but they were higher on mastery. Work is critical to single women, the quality of work affecting pleasure and occupational prestige affecting mastery. Single women who preferred a single life were high in life satisfaction. If they preferred marriage, mastery and pleasure were low, as was life satisfaction. Their networks of friends were important to both pleasure and mastery. Friendships were second only to a challenging job in their ratings of life satisfaction (Baruch et al., 1983).

Ego Resiliency

Klohnen, Vandewater, and Young (1996) proposed that ego resiliency (ER) is a personal resource that can mediate midlife stress or enable midlife women to negotiate the challenges of this period of life. It is also associated with greater life satisfaction. The definition of ER used by the researchers was a "generalized capacity for flexible and resourceful adaptation to external and internal stressors" (p. 432). The key aspects of ER that are likely to aid adaptive negotiation of midlife challenges included active and meaningful engagement in the world, autonomous and competent functioning, sense of mastery across a range of life domains, perceptiveness and insightfulness, warm and open relations with others, effective interpersonal skills, and social poise. Indicators of adaptive functioning included psychological well-being, quality of romantic relationships, engagement in work, physical health, and body image.

Outcomes of ER were evaluated in data from the Mills and Radcliffe longitudinal studies by Klohnen et al. (1996). Women from the Mills sample were assessed on ER at age 43 and again at age 52. Evaluation of the women in the Radcliffe Longitudinal Study of the class of 1964 (Stewart & Vandewater,

1993) happened at age 48, five years after assessment of ER (at age 43). The researchers evaluated whether ER assessed at age 43 could successfully predict subsequent growth or decline in adaptations regarding central tasks and issues of midlife. Results showed significant associations between prior levels of ER and later midlife adjustments in both samples. ER, at age 43, significantly predicted subsequent indicators of well-being, life satisfaction, and, additionally, in the Mills sample, low levels of psychological distress. Findings from Klohnen et al. (1996) comparing ego-resilient women with less ego-resilient women appear in Exhibit 10.1.

—— Exhibit 10.1
   High Ego-Resilient Versus Low Ego-Resilient Midlife Women ——

- Higher ER women in early midlife experienced significantly greater relationship satisfaction in later midlife (both samples). Earlier in midlife, these women tended to be in relationships that were less conflictual; they perceived their partner as satisfying their needs.

- Higher ER women in early midlife reported higher levels of work satisfaction in later midlife (both samples). An examination of other factors in the Mills sample showed that higher ER women were also more likely to expand their work involvement over the study period and were more likely to procure additional educational or vocational training.

- Higher ER women in early midlife reported positive health outcomes in later midlife (both samples). Higher ER women rated their health as better, compared to women lower in ER. Higher ER women in the Mills sample also reported fewer menopausal signs and fewer health difficulties in later midlife.

- Higher ER women in early midlife reported positive estimation of body image in later midlife (both samples), including higher self-rated attractiveness and lower negative preoccupation with appearance.

In a second evaluation of ER by Klohnen et al. (1996), the question was whether prior levels of ER could predict signs of stagnation and decline in women low in this resource, and continued well-being and positive development in women higher in it. Compared to higher ER women, women low in ER at the beginning of midlife ended up in later midlife with lower satisfaction in relationships and work, lower self-perceived general health, and higher psychological distress. In addition, low ER women experienced more negative feelings and interactions over the study period. Low ER women felt that they were less likely to reach a new level of intimacy, felt less needed by people, perceived that they were less influential in their community, felt exploited when asked to do things by others, felt they were near the end of a road and without alternatives, and felt that their lives were narrow in scope. Additional data from the Mills sample found that low ER women experienced more troubling menopausal signs and were more critical of their body image. They also experienced more conflictual romantic relationships and were less likely to increase their work involvement or pursue additional vocational training.

In summary, the lower ER women studied by Klohnen et al. (1996) experienced the midlife period as one of stagnation and decline, whereas women with higher ER experienced midlife as an *opportunity for change and growth*. In contrast with women low in the ER resource in early midlife, women with high levels of ER reported by age 48 or 52 (depending on the sample) significantly better marital quality, better general health, more positive work involvement, and greater life satisfaction. The researchers concluded that ER is an important personality resource and plays a central role in how women experience and negotiate midlife.

Regrets about Life Circumstances

Though there are many *gains* in life, there are also *losses*, which are sometimes experienced as regrets. In reports of a study of single midlife professional women, regrets about life circumstances was the third best predictor of life satisfaction (Lewis & Borders, 1995); the lower the regret, the higher the life satisfaction. In this sample, there was a low to moderate range of regrets. No significant dissimilarities regarding the types of regrets or degree of regrets occurred between the always-single and the divorced or widowed women. The top six regrets (out of 20) for always-single women reported by Lewis (1992) included: "would have saved more money, would have taken more risks, would have worked less/enjoyed life more, would have been more assertive, would have tried to please others less, and would have looked out for myself more" (p. 115). "Would have gotten married" ranked eighth and "would have had children" ranked eleventh. The top six regrets for the divorced and widowed groups included: "would have saved more money, would have waited longer before getting married, would have had children, would have tried to please others less, would have looked out for myself more, and would have divorced sooner" (p. 116).

For single women studied by Lewis (1992) and married women studied by Metha, Kinnier, and McWhirter (1989), the regrets of missed educational opportunities and not taking more risks distinguished the least satisfied from the most satisfied respondents. Dissatisfied women from both studies wished they had taken more control of their lives and looked out for themselves more.

In contrast to women studied by Metha et al., women studied by Lewis seemed to take their education more seriously but regretted not having balanced hard work and enjoyment in their lives. Another significant predictor of life satisfaction in the Lewis study involved the effect of leisure-time activities on one's enjoyment of life.

Revised Social Clock Projects

The concept of social clock projects was used by Helson and McCabe (1994) to track identity changes in a sample of women from the Mills Longitudinal Study (Helson & Wink, 1992) ranging in age from their late 30s to mid-50s. Social clock projects involve activities stemming from a desire to create oneself and to attain self-esteem by performing goal-related tasks creditably or even with distinction. Usually the tasks are in family and work arenas. The projects begin at an anticipated time in life and finish with varying degrees of success. In this study, many women in their early 40s were examining what their life was like, what was missing, and what was sacrificed. They were trying to find a new direction and to experience becoming their own person. Revisions of their social clock projects made use of and reflected substantial changes in confidence and assertiveness since their 20s (Helson & Moane, 1987). In the age 52 follow-up, the women were mostly content with the social selves they achieved. Women at this age were functioning well and knew it; they felt less pressure to continue to prove themselves. These women demonstrated the life-span concepts of *optimal development*, *vitality*, and *gains*.

EDUCATIONAL, EARNINGS, AND JOB SATISFACTION FACTORS

Educational attainment made no difference in satisfaction among the midlife women studied by McQuaide (1998b). Occupational group or whether one was in or out of the workplace also did not make any difference in well-being. An exception was lower well-being if one was forced out of the workplace through a layoff, early retirement, or because of physical disability.

In many other studies, educational attainment was a key factor in satisfaction. For example, as indicated above, data from the National Survey of Families and Households showed that the largest differences in happiness were associated with marital status and education. Educational differences had the largest effect on reported happiness and on a measure of psychological distress during midlife. Women with more education reported more happiness and less distress (Bumpass & Aquilino, 1995). Other studies, including married and single women, also found that more highly educated women experienced greater life satisfaction (for example, Carlson & Videka-Sherman, 1990; Lewis, 1992; Loewenstein et al., 1981). Carlson and Videka-Sherman reported that this finding did not vary across age or race in their sample.

Midlife women (ages 45–55) earning their own income experienced more self-esteem and less depression (Rawson et al., 1996). Life satisfaction was associated both with having a salary and with a perception of salary fairness among the midlife women studied by Loewenstein et al. (1981). Single professional women with higher salaries scored higher on satisfaction than did other women. Type of positions held, however, made no difference (Lewis, 1992). Among African American women studied by Crohan et al. (1989), high occupational status and higher earnings were associated with their feeling more in control of their lives and more satisfied with their jobs and their lives. African American women with higher earnings reported a greater sense of control than did white women. Family income of $30,000 or more per year made no difference in life satisfaction in McQuaide's (1998a) sample of midlife women. If their income was below $30,000, however, the women reported less satisfaction.

Job satisfaction is a major factor influencing the general life satisfaction of midlife women (for example, Baruch et al., 1983; Crohan et al., 1989; Lewis, 1992). Job satisfaction was the most significant predictor of life satisfaction in the Lewis (1992) study of single professional women. This association was most apparent for women in white collar, high socioeconomic, college graduate, white, and older age categories.

DIVERSITY FACTORS

As often noted in this book, the prevalent research samples of midlife women tend to be well-educated, white, and professional. In a two-wave panel study of women interviewed in 1956 and again 30 years later, Moen (1997) discovered a cumulative effect of advantage. Though personal and social resources among the women varied over the life span, women in the 1950s who possessed these kinds of resources were also most likely to possess them 30 years later. For example, more educated women (especially those with some college) sought additional educational opportunities that could benefit them after marriage and motherhood more often than did those with less education.

The findings of most studies cannot be generalized beyond the samples used because they do not address diversities among midlife women such as variations in education, social class, race, and sexual orientation. The small body of knowledge on the influence of these variables on well-being and life satisfaction are discussed here.

Poor Midlife Women

As discussed earlier and in other chapters, many midlife women are poor and never attain the sense of well-being that more advantaged women tend to experience (for example, Butler & Weatherley, 1992). A woman's social class during childhood can generate negative effects throughout her life span, including an effect on well-being in midlife (Berman & Napier, 2000; Ryff, Schmutte, & Lee, 1996). Women who are comfortable financially (likely in the upper middle class or above) may see their 50s as the most satisfying time of their lives, but others may experience this period more as "downhill." Yet, Coney (1994) found in interviews that though some midlife women were financially insecure (as well as experienced inequities in employment and felt negatively about aging), they reported satisfaction with their achievements, greater confidence and maturity than younger women, and greater knowledge of what their capabilities were than younger women. They also felt increased freedom to express their opinions and beliefs.

African American Midlife Women

Research done by Gibson (1982, 1989) indicated that midlife was the most tumultuous period for African Americans. They were poorer and less educated. They were less likely to be married and were often separated, divorced, or widowed. Separated and divorced African American women were among the least well off at midlife on measures of stress and morale. Economic difficulties were the source of much of the psychological stress and distress these women experienced. Yet, in a comparison of African American women in the underclass and the middle class, Gibson (1989) found that whereas the former were more likely stressed and distressed, the latter, especially college-educated professional women, were more likely to experience low morale (unhappy and dissatisfied with life). Gibson speculated that the reason for low morale in the latter group was the wide gap between their high aspirations and their accomplishments. Also, these women may have compared themselves with younger African American women who made greater progress in education, careers, and income in a shorter time. In addition, as emphasized by Morris (1993), all racial and ethnic women must contend with racism and sexism.

Lesbian Midlife Women

The samples available on midlife lesbians consisted mainly of white, professional, and middle to upper middle class women. Though there can be financial and other worries, this period of life appeared to be a prime time for lesbians in most of the samples studied. As summarized by Sang (1993), midlife lesbians were growing and developing, self-confident, and optimistic. Positive changes reported by Fertitta (1984) included gaining perspective and wisdom, and more self-acceptance. Sang (1990, 1991, 1992, 1993) summarized many themes that corresponded with positive changes at midlife, as shown in Exhibit 10.2.

——— Exhibit 10.2
Positive Changes in Midlife for Lesbians ————————————————

- More comfort with who they are and more self-acceptance

- Desire for more play and fun rather than pushing themselves for career or work achievements

- Increased creative expression such as writing and art

- Self-discovery in the form of increased self-knowledge

- Abandoning things not working such as unfulfilled life dreams

- Reconnection with previous interests, passions, and suppressed aspects of themselves

- Change and refocus in areas such as jobs and interests, precipitated for many lesbians by losses

- Increased use of time for meaningful activities, such as giving more time to others and to their communities

- Greater self-confidence and self-direction

- Attempts to balance diverse aspects of their lives such as work, relationships, interests (for example, music, art), and community

- Celebration of midlife with other lesbians and feminists.

The positive picture delineated by Sang (for example, 1993) is not the full picture of midlife lesbians. Over half of midlife lesbians in a national sample studied by Bradford and Ryan (1991) often experienced worries that affected their daily lives. About a quarter (24 percent) of the sample was often so worried or nervous that the women could not accomplish routine tasks; for 40 percent of the sample this happened at least some of the time. The most common worry for midlife lesbians was money (55 percent). Other worries experienced by about one-fourth of the sample included difficulties with jobs or school, too much responsibility at work, and conflict with a lover. Worries regarding family members and children, job dissatisfaction, illness or death, and discovery of one's sexual orientation characterized smaller percentages of the sample.

EXCEPTIONS TO PSYCHOLOGICAL WELL-BEING AMONG ADVANTAGED MIDLIFE WOMEN

As indicated in the studies on diversity discussed above, some studies on advantaged women show mixed findings. Not all of these women experienced "prime-time" characteristics. As reflected in the life-span concepts of *individual differences, multiple influences, diverse outcomes,* and *constraints,* considerable variation is found among midlife women, even among those who are advantaged. For example, Wink (1991, 1992, 1996) labeled a prototype of midlife women from the Mills Longitudinal Study (Helson & Wink, 1992) as "willful." Though these women were effective, happy, sociable, and confident between ages 21–27, by midlife they were maladjusted and were experiencing difficulties with drugs, careers, and relationships.

Also from the Mills data, stories of some women between the ages of 36 and 46 portrayed themes of unpleasant consequences of independence and assertiveness, such as abandonment by husbands or rejection at work. Later themes, between ages 47–53, were troubling relationships with partners, parents, and children; overload resulting from heavy work responsibilities; economic strain; and demands from others (Helson, 1992). In their early 50s, however, some of these same women rated their quality of life as high (Mitchell & Helson, 1990). Most (73 percent) of McQuaide's (1998b) sample of women rated themselves as "very happy" or "happy" during midlife but some (14 percent) rated themselves as "unhappy" or "very unhappy." Women who were unhappy did not view this period of life or the future as times of new opportunities. Instead, they longed for earlier times when they had dreamed about a happy marriage and family or a wonderful and exciting career. At midlife, dreams from the past did not offer much solace or forecasts of future events. These women lacked positive images for creating new visions and meaning in their lives.

SUMMARY

- Many factors seem to be involved in the well-being and life satisfaction of midlife women, including biological; interpersonal; social–psychological; educational, work earnings, and job satisfaction; and diversity.

- Many women, both heterosexual and lesbian, rate midlife as a time high in life satisfaction and well-being, and as the prime time of their lives. This finding, however, is reported mainly by college-educated, middle, and upper-class white women.

- Little is known about the experiences of disadvantaged groups of women at midlife. What is known generally points to lower life satisfaction and well-being for them than for more advantaged women.

IMPLICATIONS FOR PRACTICE

Professional helpers need to be informed about the multiple factors involved in the psychological well-being and life satisfaction of midlife women. Negative stereotypes of midlife women can be countered with research findings showing high satisfaction and well-being for college-educated, middle, and upper-class white women. The lower satisfaction and well-being reported by disadvantaged groups of women at midlife show that practitioners may need to address educational, work, and income issues, as well as counseling concerns related to interpersonal and social issues. Disadvantaged women also have strong social networks including extended families and religiosities. These types of resources may be able to offer assistance. It is not unusual in African American and Latino communities, for example, for persons in various family and community groups to step in and help a member when needed. Adult children may also help because of the expectation in these communities to take care of one's family, including one's extended family. These relationships and the resources they may offer can be explored in practice situations with racial or ethnic midlife women.

Professional associations, professional helpers, citizen groups, and legislators can advocate for social change to reduce the discrepancies found between the experiences of disadvantaged women and those of other midlife women. Educators in the mental health and human services fields can also encourage their students and colleagues to develop interventions to benefit these women.

VIGNETTE

Belinda, a 58-year-old African American woman, sought counseling at the suggestion of her family doctor, who was treating her for insomnia and high blood pressure. She was laid off from her job of 10 years in a food processing plant when it closed six months earlier. Belinda and her 76-year-old mother and 55-year-old sister live together in a small house in an urban neighborhood. Her three children are married with families of their own. Belinda and the father of her children are divorced.

Belinda is worried that she will not find another job at her age. Her salary provided almost half of the family's income, with her sister's salary providing the other half. She does not know how they will pay all the bills. She also feels that she and her sister are not as energetic as they used to be, and she worries about how they can continue to care for their mother. Belinda is beginning to feel that her best years, in her 20s, will not be repeated during midlife.

Questions

- *What resources in Belinda's family and community might help her?*

- *What intervention strategies would you use for Belinda? Individual, small group, family, community? Why?*

REFERENCES

Apter, T. (1995). *Secret paths: Women in the new midlife.* New York: Norton.

Baruch, G. K., Barnett, R., & Rivers, C. (1983). *Lifeprints: New patterns of love and work for today's women.* New York: McGraw-Hill.

Berman, E., & Napier, A.Y. (2000). The midlife family: Dealing with adolescents, young adults, and marriage in transition. In W. C. Nichols, M. A. Pace-Nichols, D. S. Becvar, & A. Y. Napier (Eds.), *Handbook of family development and intervention* (pp. 208–234). New York: John Wiley & Sons.

Bradford, J., & Ryan, C. (1991). Who we are: Health concerns of middle-aged lesbians. In B. J. Warshow & A. J. Smith (Eds.), *Lesbians at midlife: The creative transition* (pp.147–163). San Francisco: Spinsters.

Bumpass, L. L., & Aquilino, W. S. (1995). *A social map of midlife: Family and work over the middle life course.* Vero Beach, FL: MacArthur Foundation Research Network on Successful Midlife Development.

Butler, S. S., & Weatherley, R. A. (1992). Women at midlife and categories of neglect. *Social Work, 37,* 510–515.

Carlson, B. E., & Videka-Sherman, L. (1990). An empirical test of androgyny in the middle years: Evidence from a national survey. *Sex Roles, 23,* 305–324.

Christensen, K. A., Stephens, M.A.P., & Townsend, A. L. (1998). Mastery in women's multiple roles and well-being: Adult daughters providing care to impaired parents. *Health Psychology, 17,* 163–171.

Coney, S. (1994). *The menopause industry: How the medical establishment explains women.* Alameda, CA: Hunter House.

Crohan, S. E., Antonnucci, T. C., Adelmann, P. K., & Coleman, L. M. (1989). Job characteristics and well-being at midlife: Ethnic and gender comparisons. *Psychology of Women Quarterly, 13,* 223–235.

Fertitta, S. (1984). *Never married women in the middle years: A comparison of lesbians and heterosexuals.* Unpublished doctoral dissertation, Wright University, Los Angeles.

Frank, S. J., Towell, P. A., & Huyck, M. (1985). The effects of sex-role traits on three aspects of psychological well-being in a sample of middle-aged women. *Sex Roles, 12,* 1073–1087.

Gibson, R. C. (1982). Blacks at midlife and late life: Resources and coping. In F. M. Berardo (Ed.), *The annuals of the American academy of political and social science: Middle and late-life transitions* (pp. 79–80). Beverly Hills, CA: Sage Publications.

Gibson, R. C. (1989). Black adults in aging society. In R. L. Jones (Ed.), *Black adult development* (pp. 389–406). Berkeley, CA: Cobb & Henry.

Glenn, N. D., & McLanahan, S. (1981). The effects of offspring on the psychological well-being of older adults. *Journal of Marriage and the Family, 43,* 409–421.

Goode, E. (1999, February 16). Middle age is prime of life. *New York Times,* p. 6.

Grambs, J. D. (1989). *Women over forty: Visions and realities* (Rev. ed.). New York: Springer.

Helson, R. (1992). Women's difficult times and the rewriting of the life story. *Psychology of Women Quarterly, 16,* 331–347.

Helson, R., & McCabe, L. (1994). The social clock project at middle age. In B. F. Turner & L. E. Troll (Eds.), *Women growing older: Psychological perspectives* (pp. 68–93). Thousand Oaks, CA: Sage Publications.

Helson, R., & Moane, G. (1987). Personality change in women from college to midlife. *Journal of Personality and Social Psychology, 53,* 176–186.

Helson, R., & Wink, P. (1992). Personality change in women from the early 40s to the early 50s. *Psychology and Aging, 7,* 45–50.

Ishii-Kuntz, M (1988). The impact of informal social support on the subjective sense of well-being: Comparisons across stages of adulthood (Doctoral dissertation, Washington State University, 1988). *Dissertation Abstracts International, 51*, 350.

Keneipp, R. (1985, March). *Adult development in mid-life, childless women.* Paper presented at the meeting of the Adult Education Research Conference, Tempe, AZ.

Klohnen, E. C., Vandewater, E. A., & Young, A. (1996). Negotiating the middle years: Ego-resiliency and successful midlife adjustment in women. *Psychology and Aging, 11*, 431–442.

Koropeckyj-Cox, T. (1998). Loneliness and depression in middle and old age: Are the childless more vulnerable? *Journal of Gerontology: Social Sciences, 53*, 303–321.

Lewis, V. G. (1992). *Life satisfaction of single middle-aged professional women.* Unpublished doctoral dissertation, University of North Carolina at Greensboro.

Lewis, V. G., & Borders, D. (1995). Life satisfaction of single middle-aged professional women. *Journal of Counseling & Development, 74*, 94–99.

Loewenstein, S. F., Bloch, N. E., Campion, J., Epstein, J. S., Gale, P., & Salvatore, M. (1981). A study of satisfactions and stresses of single women in midlife. *Sex Roles, 7*, 1127–1141.

McGrath, E., Keita, G. P., Strickland, B. R., & Russo, N. F. (1992). *Women and depression: Risk factors and treatment issues.* Washington, DC: American Psychological Association.

McQuaide, S. (1998a). Opening space for alternative images and narratives of midlife women. *Clinical Social Work, 26*, 39–53.

McQuaide, S. (1998b). Women at midlife. *Social Work, 43*, 21–31.

Metha, A., Kinnier, R. T., & McWhirter, E. H. (1989). A pilot study on the regrets and priorities of women. *Psychology of Women Quarterly, 13*, 167–174.

Mitchell, V., & Helson, R. (1990). Women's prime of life. Is it the 50's? *Psychology of Women Quarterly, 14*, 451–470.

Moen, P. (1997). Women's roles and resilience: Trajectories of advantage or turning points? In J. H. Gotlib & B. Wheaton (Eds.), *Stress and adversity over the life course: Trajectories and turning points* (pp. 113–156). New York: Cambridge University Press.

Morris, J. K. (1993). Interacting oppressions: Teaching social work content on women of color. *Journal of Social Work Education, 29*, 99–110.

Rawson, K. T., McFadden, J., & Jenson, G. O. (1996). The empty-nest syndrome revisited: Women in transition at midlife. *Journal of Family and Consumer Sciences, 88*, 48–52.

Ryff, C. D. (1989). In the eye of the beholder: Views of psychological well-being among middle-aged and older adults. *Psychology and Aging, 4*, 195–210.

Ryff, C. D., Schmutte, P. S., & Lee, Y. H. (1996). How children turn out: Implications for parental self-evaluation. In C. D. Ryff & M. M. Seltzer (Eds.), *The parental experience in midlife* (pp. 383–422). Chicago: University of Chicago Press.

Sang, B. (1990). Reflections of midlife lesbians on their adolescence. *Journal of Women and Aging, 2*, 111–117.

Sang, B. (1991). Moving toward balance and integration. In B. Sang, J. Warshow, & A. Smith (Eds.), *Lesbians at midlife: The creative transition* (pp. 206–214). San Francisco: Spinsters.

Sang, B. (1992). Counseling and psychotherapy with midlife and older lesbians. In S. Dworkin & F. Gutie'rrez (Eds.), *Counseling gay men and lesbians: Journey to the end of the rainbow* (pp. 35–48). Alexandria, VA: American Association for Counseling and Development.

Sang, B. (1993). Existential issues of midlife lesbians. In L. D. Garnets & D. C. Kimmel (Eds.), *Psychological perspectives on lesbian and gay male experiences* (pp. 500–516). New York: Columbia University Press.

Schuster, D. T. (1990). Fulfillment of potential, life satisfaction, and competence: Comparing four cohorts of gifted women at midlife. *Journal of Educational Psychology, 82,* 471–478.

Stewart, A. J., & Vandewater, E. A. (1993). The Radcliffe class of 1964: Career and family social clock projects in a transitional cohort. In K. D. Hulbert & D. T. Schuster (Eds.), *Women's lives through time: Educated women of the twentieth century* (pp. 235–258). San Francisco, CA: Jossey Bass.

Thomas, S. P. (1995). Psychosocial correlates of women's health in middle adulthood. *Issues in Mental Health Nursing, 16,* 285–314.

Unger, R., & Crawford, M. (1992). *Women & gender: A feminist psychology.* New York: McGraw Hill.

Welsh, W. M., & Stewart, A. J. (1998). Relationships between women and their parents: Implications for midlife well-being. *Psychology and Aging, 10,* 181–190.

Whitley, B. E. (1983). Sex role orientation and self-esteem: A critical meta-analysis review. *Journal of Personality and Social Psychology, 44,* 765–778.

Wink, L. (1991). Self- and object-directiveness in adult women. *Journal of Personality, 63,* 769–791.

Wink, L. (1992). Three types of narcissism in women from college to midlife. *Journal of Personality, 60,* 7–30.

Wink, L. (1996). Transition from the early 40s to the early 50s in self-directed women. *Journal of Personality, 64,* 49–69.

ADDITIONAL REFERENCES

Niemela, P., & Lento, R. (1993). The significance of the 50th birthday for women's individuation. In W. O. Davis, E. Cole, & E. Rothblum (Eds.), *Faces of women and aging* (pp. 117–127). New York: Harrington Park.

Spitze, G., Logan, J. R., Joseph, G., & Lee, E. (1994). Middle generation roles and well-being of men and women. *Journal of Gerontology: Social Sciences, 49,* S107–S116.

EPILOGUE

TOWARD DEVELOPING AND APPLYING KNOWLEDGE TO INFORM PRACTICE

In this concluding chapter we examine the research approaches used to study midlife women and suggest the types of research most appropriate for this population. Developmental research, which attempts to understand intraindividual change, or how persons develop and change as they grow older, is viewed as especially promising. Important practice issues and perspectives are also discussed, including theoretical orientations, intervention approaches, and consideration of the cultural meanings of behaviors.

A LOOK AT RESEARCH ON MIDLIFE WOMEN

Most of the research studies on midlife women have used cross-sectional designs with one target group, though some studies have used longitudinal designs. The samples have ranged in size from as few as three women in case studies to samples with many thousands of women. A preponderance of the samples is of the convenience type, which raises doubts about the generalizability of the findings beyond the populations from which the participants came. Some studies used help-seeking samples, which are biased to negative experiences and personal difficulties.

Only random sampling can ensure that the respondents represent the populations from which they were drawn. Convenience samples (as well as other nonprobability samples) can be useful, however, if the purpose of the study is to determine a relationship between the independent and dependent variables with no aim to generalize the findings from the sample to a larger population (Monette, Sullivan, & Dejong, 1994). The attainment of equivalent findings in numerous studies using convenience samples might also increase the likelihood that the results are applicable to their populations or to similar groups.

The samples of midlife women to date consisted mostly of white, middle- and upper-class, well-educated women. Only a few studies had substantial numbers of members of ethnic or racial groups. A small number of studies on African American women comprise most of the research on racial and ethnic women. One notable exception was the National Survey of Families and Households study (Bumpass & Aquilino, 1995) that over-sampled ethnic and racial persons, and persons living in diverse family structures. Midlife lesbians are rarely the focus of investigation (for example, Cole & Rothblum, 1991; Sang, 1993) or even identified in samples, and no studies have identified midlife bisexual, transgender, or intersex (having varying degrees of male and female sexual reproductive organs at birth) persons.

The narrowness of samples is exemplified by the longitudinal studies conducted on white women who attended Mills College and Radcliffe College. The women in these samples were educated at prestigious colleges, so the findings are not applicable to most women. Neither the cross-sectional nor the longitudinal data available on midlife women, therefore, represent the diversity of midlife women.

Historically, white, middle-class American men have been the respondents in most studies on midlife. Although more midlife women have participated in studies conducted in the last several decades, most of the research on women (like the research conducted earlier with males) has focused on white, middle-class American females. There are also special considerations when studying sex–gender factors, such as using multiple levels of analysis (for example, interpersonal, social, and cultural). In addressing these levels and the complexity of sex–gender arrangements in society, mixed or multiple research methods are recommended (Rabinowitz & Martin, 2001). Besides one's sex–gender identification, other critical aspects of a person's identity include age, race, ethnicity, social class, sexual orientation, and disability status must also be included. We cannot view sex–gender factors as separate from these other aspects. In addition, the diversity among women (within-group diversity) is so great that generalizations about all women from the characteristics of some women are difficult to support. For example, research on the effects of ethnicity and race in considering the diverse variables that can influence respondents is just beginning to emerge (Lemme, 1999); however, the research requirements are complicated and difficult to achieve.

TYPES OF RESEARCH DESIGNS NEEDED IN THE FUTURE

Research that is appropriate for learning about midlife women is developmental. The main goals of developmental research are the description, explanation, prediction, and improvement or optimization of people's lives. More specifically, this type of research has two primary aims. The first aim is to understand intraindividual change or how persons develop and change as they grow older, that is, the origins and development of behavior within the person. So far, however, there have been minimal studies on individual development. Most of the research on development compares groups of persons of different ages. Studies describing the differences between comparison groups tend to have implications for "average" individual development and do not adequately account for individual change.

The second aim is to identify how different persons show varying patterns of change, or age-related interindividual differences, and determine the factors that account for these differences (Hoyer, Rybash, & Roodin, 1999). A related aim is to address the effects of three important factors on change: chronological age effects, cohort effects, and time-of-measurement effects (for example, Cavanaugh, 1997; Lemme, 1999). Chronological age effects, for example, are associated with normative physiological changes. Cohort effects involve the sociohistorical experiences shared by persons born during a certain period that may exert important or even greater effects than chronological age. Time-of-measurement effects include environmental influences (for example, an outbreak of HIV/AIDS or important life events such as divorce) during the time of data collection.

Developmental research encounters the same difficulties as other scientific endeavors in meeting the principles of scientific inquiry, such as finding suitable control or comparison groups, limiting generalizations to the types of groups in the research, and finding adequate means of measurement (Kausler, 1982). Textbooks on adult development and aging (for example, Cavanagh, 1997; Hoyer et al., 1999) have discussed many other difficulties in conducting developmental research, including validity, reliability, and researcher bias. The additional need in developmental research to consider multiple and diverse influences on development makes this type of research even more complicated. Rarely are many influences addressed in single projects. In addition, there is often confounding of the three factors affecting change (age effects, cohort effects, and time-of-measurement effects), making it difficult to determine which variables, singly or in combination, effect changes in behavior.

Cavanagh (1997) and Lemme (1999) addressed the advantages and disadvantages of the four research designs used in developmental research. Studies using a cross-sectional design (for example, Nydegger & Mitteness, 1996; Veevers & Mitchell, 1998) seek age-related differences among persons. These studies compare groups of respondents of different ages and different cohorts at a single point in time. Among the advantages of the cross-sectional design are no respondent dropouts and no practice effects because of repeated testing. The major limitation is the confounding of age and cohort differences. In addition, cross-sectional data can describe differences among groups, but not explain them. Although such data show age differences, they do not show developmental or age changes over time.

Studies using a longitudinal design (for example, Bromberger & Matthews, 1996a, 1996b; Li, Seltzer, & Greenberg, 1999) focus on a single group of same-age respondents (a birth cohort) and follow them over time to determine age-related changes. The advantage of the longitudinal design is the identification of individual change over time and of developmental differences among persons. This design allows the researcher to examine long-term effects of earlier events, make predictions, and identify patterns of causation. But these designs are time-consuming and costly. Another disadvantage of this design is respondent attrition or dropout that reduces the representativeness of the sample. The group of remaining study participants may be significantly different from the group that began the study. Another limitation of longitudinal studies is the practice effects on participants of being repeatedly interviewed. Because the findings from the sample may differ from those of other generations, there can be confounding of age changes with cohort effects, as well as with time of measurement. The patterns of change, therefore, may reflect the effects of age, sociohistorical experiences, or time of measurement and it will be difficult to determine which or what combination of these factors is important.

In studies using a time lag design, observations of same-age groups happen at different times, with age held constant while cohort and time of measurement vary. The advantage is the ability to observe how the same age group functions in different historical periods or contexts. The disadvantage is the confounding of cohort and time of measurement that makes it ambiguous if the results relate to being born at a particular time or are associated with the particular sociohistorical setting.

Studies using sequential designs minimize the effects of cohort and time of measurement, though they do not totally eliminate the confounding effect. These designs represent various combinations of the other developmental research designs. For example, in cohort-sequential designs, researchers follow two or more different cohorts for a period of time; in cross-sequential designs, researchers conduct comparable cross-sectional studies at different historical times. These designs help separate age-related changes from effects that are unique to specific cohorts or historical periods. They combine some of the strengths of cross-sectional and longitudinal designs while attempting to minimize confounding of age, cohort, and time-of-measurement influences. They also provide greater internal validity than the single cohort longitudinal or single time-of-measurement, cross-sectional designs. Although these designs address some of the limitations of the more traditional designs and should be in greater use, a disadvantage is their complexity, a factor that limits their widespread use.

PRACTICE ISSUES AND PERSPECTIVES

Social workers and others in the helping professions often encounter midlife women as family members of clients or as the clients themselves (Malick, 1987; Sands & Richardson, 1986). These women may initiate services for many reasons, such as counseling for family issues, including child launching, effects of the postparental period, children returning home, and caring for older parents (see Chapters 2 and 3). Relationship issues are often a concern and include couple conflicts, partners retiring or dying, divorce, and same-sex links (Anderson, Dimidjian, & Miller, 1995; Carter & McGoldrick, 1989; Ellman, 1992; McGrath, 1992; Sands & Richardson, 1986; see also Chapters 2 and 4). As shown in Chapters 6 and 7, biological issues related to health, menopause, and sexuality can affect relationships. Existential issues also come out in practice with midlife women such as changes in self-concept (for example, lost youth, altered body image, onset of physical illness, menopause); perception of time (for example, sense of urgency, limited time left); sense of meaning of one's life (for example, what priorities to pursue, anxieties about death); and views about issues of the past (for example, wanting to resolve past conflicts, trauma, and losses; see Ellman, 1992). Depression is the most common complaint of women seeking mental health services (see Chapter 8). Midlife women may also seek recommendations for work-training opportunities or ways to protect themselves from poverty (see Chapter 5). In addition, social workers and other professional helpers must strive for justice and equity for women by eliminating the numerous social constraints that impede these goals (Fitzpatrick & Gomez, 1997).

Aside from one or more of the issues discussed above, some midlife women may want to address issues associated with newly identifying as lesbians in midlife. These issues can include (a) new feelings about another woman (Bridges & Croteau, 1994); (b) making the shift to a positive self-identification as lesbian (Wyers, 1987); (c) adapting to the discrepancies between a prior heterosexual marriage and link with a lesbian partner, which can include lack of social validation for a lesbian couple, more difficulty negotiating the balance between autonomy and connection, and differences in sexual practices such as more emphasis on kissing and hugging instead of goal-oriented orgasms (Bridges & Croteau, 1994); (d) making choices about whom to tell about their lesbian identification such as families, friends, and children, and when, how, and where to tell them (Hanley-Hackenbruck, 1989); (e) fear that one's children and others will turn against one's identification as lesbian (Garnets & Kimmel, 1993; Sang, 1992); and (f) not knowing about or not taking advantage of opportunities for social support (Adelman, 1988; Kehoe, 1986; Raphael & Robinson, 1984).

Although many clients are midlife women with issues such as those identified here, research knowledge that is applicable for practice with them in social work or other helping professions is sparse. Most of the pertinent material that exists is found in psychiatric texts (for example, Colarusso & Nemiroff, 1981; Howells, 1981; Norman & Scaramella, 1980). A few special-focus resources are available such as counseling approaches for midlife marriages (Anderson et al., 1995; Guttman, 1991; Maltas, 1992; Wolinsky, 1990) and midlife divorces (Bogolub, 1991; Iwanir & Ayal, 1991); applications of the developmental concepts of the dream and life structure (Simmermon & Schwartz, 1986); and applications of life-transition frameworks (Avis, 1987; Schlossberg, 1984, 1987, 1989; Sherman, 1987). In addition, several general discussions of practice with midlife women are available (for example, Beynon & Hill, 1997; McQuaide, 1996a, 1996b, 1998a, 1998b; Sands & Richardson, 1986).

Applications of specific intervention approaches in practice are based on various theoretical orientations, such as behavioral, cognitive, psychoanalytic, existential, and feminist. Certain perspectives seem particularly relevant for practice with midlife women: developmental, feminist, interpersonal, cognitive–behavioral, and affirmative. A brief description of each of these perspectives follows.

Developmental Perspective

Ivey (1991) observed that clients often seek resolution of a difficult situation, such as separation, divorce, depression, or job choice. Traditionally, resolution was oriented to a specific end or a "cure." Cures in life, however, do not exist because life is always confronting us with new developmental challenges. The practitioner's task, therefore, is not only to help midlife women resolve difficult situations in their lives but also to consider challenges they face as developmental opportunities for growth. This view supports *the life-span human development model* presented in this book. The life-span developmental process can be applied to whatever issues a woman is dealing with in which the focus is placed on examining the choices and changes that will best facilitate her development. For example, if a midlife woman seeks vocational direction, the practitioner can help her to expand her career choices and enhance her life-planning and decision-making skills.

The lifespan approach applied in this book emphasizes *optimal development*, *individual differences*, the importance of a woman's *historical–cultural context*, and the *multifaceted*, *multidirectional*, and *complex nature of change*. It also addresses the multiple arenas that affect midlife women, such as family structures, work, and biological and health changes. This perspective can be useful in providing a more holistic framework for responding to their concerns.

Feminist Perspective

The framing of problems as day-to-day issues in living and as representations of normalcy is inherent in the feminist perspective. An emphasis on positive mental health, strengths, and adaptive strategies replaces a focus on pathology and diagnosis (Fassinger, 1991). A central objective is the empowerment of women and the creation of egalitarian relationships (McGrath, 1992). Practitioners are facilitators, educators, and advocates for clients (Fassinger, 1991). Delineating a collaborative (versus hierarchical) approach, Avis (1987) suggested that the practitioner share knowledge of adult development and life transitions with clients. Both the practitioner and the client propose and assess alternative helping strategies. The collaborative approach also considers multiple contexts and modalities, including those external to the practitioner–client context. For example, practitioners make referrals to training programs, career and educational counselors, higher education institutions, and other support systems.

Feminist practice is also critical because it focuses on cultural analysis of sexism and violence against women (McGrath, 1992). Regardless of practice setting or intervention approach, a feminist assessment of the client's circumstances involves simultaneous attention to consciousness (critical awareness of various cultural and political factors) and the contexts involving cultural variables associated with the client's situation (Bricker-Jenkins & Lockett, 1995).

Feminist interventions are both individual and environmental (Fassinger, 1991). For example, practitioners encourage women to develop useful behavioral skills and to reject sex–gender role restrictions regardless of whether they are historically associated with women or men (McGrath, 1992). Modification of social and political structures is also essential for helping women to ameliorate the various traumas induced by sexism and other forms of exploitation (Bricker-Jenkins & Lockett, 1995).

Interpersonal Perspective

The interpersonal perspective is useful for women because of the centrality of relationships in their lives (McGrath, 1992). The practitioner teaches relationship skills to women and fosters a strong interactional relationship with them (Klerman, Weissman, Rounsaville, & Chevron, 1984). It is especially important for women to connect to friends and other social networks (McQuaide, 1998b). Group work is important as a means to learn about others in comparable situations and to overcome isolation and loneliness. Groups can offer both strengths building and support (McGrath, 1992). Beynon and Hill (1997) and McQuaide (1996a) described the use of group work models in working with midlife women (see Chapter 6 for the usefulness of groups with women who have breast cancer). Group work is also an effective means for midlife lesbians to develop social support and reduce shame and alienation resulting from heterosexism and internalized oppression (Fassinger, 1991).

Cognitive–Behavioral Perspective

The cognitive–behavioral perspective can be applied to modify faulty cognitions and undesired behaviors. Cognitive interventions help women restructure negative thought patterns, especially those that contribute to their feeling helpless and victimized (McGrath, 1992). Behavioral interventions focus on the development of new skills and replacement of undesired behaviors with desired behaviors (Sundel & Sundel, 1999).

Affirmative Perspective

A nonoppressive or affirmative perspective for lesbians (and gay persons) developed from a political as well as a psychological base (for example, Brown, 1988). This perspective follows the premise that lesbians are an oppressed group. An important component of practice involves examination of the effect of this oppression on the psychological functioning of lesbian clients. Of particular concern is the effect of heterosexism and internalized oppression and their interactions with other forms of cultural oppression and self-alienation. These oppressions and negative stereotypes affect all arenas of these clients' lives. Though not specifically focused on midlife women, Comas-Di'az and Greene (1994) delineated intervention applications for various ethnic and racial populations and lesbian women.

Fassinger (1991) also recommended approaches that can be adapted for use with midlife lesbians:

- Cognitive approaches can be useful in overcoming negative thinking and self-talk about same-sex sexual orientation, and can aid in developing a positive sense of self.

- Client-centered approaches can be useful for encouraging expression of repressed affect.

- Gestalt "empty chair" techniques can help bring into awareness all sides of the ambivalence and confusion about same-sex sexual orientation, as well as help women vicariously talk to family, friends, co-workers, and others about their same-sex identity.

- Bibliotherapy, or assignment of books and articles, can present positive views of same-sex sexual orientations and diverse role models.

- Family systems and couples counseling can be useful for working with relationship issues.

- Cross-cultural approaches are important to use with culturally diverse lesbian clients.

CONCLUSION

Selecting suitable practice interventions for midlife and older adults depends on many factors; no particular intervention is currently a treatment of choice (for example, American Psychological Association, 1998). One of the essential factors in selecting an intervention is evidence for its purported efficacy. As a result of increased emphasis on the measurement of treatment outcomes, many mental health professionals are embracing empirically supported practice (for example, Sundel & Sundel, 1999; Thyer & Wodarski, 1998). A task force of the American Psychological Association categorized empirically validated psychological interventions in three categories: well-established, probably efficacious, and experimental (for example, Chambless et al., 1996). Except for family education for schizophrenia and interpersonal therapy for bulimia and depression, behavioral and cognitive–behavioral interventions are the only ones considered well-established and efficacious. There is evidence that behavioral and cognitive–behavioral interventions are effective for midlife women in the treatment of several areas of concern such as depression (Beck, Rush, Shaw, & Emery, 1979) and marital difficulties (Azrin et al., 1980; Jacobson & Follette, 1985).

Though this discussion has focused mainly on direct practice, social work addresses both social treatment and social reform as advocated by the feminist perspective. The two aspects are complementary and essential for work with midlife women. The rapid growth of specialization in social work and related helping professions sometimes leads practitioners to focus only on selected aspects of an individual's situation, instead of considering the full range of interventions that could be beneficial for women grappling with life issues. In addition, Wyche (2001) pointed out the need for practitioners to be aware of the cultural meanings of the broad ethnic and racial patterns of behaviors, such as family- and group-oriented versus individualistic patterns and cultural norms, as well as the uniqueness of each client (Rotheram-Borus & Wyche, 1994). Practitioners need to ask cultural questions that inform assessment processes and subsequent interventions (Wyche, 2001).

Human services practitioners and other professional helpers can intervene at different and multiple system levels to improve the quality of life for midlife women. Professional values, knowledge, skills, and experience can promote collaboration and constructive problem solving at the individual, couple, group, organizational, community, and societal levels. The goals are not only to improve quality of life for specific women but also to promote social and economic justice for vulnerable groups of women everywhere. This may involve going beyond the boundaries of the practitioner's office to address organizational, community, and political issues that influence women's social, emotional, and economic well-being. Practice skills used with individuals and groups are applicable not only to provide economic and social support for needy women but also to advocate for them with public authorities, organizations, community representatives, politicians, and others who lack awareness or appreciation of their circumstances. Expertise in planning, policy analysis, research, and evaluation is also necessary to facilitate and foster effective policies and programs for midlife women.

Although this book is about midlife women, men also have an important role to play in improving conditions for these women. They can become more knowledgeable about the experiences and concerns faced by midlife women, as well as gain greater appreciation of sex–gender inequities in work, family responsibilities, and other issues covered in this volume. Such understanding can lead to increased efforts by men to reduce inequities and promote improved conditions for midlife women. Men at midlife can learn more about what the women in their lives such as partners and friends are experiencing during this period, and how women's experiences can impact men during their own changes at midlife.

The research on midlife women is an evolutionary process in which knowledge becomes progressively applied and tested in the various situations encountered by professional helpers. As findings become more firmly established, professionals can apply them with greater confidence. The current era is one of rapid change that is fueled by revolutionary technological innovations and methods of communication. Professional helpers can equip themselves with updated technology and practice knowledge to improve their services.

We hope this book will be useful to students, practitioners, educators, supervisors, trainers, administrators, and others who work with midlife women. Educators of social workers and other professional helpers have a special responsibility to inform students about the knowledge base and research findings applicable to practice. The ultimate beneficiaries are women from all walks of life.

REFERENCES

Adelman, M. (1988). Quieting our fears: Lesbians and aging. *Outlook: National Lesbian and Gay Quarterly, 1,* 78–81.

American Psychological Association, Working Group on the Older Adult. (1998). What practitioners should know about working with older adults. *Professional Psychology: Research and Practice, 29,* 413–427.

Anderson, C. M., Dimidjian, S. A., & Miller, A. (1995). Redefining the past, present, and future: Therapy with long-term marriages at midlife. In N. S. Jacobson & A. S. Guttman (Eds.), *Clinical handbook of couple therapy* (pp. 247–260). New York: Guilford Press.

Avis, J. P. (1987). Collaborative counseling: A conceptual framework and approach for counselors of adults in life transitions. *Counselor Education and Supervision, 27,* 15–30.

Azrin, N. H., Besalel, V. B., Bechtel, R., Michalicek, A., Mancera, M., Carroll, D., Shuford, D., & Cox, J. (1980). Comparison of reciprocity and discussion-type counseling for marital problems. *American Journal of Family Therapy, 8,* 21–28.

Beck, A. T., Rush, A. J., Shaw, F. B., & Emery, G. (1979). Behavioral treatment of panic disorder. *Behavioral Therapy, 20,* 261–282.

Beynon, C., & Hill, G. (1997). Midlife mysteries: A group work response. *Australian Social Work, 50*, 35–40.

Bogolub, E. B. (1991). Women and mid-life divorce: Some practice issues. *Social Work, 36*, 428–433.

Bricker-Jenkins, M., & Lockett, P. W. (1995). Women: Direct practice. In R. L. Edwards (Ed.-in-Chief), *Encyclopedia of social work* (19th ed., Vol. 3, pp. 2529–2539). Washington, DC: NASW Press.

Bridges, K. L., & Croteau, J. M. (1994). Once-married lesbians: Facilitating changing life patterns. *Journal of Counseling & Development, 73*, 134–140.

Bromberger, J. T., & Matthews, K. A. (1996a). A "feminine" model of vulnerability to depressive symptoms: A longitudinal investigation of middle-aged women. *Journal of Personality and Social Psychology, 70*, 591–598

Bromberger, J. T., & Matthews, K. A. (1996b). A longitudinal study of the effects of pessimism, trait anxiety, and life stress on depressive symptoms in middle-aged women. *Psychology and Aging, 11*, 207–213.

Brown, L. S. (1988). Feminist therapy with lesbians and gay men. In M. A. Dutton & L.E.A. Walker (Eds.), *Feminist psychotherapies: Integration of therapeutic and feminist systems* (pp. 206–227). Norwood, NJ: Ablex.

Bumpass, L. L., & Aquilino, W. S. (1995). *A social map of midlife: Family and work over the middle life course*. Vero Beach, FL: MacArthur Foundation Research Network on Successful Midlife Development.

Carter, B., & McGoldrick, M. (1989). Overview: The changing family life cycle: A framework for family therapy. In B. Carter & M. McGoldrick (Eds.), *The changing family life cycle: A framework for family therapy* (2nd ed., pp. 3–28). Boston: Allyn & Bacon.

Cavanaugh, J. (1997). *Adult development and aging* (3rd ed.). Pacific Grove, CA: Brooks/Cole.

Chambless, D. L., Sanderson, W. C., Shoham, V., Johnson, S.A.B., Pope, K. S., Crits-Christoph, P., Baker, M., Johnson, B., Woody, S. R., Sue, S., Beutler, L., Williams, D. A., & McCurry, S. (1996). An update on empirically validated therapies. *Clinical Psychologist, 49*, 5–18.

Colarusso, C. A., & Nemiroff, R. A. (1981). *Adult development: A new dimension in psychoanalytic theory and practice*. New York: Plenum Press.

Cole, E., & Rothblum, E. D. (1991). Lesbian sex at menopause: As good as or better than ever. In B. Sang, J. Warshow, & A. Smith (Eds.), *Lesbians at midlife: The creative transition* (pp. 184–193). San Francisco: Spinsters.

Comas Di'az, L., & Greene, B. (Eds.). (1994). *Women of color: Integrating ethnic and gender identities in psychotherapy*. New York: Guilford Press.

Ellman, J. P. (1992). A treatment approach for patients in midlife. *Canadian Journal of Psychiatry, 37*, 564–566.

Fassinger, R. E. (1991). The hidden minority: Issues and challenges in working with lesbian and gay men. *Counseling Psychologist, 19*, 167–176.

Fitzpatrick, J. A., & Gomez, T. R. (1997). Still caught in a trap: The continued povertization of women. *Affilia, 12*, 318–341.

Garnets, L. D., & Kimmel, D. C. (Eds.). (1993). *Psychological perspectives on lesbian and gay male experiences*. New York: Columbia University Press.

Guttman, H. A. (1991). Parental death as a precipitant of marital conflict in middle age. *Journal of Marital and Family Therapy, 17*, 81–87.

Hanley-Hackenbruck, P. (1989). Psychotherapy and the "coming out" process. *Journal of Gay & Lesbian Psychotherapy, 1*, 21–39.

Howells, J. G. (Ed.). (1981). *Modern perspectives in the psychiatry of middle age*. New York: Brunner/Mazel.

Hoyer, W. I., Rybash, J. M., & Roodin, P. A. (1999). *Adult development and aging* (4th ed.). Boston: McGraw-Hill.

Ivey, A. E. (1991). *Developmental strategies for helpers: Individual, family, and network interventions*. Pacific Grove, CA: Books/Cole.

Iwanir, S., & Ayal, H. (1991). Midlife divorce initiation: From crisis to developmental transition. *Contemporary Family Therapy, 13*, 609–623.

Jacobson, N. S., & Follette, W. C. (1985). Clinical significance of improvement resulting from two behavioral marital therapy components. *Behavior Therapy, 16*, 249–262.

Kausler, D. H. (1982). *Experimental psychology and human aging*. New York: John Wiley & Sons.

Kehoe, M. (1986). Lesbians over 65: A triple invisible minority. *Journal of Homosexuality, 12*, 139–152.

Klerman, G. L., Weissman, M. M., Rounsaville, B. J., & Chevron, E. (1984). *Interpersonal psychotherapy of depression*. New York: Basic Books.

Lemme, R. H. (1999). *Development in adulthood*. Needham Heights, MA: Allyn & Bacon.

Li, L. W., Seltzer, M. M., & Greenberg, J. S. (1999). Change in depressive symptoms among daughter caregivers: An 18-month longitudinal study. *Psychology and Aging, 14*, 206–219.

Malick, M. D. (1987). A gender balancing perspective in teaching about middle age. *Report on a project to integrate scholarship on women in the professional curriculum at Hunter College* (pp. 14–24). New York: Hunter College.

Maltas, C. (1992). Trouble in paradise: Marital crises of midlife. *Psychiatry, 55*, 122–131.

McGrath, E. (1992). New treatment strategies for women in the middle. In B. R. Wainrib (Ed.), *Gender issues across the life cycle* (pp. 124–136). New York: Springer.

McQuaide, S. (1996a). Keeping the wise blood: The construction of images in a midlife women's group. *Social Work with Groups, 19*, 131–145.

McQuaide, S. (1996b). Self-hatred, the right to a life, and the tasks of midlife. *Clinical Social Work, 24*, 35–47.

McQuaide, S. (1998a). Opening space for alternative images and narratives of midlife women. *Clinical Social Work, 26*, 39–53.

McQuaide, S. (1998b). Women at midlife. *Social Work, 43*, 21–31.

Monette, D. R., Sullivan, T. J., & Dejong, C. R. (1994). *Applied social research: Tool for the human services* (3rd ed.). Fort Worth, TX: Harcourt Brace.

Norman, W. H., & Scaramella, T. J. (Eds.). (1980). *Mid-life: Developmental and clinical issues*. New York: Brunner/Mazel.

Nydegger, C. N., & Mitteness, L. S. (1996). Midlife: The prime of fathers. In C. D. Ryff & M. M. Seltzer (Eds.), *The parental experience in midlife* (pp. 533–559). Chicago: University of Chicago Press.

Rabinowitz, V. C., & Martin, D. (2001). Choices and consequences: Methodological issues in the study of gender. In R. K. Unger (Ed.), *Handbook of the psychology of woman and gender* (pp. 29–52). New York: John Wiley & Sons.

Raphael, S., & Robinson, M. (1984). The older lesbian: Love relationships and friendship patterns. In J. T. Darty & S. Potter (Eds.), *Women-identified women* (pp. 67–82). Palo Alto, CA: Mayfield.

Rotheram-Borus, M. J., & Wyche, K. F. (1994). Ethnic differences in identity development in the United States. In S. Archer (Ed.), *Interventions for adolescent identity development* (pp. 62–83). Thousand Oaks, CA: Sage Publications.

Sands, R., & Richardson, V. (1986). Clinical practice with women in their middle years. *Social Work, 31*, 36–43.

Sang, B. (1992). Counseling and psychotherapy with midlife and older lesbians. In S. Dworkin & F. Gutie'rrez (Eds.), *Counseling gay men and lesbians: Journey to the end of the rainbow* (pp. 35–48). Alexandria, VA: American Association for Counseling and Development.

Sang, B. (1993). Existential issues of midlife lesbians. In L. D. Garnets & D. C. Kimmel (Eds.), *Psychological perspectives on lesbian and gay male experiences* (pp. 500–516). New York: Columbia University Press.

Schlossberg, N. K. (1984). *Counseling adults in transition*. New York: Springer.

Schlossberg, N. K. (1987, May). Taking the mystery out of change. *Psychology Today, 21*, 74–75.

Schlossberg, N. K. (1989). *Overwhelmed: Coping with life's ups & downs*. Lexington, MA: Lexington Books.

Sherman, E. (1987). *Meaning in mid-life transitions*. Albany: State University of New York Press.

Simmermon, R., & Schwartz, K. M. (1986). Adult development and psychotherapy: Bridging the gap between theory and practice. *Psychotherapy, 23*, 404–410.

Sundel, M., & Sundel, S. (1999). *Behavior change in the human services: An introduction to principles and applications*. Thousand Oaks, CA: Sage Publications.

Thyer, B. A., & Wodarski, J. (Eds.). (1998). *Handbook of empirical social work practice* (Vol. 1). New York: John Wiley & Sons.

Veevers, J. E., & Mitchell, B. A. (1998). Intergenerational exchanges and perceptions of support within "boomerang kid" family environments. *International Journal of Human Development, 46*, 91–108.

Wolinsky, M. A. (1990). *Heart of wisdom: Marital counseling with older and elderly couples*. New York: Brunner/Mazel.

Wyche, K. F. (2001). Sociocultural issues in counseling for women of color. In R. K. Unger (Ed.), *Handbook of the psychology of women and gender* (pp. 330–340). New York: John Wiley & Sons.

Wyers, N. L. (1987). Homosexuality in the family: Lesbian and gay spouses. *Social Work, 32*, 143–148.

APPENDIX

A COMPILATION OF RESEARCH STUDIES ON MIDLIFE WOMEN

cientific research on midlife women is rare, especially studies using reliable and valid measurements.* The Appendix provides information on the designs, samples, and data collection methods used in a set of 232 studies. This collection, which is in alphabetical order, illustrates the range and type of studies conducted with midlife women. This set, which includes most of the studies cited in the book, reveals that less than half of the samples were random; therefore, the participants in the majority of the studies may not be representative of the midlife women in the populations from which they were drawn. Rarely do any of the studies that used the traditional cross-sectional and longitudinal designs, control for age effects, cohort effects, and time-of-measurement effects, the importance of which was discussed in the Epilogue.

Of the 232 studies cited, more than half (58 percent) used cross-sectional designs and over one-fourth (28 percent) used longitudinal or panel designs. One study used a cross-sequential design. Some (13 percent) studies reported data from both cross-sectional and longitudinal designs. A few (2 percent) studies were qualitative. The samples used in this collection ranged from case studies with as few as three women to studies using thousands of women. About 40 percent used sampling methods identified as random, probability, representative, stratified, or clustered. The remaining studies used other types of sampling methods mostly defined as convenience. Only about 9 percent included substantial proportions of nonwhite women, predominantly African American women.

*See M. E. Lachman. (Ed.). (2001). *Handbook of Midlife Development.* New York: John Wiley & Sons.

APPENDIX INDEX OF RESERACH STUDIES

CHAPTER 9 | **Personality, Identity, and Generativity**
41, 52, 75, 76, 77, 86, 89, 90, 93, 124, 139, 160, 231

CHAPTER 10 | **Psychological Well-Being and Life Satisfaction**
30, 36, 45, 48, 75, 77, 98, 99, 115, 119, 144, 147, 151, 156, 174, 184, 186, 190, 199, 205, 206, 222, 227, 228

Epilogue
24, 25, 40, 76, 116, 144, 216

1

RESEARCHERS: Adelmann, P. K., Antonucci, T. C., Crohan, S. E., & Coleman, L. M. (1989). Empty nest, cohort, and employment in the well-being of mid-life women. *Sex Roles, 20,* 173–189.
RESEARCH DESIGN: cross-sectional
SAMPLING METHOD: area-sampling probability method
SAMPLE: 374 mothers in 1957, 312 mothers in 1976; ages 40–69 in both samples
DATA COLLECTION METHOD: person-to-person interviews

2

RESEARCHERS: Adelmann, P. K., Antonucci, T. C., Crohan, S. E., & Coleman, L. M. (1990). A causal analysis of employment and health in midlife women. *Women & Health, 16,* 5–20.
RESEARCH DESIGN: cross-sectional
SAMPLING METHOD: nationally representative
SAMPLE: subset of 463 women, ages 40–64, and a comparison sample of 566 women, ages 21–39, drawn from 2,264 adults in the Americans View Their Mental Health data set
DATA COLLECTION METHOD: secondary analyses

3

RESEARCHERS: Allen, K. R. (1994). Feminist reflections on lifelong single women. In D. L. Sollie & L. A. Leslie (Eds.), *Gender, families, and close relationships: Feminist research journeys* (pp. 97–119). Thousand Oaks, CA: Sage Publications.
RESEARCH DESIGN: cross-sectional
SAMPLING METHOD: self-selected

SAMPLE: 30 working-class women: 15 did not marry or bear children, 15 married and had at least one child; birth cohorts 1907–1914
DATA COLLECTION METHOD: life history person-to-person interviews

4

RESEARCHERS: Allen, L., Aber, J. L., Seidman, E., Denner, J., & Mitchell, C. (1996). Mother's parental efficacy at midlife in a Black and Latina SAMPLE: Effects of adolescent change across a school transition. In C. D. Ryff & M. M. Seltzer (Eds.), *The parental experience of midlife* (pp. 301–335). Chicago: University of Chicago Press.
RESEARCH DESIGN: longitudinal
SAMPLING METHOD: self-selected
SAMPLE: 904 poor youths, diverse ethnic/racial backgrounds, ages 9–15, from the young cohort of the Youth Study of the Adolescent Pathways Project and 246 parents (*mean age* 38.94)
DATA COLLECTION METHOD: paper–pencil surveys with adolescents, person-to-person interviews with parents

5

RESEARCHERS: Allen, S. F., & Stoltenberg, C. D. (1995). Psychological separation of older adolescents and young adults from their parents: An investigation of gender differences. *Journal of Counseling & Development, 73,* 542–546.
RESEARCH DESIGN: cross-sectional
SAMPLING METHOD: convenience
SAMPLE: 182 first-year college students (98 men, 93 women; *mean age* 18.97)
DATA COLLECTION METHOD: paper–pencil questionnaires

6

RESEARCHERS: Amato, P. R., Rezac, S. J., & Booth, A. (1995). Helping between parents and young adult offspring: The role of parental marital quality, divorce, and remarriage. *Journal of Marriage and the Family, 57,* 363–374.
RESEARCH DESIGN: cross-sectional, longitudinal (5 years)
SAMPLING METHOD: random, national probability
SAMPLE: subset of 471 parents and their adult children, from the National Survey of Families and Households data
DATA COLLECTION METHOD: person-to-person interviews, paper–pencil questionnaires

7

RESEARCHERS: Aquilino, W. S. (1996). The returning adult child and parental experience at midlife. In C. D. Ryff & M. M. Seltzer (Eds.), *The parental experience in midlife* (pp. 423–455). Chicago: University of Chicago Press.
RESEARCH DESIGN: cross-sectional, longitudinal (5 years)
SAMPLING METHOD: random, national probability
SAMPLE: subset of 4,922 women, ages 19–34, who had left home at least once, drawn from the National Survey of Families and Households data
DATA COLLECTION METHOD: person-to-person interviews, paper–pencil questionnaires

8

RESEARCHERS: Avis, N. E., Brambilla, D., Vass, K., & McKinlay, S. M. (1991). The effect of widowhood on health: A prospective analysis from the Massachusetts Women's Health Study. *Social Science & Medicine, 33,* 1063–1070.
RESEARCH DESIGN: longitudinal (5 years)
SAMPLING METHOD: convenience
SAMPLE: subset of 76 widowed women, ages 45–55 at baseline
DATA COLLECTION METHOD: paper–pencil questionnaires, telephone interviews

9

RESEARCHERS: Avis, N. E., & McKinlay, S. M. (1991). A longitudinal analysis of women's attitudes toward the menopause: Results from the Massachusetts Women's Health Study. *Maturitas, 13,* 65–79.
RESEARCH DESIGN: longitudinal (5 years)
SAMPLING METHOD: random
SAMPLE: 2,565 women, ages 45–55
DATA COLLECTION METHOD: person-to-person interviews, paper–pencil questionnaires

10

RESEARCHERS: Bachmann, G. A., Notelovitz, M., Gonzales, S. J., Thompson, C., & Morecraft, B. A. (1991). Vaginal dryness in menopausal women: Clinical characteristics and nonhormonal treatment. *Clinical Practice and Sexuality, 7,* 1–8.
RESEARCH DESIGN: cross-sectional
SAMPLING METHOD: recruited
SAMPLE: 89 perimenopausal and postmenopausal women, age 40 and older
DATA COLLECTION METHOD: self-reports

11

RESEARCHERS: Barbee, E. L., & Bauer, J. A. (1988). Aging and life experiences of low-income, middle-aged African-American and Caucasian women. *Canadian Journal of Nursing Research, 20,* 5–17.
RESEARCH DESIGN: cross-sectional
SAMPLING METHOD: convenience
SAMPLE: 100 mothers, ages 32–56 (54 African American, 46 Caucasian)
DATA COLLECTION METHOD: paper–pencil questionnaires

12

RESEARCHERS: Bartman, B. A., & Moy, E. (1998). Racial differences in estrogen use among middle-aged and older women. *Women's Health Issues, 8,* 32–44.
RESEARCH DESIGN: cross-sectional, longitudinal (15 years)
SAMPLING METHOD: population-based surveys
SAMPLE: subsets of women from three data sets: 1987 National Medical Expenditure Survey, age 45 and older ($n = 615$); 1987 National Health Interview Survey, age 45 and older ($n = 1,619$); and the 1980, 1985, and 1990–1995 National Ambulatory Medical Care Surveys (physicians to women)
DATA COLLECTION METHOD: secondary analyses

13

RESEARCHERS: Bastian, L. A., Couchman, G. M., Rimer, B. K., McBride, C. M., Feaganes, J. R., & Siegler, I. C. (1998). Perceptions of menopausal stage and patterns of hormone replacement therapy use. *Journal of Women's Health, 6,* 467–475.
RESEARCH DESIGN: cross-sectional
SAMPLING METHOD: recruitment
SAMPLE: subset of 1,080 women, ages 45–51, from the University of North Carolina Alumni Heart Study
DATA COLLECTION METHOD: paper–pencil questionnaires

14

RESEARCHERS: Bebbington, P. E., Dunn, G., Jenkins, J. R., Lewis, G., Brugha, T., Farrell, M., & Meltzer, H. (1998). The influence of age and sex on the prevalence of depressive conditions: Report from the national survey of psychiatric morbidity. *Psychological Medicine, 28,* 9–19.
RESEARCH DESIGN: cross-sectional
SAMPLING METHOD: random
SAMPLE: 9,792 adults, ages 16–64
DATA COLLECTION METHOD: person-to-person interviews

15

RESEARCHERS: Bell, M. L. (1995). Attitudes toward menopause among Mexican American Women, *Health Care Women International, 16,* 425–435.
RESEARCH DESIGN: cross-sectional
SAMPLING METHOD: convenience
SAMPLE: 130 Mexican American women, ages 28–75
DATA COLLECTION METHOD: paper–pencil questionnaires

16

RESEARCHERS: Berg-Weger, M., Rubio, D. M., & Tebb, S. S. (2000). Living with and caring for older family members: Issues related to caregiver well-being. *Journal of Gerontological Social Work, 33,* 47–62.
RESEARCH DESIGN: cross-sectional
SAMPLING METHOD: convenience
SAMPLE: 118 family caregivers (64 spouse, 54 adult child), 136 caregivers in a coresidential arrangement with care recipients
DATA COLLECTION METHOD: paper–pencil questionnaires

17

RESEARCHERS: Binson, D., Pollack, L., & Catania, J. A. (1997). AIDS-related risk behaviors and safer sex practices of women in midlife and older in the United States: 1990–1992. *Health Care for Women International, 18,* 343–354.
RESEARCH DESIGN: longitudinal (Wave 1 data collected from June 1990 to February 1991; Wave 2 data from January to September, 1992)
SAMPLING METHOD: nationwide and in metropolitan cities and areas that have large numbers of AIDS cases and large Hispanic and African American populations
SAMPLE: 887 women, national sample; 2,111 women, urban sample; ages 40–75; follow-up national sample of 625 women from the National AIDS Behavioral Surveys
DATA COLLECTION METHOD: telephone interviews

18

RESEARCHERS: Bird, G. W., & Kemerait, L. N. (1990). Stress among early adolescents in two-earner families. *Journal of Early Adolescence, 10,* 344–365.
RESEARCH DESIGN: cross-sectional
SAMPLING METHOD: purposive
SAMPLE: subset of 173 eighth-grade adolescents (79 males, 94 females), ages 12–14, and their dual-career parents (father: *mean age* 41; mother: *mean age* 38) from the Work and Family Project

DATA COLLECTION METHOD: paper–pencil questionnaires

19

RESEARCHERS: Blumstein, P. W., & Schwartz, P. (1983). *American couples*. New York: William Morrow.
RESEARCH DESIGN: longitudinal (18 months)
SAMPLING METHOD: convenience
SAMPLE: 3,574 married couples, 642 cohabiting couples, 957 gay couples, 772 lesbian couples
DATA COLLECTION METHOD: paper–pencil questionnaires

20

RESEARCHERS: Bradford, J., & Ryan, C. (1987). *The National Lesbian Health Care Survey*. Washington, DC: National Lesbian and Gay Health Foundation.
RESEARCH DESIGN: cross-sectional
SAMPLING METHOD: recruitment, convenience
SAMPLE: 1,925 lesbian respondents in the National Lesbian Health Care Survey (1984–1985), ages 17–80 (four-fifths ages 25–44)
DATA COLLECTION METHOD: paper–pencil questionnaires

21

RESEARCHERS: Brody, E. M., Litvin, S. J., Albert, S. M., & Hoffman, C. J. (1994). Marital status of daughters and patterns of parent care. *Journal of Gerontology: Social Sciences, 49*, S95–S103.
RESEARCH DESIGN: cross-sectional
SAMPLING METHOD: recruitment, convenience
SAMPLE: initial baseline interviews as part of a longitudinal study on 492 parent-caring daughters, ages 25–75, divided into five groups: married ($n = 234$), remarried ($n = 56$), separated/divorced ($n = 91$), widowed ($n = 52$), and never married ($n = 59$); mostly well-educated
DATA COLLECTION METHOD: paper–pencil questionnaires for daughters; several scales that assessed parents' functional capacities

22

RESEARCHERS: Brody, E. M., Litvin, S. J., Hoffman, C., & Kleban, M. H. (1995). Marital status of caregiving daughters and co-residence with dependent parents. *Gerontologist, 35*, 75–85.
RESEARCH DESIGN: cross-sectional
SAMPLING METHOD: recruitment, convenience
SAMPLE: subset of 364 daughters, ages 25–75, of different marital statuses coresiding with their elderly parents from the Caring Families:

Helping Across the Generations study
DATA COLLECTION METHOD: paper–pencil questionnaires for daughters; several scales that assessed parents' functional capacities

23

RESEARCHERS: Bromberger, J. T., & Matthews, K. A. (1994). Employment status and depressive symptoms in middle-aged women: A longitudinal investigation. *American Journal of Health, 84*, 202–206.
RESEARCH DESIGN: longitudinal (3 years)
SAMPLING METHOD: random
SAMPLE: 541 women, ages 42–50
DATA COLLECTION METHOD: evaluation of blood-pressure levels, measures of biological characteristics and health behaviors, paper–pencil inventories, 3 years later employment history questionnaires

24

RESEARCHERS: Bromberger, J. T., & Matthews, K. A. (1996). A "feminine" model of vulnerability to depressive symptoms: A longitudinal investigation of middle-aged women. *Journal of Personality and Social Psychology, 70*, 591–598.
RESEARCH DESIGN: longitudinal (3 years)
SAMPLING METHOD: random
SAMPLE: subset of 460 midlife women, ages 42–50, part of larger sample of 541 recruited between 1983 and 1985
DATA COLLECTION METHOD: paper–pencil scales

25

RESEARCHERS: Bromberger, J. T., & Mathews, K. T. (1996). A longitudinal study of the effects of pessimism, trait anxiety, and life stress on depressive symptoms in middle-aged women. *Psychology and Aging, 11*, 207–213.
RESEARCH DESIGN: longitudinal (3 years)
SAMPLING METHOD: randomly recruited between 1983 and 1985
SAMPLE: subset of 460 women, ages 42–50, from 541 women
DATA COLLECTION METHOD: paper–pencil scales

26

RESEARCHERS: Buenting, J. A. (1992). Health life-styles of lesbian and heterosexual women. *Health Care for Women International, 13*, 165–173.
RESEARCH DESIGN: cross-sectional
SAMPLING METHOD: recruited, snowball technique (one person recommends another person, who recommends another...)

SAMPLE: 79 women, 34 percent lesbian, ages 21–43; 66 percent heterosexual, ages 20–66
DATA COLLECTION METHOD: paper–pencil questionnaires

27

RESEARCHERS: Bumpass, L. L., Sweet, J. A., & Cherlin, A. (1991). The
role of cohabitation in the declining rates of marriage. *Journal of
Marriage and the Family, 53,* 913–927.
RESEARCH DESIGN: cross-sectional, longitudinal (5 years)
SAMPLING METHOD: national probability sample
SAMPLE: 13,017 households, including 9,643 adults (one adult randomly
self-selected per household), and 3,374 persons who were either their
spouse or cohabiting partner, from the National Survey of Families and
Households study
DATA COLLECTION METHOD: person-to-person interviews,
paper–pencil questionnaires

28

RESEARCHERS: Burnley, C. S., & Kurth, S. B. (1992). Never married
women: Alone and lonely? *Humboldt Journal of Social Relations, 18,* 57–83.
RESEARCH DESIGN: cross-sectional
SAMPLING METHOD: snowball technique (one person recommends
another person, who recommends another…)
SAMPLE: 30 never married women, ages 30–40
DATA COLLECTION METHOD: person-to-person interviews,
paper–pencil surveys

29

RESEARCHERS: Busch, C. M., Zonderman, A. B., & Costa, P. T. (1994).
Menopausal transition and psychological distress in a nationally repre-
sentative SAMPLE: Is menopause associated with psychological distress.
Journal of Aging and Health, 6, 209–228.
RESEARCH DESIGN: longitudinal (10 years)
SAMPLING METHOD: stratified probability
SAMPLE: 3,049 women, ages 40–60, from the National Health
Examination Follow-Up Study: premenopause ($n = 989$), perimenopause
($n = 312$), natural menopause ($n = 781$), surgical menopause ($n = 967$)
DATA COLLECTION METHOD: paper–pencil scales

30

RESEARCHERS: Butler, S. S., & Weatherley, R. A. (1995). Women at
midlife and categories of neglect. *Social Work, 37,* 510–515.

RESEARCH DESIGN: cross-sectional
SAMPLING METHOD: recruited
SAMPLE: 11 unattached midlife homeless women, ages 45–65
DATA COLLECTION METHOD: phenomenological, person-to-person interviews

---

31

RESEARCHERS: Cacace, M. F., & Williamson, E. (1996). Grieving the death of an adult child. *Journal of Gerontological Nursing, 22,* 16–22.
RESEARCH DESIGN: cross-sectional
SAMPLING METHOD: convenience, snowball technique (one person recommends another person, who recommends another...)
SAMPLE: 2 married couples, 1 single divorced mother, 1 divorced but remarried mother, 1 man whose wife was in a nursing home; ages 60–72
DATA COLLECTION METHOD: person-to-person interviews

32

RESEARCHERS: Cantor, M. H. (1983). Strain among caregivers: A study of the experience in the U.S. *Gerontologist, 17,* 597–624.
RESEARCH DESIGN: cross-sectional
SAMPLING METHOD: convenience
SAMPLE: subset of 111 elderly parents (over half age 60 and over, the remainder age 75 and over) and their primary caregivers, ages 20–75 and over, from larger study called "Impact of the Entry of the Formal Organization on the Informal Support System of Older Americans Study"
DATA COLLECTION METHOD: person-to-person interviews

33

RESEARCHERS: Carr, D. (1997). The fulfilment of career dreams at midlife: Does it matter for women's mental health? *Journal of Health and Social Behavior, 38,* 331–344.
RESEARCH DESIGN: longitudinal, interviewed three times: 1957 (ages 17–18), 1975 (ages 35–36), 1992–1993 (ages 52–53)
SAMPLING METHOD: self-selected
SAMPLE: 2,624, a subset of 3,499 women respondents to the Wisconsin Longitudinal Study, graduated from high school in 1957
DATA COLLECTION METHOD: person-to-person interviews, paper–pencil questionnaires

---

34

RESEARCHERS: Cate, M. A., & Corbin, D. E. (1992). Age differences in knowledge and attitudes toward menopause. *Journal of Women & Aging, 4,* 33–46.

RESEARCH DESIGN: cross-sectional
SAMPLING METHOD: recruited
SAMPLE: 286 women, ages 19–92
DATA COLLECTION METHOD: paper–pencil questionnaires

35

RESEARCHERS: Chiriboga, D. A., Yee, B.W.K., & Weiler, P. G. (1992). Stress and coping in the context of caring. In L. Montada, S. H. Filipp, & M. J. Lerner (Eds.), *Life crises and experience of loss in adulthood* (pp. 95–118). Hillsdale, NJ: Lawrence Erlbaum.
RESEARCH DESIGN: two-wave panel design, separated by about 10 months
SAMPLING METHOD: the target source, parents, recruited
SAMPLE: 385 adult children (142 sibling pairs, ages 27–67, 70 percent women, 90 percent white) with parents (*n* = 201) with a diagnosis of probable Alzheimer's disease
DATA COLLECTION METHOD: person-to-person interviews of adult children, whenever possible, including 2 adult children from a family

36

RESEARCHERS: Christensen, K. A., Stephens, M .A. P., & Townsend, A. L. (1998). Mastery in women's multiple roles and well-being: Adult daughters providing care to impaired parents. *Health Psychology, 17,* 163–171.
RESEARCH DESIGN: longitudinal, first wave of a study of midlife women caregivers
SAMPLING METHOD: recruited, self-selected
SAMPLE: 296 adult-daughter primary caregivers of chronically ill or disabled parent or parent-in-law, mother to children living at home, wife, and employee, average age 43.9 years, approximately 88 percent white, 12 percent African American
DATA COLLECTION METHOD: paper–pencil scales

37

RESEARCHERS: Cicirelli, V. G. (2000) An examination of the trajectory of the adult child's caregiving for an elderly parent. *Family Relations, 49,* 169–175.
RESEARCH DESIGN: cross-sectional
SAMPLING METHOD: random sample of residential blocks
SAMPLE: 53 parents, ages 65 and older, 53 of their adult children (*mean age* 45.83)
DATA COLLECTION METHOD: in-home structured interview questionnaires

38

RESEARCHERS: Clark, M., & Huttlinger, K. (1998). Elder care among Mexican American families. *Clinical Nursing Research, 7,* 64–81.
RESEARCH DESIGN: cross-sectional
SAMPLING METHOD: purposive
SAMPLE: 8 Latino women, ages 32–67, who cared for elderly family members
DATA COLLECTION METHOD: person-to-person interviews, observations

39

RESEARCHERS: Cole, E. (1988). Sex at menopause: Each in her own way. In E. Cole & E. Rothblum (Eds.), *Women and sex therapy: Closing the circle of sexual knowledge* (pp. 159–168). New York: Harrington.
RESEARCH DESIGN: cross-sectional
SAMPLING METHOD: random
SAMPLE: 100 women
DATA COLLECTION METHOD: person-to-person interviews

40

RESEARCHERS: Cole, E., & Rothblum, E. D. (1991). Lesbian sex at menopause: As good as or better than ever. In B. Sang, J. Warshow, & A. Smith (Eds.), *Lesbians at midlife: The creative transition* (pp. 184–193). San Francisco: Spinsters.
RESEARCH DESIGN: cross-sectional
SAMPLING METHOD: convenience
SAMPLE: 41 self-identified lesbians, ages 43–68
DATA COLLECTION METHOD: paper–pencil questionnaires

41

RESEARCHERS: Cole, E. R., & Stewart, A. J. (1996). Meanings of political participation among Black and White women: Political identity and social responsibility. *Journal of Personality and Social Psychology, 71,* 130–140.
RESEARCH DESIGN: cross-sectional, longitudinal
SAMPLING METHOD: African American women recruited through alumni association and African American alumni newsletter; white women drawn from the fourth wave of Women's Life Paths Study initiated in 1967
SAMPLE: 64 African American women, 107 white women from classes 1967–1973, University of Michigan
DATA COLLECTION METHOD: mailed paper–pencil questionnaires in 1992

42

RESEARCHERS: Cole, E. R., Zucker, A. N., & Ostrove, J. M. (1998). Political participation and feminist consciousness among women activists of the 1960s. *Political Psychology, 19*, 349–371.
RESEARCH DESIGN: cross-sectional, longitudinal
SAMPLING METHOD: self-selected for political activity or political inactivity
SAMPLE: 39 alumnae of University of Michigan, politically active, from classes 1967–1973 (year of birth: *mean* 1948); 107 nonactivist women from the fourth wave of the Women's Life Path Study, class of 1967 (year of birth: *mean* 1945)
DATA COLLECTION METHOD: mailed questionnaires

43

RESEARCHERS: Coleman, L. M., Antonucci, T. C., Adelmann, P. K., & Crohan, S. E. (1987). Social roles in the lives of middle-aged and older Black women. *Journal of Marriage and the Family, 49*, 761–771.
RESEARCH DESIGN: cross-sectional
SAMPLING METHOD: multistage probability, stratified, using 1970 census
SAMPLE: subset of 451 African American women, ages 40–64, 215 African American women, ages 65–101; from the National Survey of African Americans
DATA COLLECTION METHOD: paper–pencil scales, secondary analyses

44

RESEARCHERS: Connidis, I. A., & McMullin, J. A. (1993). To have or have not: Parent status and the subjective well-being of older men and women. *Gerontologist, 33*, 630–636.
RESEARCH DESIGN: cross-sectional
SAMPLING METHOD: multistage quota sample, random selection
SAMPLE: 678 men and women, ages 55–75 and over
DATA COLLECTION METHOD: person-to-person interviews

45

RESEARCHERS: Cooney, T. M. (1994). Young adult's relations with parents: the influence of recent parental divorce. *Journal of Marriage and the Family, 56*, 45–56.
RESEARCH DESIGN: cross-sectional
SAMPLING METHOD: random
SAMPLE: subset of 257 young adults, ages 18–23, and their parents, from a larger study on the effects of recent parental divorce on sample of 485 young adults

DATA COLLECTION METHOD: paper–pencil scales, self-reports, other questions

---

46

RESEARCHERS: Coplon, J. K. (1997). *Single older women in the workforce: By necessity or choice?* New York: Garland.
RESEARCH DESIGN: cross-sectional
SAMPLING METHOD: selected
SAMPLE: 395 single women workers, 2,166 nonworking single women, ages 55–70 and over; varied race, educational level, and geographic area
DATA COLLECTION METHOD: paper–pencil questionnaires

47

RESEARCHERS: Costello, E. J. (1991). Married with children: Predictors of mental and physical health in middle-aged women. *Psychiatry, 54,* 292–305.
RESEARCH DESIGN: longitudinal (5 years)
SAMPLING METHOD: random
SAMPLE: 541 women, ages 42–50
DATA COLLECTION METHOD: paper–pencil scales

48

RESEARCHERS: Crohan, S. E., Antonnucci, T. C., Adelmann, P. K., & Coleman, L. M. (1989). Job characteristics and well-being at midlife: Ethnic and gender comparisons. *Psychology of Women Quarterly, 13,* 223–235.
RESEARCH DESIGN: cross-sectional
SAMPLING METHOD: samples drawn from a national survey
SAMPLE: subset of employed middle-age women and men, white (202 men, 186 women), African American (169 men, 255 women); ages 40–64; from two nationwide surveys: Americans View Their Mental Health and National Survey of African Americans
DATA COLLECTION METHOD: secondary analyses

49

RESEARCHERS: Dalton, S. T. (1992). Lived experience of never-married women. *Issues in Mental Health Nursing, 13,* 69–80.
RESEARCH DESIGN: cross-sectional
SAMPLING METHOD: self-selected
SAMPLE: 9 heterosexual women, childless, never married: 8 white, 1 African American; ages 32–54
DATA COLLECTION METHOD: person-to-person interviews

50

RESEARCHERS: Daly, J. (1995). Caught in the web: The social construction of menopause as disease. *Journal of Reproductive and Infant Psychology, 13,* 115–126.
RESEARCH DESIGN: qualitative
SAMPLING METHOD: self-selected
SAMPLE: subset of 20 women, ages 35–53, from a larger study of 150 women
DATA COLLECTION METHOD: individual and group interviews

51

RESEARCHERS: Davies, L. (1995). A closer look at gender and distress among the never married. *Women & Health, 23,* 13–30.
RESEARCH DESIGN: cross-sectional, longitudinal (5 years)
SAMPLING METHOD: random, mulitistage probability
SAMPLE: subset of 1,139 single, noncohabiting persons, ages 19–64, never (or not yet) married; 4,128 never-married parents (198 women, 4 men, excluding biological child under 18 living in home); about evenly divided by gender, white (89.9 percent), African American (10.1 percent); from National Survey of Families and Households
DATA COLLECTION METHOD: person-to-person interviews, paper–pencil questionnaires

52

RESEARCHERS: De Haan, L. G., & MacDermid, S. M. (1994). Is women's identity achievement associated with the expression of generativity? Examining identity and generativity in multiple roles. *Journal of Adult Development, 1,* 235–247.
RESEARCH DESIGN: cross-sectional
SAMPLING METHOD: volunteers and convenience
SAMPLE: 2 samples: 40 midlife mothers (*mean age* 40) employed at a medium-size bank, 136 college women (*mean age* 20.4) representing over 25 majors; predominantly European American
DATA COLLECTION METHOD: paper–pencil questionnaires

53

RESEARCHERS: Dennerstein, L., Dudley, E., & Burger, H. (1997). Well-being and the menopausal transition. *Journal of Psychosomatic Obstetrics and Gynecology, 18,* 95–101.
RESEARCH DESIGN: longitudinal
SAMPLING METHOD: random, population based

SAMPLE: 2,001 women from the first 4 years of Melbourne Women's Midlife Health project, ages 45–55
DATA COLLECTION METHOD: person-to-person interviews

54

RESEARCHERS: Dennerstein, L., Smith, A. M. A., Morse, C. A., & Burger, H. G. (1994). Sexuality and menopause. *Journal of Psychosomatic Obstetrics and Gynecology, 15,* 59–66.
RESEARCH DESIGN: cross-sectional
SAMPLING METHOD: random
SAMPLE: 2,001 women, ages 45–55, from Melbourne Women's Midlife Health Project
DATA COLLECTION METHOD: paper–pencil questionnaires

55

RESEARCHERS: Doty, P., Jackson, M. W., & Crown, W. (1998). The impact of female caregivers' employment status on patterns of formal and informal eldercare. *Gerontologist, 38,* 331–341.
RESEARCH DESIGN: longitudinal (1989, 1994, 1999)
SAMPLING METHOD: nationally representative
SAMPLE: 818 primary informal caregiver/care recipient pairs; caregiver average age 60.3 years, care recipient average age 78.3 years; from the 1989 National Long-Term Care Survey and a companion Informal Caregivers Survey
DATA COLLECTION METHOD: secondary analyses, paper–pencil questionnaires

56

RESEARCHERS: Drebing, C., Gooden, W., Drebing, S., Van De Kemp, H., & Malony, H. N. (1995). The dream in midlife women: Its impact on mental health. *International Journal of Aging and Human Development, 40,* 73–87.
RESEARCH DESIGN: cross-sectional
SAMPLING METHOD: self-selected
SAMPLE: 90 women, ages 38–52
DATA COLLECTION METHOD: paper–pencil questionnaires

57

RESEARCHERS: Duxbury, L., & Higgins, C. (1994). Interference between work and family: A status report on dual-career and dual-earner mothers and fathers. *Employee Assistance Quarterly, 9,* 55–80.

RESEARCH DESIGN: cross-sectional
SAMPLING METHOD: random public sample, self-selected private sample
SAMPLE: 20,836 respondents from public and private work sectors
DATA COLLECTION METHOD: paper–pencil questionnaires

58

RESEARCHERS: Earle, J. R., Smith, M. H., Harris, C. T., & Longino, C. F., Jr. (1998). Women, marital status, and symptoms of depression in a midlife national sample. *Journal of Women & Aging, 10*, 41–57.
RESEARCH DESIGN: cross-sectional
SAMPLING METHOD: recruited
SAMPLE: subset of 6,054 women, 4,842 men; ages 45–65; from the Health and Retirement Survey, Wave 1
DATA COLLECTION METHOD: paper–pencil scales, self-reports

59

RESEARCHERS: Elman, C., & O'Rand, A. M. (1998). Midlife work pathways and educational entry. *Research on Aging, 20*, 475–505.
RESEARCH DESIGN: cross-sectional, longitudinal (5 years)
SAMPLING METHOD: random
SAMPLE: 3,417 persons from two linked waves of the National Survey of Families and Households; ages 42–62 at the second wave (1992–1994)
DATA COLLECTION METHOD: person-to-person interviews, paper–pencil questionnaires

60

RESEARCHERS: England, M. (1995). Crisis and the filial caregiving situation of African American adult offspring. *Issues in Mental Health Nursing, 16*, 143–163.
RESEARCH DESIGN: cross-sectional
SAMPLING METHOD: self-selected
SAMPLE: 38 African American adult children caregivers of parents
DATA COLLECTION METHOD: person-to-person interviews in homes

61

RESEARCHERS: Fox, C., & Halbrook, B. (1994). Terminating relationships at midlife: A qualitative investigation of low-income women's experiences. *Journal of Mental Health Counseling, 16*, 143–154.
RESEARCH DESIGN: qualitative
SAMPLING METHOD: convenience
SAMPLE: 8 women, ages 33–42
DATA COLLECTION METHOD: person-to-person interviews

62

RESEARCHERS: Franklin, S. T., Ames, B. D., & King, S. (1994). Acquiring the family eldercare role. *Research on Aging, 16,* 27–42.
RESEARCH DESIGN: longitudinal (18 months)
SAMPLING METHOD: convenience
SAMPLE: subset of 119 employed women (*mean age* 50.67) caregivers of elderly relatives from a larger sample of 236 women
DATA COLLECTION METHOD: paper–pencil scales

63

RESEARCHERS: Gallo, J. J., Royall, D. R., & Anthony, J. C. (1993). Risk factors on the onset of depression in middle age and later life. *Social Psychiatry and Psychiatric Epidemiology, 28,* 101–108.
RESEARCH DESIGN: longitudinal (1 year)
SAMPLING METHOD: probability sampling of census tracts and households in 1980 and 1984, by the National Institute of Mental Health Epidemologic Catchment Area (ECA) Program
SAMPLE: 7,737 middle-age and older adults (age 40 and older) not currently working for pay and with less than 12 years formal schooling
DATA COLLECTION METHOD: diagnostic interviews

64

RESEARCHERS: Globerman, J. (1996). Motivations to care: Daughters- and sons-in-law caring for relatives with Alzheimer's disease. *Family Relations, 45,* 37–45.
RESEARCH DESIGN: qualitative
SAMPLING METHOD: recruited
SAMPLE: subset of 16 caregiving daughters- and sons-in-law and their 16 spouses from a longitudinal interpretive study of kins' experiences with relatives who have Alzheimer's disease
DATA COLLECTION METHOD: person-to-person interviews

65

RESEARCHERS: Goldscheider, F. K., & Goldscheider, C. (1998). The effects of childhood family structure on leaving and returning home. *Journal of Marriage and the Family, 60,* 745–756.
RESEARCH DESIGN: cross-sectional, longitudinal (5 years)
SAMPLING METHOD: random, national probability
SAMPLE: children who left home between ages 15–25; data from the National Survey of Families and Households
DATA COLLECTION METHOD: person-to-person interviews, paper–pencil questionnaires

66

RESEARCHERS: Gordon, J. R., & Whelan, K. S. (1998). Successful professional women in midlife: How organizations can more effectively understand and respond to the challenges. *Academy of Management Executives, 12,* 8–27.
RESEARCH DESIGN: cross-sectional
SAMPLING METHOD: self-selected
SAMPLE: 36 professional women, ages 35–50, who combined parenting with relatively uninterrupted full-time work
DATA COLLECTION METHOD: qualitative

67

RESEARCHERS: Gottlieb, B. H., Kelloway, E. K., & Fraboni, M. (1994). Aspects of eldercare that place employees at risk. *Gerontologist, 34,* 815–821.
RESEARCH DESIGN: cross-sectional
SAMPLING METHOD: stratified for employment sectors
SAMPLE: subset of 1,302 employees age 35 and over who provided assistance to elderly relatives from Work and Family Survey, Canadian Aging Research Network
DATA COLLECTION METHOD: paper–pencil surveys

68

RESEARCHERS: Guthrie, J. R., Dennerstein, L., Hopper, J. L., & Burger, H. G. (1996). Hot flushes, menstrual status, and hormone levels in a population-based sample of midlife women. *Obstetrics and Gynecology, 88,* 437–442.
RESEARCH DESIGN: longitudinal (ongoing)
SAMPLING METHOD: population based
SAMPLE: 453 pre-, peri-, and postmenopausal women, ages 48–59, from the third wave of annual follow-up interviews
DATA COLLECTION METHOD: in-home person-to-person interviews

69

RESEARCHERS: Haley, W. E., Wadley, V. G., West, C. A., & Vetzel, L. L. (1994). How caregiving stressors change with severity of dementia. *Seminars in Speech and Language, 15,* 195–205.
RESEARCH DESIGN: cross-sectional
SAMPLING METHOD: recruited
SAMPLE: subset of 170 patients diagnosed with Alzheimer's disease or other progressive dementia from larger, ongoing project focused on stress and coping in African American and white caregiving families

DATA COLLECTION METHOD: person-to-person assessments

70

RESEARCHERS: Hallstrom, T., & Samuelsson, S. (1990). Changes in women's sexual desire in middle life: The longitudinal study of women in Gothenberg. *Archives of Sexual Behavior, 19,* 259–268.
RESEARCH DESIGN: longitudinal, interviewed twice, 6 years apart
SAMPLING METHOD: stratified, representative
SAMPLE: 475 urban women, ages 38–54, from an original study of 800 participants from Longitudinal Study of Women in Gothenberg
DATA COLLECTION METHOD: person-to-person interviews by psychiatrist

---

71

RESEARCHERS: Hamill, S. B., & Goldberg, W. A. (1997). Between adolescents and aging grandparents: Midlife concerns of adults in the "sandwich generation." *Journal of Adult Development, 4,* 135–147.
RESEARCH DESIGN: cross-sectional
SAMPLING METHOD: recruited from multiple sources
SAMPLE: 62 mothers (*mean age* 44.5) and fathers (*mean age* 46.4), 62 adolescent children (34 males, 28 females; *mean age* 16.9)
DATA COLLECTION METHOD: paper–pencil questionnaires

72

RESEARCHERS: Hanna, E., Dufour, M. C., Elliott, S., Stinson, F., & Harford, T. C. (1992). Dying to be equal: Women, alcohol, and cardiovascular disease. *British Journal of Addiction, 87,* 1593–1597.
RESEARCH DESIGN: cross-sectional
SAMPLING METHOD: nationally representative probability sample
SAMPLE: subset of 8,164 deaths attributed to cardiovascular disease from 1986 National Mortality Followback Study of 18,733 decedents, age 25 and older; over sampled for race, age, and female decedents, ages 25–54, and male decedents, ages 35–64
DATA COLLECTION METHOD: collected from death certificates

73

RESEARCHERS: Hawton, K., Gath, D., & Day, A. (1994). Sexual function in a community sample of middle-aged women with partners: Effects of age, marital, socioeconomic, psychiatric, gynecological, and menopausal factors. *Archives of Sexual Behavior, 23,* 375–395.
RESEARCH DESIGN: cross-sectional
SAMPLING METHOD: random

SAMPLE: 436 women, ages 35–59, with partners
DATA COLLECTION METHOD: in-home person-to-person interviews

74

RESEARCHERS: Hayes, C. L., & Anderson, D. (1993). Psycho-social and economic adjustment of mid-life women after divorce: A national study. *Journal of Women & Aging, 4*, 83–99.
RESEARCH DESIGN: cross-sectional
SAMPLING METHOD: obtained from the mailing list of the National Center for Women and Retirement Research
SAMPLE: 338 recently divorced women, ages 40–75 (*mean age* 50), previously in long-term marriages ranging 20–48 years (*mean year* 23)
DATA COLLECTION METHOD: paper–pencil questionnaires

75

RESEARCHERS: Helson, R., & McCabe, L. (1994). The social clock project at middle age. In B. F. Turner & L. E. Troll (Eds.), *Women growing older: Psychological perspectives* (pp. 68–93). Thousand Oaks, CA: Sage Publications.
RESEARCH DESIGN: longitudinal, began in 1958 and 1960 with 142 women from two graduating classes from Mills College; follow-ups in 1963–1964, 1981, and 1989 when the women were in late 20s, early 40s, and early 50s
SAMPLING METHOD: representative of two-thirds of two senior classes
SAMPLE: subset of women, ages 43 and 52, from the 142 predominantly white, upper middle class participants from the study of Mills College classes of 1958 and 1960
DATA COLLECTION METHOD: paper–pencil inventories and questionnaires

---

76

RESEARCHERS: Helson, R., Stewart, A. J., & Ostrove, J. (1995). Identity in three cohorts of midlife women. *Journal of Personality and Social Psychology, 69*, 644–557.
RESEARCH DESIGN: longitudinal; participants from three studies: the Berkeley Guidance Study that began in 1928 and studied the sample during childhood, adolescence, and at ages 30, 40, and 53; the Mills study that began in 1958 and 1960 with 142 women from two graduating classes from Mills College with follow-ups in 1963–1964, 1981, and 1989 when the women were in late 20s, early 40s, and early 50s; the Radcliffe study that began in 1986 with 264 women from the 1964 graduating class with follow-ups on 103 participants at approximately age 43

and 89 of the 103 participants at approximately age 48
SAMPLING METHOD: representative (Mills, Radcliffe), random (Berkeley)
SAMPLE: women from three samples: 76 women, age 40, in 1969, 58 women, age 53, from Berkeley Guidance Study, Institute of Human Development; 96 women, ages 21 and 52, 105 women, age 43, from Mills Longitudinal Study; 103 women, age 43, 89 of the 103 women at age 48, from Radcliffe Longitudinal Study
DATA COLLECTION METHOD: *Q* sorts and other measures

77

RESEARCHERS: Helson, R., & Wink, P. (1992). Personality change in women from the early 40s to the early 50s. *Psychology and Aging, 7,* 45–50.
RESEARCH DESIGN: longitudinal, began in 1958 and 1960 with 142 women from two graduating classes from Mills College; follow-ups in 1963–1964, 1981, and 1989 when the women were in late 20s, early 40s, and early 50s
SAMPLING METHOD: representative of two-thirds of two senior classes
SAMPLE: 141 women seniors in 1958, contacted again at ages 27, 43, 52
DATA COLLECTION METHOD: paper–pencil inventories and question-naires

---

78

RESEARCHERS: Helstrom, L. (1994). Sexuality after hysterectomy: A model based on quantitative and qualitative analysis of 104 women before and after subtotal hysterectomy. *Journal of Psychosomatic and Obstetrical Gynecology, 15,* 219–229.
RESEARCH DESIGN: longitudinal (1 year)
SAMPLING METHOD: convenience
SAMPLE: 104 women, ages 33–45
DATA COLLECTION METHOD: person-to-person interviews 1 month before and 1 year after subtotal hysterectomy

---

79

RESEARCHERS: Hiedemann, B., Suhomlinova, O., & O'Rand, A. M. (1998). Economic independence, economic status, and empty nest in midlife marital disruption. *Journal of Marriage and the Family, 60,* 219–231.
RESEARCH DESIGN: an analysis of panel data (22 years)
SAMPLING METHOD: self-selected
SAMPLE: subset of 2,484 women, ages 52–66, from the 1967–1989 waves of the National Longitudinal Survey of Mature Women

DATA COLLECTION METHOD: secondary analyses

80

RESEARCHERS: Higgins, C., Duxbury, L., & Lee, C. (1994). Impact of life-cycle stage and gender on the ability to balance work and family responsibilities. *Family Relations, 43,* 144–150.
RESEARCH DESIGN: cross-sectional
SAMPLING METHOD: random
SAMPLE: subset of 3,616 men and women from 1990–1992 Canadian study of 6,287 Canadian federal public-sector employees in the National Capital region and cross-section of 14,549 private-sector employees
DATA COLLECTION METHOD: paper–pencil survey instruments

81

RESEARCHERS: Himes, C. (1994). Parental caregiving by adult women: A demographic perspective. *Research on Aging, 16,* 191–211.
RESEARCH DESIGN: cross-sectional, longitudinal (5 years)
SAMPLING METHOD: nationwide
SAMPLE: subset of 3,543 women, over age 19, with at least one surviving parent, from National Survey of Families and Households data
DATA COLLECTION METHOD: person-to-person interviews, paper–pencil questionnaires

---

82

RESEARCHERS: Hochschild, A. R. (1989). *The second shift.* New York: Viking Press.
RESEARCH DESIGN: cross-sectional
SAMPLING METHOD: selected
SAMPLE: 100 husbands (*mean age* 33 years) and wives (*mean age* 31 years); 70 percent white, 24 percent African American, 3 percent Latino, 3 percent Asian; 50 of this group were two-job couples; 45 other persons were babysitters, school teachers, divorced persons who had been in two-job couples, and partners in traditional couples with small children
DATA COLLECTION METHOD: person-to-person interviews

83

RESEARCHERS: Hooker, K., & Kaus, C. R. (1994). Health-related possible selves in young and middle adulthood. *Psychology and Aging, 9,* 126–133.
RESEARCH DESIGN: cross-sectional
SAMPLING METHOD: recruited from student nominations
SAMPLE: 171 young, ages 24–39, and middle-aged, ages 40–59, adults

DATA COLLECTION METHOD: person-to-person interviews, paper–pencil questionnaires

---

84

RESEARCHERS: Humphrey, J. A., & Palmer, S. (1990–1991). The effects of race, gender, and marital status of suicides among young adults, middle-aged adults, and older adults. *Omega, 22,* 277–285.
RESEARCH DESIGN: cross-sectional
SAMPLING METHOD: representative
SAMPLE: 3,187 officially recorded suicides, age 25 and older, between 1980–1984
DATA COLLECTION METHOD: all officially recorded suicides

85

RESEARCHERS: Huyck, M. H. (1989). Midlife parental imperatives. In R. A. Kalish (Ed.), *Midlife loss: Coping strategies* (pp. 115–148). Newbury Park, CA: Sage Publications.
RESEARCH DESIGN: cross-sectional
SAMPLING METHOD: random
SAMPLE: 74 male and 76 female young adults, ages 22 and 32; 134 of their mothers, ages 43–69, and 108 of their fathers, ages 44–70
DATA COLLECTION METHOD: person-to-person interviews

86

RESEARCHERS: Hyde, J. S., Krajnik, M., & Skuldt-Niederberger, K. (1991). Androgyny across the life span: A replication and longitudinal follow-up. *Developmental Psychology, 27,* 516–519.
RESEARCH DESIGN: (1) cross-sectional; (2) longitudinal (recontacted 10 years later)
SAMPLING METHOD: convenience
SAMPLE: 2 samples: (1) 300 respondents, including 38 men and 62 women college students, 112 women and 88 men, ages 13–86; (2) 89 respondents, ages 24–81 in 1987, recontacted from a previous 1977 study
DATA COLLECTION METHOD: paper–pencil questionnaires

87

RESEARCHERS: Jacobson, J. M. (1993). Midlife baby boom women compared with their older counterparts in midlife. *Health Care for Women International, 14,* 427–436.
RESEARCH DESIGN: cross-sectional
SAMPLING METHOD: stratified random

SAMPLE: 992 women who graduated from college during 1955–1975
DATA COLLECTION METHOD: paper–pencil questionnaires

88

RESEARCHERS: Jacobson, J. M. (1995). *Midlife women: Contemporary issues.* Boston: Jones and Bartlett.
RESEARCH DESIGN: cross-sectional
SAMPLING METHOD: self-selected
SAMPLE: 962 midlife women from 21 graduating university classes, ages 35–55
DATA COLLECTION METHOD: mailed paper–pencil questionnaires

89

RESEARCHERS: James, J. B., Lewkowicz, C., Libhaber, J., & Lachman, M. (1995). Rethinking the gender identity crossover hypothesis: A test of a new method. *Sex Roles, 32,* 185–207.
RESEARCH DESIGN: cross-sectional
SAMPLING METHOD: recruited
SAMPLE: 150 predominantly white men and women, ages 20–84
DATA COLLECTION METHOD: paper–pencil questionnaires

90

RESEARCHERS: John, O. P., Pals, J. L., & Westenberg, P. W. (1998). Personality prototypes and ego development: Conceptual similarities and relations in adult women. *Journal of Personality and Social Psychology, 74,* 1093–1108.
RESEARCH DESIGN: longitudinal, the Mills study begun 1958 and 1960, 142 women from two graduating classes from Mills College; follow-ups in 1963–1964, 1981, and 1989 when the women were in late 20s, early 40s, and early 50s
SAMPLING METHOD: representative of the graduating classes
SAMPLE: subset of 83 women from the Mills Longitudinal Study, approximately age 43
DATA COLLECTION METHOD: paper–pencil measures

91

RESEARCHERS: Jones, P. S. (1995). Paying respect: Care of elderly parents by Chinese and Filipino American women. *Health Care for Women International, 16,* 385–398.
RESEARCH DESIGN: cross-sectional
SAMPLING METHOD: convenience

SAMPLE: 20 Asian American women (10 Chinese, 10 Filipino), age 55 and older
DATA COLLECTION METHOD: person-to-person interviews

92

RESEARCHERS: Karon, S. L., Egan, J., Jacobson, M., Nugent, J., Settersten, L., & Shaw, V. (1999). Understanding lesbians' mammography utilization. *Women's Health Issues, 9*, 264–274.
RESEARCH DESIGN: cross-sectional
SAMPLING METHOD: snowball technique (one person recommends another person, who recommends another…)
SAMPLE: 107 lesbians, ages 51–80
DATA COLLECTION METHOD: paper–pencil questionnaires

93

RESEARCHERS: Karp, D. A. (1988). A decade of reminders: Changing age consciousness between fifty and sixty year olds. *Gerontologist, 28*, 727–738.
RESEARCH DESIGN: cross-sectional
SAMPLING METHOD: snowball technique (one person recommends another person, who recommends another…)
SAMPLE: 30 male and 33 female professionals, ages 50–60
DATA COLLECTION METHOD: person-to-person interviews

94

RESEARCHERS: Kaufert, P. A. (1986). Menstruation and menstrual change: Women in midlife. *Health Care for Women International, 7*, 63–76.
RESEARCH DESIGN: cross-sectional
SAMPLING METHOD: random
SAMPLE: 2,493 women, ages 40–59, in stage one of a three-stage project
DATA COLLECTION METHOD: paper–pencil mailed questionnaires

95

RESEARCHERS: Kawachi, I., Colditz, G. A., Stampfer, M. J., Willett, W. C., Manson, J. E., Rosner, B., Speizer, F. E., & Hennekens, C. H. (1994). Smoking cessation and time course of decreased risks of coronary heart disease in middle-aged women. *Archives of International Medicine, 154*, 169–175.
RESEARCH DESIGN: longitudinal, 12-year follow-up data between 1976–1988

SAMPLING METHOD: selected
SAMPLE: 117,006 female registered nurses, ages 30–55, from Nurses'
Health Study
DATA COLLECTION METHOD: paper–pencil questionnaires

96

RESEARCHERS: Kinsey, A. C., Pomeroy, W. B., Martin, C. E., &
Gebhard, P. H. (1953). *Sexual behavior in the human female.* Philadelphia:
W. B. Saunders.
RESEARCH DESIGN: cross-sectional
SAMPLING METHOD: convenience
SAMPLE: 5,940 females
DATA COLLECTION METHOD: person-to-person interviews

97

RESEARCHERS: Kittell, L. A., Mansfield, P. K., & Voda, A. M. (1998).
Keeping up appearances: The basic social process of the menopausal
transition. *Qualitative Health Research, 8,* 618–633.
RESEARCH DESIGN: longitudinal (ongoing since 1991)
SAMPLING METHOD: 61 women, ages 41–54, mostly white, middle
class, college educated, and employed outside home, recruited from
Midlife Women's Health Study initiated in 1991
SAMPLE: 61 perimenopausal women experiencing changes in menstrual
bleeding
DATA COLLECTION METHOD: interviews by phone

98

RESEARCHERS: Klohnen, E. C., Vandewater, E. A., & Young, A. (1996).
Negotiating the middle years: Ego-resiliency and successful midlife
adjustment in women. *Psychology and Aging, 11,* 431–442.
RESEARCH DESIGN: longitudinal, the Mills study begun 1958 and 1960,
142 women from two graduating classes from Mills College; follow-ups
in 1963–1964, 1981, and 1989 when the women were in late 20s, early
40s, and early 50s; Radcliffe study begun 1986 with 264 women from
the 1964 graduating class, 103 participants responded to a questionnaire, approximately age 43, and 89 of the 103 participants completed
the California Personality Inventory, approximately age 48
SAMPLING METHOD: representative of college classes
SAMPLE: subset of 141 women from the Mills study (1958 and 1960
graduating classes), ages 43 and 53; Radcliffe study (1964 graduating
class), ages 52 and 48
DATA COLLECTION METHOD: paper–pencil scales, observer measures

99

RESEARCHERS: Koropeckyj-Cox, T. (1998). Loneliness and depression in middle and old age: Are the childless more vulnerable? *Journal of Gerontology: Social Sciences, 53*, 303–321.
RESEARCH DESIGN: cross-sectional, longitudinal (5 years)
SAMPLING METHOD: random, national probability
SAMPLE: subset of 3,820 respondents, ages 50–84, from National Survey of Families and Households
DATA COLLECTION METHOD: person-to-person interviews, paper–pencil questionnaires

100

RESEARCHERS: Kramer, B. J., & Kipnis, S. (1995). Eldercare and work-role conflict: Toward an understanding of gender differences in caregiver burden. *Gerontologist, 35*, 340–348.
RESEARCH DESIGN: cross-sectional
SAMPLING METHOD: random probability sample
SAMPLE: 413 employed, nonspousal caregivers, ages 18–59
DATA COLLECTION METHOD: random-digit dialing surveys

101

RESEARCHERS: Kritz-Silverstein, D., Wingard, D. L., & Barrett-Connor, E. (1992). Employment status and heart disease risk factors in middle-aged women: The Rancho Bernardo study. *American Journal of Public Health, 82*, 215–219.
RESEARCH DESIGN: longitudinal
SAMPLING METHOD: self-selected
SAMPLE: subset of 242 women, ages 40–59, from Rancho Bernardo Heart and Chronic Disease Survey done between 1972 and 1974; follow-up clinic visit between 1984 and 1987
DATA COLLECTION METHOD: person-to-person interviews

102

RESEARCHERS: Kuh, D. L., Wadsworth, M., & Hardy, R. (1997). Women's health in midlife: The influence of the menopause, social factors, and health in earlier life. *British Journal of Obstetrics and Gynaecology, 104*, 923–933.
RESEARCH DESIGN: cross-sectional
SAMPLING METHOD: stratified
SAMPLE: subset of 1,498 women, age 47, from Medical Research Council National Survey of Health and Development
DATA COLLECTION METHOD: paper–pencil questionnaires

103

RESEARCHERS: Kurdek, L. A. (1988). Perceived social support in gays and lesbians in cohabitating relationships. *Journal of Personality and Social Psychology, 54,* 504–509.
RESEARCH DESIGN: cross-sectional
SAMPLING METHOD: convenience and recruitment
SAMPLE: 65 gay (*mean age* 36.46), 47 lesbian cohabitating couples (*mean age* 35.82)
DATA COLLECTION METHOD: paper–pencil questionnaires

104

RESEARCHERS: Kurdek, L. A. (1991). The dissolution of gay and lesbian couples. *Journal of Social and Personal Relationships, 8,* 265–278.
RESEARCH DESIGN: longitudinal (4 years)
SAMPLING METHOD: recruitment; referrals
SAMPLE: subset of both partners of gay and lesbian couples, 26 individuals, both partners from 6 gay (*mean age* 31.50) and 7 lesbian (*mean age* 33.07) couples who separated during a 4-year longitudinal study
DATA COLLECTION METHOD: paper–pencil questionnaires

105

RESEARCHERS: Kurdek, L. A. (1994). The nature and correlates of relationship quality in gay, lesbian, and heterosexual cohabitating couples: A test of the contextual, investment, and discrepancy models. In B. Greene & G. M. Herek (Eds.), *Lesbian and gay psychology: Theory, research, and clinical applications* (pp. 133–135). Thousand Oaks, CA: Sage Publications.
RESEARCH DESIGN: longitudinal (1 year)
SAMPLING METHOD: recruitment; referrals
SAMPLE: both partners from 75 gay (*mean age* 32.64), 51 lesbian (*mean age* 33.88), and 108 heterosexual (*mean age* 30.65) couples who did not reside with children
DATA COLLECTION METHOD: paper–pencil questionnaires

106

RESEARCHERS: Kurdek, L. A. (1995). Developing changes in relationship quality in gay and lesbian cohabitating couples. *Developmental Psychology, 31,* 86–94.
RESEARCH DESIGN: longitudinal (3 years)
SAMPLING METHOD: recruitment; referrals

SAMPLE: 61 gay couples (partner 1: *mean age* 42.9; partner 2: *mean age* 42.11); 42 lesbian couples (partner 1: *mean age* 41.26; partner 2: *mean age* 40.76), mostly white
DATA COLLECTION METHOD: paper–pencil surveys

107

RESEARCHERS: Kurdek, L. A., & Schmitt, J. P. (1986). Relationship quality of partners in heterosexual married, heterosexual cohabitating, and gay and lesbian relationships. *Journal of Personality and Social Psychology, 51,* 711–720.
RESEARCH DESIGN: cross-sectional
SAMPLING METHOD: convenience; recruited
SAMPLE: partners in 44 married (*mean age* 29.68), 35 heterosexual cohabiting (*mean age* 28.68), 50 gay (*mean age* 31.28), and 56 lesbian (*mean age* 31.18) couples
DATA COLLECTION METHOD: paper–pencil questionnaires

108

RESEARCHERS: Kurdek, L. A., & Schmitt, J. P. (1987). Perceived emotional support from family and friends in members of homosexual, married, and heterosexual cohabiting couples. *Journal of Homosexuality, 14,* 57–68.
RESEARCH DESIGN: cross-sectional
SAMPLING METHOD: self-selected; responses obtained from three gay periodicals
SAMPLE: 98 gay men in monogamous links, 34 gay men in nonmonogomous links (*mean length of time* 33.92 years)
DATA COLLECTION METHOD: paper–pencil questionnaires to both members of couples

---

109

RESEARCHERS: Lachman, M. E., Lewkowicz, C., Marcus, A., & Peng, Y. (1994). Images of midlife development among young, middle aged, and older adults. *Journal of Adult Development, 1,* 201–211.
RESEARCH DESIGN: cross-sectional
SAMPLING METHOD: self-selected
SAMPLE: 121 young (*mean age* 19.8), middle-aged (*mean age* 47.9), and older (*mean age* 74.6) men and women; 84 percent white
DATA COLLECTION METHOD: paper–pencil questionnaires, scales

110

RESEARCHERS: Lechner, V. M., & Gupta, C. (1996). Employed caregivers: A four-year follow-up. *Journal of Applied Gerontology, 15,* 102–115.
RESEARCH DESIGN: longitudinal (4 years)
SAMPLING METHOD: convenience
SAMPLE: 24 employed persons caring for frail persons
DATA COLLECTION METHOD: paper–pencil questionnaires

111

RESEARCHERS: Lee, G. R., Dwyer, J. W., & Coward, R. T. (1993). Gender differences in parent care: Demographic factors and same-gender preferences. *Journal of Gerontology: Social Sciences, 48,* S9–S16.
RESEARCH DESIGN: cross-sectional
SAMPLING METHOD: nationally representative of Medicare enrollment files
SAMPLE: subset of 4,371 infirm elders, age 65 and older, and their 13,172 adult children from the 1982 National Long-Term Care Survey
DATA COLLECTION METHOD: paper–pencil surveys

112

RESEARCHERS: Lee, Y-J, & Aytac, I. A. (1998). Intergenerational financial support among whites, African Americans, and Latinos. *Journal of Marriage and the Family, 60,* 426–441.
RESEARCH DESIGN: cross-sectional, longitudinal (5 years)
SAMPLING METHOD: random, national probability
SAMPLE: subset of whites, Latinos, and African Americans, ages 25–65, from the National Survey of Families and Households
DATA COLLECTION METHOD: person-to-person interviews, paper–pencil questionnaires

113

RESEARCHERS: Lemaire, G. S., & Lenz, E. R. (1995). Perceived uncertainty about menopause in women attending an educational program. *International Journal of Nursing Studies, 32,* 39–48.
RESEARCH DESIGN: cross-sectional, pretest–posttest design
SAMPLING METHOD: convenience
SAMPLE: 177 women, ages 30–71, attending an educational program on menopause
DATA COLLECTION METHOD: paper–pencil scales

114

RESEARCHERS: Lewis, K. G., & Moon, S. (1997). Always single and single again women: A qualitative study. *Journal of Marital and Family therapy, 23,* 115–134.
RESEARCH DESIGN: cross-sectional
SAMPLING METHOD: selected focus groups
SAMPLE: 37 single women
DATA COLLECTION METHOD: two phases: (1) open-ended questions to 37 single women in focus groups; (2) structured questionnaire based on findings from the first interviews administered to 39 additional single women

115

RESEARCHERS: Lewis, V. G. (unpublished doctoral dissertation, 1992); Lewis, V. G., & Borders, D. (1995). Life satisfaction of single middle-aged professional women. *Journal of Counseling & Development, 74,* 94–99.
RESEARCH DESIGN: cross-sectional
SAMPLING METHOD: self-selected
SAMPLE: 152 single professional women in higher education institutions, ages 35–65, most never married, no children, highly educated
DATA COLLECTION METHOD: paper–pencil questionnaires

116

RESEARCHERS: Li, L. W., Seltzer, M. M., & Greenberg, J. S. (1999). Change in depressive symptoms among daughter caregivers: An 18-month longitudinal study. *Psychology and Aging, 14,* 206–219.
RESEARCH DESIGN: longitudinal (18 months)
SAMPLING METHOD: random-digit dialing
SAMPLE: subset of 115 daughter caregivers (average age 56 at Wave 1) from a larger probability sample of 2,250 persons, age 60 and older, and 500 persons, younger than age 60, drawn for the State of Wisconsin Bureau on Aging in 1991; a supplemental sample of 1,000 households
DATA COLLECTION METHOD: secondary analyses, first two of a three-wave study of women caregivers

117

RESEARCHERS: Liao, K.L.M., & Hunter, M. S. (1998). Preparation for menopause: Prospective evaluation of a health education intervention for mid-aged women. *Maturitas, 29,* 215–224.

RESEARCH DESIGN: longitudinal (3 years)
SAMPLING METHOD: self-selected then randomly assigned to two groups
SAMPLE: 86 women, age 45
DATA COLLECTION METHOD: paper–pencil questionnaires

118

RESEARCHERS: Liebig, P. S. (1993). Factors affecting the development of employer-sponsored eldercare programs: Implications for employed caregivers. *Journal of Women & Aging, 5,* 59–78.
RESEARCH DESIGN: cross-sectional
SAMPLING METHOD: nonprobability cluster sampling
SAMPLE: 33 employers
DATA COLLECTION METHOD: paper–pencil questionnaires

119

RESEARCHERS: Loewenstein, S. F., Bloch, N. E., Campion, J., Epstein, J. S., Gale, P., & Salvatore, M. (1981). A study of satisfactions and stresses of single women at midlife. *Sex Roles, 7,* 1127–1141.
RESEARCH DESIGN: cross-sectional
SAMPLING METHOD: self-selected
SAMPLE: 60 self-defined single women, ages 35–65, previously married or never married, 58 white, 2 African American
DATA COLLECTION METHOD: semistructured in-person interviews

120

RESEARCHERS: Logan, J. R., Ward, R., & Spitze, G. (1992). As old as you feel: Age identity in middle and later life. *Social Forces, 71,* 451–467.
RESEARCH DESIGN: cross-sectional
SAMPLING METHOD: probability sample
SAMPLE: 807 persons, age 40 and older
DATA COLLECTION METHOD: person-to-person interviews

121

RESEARCHERS: Loomis, L. S., & Booth, A. (1995). Multigenerational caregiving and well-being: The myth of the beleaguered sandwich generation. *Journal of Family Issues, 16,* 131–148.
RESEARCH DESIGN: longitudinal (12 years)
SAMPLING METHOD: nationwide sample of married persons, cluster random-digit dialing
SAMPLE: subset of 848 persons married in 1988 and 1992, not divorced

or widowed between 1988 and 1992 interviews, ages 30–68, from a 12-year study of 2,033 married persons, ages 16–55, drawn from the Marital Instability over the Life Course Study
DATA COLLECTION METHOD: interviews, secondary analyses

122

RESEARCHERS: Loos, C., & Bowd, A. (1997). Caregivers of persons with Alzheimer's disease: Some neglected implications of the experience of personal loss and grief. *Death Studies, 21,* 501–504.
RESEARCH DESIGN: cross-sectional
SAMPLING METHOD: self-selected
SAMPLE: 68 caregivers, ages 40–80, of persons with Alzheimer's disease
DATA COLLECTION METHOD: paper–pencil questionnaires

123

RESEARCHERS: Lucas, V. A. (1992). An investigation of the health care preferences of the lesbian population. *Health Care for Women International, 13,* 221–228.
RESEARCH DESIGN: cross-sectional
SAMPLING METHOD: convenience
SAMPLE: 178 self-identified lesbians (*mean age* 28)
DATA COLLECTION METHOD: paper–pencil questionnaires

124

RESEARCHERS: MacDermid, S. M., Heilbrum, G., & DeHaan, L. G. (1997). The generativity of employed mothers in multiple roles: 1979 and 1991. In M. E. Lachman & J. Boone James (Eds.), *Multiple paths of midlife development* (pp. 207–240). Chicago: University of Chicago Press.
RESEARCH DESIGN: cross-sectional
SAMPLING METHOD: convenience, community voting lists and bank volunteers
SAMPLE: subset of 45 women, ages 35–55, who were mothers, workers, and wives from 1978–1979 sample developed by Baruch, Barnett, & Rivers (1983)[1]; subset of 45 mothers, ages 35–55, from data set from medium-sized bank, described by De Haan & MacDermid (1994).[2]
DATA COLLECTION METHOD: multiple paper–pencil measures

[1]*Lifeprints: New patterns of love and work for today's women.* New York: McGraw-Hill.
[2]Is women's identity achievement associated with the expression of generativity? Examining identity and generativity in multiple roles. *Journal of Adult Development, 1,* 235–247.

RESEARCHERS: Mansfield, P. K., Koch, P. B., & Voda, A. M. (1998). Qualities midlife women desire in their sexual relationships and their changing sexual response. *Psychology of Women Quarterly*, *22*, 285–303.
RESEARCH DESIGN: longitudinal (ongoing since 1990)
SAMPLING METHOD: convenience
SAMPLE: 280 women, ages 35–55, still menstruating, participating in the ongoing Midlife Women's Health Survey
DATA COLLECTION METHOD: paper–pencil surveys, menstrual bleeding calendar

RESEARCHERS: Manson, J. E., Colditz, G. A., Stampfer, M. J., Willett, W. C., Rosner, B., Monson, R. R., Speizer, F. E., & Hennekens, C. H. (1990). A prospective study of obesity and risk of coronary heart disease in women. *New England Journal of Medicine*, *322*, 882–889.
RESEARCH DESIGN: longitudinal (8 years)
SAMPLING METHOD: selected
SAMPLE: subset of 115,886 women, ages 30–55, from a sample of 121,700 registered female nurses from the Nurses' Health Study
DATA COLLECTION METHOD: paper–pencil questionnaires

RESEARCHERS: Marks, N. F. (1991). *Remarried and single parents in middle adulthood: Differences in psychological well-being and relationships with adult children* (NSFH Working Paper No. 47). Madison: University of Wisconsin, Center for Demography and Ecology.
RESEARCH DESIGN: cross-sectional, longitudinal (5 years)
SAMPLING METHOD: random, national probability
SAMPLE: subset 3,002 respondents (1,090 fathers, 1,912 mothers), ages 35–64, parents of at least 1 biological, adopted, or step child, age 19 and older, living out of the household, from National Survey of Families and Households data
DATA COLLECTION METHOD: person-to-person interviews, paper–pencil questionnaires

RESEARCHERS: Marks, N. F. (1993). *Contemporary social demographics of American midlife parents* (NSFH Working Paper No. 54). Madison: University of Wisconsin, Center for Demography and Ecology.
RESEARCH DESIGN: cross-sectional, longitudinal (5 years)
SAMPLING METHOD: random, national probability

SAMPLE: subset of 9,643 respondents with additional oversample of 3,374 African Americans, Mexican Americans, Puerto Ricans, one-parent families, families with stepchildren, cohabitors, and recently married persons, from National Survey of Families and Households data
DATA COLLECTION METHOD: person-to-person interviews, paper–pencil questionnaires

---

129

RESEARCHERS: Marks, N. F. (1994). *Midlife caregiving: Do effects differ by gender* (NSFH Working Paper No. 64). Madison: University of Wisconsin, Center for Demography and Ecology.
RESEARCH DESIGN: cross-sectional, longitudinal (5 years)
SAMPLING METHOD: random, national probability
SAMPLE: subset of 5,643 male and female caregivers, ages 35–64, from the first wave of National Survey of Families and Households survey
DATA COLLECTION METHOD: person-to-person interviews, paper–pencil questionnaires

---

130

RESEARCHERS: Marks, N. F. (1995). *Flying solo at midlife: Gender, marital status, and psychological well-being* (CDE Working Paper No. 95-03). Madison: University of Wisconsin, Center for Demography and Ecology.
RESEARCH DESIGN: longitudinal (data collected 1957, 1964, 1975, 1992–1993)
SAMPLING METHOD: random
SAMPLE: 10,317 men and women, graduated from Wisconsin high schools 1957, most ages 53 or 54, when interviewed in 1992 and 1993
DATA COLLECTION METHOD: computer-assisted telephone interviews with 6,877 still living men and women

---

131

RESEARCHERS: Marks, N. F. (1995). Midlife marital status differences in social support relationships with adult children and psychological well-being. *Journal of Family Issues, 16,* 5–28.
RESEARCH DESIGN: cross-sectional, longitudinal (5 years)
SAMPLING METHOD: random, national probability
SAMPLE: subset of 3,002 respondents (1,090 fathers, 1,912 mothers), ages 35–64, parents of at least 1 biological, adopted, or stepchild, age 19 and older, and living out of the household (other than those away from school), from National Survey of Families and Households data
DATA COLLECTION METHOD: person-to-person interviews, paper–pencil questionnaires

132

RESEARCHERS: Marks, N. F. (1996). Caregiving across the lifespan: National prevalence and predictors. *Family Relations, 45,* 27–35.
RESEARCH DESIGN: cross-sectional, longitudinal (5 years)
SAMPLING METHOD: random, national probability
SAMPLE: first wave of 13,017 adults, age 19 and older, from National Survey of Families and Households
DATA COLLECTION METHOD: person-to-person interviews, paper–pencil questionnaires

133

RESEARCHERS: Marks, N. F. (1996). Social demographic diversity among American midlife parents. In C. D. Ryff & M. M. Seltzer (Eds.), *The parental experience in midlife* (pp. 29–75). Chicago: University of Chicago Press.
RESEARCH DESIGN: cross-sectional, longitudinal (5 years)
SAMPLING METHOD: random, national probability
SAMPLE: subset of the first wave of National Survey of Families and Households, including 4,992 parents, ages 35–64, of biological, adopted, and/or stepchildren
DATA COLLECTION METHOD: person-to-person interviews, paper–pencil questionnaires

134

RESEARCHERS: Marks, N. F. (1998). Does it hurt to care? Caregiving, work–family conflict, and midlife well-being. *Journal of Marriage and the Family, 60,* 951–966.
RESEARCH DESIGN: longitudinal
SAMPLING METHOD: high school graduates in Wisconsin in 1957
SAMPLE: subset of 5,782 employed midlife men and women from the Wisconsin Longitudinal Study, 1992–1993 (N = 10,317), mostly ages 53 or 54
DATA COLLECTION METHOD: computer-assisted telephone interviews

135

RESEARCHERS: Martire, L. M., Stephens, M.A.P., & Franks, M. M. (1997). Multiple roles of women caregivers: Feelings of mastery and self-esteem as predictors of psychological well-being. *Journal of Women & Aging, 9,* 117–131.
RESEARCH DESIGN: longitudinal (2 months)
SAMPLING METHOD: recruited from variety of sources
SAMPLE: 75 women, average age 43.3, who occupied the roles of care-

giver, mother, and wife
DATA COLLECTION METHOD: paper–pencil questionnaires

136

RESEARCHERS: Martire, L. M., Stephens, M.A.P., & Townsend, A. L. (1998). Emotional support and well-being of midlife women: Role-specific mastery as a mediational mechanism. *Psychology and Aging, 13,* 396–404.
RESEARCH DESIGN: longitudinal (2 months)
SAMPLING METHOD: multiple recruitment sources with special efforts to recruit African American women
SAMPLE: subset of 264 of the first wave of midlife women, average age 44, 13 percent African American, who occupied the roles of primary caregiver to an impaired parent or parent-in-law, wife, mother to at least 1 child living at home, age 25 or younger, and employee
DATA COLLECTION METHOD: paper–pencil questionnaires

137

RESEARCHERS: Matthews, K. A., Kuller, L. H., Wing, R. R., & Meilahn, E. N. (1994). Biobehavioral aspects pf menopause: Lessons from the healthy women study. *Experimental Gerontology, 29,* 337–342.
RESEARCH DESIGN: longitudinal (8 years)
SAMPLING METHOD: recruited
SAMPLE: 541 women, ages 42–50
DATA COLLECTION METHOD: medical evaluations, paper–pencil questionnaires

---

138

RESEARCHERS: Matthews, K. A., Wing, R., Kuller, L., Meilahn, E., Kelsey, S., Costello, E., & Caggiula, A. (1990). Influences of natural menopause on psychological characteristics and symptoms of middle-aged healthy women. *Journal of Consulting and Clinical Psychology, 58,* 345–351.
RESEARCH DESIGN: longitudinal (3 years)
SAMPLING METHOD: random
SAMPLE: 541 initially premenopausal healthy women, ages 42–50
DATA COLLECTION METHOD: paper–pencil scales

139

RESEARCHERS: McAdams, D. P., de St. Aubin, E., & Logan, R. L. (1993). Generativity among young, midlife, and older adults. *Psychology and Aging, 8,* 221–230.

RESEARCH DESIGN: cross-sectional
SAMPLING METHOD: stratified random
SAMPLE: 152 men and women, ages 22–72, of which 53 were midlife adult
DATA COLLECTION METHOD: paper–pencil scales

140

RESEARCHERS: McGrew, K. B. (1998). Daughter's caregiving decisions: From an impulse to a balancing point of care. *Journal of Women & Aging, 10*, 49–65.
RESEARCH DESIGN: cross-sectional
SAMPLING METHOD: purposive
SAMPLE: 10 women, ages 43–60, married with children, upper-middle socioeconomic status; 4 of which worked outside home
DATA COLLECTION METHOD: person-to-person interviews, paper–pencil questionnaires

---

141

RESEARCHERS: McKinlay, J. B., & McKinlay, S. M. (1987). Depression in middle-aged women: Social circumstances versus estrogen deficiency. In R. Walsh (Ed.), *The psychology of women* (pp. 157–161). New Haven, CT: Yale University Press.
RESEARCH DESIGN: cross-sectional
SAMPLING METHOD: random
SAMPLE: 2,500 women, ages 45–55
DATA COLLECTION METHOD: paper–pencil scales

142

RESEARCHERS: McKinlay, S. M., Brambilla, D. J., & Posner, J. G. (1992). The normal menopause transition. *Maturitas, 14*, 103–115.
RESEARCH DESIGN: cross-sectional, longitudinal (5 years)
SAMPLING METHOD: 2-stage clustering sample
SAMPLE: 2,570 women, ages 44–55, as of 01/01/1982 (study begun late 1981 with 8,050 women)
DATA COLLECTION METHOD: telephone interviews, mailed questionnaires

---

143

RESEARCHERS: McKirnan, D. J., & Peterson, P. L. (1989). Alcohol and drug use among homosexual men and women: Epidemiology and population characteristics. *Addictive Behaviors, 14*, 545–553.
RESEARCH DESIGN: cross-sectional

SAMPLING METHOD: convenience
SAMPLE: 2,652 men (*mean age* 35), 748 women (*mean age* 32), 83 percent primarily or exclusively gay or lesbian, 15 percent more gay or lesbian than heterosexual, 2 percent bisexual
DATA COLLECTION METHOD: paper–pencil questionnaires

144

RESEARCHERS: McQuaide, S. (1998). Women at midlife. *Social Work, 43,* 21–31.
RESEARCH DESIGN: cross-sectional
SAMPLING METHOD: recruited
SAMPLE: 103 women, ages 40–59
DATA COLLECTION METHOD: paper–pencil questionnaires

145

RESEARCHERS: McWhirter, D. P., & Mattison, A. M. (1984). *The male couple.* Englewood, Cliffs, NJ: Prentice-Hall.
RESEARCH DESIGN: cross-sectional
SAMPLING METHOD: convenience
SAMPLE: 156 gay male couples
DATA COLLECTION METHOD: case studies

146

RESEARCHERS: Merrill, D. M. (1996). Conflict and cooperation among adult siblings during the transition to the role of filial caregiver. *Journal of Social and Personal Relationships, 13,* 399–413.
RESEARCH DESIGN: cross-sectional
SAMPLING METHOD: self-selected
SAMPLE: 40 working, middle-class adult children and children-in-law currently caring for an elderly parent
DATA COLLECTION METHOD: person-to-person interviews

147

RESEARCHERS: Metha, A., Kinnier, R. T., & McWhirter, E. H. (1989). A pilot study on the regrets and priorities of women. *Psychology of Women Quarterly, 13,* 167–174.
RESEARCH DESIGN: cross-sectional
SAMPLING METHOD: convenience
SAMPLE: 178 women in 3 groups: 20–29 (young), 35–55 (middle aged), 65 and older (older)
DATA COLLECTION METHOD: paper–pencil questionnaires

148

RESEARCHERS: Meyer, D. R (1996). The economic vulnerability of
midlife single parents. In C. D. Ryff & M. M. Seltzer (Eds.), *The
parental experience in midlife* (pp. 77–102). Chicago: University of
Chicago Press.
RESEARCH DESIGN: cross-sectional
SAMPLING METHOD: drawn from individuals participating in a court
process
SAMPLE: two data sets: (1) Current Population Survey (a representative
sample) 478 single midlife fathers, ages 35–54; 354 single fathers, age 34
and younger; 2,170 single midlife mothers, ages 35–54; 3,042 single
mothers, age 34 and younger; (2) Wisconsin Court Record Database
(provides child support data), 392 custodial fathers, ages 35–54; 165 custodial fathers, age 35 and younger; 4,680 custodial mothers, ages 35–54;
3,127 mothers, age 35 and younger
DATA COLLECTION METHOD: two preexisting data sets

149

RESEARCHERS: Mitchell, E. S., & Woods, N. F. (1996). Symptom
experiences of midlife women: Observations from the Seattle midlife
women's health study. *Maturitas, 25,* 1–10.
RESEARCH DESIGN: longitudinal (3 years)
SAMPLING METHOD: population based
SAMPLE: 301 women, ages 35–55
DATA COLLECTION METHOD: daily symptom diary for at least
1 menstrual cycle for 3 consecutive years; person-to-person
interviews

150

RESEARCHERS: Mitchell, V., & Helson, R. (1990). Women's prime of
life. Is it in the 50's? *Psychology of Women Quarterly, 14,* 451–470.
RESEARCH DESIGN: (1) cross-sectional, (2) longitudinal; the Mills
study begun 1958 and 1960, 142 women from two graduating classes;
follow-ups in 1963–1964, 1981, and 1989 when the women were in
their late 20s, early 40s, and early 50s
SAMPLING METHOD: representative of graduating
classes
SAMPLE: (1) 700 college alumnae, ages 26–80, studied in
1983; 60 alumnae in early 50s; (2) longitudinal sample,
118 alumnae from the same institution in 1989, early 40s and
early 50s
DATA COLLECTION METHOD: paper–pencil questionnaires

151

RESEARCHERS: Moen, P., Robinson, J., & Fields, V. (1994). Women's work and caregiving roles: A life-course approach. *Journal of Gerontology: Social Sciences, 49*, S176–S186.
RESEARCH DESIGN: cross-sectional
SAMPLING METHOD: random
SAMPLE: 293 women from 4 birth cohorts
DATA COLLECTION METHOD: person-to-person interviews

152

RESEARCHERS: Montgomery, R. J. V., & Kamo, Y. (1989). Parent care by sons and daughters. In J. A. Mancini (Ed.), *Aging parents and adult children* (pp. 213–227). Lexington, MA: D. C. Heath.
RESEARCH DESIGN: longitudinal (ongoing)
SAMPLING METHOD: selected
SAMPLE: subset of 347 families with adult child as caregiver (sons: m*edian* = 51 years; daughters: *median* = 55 years), from a larger, ongoing study of family units consisting of elderly impaired person and at least 1 family member who has provided assistance to the elder person
DATA COLLECTION METHOD: person-to-person interviews

153

RESEARCHERS: Morgan, L. A. (1989). Economic well-being following marital termination: A comparison of widowed and divorced women. *Journal of Family Issues, 10*, 86–101.
RESEARCH DESIGN: longitudinal (15 years)
SAMPLING METHOD: weighted
SAMPLE: 5,000 women, ages 30–44 in 1967, ages 45–59 in 1982, many experienced widowhood or divorce, from the National Longitudinal Surveys cohort of mature women (1967–1982)
DATA COLLECTION METHOD: secondary analyses

154

RESEARCHERS: Murphy, S. A., Gupta, A. D., Cain, K. C., Johnson, L. C., Lohan, J., Wu, L., & Mekwa, J. (1999). Changes in parents' mental distress after the violent death of an adolescent or young adult child: A longitudinal prospective analysis. *Death Studies, 23*, 129–159.
RESEARCH DESIGN: longitudinal data collected at 4, 12, and 24 months on an experimental intervention
SAMPLING METHOD: recruited
SAMPLE: 171 bereaved mothers and 90 fathers
DATA COLLECTION METHOD: paper–pencil questionnaires

RESEARCHERS: Newton, K. M., LaCroix, A. Z., Leveille, S. G., Rutter, C., Keenan, N. L., & Anderson, L. A. (1997). Women's beliefs and decisions about hormone replacement therapy. *Journal of Women's Health, 6,* 459–465.
RESEARCH DESIGN: cross-sectional
SAMPLING METHOD: convenience
SAMPLE: 1,082 women, ages 50–80
DATA COLLECTION METHOD: computer-assisted telephone interviews

RESEARCHERS: Niemela, P., & Lento, R. (1993). The significance of the 50th birthday for women's individuation. In W. O. Davis, E. Cole, & E. Rothblum (Eds.), *Faces of women and aging* (pp. 117–127). New York: Harrington Park.
RESEARCH DESIGN: cross-sectional
SAMPLING METHOD: convenience
SAMPLE: 17 women, ages 49–51, 13 women, ages 52–55
DATA COLLECTION METHOD: person-to-person interviews

RESEARCHERS: Nunley, B. L., Hall, L. A., & Rowles, G. D. (2000). Effects of the quality of dyadic relationships on the psychological well-being of elderly care-recipients. *Journal of Gerontological Nursing, 26,* 23–31.
RESEARCH DESIGN: cross-sectional
SAMPLING METHOD: convenience
SAMPLE: 37 community-dwelling persons, age 75 and older, indicating instrumental assistance from primary caregivers
DATA COLLECTION METHOD: home interviews, assorted scales

RESEARCHERS: Nydegger, C. N., & Mitteness, L. S. (1996). Midlife: The prime of fathers. In C. D. Ryff & M. M. Seltzer (Eds.), *The parental experience in midlife* (pp. 533–559). Chicago: University of Chicago Press.
RESEARCH DESIGN: cross-sectional
SAMPLING METHOD: random
SAMPLE: drawn from two studies in the Fatherhood Project: (1) more than 250 men, ages
45–80, college educated, largely economically advantaged or middle class; (2) a later study used part of a random sample of adult children of

the previously interviewed fathers, ages 20–50 (*mean age* 32)
DATA COLLECTION METHOD: secondary analyses

159

RESEARCHERS: O'Connor, T. G., Allen, J. P., Bell, K. L., & Hauser, S. T. (1996, Spring). Adolescent–parent relationships and leaving home in young adulthood. *New Directions for Child Development*, pp. 39–52.
RESEARCH DESIGN: longitudinal; data collected when respondents were on average ages 14, 16, and 25
SAMPLING METHOD: self-selected
SAMPLE: subset of 146 adolescents and their families initially studied when adolescents were approximately 14 years old; half from the 9th grade; half self-selected from a psychiatric hospital, diagnoses of mood or conduct disorders; predominantly middle and upper middle class
DATA COLLECTION METHOD: paper–pencil questionnaires, *Q*-sort rating of personality and adjustment obtained from peer whom the target young adult named as knowing well

160

RESEARCHERS: Parker, R. A., & Aldwin, C. M. (1997). Do aspects of gender identity change from early to middle adulthood? Disentangling age, cohort, and period effects. In M. E. Lachman & J. Boone James (Eds.), *Multiple paths of midlife development* (pp. 67–107). Chicago: University of Chicago Press.
RESEARCH DESIGN: cross-sequential analysis
SAMPLING METHOD: self-selected
SAMPLE: 645 respondents from Davis Longitudinal Study (DLS), Transition Study (TS); both followed a cohort of 20 year olds from 1969–1979; TS also followed cohort of 40 year olds; DLS also followed 20 and 30 year olds from 1979–1991
DATA COLLECTION METHOD: personality instruments and questionnaires

161

RESEARCHERS: Parks, S. H., & Pillsuk, M. (1991). Caregiver burden: Gender and the psychological costs of caregiving. *American Journal of Orthopsychiatry*, 6, 501–509.
RESEARCH DESIGN: cross-sectional
SAMPLING METHOD: recruited from university medical center's Alzheimer's disease clinic
SAMPLE: 176 adults (60 percent women) providing some caregiving for parent with Alzheimer's disease
DATA COLLECTION METHOD: paper–pencil questionnaires

RESEARCHERS: Pavalko, E. K., & Artis, J. E. (1997). Women's caregiving and paid work: Casual relationships in late midlife. *Journal of Gerontology, 52B,* S170–S179.

RESEARCH DESIGN: longitudinal (interviews approximately every 2 years since 1967)

SAMPLING METHOD: nationally representative

SAMPLE: subset of 3,083 women, ages 30–44, from 1984 and 1987 waves of National Longitudinal Survey of Mature Women; African American women over sampled for racial comparisons; comparison sample of 1,389 women provided information on wage and salary

DATA COLLECTION METHOD: secondary analyses

RESEARCHERS: Penning, M. J. (1998). In the middle: Parental caregiving in the context of other roles. *Journal of Gerontology: Social Sciences, 53B,* 188–197.

RESEARCH DESIGN: cross-sectional

SAMPLING METHOD: systematically narrowed probability sample

SAMPLE: 687 caregivers (*mean age* 47.85)

DATA COLLECTION METHOD: telephone interviews

RESEARCHERS: Pett, M. A., Caserta, M. S., Hutton, A. P., & Lund, D. A. (1988). Intergenerational conflict: Middle aged women caring for demented older relatives. *American Journal of Orthopsychiatry, 58,* 405–407.

RESEARCH DESIGN: cross-sectional

SAMPLING METHOD: convenience, mailing lists of support groups

SAMPLE: subset of 181 women, ages 24–67, from larger sample of 888 women who were primary caregivers of institutionalized and community-based dementia patients

DATA COLLECTION METHOD: paper–pencil questionnaires

RESEARCHERS: Pienta, A. M., Burr, J. A., & Mutchler, J. E. (1994). Women's labor force participation in later life: The effects of early work and family experiences. *Journal of Gerontology: Social Sciences, 49,* S231–S239.

RESEARCH DESIGN: panel (2-1/2 years; respondents interviewed at 4-month intervals)

SAMPLING METHOD: random

SAMPLE: subset of 1,108 women, ages 55–64, from 1984 Survey of Income and Program Participation
DATA COLLECTION METHOD: secondary analyses

166

RESEARCHERS: Piercy, K. W. (1998). Theorizing about family caregiving: The role of responsibility. *Journal of Marriage and the Family, 60,* 109–118.
RESEARCH DESIGN: cross-sectional
SAMPLING METHOD: recruited
SAMPLE: 15 male adults, 28 female adults; all representing two or three generations of 15 families
DATA COLLECTION METHOD: person-to-person interviews

167

RESEARCHERS: Pohl, J. M., Boyd, C., & Given, B. A. (1997). Mother–daughter relationships during the first year of caregiving: A qualitative study. *Journal of Women & Aging, 9,* 133–149.
RESEARCH DESIGN: cross-sectional
SAMPLING METHOD: self-selected
SAMPLE: subset of 8 daughters caring for mothers (age 55 and older) from National Institute on Aging project
DATA COLLECTION METHOD: person-to-person interviews

168

RESEARCHERS: Pot, A. M., Deeg, D.J.H., van Dyck, R., & Jonker, C. (1998). Psychological stress of caregivers: The mediator effect of caregiving appraisal. *Patient Education and Counseling, 34,* 43–51.
RESEARCH DESIGN: cross-sectional
SAMPLING METHOD: self-selected
SAMPLE: 175 demented elderly persons (*mean age* 75.6) and their informal caregivers (*mean age* 75.1)
DATA COLLECTION METHOD: paper–pencil questionnaires

169

RESEARCHERS: Pruchno, R. A., Peters, N. D., & Burant, C. J. (1996). Child life events, parent–child disagreements, and parent well-being: Model development and testing. In C. D. Ryff & M. M. Seltzer (Eds.), *The parental experience in midlife* (pp. 561–606). Chicago: University of Chicago Press.
RESEARCH DESIGN: cross-sectional
SAMPLING METHOD: convenience

SAMPLE: 171 three-generational families, parents ages 32–75, children ages 13–25
DATA COLLECTION METHOD: person-to-person structured interviews conducted with daughter, daughter-in-law, her husband, and their child

170

RESEARCHERS: Quinn, P., & Walsh, P. K. (1995). Midlife women with disabilities: Another challenge for social workers. *Affilia, 10*, 235–254.
RESEARCH DESIGN: qualitative
SAMPLING METHOD: convenience
SAMPLE: 25 women, ages under 35 to 55 and over
DATA COLLECTION METHOD: person-to-person interviews, follow-up phone calls

171

RESEARCHERS: Raley, R. K. (1995). Black–white differences in kin contact and exchange among never married adults. *Journal of Family Issues, 16*, 77–103.
RESEARCH DESIGN: cross-sectional, longitudinal (5 years)
SAMPLING METHOD: random, national probability
SAMPLE: subset of 147 African American men, 222 African American women, 289 white men, 296 white women, all ages 19–29, from National Survey of Families and Households project
DATA COLLECTION METHOD: person-to-person interviews, paper–pencil questionnaires

172

RESEARCHERS: Rankow, E. J., & Tessaro, I. (1998). Mammography and risk factors for breast cancer in lesbian and bisexual women. *American Journal of Health Behavior, 22*, 403–410.
RESEARCH DESIGN: cross-sectional
SAMPLING METHOD: outreach, self-selected
SAMPLE: 570 lesbians, age 40 and older
DATA COLLECTION METHOD: anonymous paper–pencil questionnaires

173

RESEARCHERS: Rawson, K. T., & Jenson, G. O. (1995). Depression as a measurement of well-being in women at midlife. *Family Perspective, 29*, 297–313.
RESEARCH DESIGN: cross-sectional
SAMPLING METHOD: random

SAMPLE: 2,887 women, ages 34–66, from Brigham Young University's Center for Studies of the Family
DATA COLLECTION METHOD: paper–pencil questionnaires

174

RESEARCHERS: Rawson, K. T., McFadden, J., & Jenson, G. O. (1996). The empty-nest syndrome revisited: Women in transition at midlife. *Journal of Family and Consumer Sciences, 88*, 48–52.
RESEARCH DESIGN: cross-sectional
SAMPLING METHOD: women in a certain area of Utah
SAMPLE: subset of mothers, ages 56–66, from larger sample of 1,041 women, ages 34–66, from Women's Experience in Family, Work, Religion, and Community study
DATA COLLECTION METHOD: mailed paper–pencil scales

175

RESEARCHERS: Reeves, J. B., & Darville, R. L. (1992). Aging couples in dual-career/earner families: Patterns of role sharing. *Journal of Women & Aging, 4*, 39–55.
RESEARCH DESIGN: cross-sectional
SAMPLING METHOD: self-selected
SAMPLE: 611 women in dual-career or dual-earner couples, age 50 and over, at least 1 partner a member of the National Retired Teacher's Association and retired
DATA COLLECTION METHOD: person-to-person interviews, paper–pencil questionnaires

176

RESEARCHERS: Reitzes, D. C., & Mutran, E. J. (1994). Multiple roles and identities: Factors influencing self-esteem among middle-aged working men and women. *Social Psychology Quarterly, 57*, 313–325.
RESEARCH DESIGN: cross-sectional
SAMPLING METHOD: self-selected
SAMPLE: 818 full-time working (at least 35 hours a week) men (397), women (421), ages 58–64, 64 percent white, 54 percent African American; subset of 599 married men and women
DATA COLLECTION METHOD: telephone interviews

RESEARCHERS: Roberts, B. W., & Friend, W. (1998). Career momentum in midlife women: Life context, identity, and personality correlates. *Journal of Occupational Health Psychology, 3*, 195–208.

RESEARCH DESIGN: longitudinal, Mills study begun 1958 and 1960, 142 women from two graduating classes from Mills College; follow-ups in 1963–1964, 1981, and 1989 when the women were in late 20s, early 40s, and early 50s
SAMPLING METHOD: representative of the senior classes in 1985 and 1960
SAMPLE: subset of 83 women in their early 50s from Mills Longitudinal Study of approximately 100 predominantly white, middle-class women; subset of 420 spouses
DATA COLLECTION METHOD: paper–pencil scales

RESEARCHERS: Rogers, L. P., & Markides, K. S. (1989). Well-being in the postparental stage in Mexican–American women. *Research on Aging, 11*, 508–516.
RESEARCH DESIGN: cross-sectional
SAMPLING METHOD: random
SAMPLE: subset of 243 Mexican American women, ages 32–50, from larger three-generational study
DATA COLLECTION METHOD: paper–pencil scales

RESEARCHERS: Rosenthal, C. J., Matthews, S. H., & Marshall, V. W. (1989). Is parent care normative? The experiences of a sample of middle-age women. *Research on Aging, 11*, 244–260.
RESEARCH DESIGN: cross-sectional
SAMPLING METHOD: random
SAMPLE: subset of 163 women, ages 40–69, from a larger project of 458 respondents
DATA COLLECTION METHOD: home interviews

RESEARCHERS: Rosenthal, M., & Morith, N. P. (1993). Women and long term care planning: The adverse impact of women's perceptions. In C. L. Hayes (Ed.), *Women in mid-life: Planning for tomorrow* (pp. 67–81). New York: Haworth Press.
RESEARCH DESIGN: cross-sectional
SAMPLING METHOD: clinical
SAMPLE: 4 clinical cases
DATA COLLECTION METHOD: unavailable

181

RESEARCHERS: Rossi, A. S., & Rossi, P. H. (1990). *Of human bonding: Parent–child relations across the life course.* Hawthorne, NY: Aldine de Gryter.
RESEARCH DESIGN: cross-sectional
SAMPLING METHOD: random, probability
SAMPLE: 1,393 respondents in the main sample (ages 19–71 and over), spin-off samples of 323 parents and 278 adult children
DATA COLLECTION METHOD: in-person interviews, telephone interviews, paper–pencil questionnaires

182

RESEARCHERS: Ryff, C. D. (1989). In the eye of the beholder: Views of psychological well-being among middle-aged and older adults. *Psychology and Aging, 4,* 195–210.
RESEARCH DESIGN: cross-sectional
SAMPLING METHOD: convenience
SAMPLE: 171 younger (*mean age* 52.5) and older (*mean age* 73.5) women and men
DATA COLLECTION METHOD: person-to-person interviews

183

RESEARCHERS: Ryff, C. D., Lee, Y. H., Essex, M. J., & Schmutte, P. S. (1994). My children and me: Midlife evaluations of grown children and of self. *Psychology and Aging, 9,* 195–205.
RESEARCH DESIGN: cross-sectional
SAMPLING METHOD: random
SAMPLE: 215 midlife parents (114 mothers, 101 fathers; *mean age* 53.7)
DATA COLLECTION METHOD: person-to-person interviews

184

RESEARCHERS: Ryff, C. D, Schmutte, P. S., & Lee, Y. H. (1996). How children turn out: Implications for parental self-evaluation. In C. D. Ryff & M. M. Seltzer (Eds.), *The parental experience in midlife* (pp. 383–422). Chicago: University of Chicago Press.
RESEARCH DESIGN: cross-sectional
SAMPLING METHOD: random
SAMPLE: 215 midlife parents (114 mothers, 101 fathers; *mean age* 53.7)
DATA COLLECTION METHOD: person-to-person interviews

RESEARCHERS: Saghir, M. T., & Robins, E. (1973). *Male and female homosexuality*. Baltimore: Williams & Williams.
RESEARCH DESIGN: cross-sectional
SAMPLING METHOD: convenience
SAMPLE: 89 gay men, 57 lesbians, 87 heterosexual males, 44 heterosexual females; all roughly comparable in age
DATA COLLECTION METHOD: person-to-person interviews

RESEARCHERS: Sang, B. (1990). Reflections of midlife lesbians on their adolescence. *Journal of Women and Aging, 2*, 111–117.
RESEARCH DESIGN: cross-sectional
SAMPLING METHOD: recruited from multiple sources
SAMPLE: 110 self-identified lesbians, ages 40–59
DATA COLLECTION METHOD: paper–pencil questionnaires

RESEARCHERS: Saunders, J. M., Tupac, J. D., & MacCulloch, B. (1988). *A lesbian profile: A survey of 1000 lesbians*. West Hollywood: Southern California Women for Understanding.
RESEARCH DESIGN: cross-sectional
SAMPLING METHOD: selected
SAMPLE: 996 lesbians
DATA COLLECTION METHOD: paper–pencil questionnaires

RESEARCHERS: Scharlach, A. E. (1994). Caregiving and employment: Competing or complementary roles? *Gerontologist, 34*, 378–385.
RESEARCH DESIGN: cross-sectional
SAMPLING METHOD: recruited
SAMPLE: 94 employed caregivers, ages 30 and under to 60 and over, caring for a relative, age 60 and older
DATA COLLECTION METHOD: paper–pencil questionnaires

RESEARCHERS: Scharlach, A. E., & Fredriksen, K. I. (1994). Elder care versus adult care: Does care recipient age make a difference. *Research on Aging, 16*, 43–68.
RESEARCH DESIGN: cross-sectional
SAMPLING METHOD: stratified random

SAMPLE: university employees, age 30 and over, caring for 329 disabled adults, ages 18–64, and 749 disabled adults, age 65 and over
DATA COLLECTION METHOD: paper–pencil questionnaires

190

RESEARCHERS: Schuster, D. T. (1990). Fulfillment of potential, life satisfaction, and competence: Comparing four cohorts of gifted women at midlife. *Journal of Educational Psychology, 82,* 471–478.
RESEARCH DESIGN: longitudinal, cross-cohort comparisons
SAMPLING METHOD: selected
SAMPLE: compared data from 4 studies of gifted midlife women, including 1910 cohort, early 1920s cohort, 1920s–1930s cohort, and 1940 cohort
DATA COLLECTION METHOD: secondary analyses

191

RESEARCHERS: Schwarz, K. A., & Roberts, B. L. (2000). Social support and strain of family caregivers of older adults. *Holistic Nursing Practice, 14,* 77–90.
RESEARCH DESIGN: longitudinal (3 months)
SAMPLING METHOD: convenience
SAMPLE: 100 primary caregivers to older adults who resided with the care recipients; caregivers ages 29–88
DATA COLLECTION METHOD: person-to-person interviews, paper–pencil scales

---

192

RESEARCHERS: Schwiebert, V. L., & Myers, J. E. (1994). Midlife care givers: Effectiveness of a psychoeducational intervention for midlife adults with parent-care responsibilities. *Journal of Counseling & Development, 72,* 627–632.
RESEARCH DESIGN: longitudinal (7 weeks)
SAMPLING METHOD: recruited through various resources to attend a psychoeducational group SAMPLE: 51 adult children, ages 54–72, caring for aging parents, age 60 and over
DATA COLLECTION METHOD: paper–pencil questionnaires

193

RESEARCHERS: Seccombe, K., & Ishii-Kuntz, M. (1994). Gender and social relationships among the never-married. *Sex Roles, 30,* 585–603.
RESEARCH DESIGN: cross-sectional, longitudinal (5 years)

SAMPLING METHOD: random, national probability
SAMPLE: subset of 193 never-married men, 217 never-married women; 16 percent men, 20 percent women African American, from the National Survey of Families and Households study
DATA COLLECTION METHOD: person-to-person interviews, paper–pencil questionnaires

194

RESEARCHERS: Seltzer, M. M., Krauss, M. W., Choi, S. C., & Hong, J. (1996). Midlife and later-life parenting of adult children with mental retardation. In C. D. Ryff & M. M. Seltzer (Eds.), *The parental experience in midlife* (pp. 459–489). Chicago: University of Chicago Press.
RESEARCH DESIGN: longitudinal (ongoing)
SAMPLING METHOD: volunteers
SAMPLE: subset of the 461 families in which mothers, ages 57–86, had son or daughter with mental retardation (ages 17–68) who lived at home at the time of entry into the study; current analysis on 387 mothers.
DATA COLLECTION METHOD: person-to-person interviews

195

RESEARCHERS: Sherman, S. S. (1993). Gender, health, and responsible research. *Clinics in Geriatric Medicine, 9,* 261–269.
RESEARCH DESIGN: cross-sectional
SAMPLING METHOD: purposive
SAMPLE: 67 women, 34 men, ages 41–96
DATA COLLECTION METHOD: person-to-person interviews

196

RESEARCHERS: Silverberg, S. B. (1996). Parents' well-being at their children's transition to adolescence. In C. D. Ryff & M. M. Seltzer (Eds.), *The parental experience in midlife* (pp. 215–254). Chicago: University of Chicago Press.
RESEARCH DESIGN: cross-sectional, longitudinal (5 years)
SAMPLING METHOD: random, national probability
SAMPLE: subset of 129 two-parent intact families with firstborn child (target) between ages 10–15 at time of first wave of data collection; adolescents evenly divided by gender, from the National Survey of Families and Households project
DATA COLLECTION METHOD: person-to-person interviews, paper–pencil questionnaires

RESEARCHERS: Silverstein, M., & Angelelli, J. J. (1998). Older parents' expectations of moving closer to their children. *Journal of Gerontology: Social Sciences, 53B*, 153–163.
RESEARCH DESIGN: cross-sectional
SAMPLING METHOD: national probability
SAMPLE: subset of 5,382 older parents from sample of 8,223, studied in 1993–1994 Asset and Health Dynamics of the Oldest Old survey; over-sampled for blacks, Hispanics, and residents of Florida
DATA COLLECTION METHOD: telephone interviews, person-to-person interviews, secondary analyses

RESEARCHERS: Spitze, G., & Logan, J. R. (1990). More evidence on women (and men) in the middle. *Research on Aging, 12*, 182–198.
RESEARCH DESIGN: cross-sectional
SAMPLING METHOD: probability
SAMPLE: 505 women, ages 40–64
DATA COLLECTION METHOD: person-person interviews

RESEARCHERS: Spitze, G., Logan, J. R., Joseph, G., & Lee, E. (1994). Middle generation roles and well-being of men and women. *Journal of Gerontology: Social Sciences, 49*, S107–S116.
RESEARCH DESIGN: cross-sectional
SAMPLING METHOD: random
SAMPLE: 1,200 persons, age 40 and over
DATA COLLECTION METHOD: person-to-person interviews

RESEARCHERS: Stevens, P. E. (1994). Lesbians' health-related experiences of care and noncare. *Western Journal of Nursing Research, 16*, 639–659.
RESEARCH DESIGN: cross-sectional
SAMPLING METHOD: recruitment, snowball technique (one person recommends another person, who recommends another...)
SAMPLE: 45 self-identified lesbians, ages 21–56, racially and economically diverse
DATA COLLECTION METHOD: person-to-person interviews, focus groups

RESEARCHERS: Stevens, P. E. (1994). Protective strategies of lesbian clients in health care environments. *Research in Nursing & Health, 17,* 217–229.

RESEARCH DESIGN: cross-sectional

SAMPLING METHOD: recruitment, snowball technique (one person recommends another person, who recommends another…)

SAMPLE: subset of original sample of 45 self-identified lesbians, ages 21–56, racially and economically diverse

DATA COLLECTION METHOD: person-to-person interviews, focus groups

RESEARCHERS: Stevens, P. E. (1995). Structural and interpersonal impact of heterosexual assumptions on lesbian health care clients. *Nursing Research, 44,* 25–30.

RESEARCH DESIGN: cross-sectional

SAMPLING METHOD: recruitment, snowball technique (one person recommends another person, who recommends another…)

SAMPLE: 45 self-identified lesbians, ages 21–56, racially and economically diverse

DATA COLLECTION METHOD: person-to-person interviews, focus groups

RESEARCHERS: Stevens, P. E. (1998). The experiences of lesbians of color in health care encounters: Narrative insights for improving access and quality. In C. M. Ponticelli (Ed.), *Gateways to improving lesbian health and health care: Opening doors* (pp. 77–94). New York: Haworth Press.

RESEARCH DESIGN: cross-sectional

SAMPLING METHOD: feminist narrative

SAMPLE: 45 lesbians, half with diverse ethnic/racial backgrounds, ages 21–56

DATA COLLECTION METHOD: person-to-person interviews for 32, focus groups for 13

RESEARCHERS: Stevens, P. E., & Hall, J. M. (1990). Abusive health care interactions experienced by lesbians: A case of institutional violence in the treatment of women. *Response, 13,* 23–27.

RESEARCH DESIGN: cross-sectional

SAMPLING METHOD: snowball technique (one person recommends another person, who recommends another...)
SAMPLE: 25 self-identified lesbians, ages 21–58, college educated
DATA COLLECTION METHOD: person-to-person interviews

205

RESEARCHERS: Stewart, A. J., & Gold-Steinberg, S. (1990). Midlife women's political consciousness: Case studies of psychosocial development and political commitment. *Psychology of Women Quarterly, 14,* 543–566.
RESEARCH DESIGN: case study
SAMPLING METHOD: self-selected
SAMPLE: 3 case studies of women who finished college in 1964 who were part of Radcliffe sample and among the most politically engaged
DATA COLLECTION METHOD: person-to-persons interviews, paper–pencil questionnaires

206

RESEARCHERS: Stewart, A. J., Settles, I. H., & Winter, N. J. G. (1998). Women and the social movements of the 1960s: Activists, engaged observers, and nonparticipants. *Political Psychology, 19,* 63–94.
RESEARCH DESIGN: cross-sectional, graduates University of Michigan, 1967 (almost all white women), sample of African American women who graduated 1967–1973; longitudinal, Radcliffe study began 1986 with 264 women from 1964 graduating class; 103 participants responded to questionnaires, approximately age 43, and 89 of 103 participants that responded completed California Personality Inventory at approximately age 48
SAMPLING METHOD: convenience
SAMPLE: 2 studies: Study 1: African American and white women alumnae linked to social movements: (1) subset of 107 women of the fourth wave of 2 longitudinal samples of women who were graduates of University of Michigan, 1967 (Women's Life Paths Studies; almost all white, *mean age* 46.91); (2) sample of 68 African American women (*mean age* 43.17) who graduated from University of Michigan 1967–1973. Study 2: Perceived effects of social movements on lives of women in Radcliffe Longitudinal Study: subset of 96 seventh wave women (*mean age* 53.32) from Radcliffe Longitudinal Study of women who graduated from Radcliffe College, 1964
DATA COLLECTION METHOD: Study 1: multiple paper–pencil scales; Study 2: mailed questionnaires

RESEARCHERS: Stewart, D. E., Boydell, K., Derzko, C., & Marshall, V.
(1992). Psychologic distress during menopausal years in women attending a menopause clinic. *International Journal of Psychiatry in Medicine, 22,*
213–220.
RESEARCH DESIGN: cross-sectional
SAMPLING METHOD: convenience
SAMPLE: 259 menopause clinic women, 113 perimenopasual (*mean age*
46.8), 146 menopausal (*mean age* 55.1)
DATA COLLECTION METHOD: paper–pencil questionnaires

RESEARCHERS: Suitor, J. J., & Pillemer, K. (1994). Family caregiving
and marital satisfaction: Findings from a 1-year panel study of women
caring for parents with dementia. *Journal of Marriage and the Family, 56,*
681–690.
RESEARCH DESIGN: longitudinal (3 years)
SAMPLING METHOD: mostly physician referrals, others from psychia-
trists and neurologists
SAMPLE: 94 caregiving daughters, daughters-in-law (*mean age* 46.2)
DATA COLLECTION METHOD: person-to-person interviews

RESEARCHERS: Thompson, E. H., Futterman, A. M., Gallagher-
Thompson, D., Rose, J. M., & Lovett, S. B. (1993). Social support and
caregiver burdens in family caregivers of frail elderly. *Journal of
Gerontology: Social Sciences, 48,* S245–S254.
RESEARCH DESIGN: cross-sectional
SAMPLING METHOD: recruited
SAMPLE: 217 family caregivers of frail elderly relative
DATA COLLECTION METHOD: person-to-person interviews,
paper–pencil questionnaires

RESEARCHERS: Thornton, A., Orbuch, T. L., & Axinn, W. G. (1995).
Parent–child relationships during the transition to adulthood. *Journal of
Family Issues, 16,* 518–564.
RESEARCH DESIGN: panel (mothers interviewed 7 times between
1962–1985; children in 1980 and 1985); data for this analysis from 1980
and 1985 interviews
SAMPLING METHOD: probability sample

SAMPLE: 867 families with mothers and adult children when the children moved from 18 to 23 years old

DATA COLLECTION METHOD: telephone interviews with mothers, person-to-person interviews with children, telephone interviews if children out of area

211

RESEARCHERS: Tirrito, T., & Nathanson, I. (1994). Ethnic differences in caregiving: Adult daughters and elderly mothers. *Affilia, 9*, 71–84.

RESEARCH DESIGN: cross-sectional

SAMPLING METHOD: recruited

SAMPLE: 118 daughters in nuclear family structure (Irish, Italian, Jewish) and in extended family structure (Asian, African American, Latino), ages 20–70 and over

DATA COLLECTION METHOD: paper–pencil questionnaires

212

RESEARCHERS: Trippet, S. E., & Bain, J. (1990). Preliminary study of lesbian health concerns. *Health Values, 14*, 30–36.

RESEARCH DESIGN: cross-sectional

SAMPLING METHOD: convenience

SAMPLE: 41 mostly self-identified lesbians, ages 20–39

DATA COLLECTION METHOD: paper–pencil questionnaires

213

RESEARCHERS: Turner, M. J., Bailey, W. C., & Scott, J. P. (1994). Factors influencing attitude toward retirement and retirement planning among midlife university employees. *Journal of Applied Gerontology, 13*, 143–156.

RESEARCH DESIGN: cross-sectional

SAMPLING METHOD: self-selected

SAMPLE: 2,760 university employees with professional status, ages 40–65

DATA COLLECTION METHOD: mailed paper–pencil questionnaires

214

RESEARCHERS: Uhlenberg, P., Cooney, T., & Boyd, R. (1990). Divorce for women after midlife. *Journal of Gerontology, 45*, S3–S11.

RESEARCH DESIGN: cross-sectional

SAMPLING METHOD: nationwide, representative

SAMPLE: women, age 40 and over

DATA COLLECTION METHOD: data examined from nationwide vital statistics, nationwide population censuses, current population surveys

215

RESEARCHERS: Utian, W., & Boggs, P. B. (1999). The North American Menopause Society 1998 menopause survey. Part I: Postmenopausal women's perceptions about menopause and midlife. *Menopause, 6,* 122–128.
RESEARCH DESIGN: cross-sectional
SAMPLING METHOD: random
SAMPLE: 752 postmenopausal women, ages 50–65
DATA COLLECTION METHOD: telephone interviews

216

RESEARCHERS: Veevers, J. E., & Mitchell, B. A. (1998). Intergenerational exchanges and perceptions of support within "boomerang kid" family environments. *International Journal of Human Development, 46,* 91–108.
RESEARCH DESIGN: cross-sectional
SAMPLING METHOD: snowball technique (one person recommends another person, who recommends another…)
SAMPLE: subset of 218 families in which adult children, ages 19–35, recently returned home, from larger study of 420 families
DATA COLLECTION METHOD: telephone interviews

217

RESEARCHERS: Waldrop, D. P., & Weber, J. A. (2001). From grandparenthood to caregivier: The stress and satisfaction of raising grandchildren. *Families in Society: Journal of Contemporary Human Services, 82,* 461–472.
RESEARCH DESIGN: qualitative
SAMPLING METHOD: recruitment, snowball technique (one person recommends another person, who recommends another…)
SAMPLE: Fifty-four grandparent caregivers (37 grandmothers, 17 grandfathers)
DATA COLLECTION METHOD: interviews

218

RESEARCHERS: Wanamaker, N. J., & Bird, G. W. (1990). Coping with stress in dual-career marriages. *International Journal of Sociology of the Family, 20,* 198–211.
RESEARCH DESIGN: cross-sectional
SAMPLING METHOD: self-selected
SAMPLE: 190 dual-career parents (men: *mean age* 40; women: *mean age* 38)
DATA COLLECTION METHOD: paper–pencil scales

RESEARCHERS: Ward, D. H., & Carney, P. A. (1994). Caregiving women and the U.S. welfare state: The case of elder kin care by low-income women. *Holistic Nursing Practice, 8,* 44–58.
RESEARCH DESIGN: cross-sectional
SAMPLING METHOD: convenience
SAMPLE: 12 ethnically diverse women caregivers, ages 41–102
DATA COLLECTION METHOD: paper–pencil questionnaires

RESEARCHERS: Ward, R. A., & Spitze, G. (1996). Gender differences in parent–child coresidence experience. *Journal of Marriage and the Family, 58,* 718–725.
RESEARCH DESIGN: cross-sectional
SAMPLING METHOD: random, nationwide probability
SAMPLE: subset of 661 adult children who lived in parent household, younger than age 40, from National Survey of Families and Households data
DATA COLLECTION METHOD: person-to-person interviews, paper–pencil questionnaires

RESEARCHERS: Ward, R. A., & Spitze, G. (1996). Will the children ever leave? Parent–child coresidence history and plans. *Journal of Family Issues, 17,* 514–539.
RESEARCH DESIGN: cross-sectional, longitudinal (5 years)
SAMPLING METHOD: random
SAMPLE: subset of 716 adult children (*mean age* 23.8) who lived in parent household, from National Survey of Families and Households study
DATA COLLECTION METHOD: person-to-person interviews, paper–pencil questionnaires

RESEARCHERS: Welsh, W. M., & Stewart, A. J. (1998). Relationships between women and their parents: Implications for midlife well-being. *Psychology and Aging, 10,* 181–190.
RESEARCH DESIGN: longitudinal, Radcliffe study began in 1986 with 264 women from 1964 graduating class, 103 participants responded to questionnaires, approximately age 43, and 89 of 103 participants that responded completed the California Personality Inventory at approximately age 48
SAMPLING METHOD: representative of the graduating class

SAMPLE: subset of 89 Radcliffe graduates (class of 1964) including the waves 1980, 1986, and 1990
DATA COLLECTION METHOD: paper–pencil questionnaires

RESEARCHERS: White, L., & Edwards, J. N. (1990). Emptying the nest and parental well-being: An analysis of national panel data. *American Sociological Review, 55,* 235–242.
RESEARCH DESIGN: panel (5 years)
SAMPLING METHOD: random
SAMPLE: 402 parents of at least one child, age 14 and over, in home in 1983
DATA COLLECTION METHOD: telephone interviews

RESEARCHERS: White, L. K., & Rogers, S. J. (1997). Strong support but uneasy relationships: Coresidence and adult children's relationships with their parents. *Journal of Marriage and the Family, 59,* 62–76.
RESEARCH DESIGN: cross-sectional
SAMPLING METHOD: clustered random-digit dialing
SAMPLE: subset of 435 young adults, ages 19–40, interviewed in 1992, and their parents interviewed in 1988 (N = 2,034 married persons under age 55) from the Marital Instability over the Life Course Study that began 1980
DATA COLLECTION METHOD: telephone surveys

RESEARCHERS: Wight, R. G., LeBlanc, A. J., & Aneshensel, C. S. (1998). AIDS caregiving and health among midlife and older women. *Health Psychology, 17,* 130–137.
RESEARCH DESIGN: cross-sectional
SAMPLING METHOD: recruited through variety of sources
SAMPLE: subset of 121 women, age 35 and over, from sample of 642 informal AIDS caregivers in University of California AIDS care study
DATA COLLECTION METHOD: paper–pencil questionnaires

RESEARCHERS: Wilk, C. A., & Kirk, M. A. (1995). Menopause: A developmental stage, not a deficiency disease. *Psychotherapy, 32,* 233–241.
RESEARCH DESIGN: cross-sectional
SAMPLING METHOD: random
SAMPLE: 157 therapists, 90 percent over age 40

DATA COLLECTION METHOD: paper–pencil questionnaires

RESEARCHERS: Wink, L. (1992). Three types of narcissism in women from college to midlife. *Journal of Personality, 60,* 7–30.
RESEARCH DESIGN: longitudinal, Mills study begun 1958 and 1960 with 142 women from two graduating classes from Mills College; follow-ups in 1963–1964, 1981, and 1989 when women were in late 20s, early 40s, and early 50s
SAMPLING METHOD: representative two-thirds of senior class, Mills College, 1958 and 1960
SAMPLE: subset of Mills College sample, 81 women, ages 40–50
DATA COLLECTION METHOD: paper–pencil questionnaires

RESEARCHERS: Wink, L. (1996). Transition from the early 40s to the early 50s in self-directed women. *Journal of Personality, 64,* 49–69.
RESEARCH DESIGN: longitudinal, Mills study begun 1958 and 1960, 142 women from two graduating classes, Mills College; follow-ups 1963–1964, 1981, and 1989, when women were in late 20s, early 40s, and early 50s
SAMPLING METHOD: representative two-thirds of graduating class, 1958 and 1960
SAMPLE: subset of 76 women from Mills Longitudinal Study
DATA COLLECTION METHOD: *Q* sorts at age 43

RESEARCHERS: Woods, N. F., & Mitchell, E. S. (1996). Patterns of depressed mood in midlife women: Observations from the Seattle midlife women's health study. *Research in Nursing & Health, 19,* 111–123.
RESEARCH DESIGN: cross-sectional
SAMPLING METHOD: random
SAMPLE: subset of 347 women enrolled in Seattle Midlife Women's Health Study ($N = 508$); ages 35–55; 80 percent European American, 8 percent African American, 8 percent Asian American
DATA COLLECTION METHOD: paper–pencil measures

RESEARCHERS: Woods, N. F., & Mitchell, E. S. (1997). Women's images of midlife: Observations from the Seattle midlife women's health study. *Health Care for Women International, 18,* 439–453.

RESEARCH DESIGN: cross-sectional
SAMPLING METHOD: random
SAMPLE: subset of 131 women enrolled in Seattle Midlife Women's
Health Study ($N = 508$), ages 35–55, 80 percent European American, 8
percent African American, 8 percent Asian American
DATA COLLECTION METHOD: telephone interviews

231

RESEARCHERS: York, K. L., & John, O. P. (1992). The four faces of
Eve: A typological analysis of women's personality at midlife: *Journal of
Personality and Social Psychology, 63,* 494–508.
RESEARCH DESIGN: longitudinal, Mills study begun 1958 and 1960, 142
women from two graduating classes from Mills College; follow-ups
1963–1964, 1981, and 1989, when women were in late 20s, early 40s,
and early 50s
SAMPLING METHOD: representative of two senior classes
SAMPLE: subset of women from Mills Longitudinal Study, 51 from 1958
cohort, 52 from 1960 cohort, ages 42–45
DATA COLLECTION METHOD: paper–pencil questionnaires

232

RESEARCHERS: Young, R. F., & Kahana, E. (1994). Gender, recovery
from late life heart attack, and medical care. *Women & Health, 20,*
11–31.
RESEARCH DESIGN: longitudinal (1 year)
SAMPLING METHOD: self-selected
SAMPLE: women 36 percent of a sample at time 1 of 246 myocardial
infarction patients (ages 43–87; women: *mean age* 69.7, men: *mean age*
65.5); 166 patients available at time 2 (32 percent women)
DATA COLLECTION METHOD: person-to-person in-home interviews
with patients and their informal caregivers

INDEX

D

E

M

Women at Midlife
Life Experiences and Practice Implications

Cover design by Suzani Pavone, Eye to Eye Design Studio

Interior Design and Composition by
MidAtlantic Books & Journals, Inc.

Typeset in Janson

Printed by Boyd Printing

MORE RESOURCES FROM NASW PRESS!

Women at Midlife: *Life Experiences and Implications for the Helping Professions, by Ski Hunter, Sandra S. Sundel, and Martin Sundel.* The number of women at midlife served by the helping professions is substantial. *Women at Midlife* fills a gap in the organized research knowledge on this population and examines a wide variety of the issues and concerns that women encounter during this life period, including family contexts and relationships, physical health, menopause and sexuality, emotional concerns, personality and identity, and life satisfaction.

ISBN: 0-87101-351-7. August 2002. Item #3517. $44.99.

Feminist Practice in the 21st Century, *Nan Van Den Bergh, Editor.* This important work demonstrates how the feminist standpoints of knowing, connecting, caring, and diversity can help practitioners build communities and solve problems. *Feminist Practice in the 21st Century* contains 18 chapters organized by method, field of practice, and special populations, and sets forth a feminist model for social work theory and practice. Educators, students, and practitioners find the book a compelling resource on the feminist perspective on clinical social work, administration, family-centered practice, culturally competent practice, substance abuse, AIDS, violence against women, and more.

ISBN: 0-87101-244-8. 1995. Item #2448. $34.95.

Resiliency: *An Integrated Approach to Practice, Policy and Research, Roberta R. Greene, Editor.* Social workers require both the understanding of how people successfully meet life challenges and the knowledge to build client strengths, adaptation, healing, and self-efficacy. This comprehensive volume integrates social work theory, policy, research, and method to promote and improve resilience-based practice. Faculty across curriculum, students, and practitioners will find this timely book an invaluable text.

ISBN: 0-87101-350-9. January 2002. Item #3509. $44.99.

Affirmative Practice: *Understanding and Working with Lesbian, Gay, Bisexual, and Transgendered Persons, by Ski Hunter and Jane Hickerson. Affirmative Practice* is a groundbreaking new book that contributes to the intellectual and emotional capacity of social workers and social work students who work with or will work with lesbian, gay, bisexual, and transgendered clients. Specific topics include the development of communities among LGBT persons, social and legal issues and advances, coming out and disclosure, and more.

ISBN: 0-87101-352-5. October 2002. Item #3525. $44.99.

Alcohol, Tobacco, and Other Drugs: *Challenging Myths, Assessing Theories, Individualizing Interventions, Ann A. Abbott, Editor. Alcohol, Tobacco, and Other Drugs* is an important addition to the limited material written expressly for human services professionals dealing with clients who misuse substances. This much-needed text provides an empirically based approach to social work practice with individuals, groups, and families that are experiencing problems stemming from the misuse of alcohol, tobacco, and other drugs. The book also addresses the importance of culture, race, ethnicity, and gender in treating substance abuse.

ISBN: 0-87101-316-9. 2000. Item #3169. $39.99.

(Order form and information on reverse side)

ORDER FORM

Qty.	Title	Item #	Price	Total
__	Women at Midlife	3517	$44.99	_____
__	Feminist Practice in the 21st Century	2448	$34.95	_____
__	Resiliency	3509	$44.99	_____
__	Affirmative Practice	3525	$44.99	_____
__	Alcohol, Tobacco, and Other Drugs	3169	$39.99	_____

			Subtotal	_____
			Postage and Handling	_____
			DC residents add 6% sales tax	_____
			MD residents add 5% sales tax	_____
			Total	_____

POSTAGE AND HANDLING
Minimum postage and handling fee is $4.95. Orders that do not include appropriate postage and handling will be returned.

DOMESTIC: Please add 12% to orders under $100 for postage and handling. For orders over $100 add 7% of order.

CANADA: Please add 17% postage and handling.

OTHER INTERNATIONAL: Please add 22% postage and handling.

❐ **Check** or **money order** (payable to NASW Press) for $ _____.

❐ **Credit card**
   ❐ NASW Visa* I ❐ Visa I ❐ NASW MasterCard* I ❐ MasterCard I ❐ Amex

_____   _____
Credit Card Number   Expiration Date

Signature _____

        Use of these cards generates funds in support of the social work profession.

Name _____

Address _____

City _____ State/Province _____

Country _____ Zip _____

Phone _____ E-mail _____

NASW Member # (if applicable) _____

     (Please make checks payable to NASW Press. Prices are subject to change.)

NASW PRESS
P. O. Box 431
Annapolis JCT, MD 20701
USA

Credit card orders call
1-800-227-3590
(In the Metro Wash., DC, area, call 301-317-8688)
Or fax your order to 301-206-7989
Or order online at http://www.naswpress.org

Visit our Web site at http://www.naswpress.org.   CPWM02